CONVERSATIONS WITH CRITICS

Also by Nicolas Tredell from Carcanet

The Critical Decade

CONVERSATIONS WITH CRITICS

NICOLAS TREDELL

CARCANET

SHEEP MEADOW PRESS

First published in Great Britain in 1994 by
Carcanet Press Limited
208-212 Corn Exchange Buildings
Manchester M4 3BQ

First published in United States of America in 1994 by
Sheep Meadow Press
Post Office Box 1345
Riverdale-on-Hudson
New York 10471

A CIP catalogue record for this book
is available from the British Library.
ISBN 1 85754 016 6

Carcanet Press acknowledges financial assistance
from the Arts Council of Great Britain

Set in 10pt Sabon by Bryan Williamson, Frome, Somerset
Printed and bound in England by SRP Ltd, Exeter

Contents

Introduction

The interviews collected in this book were originally conducted for the magazine *PN Review* in the years 1990 to 1993. *PN Review* has always aimed to chart changes in contemporary culture and to promote dialogue between those of differing persuasions. Much of this mapping and dialogue takes the form of essays, reviews and letters. But today's cultural ferment seemed to call for a further form of exploration: the interview. Most of the writers and critics whose work we discussed were very much alive and kicking. Surely it was time to get out there and talk to them?

The interview might itself be seen as a distinctive contemporary form. It is not new: the narrator of Henry James's *The Aspern Papers* (1888), speaks of 'the latter half of the nineteenth century' as 'the age of newspapers and telegrams and photographs and interviewers' (1984 edn, p. 48). James registers the link between the interview and the development of technologies of communication and mechanical reproduction; it is the further development of those technologies, shaped by and shaping a certain sort of society, which have made the interview much more prominent today. There are different sorts of interviews, of course: one task for modern cultural studies – perhaps it is already under way – is the analysis and classification of the varieties of this particular form. Two varieties are notable today. One – associated mainly with the magazine, newspaper and colour supplement – presents a profile of the subject of the interview, incorporating some of his or her spoken discourse in direct speech, but framing this within an often slick anecdotal perspective supplied by the interviewer. The other – associated primarily with television – intercuts fragments of interviews with a range of people to produce a montage of 'soundbites'.

Neither of these varieties offered an appropriate model for the explorations assembled in this book. A much better model was offered by the interviews with Raymond Williams conducted by

Perry Anderson, Anthony Barnett and Francis Mulhern, then of the
editorial committee of *New Left Review,* which were collected in the
book *Politics and Letters* (1979). Allowing for the difference that the
interviews with Williams were conducted over a period of months,
while each interview in this volume was a one-off occasion, it was the
model of *Politics and Letters* that was adopted and adapted. It
entailed a sustained and attentive reading of the texts of those who
were to be interviewed – a reading which tried both to enter into their
thought-worlds and to take a critical distance from them. It was this
kind of reading which generated the questions that would be posed,
challenged, diverted, developed and departed from in the human
encounter of the interview itself. The aim was always to give the person being interviewed the scope to explore his or her own ideas and
concerns in a context that was informed, open, but probing. The
interview was recorded on cassette tape, transcribed, edited, and sent
to the person who had been interviewed for approval and for any
desired amendments.

All these interviews were conducted in Britain, though by no
means all those interviewed are British by provenance or primary
location. They thus refer, to a greater or lesser extent, to a British
context which is itself fraught, threatened and mobile, which can no
longer be taken for granted. Among those interviewed, George
Steiner, educated in France and America, darkly aware of the interfusion of culture and barbarism in Europe, now a Professor at the
University of Geneva but still based in Cambridge and an Extraordinary Fellow of Churchill College, is the figure who, in the postwar
era, presented the most dramatic challenge to English insularity and
parochialism. A sustained if more distant challenge was presented by
Christine Brooke-Rose, prominent as a novelist and critic in 1950s
London, but long resident in France and deeply versed in French cultural and literary theory. Challenges were also to be mounted by
Donald Davie, particularly because of his engagement with Ezra
Pound and with Russian and Polish and American poetry, and by
those who, in the later sixties, encountered French ideas about literature and culture and tried to bring them back home, particularly
Frank Kermode and Stephen Heath. The question of British identity,
of its relationship to other cultures in Europe and beyond, is a recurrent concern in this book. Among those interviewed, it is Robert
Hewison who has provided the most comprehensive chronicle of
British culture since 1939 and the most swingeing attack on what he
sees as its insular and nostalgic tendencies.

Between them, the lifetimes of those in this volume cover much of the century. C.H. Sisson lived through the 1930s as a young man and his interview provides a vivid record of that decade, especially of his time in France and Nazi Germany. For Frank Kermode, Donald Davie and Richard Hoggart, the 1930s was the time of the passage from boyhood to manhood. Sisson, Kermode, Davie and Hoggart all served in the Second World War – Sisson in the ranks of the Army, Davie and Kermode in the Royal Navy, Hoggart in the Royal Artillery – and for all four, that experience was, necessarily, of deep significance. After the War, in the 1950s, there emerged in Britain that loose assembly of poets and novelists which came to be called the Movement – a movement which, rejecting modernism, updated traditional verse forms and the picaresque novel by marrying them to modern themes and idioms. Of those interviewed in this book, Donald Davie was both the most prominently involved in the Movement and one of its harshest later critics: he now offers a summing-up from the perspective of the 1990s. Bernard Bergonzi allied himself with the Movement as a poet and critic, Karl Miller did so as an editor, and Frank Kermode was close to one of its leading protagonists and publicists, John Wain. All speak enthusiastically about this period in British cultural history. As Karl Miller has pointed out, the Movement is not the only story that can be told of the 1950s; and doubtless there are other stories that can be – that are being – told, from feminist or black or gay or working-class viewpoints; but it remains a significant and interesting story, for its exclusions as much as for its emphases.

The moment of the Movement was, as Bergonzi points out, short-lived, born of cultural circumstances that could not long hold. Things started to loosen up, or break up, in the later fifties: 1956 – the year of Hungary and Suez, of John Osborne's *Look Back in Anger* and Colin Wilson's *The Outsider* – is the conventional but convenient marker of the turning-point. It was in the following year that David Caute published a first novel which, in its themes, technical variety, and political engagement, differed sharply from the Movement ideal of fiction: in his interview, Caute talks about that novel and about the writing that followed, in which he tried to keep pace with the changes of the 1960s: the decade of pop music and protest, drugs and dropouts, Vatican II and Vietnam; of the expansion of higher education in Britain and the creation of new universities; of the first Labour government for 13 years; of rebellion in Rhodesia and Enoch Powell's vision of race war in Britain. It was a time that produced strong reactions and which remains embroiled in controversy and myth. Of those interviewed in this book, two figures of different generations, Donald Davie and Roger Scruton, reacted strongly against it; Bernard Bergonzi disliked some of its aspects, but his repudiation is less total; it was a formative period for Terry Eagleton in terms of his relationship to Catholicism and Marxism; its apparent impending dissolution of class and cultural barriers found an enthusiastic partisan in Colin MacCabe. One of the new universities, Essex, became a key site of student protest: three of those interviewed in this volume, Donald Davie, Lisa Jardine and John Barrell were involved in the troubles there, and each offers a perspective upon them.

The tumults of the sixties subsided into a decade dominated by economic difficulty and by growing disillusionment, on left and right, with an increasingly strained and shabby Welfare State consensus. Left-wing hopes for socialist revolution declined as North Vietnam and China pursued familiar paths of repression, and as militancy at home was defused by a Labour Government. But the legacies of the sixties were manifold. One of them was feminism – or, rather, a range of feminisms, emerging in conjunction with, but also often against, a New Left which, as Lisa Jardine suggests, had proved no better than the Old Left in acknowledging the claims of women. Christine Brooke-Rose, A.S. Byatt, Catherine Belsey, Marina Warner, and Lisa Jardine, from different generations and backgrounds, each offer perspectives on feminism in relation to writing, criticism, culture and society. Karl Miller, David Caute, Terry Eagleton and Roger Scruton offer a perspective from the other side of what Marina Warner has called the ring-fence of gender.

The 1960s was also the era in which, as Philip Larkin mordantly put it, sexual intercourse began; or at least went public. Affluence, consumer pressures, more convenient contraception, contributed to changes in sexual attitudes and behaviour which were presented, sometimes euphorically, as a form of liberation. In these interviews, Roger Scruton and Stephen Heath, from very different positions, question the reality of such liberation. Larkin's prelude to the start of sexual intercourse was the end of the ban on D.H. Lawrence's *Lady Chatterley's Lover*: the lifting of that ban also stands as a metonymy for the loosening of censorship, another proclaimed liberation which was later to pose problems, not least in the light of feminism. George Steiner, Robert Hewison and Stephen Heath all tackle the issue of censorship and present a range of responses to it.

On the more explicitly political front, the sixties saw the growth of a New Left which had its origins in the late fifties, with the attempts of cultural critics and historians such as Raymond Williams and

E.P. Thompson to find a third path between the Communist and Labour Parties. In the sixties the New Left took on a distinctive and apparently powerful profile, reshaped and reinforced by the protests against the Vietnam War and the revival and revision of Marxist ideas by such figures as Louis Althusser, transmitted to England by the journal *New Left Review*. But the political aims of the New Left were not realized; and a converse political consequence of the sixties – one which grew during the 1970s and became fully visible in the 1980s – was the development of the New Right, a process recalled in this volume by Roger Scruton, its most prominent British intellectual representative.

In the field of higher education, the dissatisfaction with existing curricula, particularly in the humanities, which had broken out in the sixties, began to produce more radical and enduring changes in the seventies, and these were consolidated in the ensuing decade. Crucial here was the French connection – the introduction into Britain, by means of translation, explication, and application, of the structuralist, poststructuralist and deconstructionist ideas which, in the sixties, had been generated in France by Althusser, Lacan, Derrida, Barthes, Julia Kristeva, Philippe Sollers, and the journal *Tel Quel*. Stephen Heath recalls the excitement of the moment when the ideas of Barthes and *Tel Quel* were reaching the heights of a revolutionary semiotics. But bringing it all back home was hard. Frank Kermode's informal seminars at University College London were very important in disseminating the new ideas in British intellectual life: Kermode himself, Stephen Heath, and A.S. Byatt each recall them in this volume. Such ideas were also very important in the development of the analysis of film and cinema in the magazine *Screen* – a magazine with which, as they recall here, both Stephen Heath and Colin MacCabe were prominently involved, and to the influence of which Catherine Belsey testifies. But more generally in British culture these new ideas were met with incomprehension and hostility. They seemed to strike at the very basis of literary study as it had been constituted in England, where it had come to seem a means of personal self-development, and perhaps of gradual social amelioration, by means of a succession of close encounters with a mature and reverent sensibility enacting its judgements in an organically unified text. The links between poststructuralist and deconstructionist ideas, and notions – if sometimes rather vague ones – of radical social and political change, increased the sense of threat to a subject that had come to be seen as offering, contradictorily, both an escape from politics and an engagement with it at a more profound level than that of mere commitment. A range of struggles ensued: they were to become most public in Cambridge in 1980, with the refusal to appoint Colin Mac-Cabe to a permanent post as lecturer in English. In this book, Colin MacCabe himself, Stephen Heath, John Barrell, Lisa Jardine, and Frank Kermode all give an account of the MacCabe affair and of its broader causes and consequences. It should be said that Christopher Ricks, generally identified as the leading figure in the opposition to what MacCabe seemed to represent, was approached for an interview, but declined.

As Stephen Heath points out, the MacCabe affair occurred in the heady early days of Thatcherism, and can be seen as part of a much more general attempt – in Britain and the USA – to roll back both socialism and the sixties, to promote the free market, a strong state, and family values. This attempt radically reshaped the cultural and political landscape in both countries. In the sixties the Yardbirds had produced a song which questioned whether it was possible any longer to say that people must die for their monarch and country; the Falklands/Malvinas War proved that it was possible both to say and to do it, and produced an upsurge of patriotic and martial emotion that would have seemed atavistic fifteen years previously. The vision of working-class solidarity which had surged up briefly in 1972 as the gates of Saltley Coke Depot clanged shut met its Waterloo in 1984 on the fields of Orgreave. With the defeat of the 1984-5 miners's strike, the possibilities of socialist resistance almost evaporated. A bloc of support for Conservatism was created which, under the British electoral system, enabled the Conservatives to hold power into the 1990s.

If the foreign devils were driven from English soil, the attempt to expel them from English studies backfired: the MacCabe affair provided a symbol and a myth to which those drawn to the new ideas could rally. Moreover, the Conservative emphasis on market forces, and the drive to restructure academic institutions in the supposed interests of greater productivity and efficiency, favoured the new ideas and approaches since these, in contrast to the vaguer humanistic notions of conventional literary study, could be packaged, marketed and modularized for teaching. They were explicated in lively fashion in a range of books, most notably those of Methuen's 'New Accents' series. One title in that series was to prove particularly provocative, becoming both a prime target for hate sessions that lasted considerably longer than two minutes, and a set text on student reading lists: Catherine Belsey's *Critical Practice* (1980), a trenchant synthesis of ideas drawn from Barthes, Lacan and Althusser which was brought to bear primarily on those 'classic realist' texts which had been at the heart of conventional English studies. In her interview, Belsey talks about what led up to *Critical Practice* and about her subsequent view of the book and of its implications. A second crucial text appeared from Blackwell in 1983: Terry Eagleton's *Literary Theory* which vividly conjoined exposition and polemic, combining a lively guide to a range of literary theories with an impassioned sense of political mission. It has since sold over 100,000 copies. In his interview, Eagleton discusses that book and his other texts, which now comprise a considerable body of work.

In the early 1980s, it could still seem possible to assimilate or avert new critical practices and to preserve literary studies in England in broadly the form which had become established in the mid-twentieth-century. By the later eighties, this seemed much less likely. Bernard Bergonzi recalls his realization that the system which had sustained English studies since the 1950s had collapsed. What then of an English curriculum for the 1990s? The figure who was most centrally and practically involved in this was Brian Cox, a founder of *Critical Quarterly* in the late fifties, a begetter of the Black Papers on Education in the sixties and seventies, and chairman in 1988-9 of the committee set up by Margaret Thatcher's government which produced the report *English from ages 5 to 16*. In his interview, Cox talks about *Critical Quarterly*, the Black Papers, and the Cox Report and defends the Report against the attacks that have been made on it. But it may be, as Bergonzi suggests, that English will have to take second place to, or be assimilated into, cultural studies: certainly there is now, in higher education, a strong movement in this direction. The problems and possibilities of this change, the relationship that literary studies may have with cultural studies, the whole question of the future of literary studies, are discussed by Bergonzi, Eagleton, Cox, Lisa Jardine, and one of the founding fathers of cultural studies in England, Richard Hoggart.

One result of the new critical practices is that literary and cultural studies have, ostensibly at least, become much more thoroughly secularized. Older ideas of literature and culture have, however, close and difficult connections with religion. Some of these connections are considered by Frank Kermode, George Steiner and Roger Scruton. Terry Eagleton and Marina Warner talk about their formative Catholicism and subsequent attitude to Christianity, Brian Cox recalls his attempts to make a relationship with the Christian Church, and Donald Davie and C.H. Sisson consider their continuing Christian involvement.

If literature and culture could once be seen as displacements of, or even replacements for, religion, they have now, in their academic manifestations, become the sites in which radical politics can gain a purchase which has increasingly been denied to them in the wider world. But if the spiritualization of literature and culture took place at a time when Christianity was on the wane, the left-wing politicalization of literary and cultural studies took place at a time when socialism and Marxism were beating the retreat which ended in the rout of actually existing socialism in the USSR and Eastern Europe. Many socialists and Marxists, as Terry Eagleton points out, had made their retreat from Moscow long ago. Nonetheless, the dissolution of the empire over which the Red Flag had flown for so long, in which the symbols of October 1917 had so assiduously been embalmed and enshrined, could not but resound like the fall of a thousand colossal statues. The consequences of that collapse are considered, from a Marxist viewpoint, by Terry Eagleton, from a left-postmodernist viewpoint by Catherine Belsey, from a cultural viewpoint by George Steiner, and from the viewpoint of a 'plain old-fashioned socialist' by Lisa Jardine. Roger Scruton provides a conservative perspective on the aftermath of the fall of actually existing socialism.

If the collapse of communism could be seen, from one viewpoint, to vindicate capitalism and conservatism, from another it could be seen to vindicate postmodernism, with its distrust of *grands récits*, the big stories or tall tales – whether those of Christianity, the Enlightenment, or Marxism – which assure us that we are all, if in sometimes mysterious ways, moving towards one ultimate goal. Postmodernism has come to be the term most often used to denote our current condition: it is, at the same time, a contested and questionable notion. Frank Kermode, Terry Eagleton, Robert Hewison and Catherine Belsey all consider the issue of postmodernism as a characterization of the current epoch. Questions, related to postmodernism, about how to combine an awareness of cultural relativity with an affirmation of certain values are considered by Frank Kermode and Stephen Heath while John Barrell and Lisa Jardine both address the issue of the 'truth' of history and of representation.

In current debates about literature, culture and politics, it sometimes happens that the production of those specific cultural artefacts – in the shape of poems and novels and plays – which were once thought to be the critic's *raison d'être*, is pushed aside. Of those interviewed in this volume, Christine Brooke-Rose, A.S. Byatt, Bernard Bergonzi, David Caute, George Steiner, Terry Eagleton, Roger

Scruton, Marina Warner, and C.H. Sisson have all published novels, and in some cases it is as novelists that they are best known; Caute and Eagleton have also written plays. Donald Davie and C.H. Sisson have produced substantial bodies of poetry, Brian Cox's *Collected Poems* was published in 1993, and Bernard Bergonzi, John Barrell and Terry Eagleton all published poetry in earlier life. Richard Hoggart's *The Uses of Literacy* and his autobiographical trilogy evoke 'felt life' in a way which is characteristic of a certain kind of realistic fiction. A crucial topic in the interviews with each of these figures is the relationship between their writing in these forms and their other work. Today, of course, poems and novels and plays are being displaced not only by criticism but also by film, television and video. The omnipresence of these media makes the future of broadcasting a central issue, and it is discussed here by Marina Warner, Colin MacCabe and Richard Hoggart.

These are some of the concerns explored in these interviews. Readers will discover others for themselves. I stated near the start of this introduction that one of the aims of this project was to give those who were being interviewed the scope to explore their own ideas and concerns. A further aim can now be stated: that of giving readers the scope to explore the interviews for themselves: to make their own maps, find their own connections, ask their own questions, draw their own conclusions. It is time to step aside, to let the dialogue between the interview and the reader commence.

Christine Brooke-Rose

Park Court Hotel, Lancaster Gate, London
6 March 1990

NICOLAS TREDELL: *Your latest novel,* Verbivore, *is a very inventive, very witty work, but it also seems to me to have a very sombre resonance. There's a strong sense of an ending, an apprehension of a fall, after an excess of noise, into a possibly terminal silence. How do you feel yourself about the book?*

CHRISTINE BROOKE-ROSE: Yes, I was trying to explore the possibility of our minds being completely altered by the media, and if the media suddenly collapse, which is what the book is about, can we actually go back to a premedia mentality? And we can't. Society was very structured and layered, but everyone knew where they were. This was not necessarily a good society, but there were all sorts of ways of communicating at different levels, and above all, people read. Perhaps only an élite, I'm not going to go into the sociology of it, but nowadays people read less and less, and they want easy books, and they're so formed by television. I saw this as a teacher. It was very difficult to get students to read even a short story, where I in my youth just read, that was it, that was the centre of my life, to read, and there was this notion of completion, I wanted to read *all* Balzac, for instance, I wanted to cover the whole terrain. Reading was always central and still is now, though I listen a lot to the radio and I look at television and I'm very much more interested in the world and what goes on around me than I was when I was young – I was very much a bluestocking, stuck in my books. So I was interested in the notion that people have lost the art of communicating. In this highly 'communications' age, we are in fact all isolated, looking at our television sets and identifying with these soap characters and newscasters. What would happen if this were taken away from us? We've lost the previous ways and if we lose this way, this televisual age, what is left?

So it does give me a rather pessimistic idea that there's nothing left. In fact, I don't believe that. Something always comes after something, because obviously in many ways – people travel more and so on and communicate like that, but it's much more an illiterate form of communication.

This leads on to a question which also relates to your novel Amalgamemnon, *published in 1984. In modernism or at least in the critical ideology that developed around modernism, there is a kind of nostalgia – you could call it, in a reductive way, an élitist nostalgia – for a vanished past of high literacy. How much do you think this emerges from both* Verbivore *and* Amalgamemnon?

I think that whereas in the past there was a highly literate and cultured élite and all the rest practically couldn't read, after the Second World War, and perhaps before, we were moving towards a much more egalitarian society. Many more people were going to university and so on. After all, I was a beneficiary of this, I went to Oxford on a grant, I would never have gone to university at all without these changes. What's happening now is that all these people who go to university and get diplomas – universities have become diploma-churning factories – don't even get jobs, many of them, they just fill up the unemployment figures, and there's a super-élite of high technologists. I think already in *Amalgamemnon* I make that comparison between the computer programmer who knows all about how computers work and the users who are just typists, so that even in computers, there's already a social hierarchy. We're producing this new élite who run society, and then there's all the rest, so it's almost as though we'd gone back. This dream of an egalitarian society after the Second World War has frittered away, and I find this rather serious.

So you see a kind of technological élite developing. And you're not nostalgic in the way that perhaps some modernist writers seem to be for a literary élite?

Oh no. I'm not a modernist at all. I don't think you've just got to know all about Greek gods to run the country. That was the idea in the nineteenth century: you read Classics and you went into the Foreign Office.

I felt that in Amalgamemnon *particularly you do, to some extent, sound this note of high modernist regret for a vanished past, and yet at the same time your novels, especially your recent novels, are* absolument moderne, *in Rimbaud's phrase, they are very much up-to-date. I'm interested in a kind of ambivalence in your work.*

Yes, you're right. You see when a writer advances in years, he or she can simply write about his or her own childhood and youth and what they know best, and be nostalgic, and I've got all this capital, as it were, inside me, but I'm extremely interested in what's going on around me, and concerned. I read a lot of non-literary things, and I've always been interested in other disciplines, like psychoanalysis and linguistics. I think you've got to be aware of what's going on and the implications of what's going on, so that I'm axed in one sense in the past but also in the future.

Both Verbivore *and your previous novel,* Xorandor *, which came out in 1986, have the shifting ontological levels and the wordplay that characterize your earlier fiction, but these recent novels seem more user-friendly, so to speak. Do they mark for you a certain acknowledgement of the claims of narrative which you seemed to be repudiating in* Out, *which appeared in 1964, or particularly* Thru, *published in 1975?*

Oh yes. Well, it's a long road I've followed. You see, my first four novels, which are completely out of print and which I never even talk about, were really quite traditional novels, light satires on society, more influenced by Evelyn Waugh and people like that. But then I was very dissatisfied, because it really seemed too easy, and from *Out* onwards, I really was trying to expand the possibilities of the novel form. *Out* is, in a way, a very sick book, because I was very ill when I wrote it, and I was very influenced by Robbe-Grillet, so you have this obsessive description. But what Robbe-Grillet wouldn't approve of in that book is the science fiction element, because it's staged at a time when the colour bar has been reversed, and it all goes on in the mind of this old white man who queues to get a job and so on, and he's completely obsessed with detail. But after that – you know I never repeat myself – I went on getting the label of '*nouveau roman* in English'; but that's the only one which is directly influenced by the *nouveau roman*. With *Such*, which came out in 1966, I went off into a kind of metaphysical science fiction. *Between*, which appeared in 1968, was about a simultaneous interpreter who was travelling from hotel room to hotel room and conference to conference, and there

I used a lot of different languages, which of course is not very user-friendly, but I was exploring what it's like to be bilingual, and what it's like also *not* to know all the languages. You travel and see 'Toilets' in Bulgaria in Cyrillic script, and it acts like a block, rather like the ideograms in Pound. So I had a lot of fun with that, but that's something different again, it's no longer anything to do with the *nouveau roman*.

Then I became a university teacher and plunged myself into literary theory and got completely split apart, the critic and the writer, and I wrote *Thru*, which is probably my most difficult novel, because it's a novel about the theory of the novel. And I had tremendous fun with the different structuralist and poststructuralist theories and so on, and I knew I would be rapped on the knuckles for that, because it's really written for a handful of narratologists. Afterwards I really felt I'd gone too far, and I took a long time before writing *Amalgamemnon*, I took nine years and rewrote it many times. That was the beginning of an effort towards more readability, but obviously some people still found it difficult. And then I wrote *Xorandor*, which was science fiction, and there I really thought, well now, I'm going to write a bestseller. But it's no use, I can't write a bestseller, because there's still difficult things in it.

There's the slang invented for the kids, for one, which actually was a purely practical thing; I simply didn't know, partly because of the generation gap, and partly because of living in France, how kids talk today. In the first version, they were saying things like 'Crikey!', which *I* said as a child. Who says 'Crikey!' today? That's no use, so the only way out was to invent a language based on computer words and so on. Though I don't think that's a real difficulty: *Xorandor* is probably the most straightforward. *Verbivore* I thought was even more straightforward, but I don't know whether it is or not. There is perhaps a difficulty: in *Amalgamemnon*, Mira Enketei, who's a Greek scholar, a teacher of the classics who's been made redundant and who has nothing to do but listen to the radio while reading Herodotus, hears Perry Someone on the radio presenting some sort of late-night show, and she invents this character called Perry Hupsos, which in Greek means 'on the sublime', an allusion to Longinus – that was just an in-joke. Perry Hupsos comes back in *Verbivore* as a 'real' character who also calls himself Perry Striker and who writes a radio play, and inside that radio play there's a character called Julian Freeman who has brief appearances at the level of the main plot. But there's also a character called Decibel in the play, who lives on noise and dies of silence, and she also reappears at the end at the level of the main plot. This play with narrative levels is well-known in theory, it's called metalepsis, where you go from one level to another, so that if there's a story within a story, and a character from the inner story appears within the outer story, there's a transgression of narrative levels. But obviously it's a little disconcerting to the reader who expects a straight story.

Can we go on from that to the general question of an audience for your work? It seems to me that if you had been an American writer, there would now be one, perhaps more, critical monographs, a sheaf of essays, parts of many academic courses that would be devoted to your work –

Well, there are, you see, in America.

In America, but not in England. How do you feel about that?

I don't know how to feel about it. I mean, it's the old story of a prophet being recognized elsewhere, though I'm not a prophet. But even in France, for instance, where I've been living for 21 years, the *anglicistes* who would be teaching a course on, say Emma Tennant, had me there all the time, and they never even came to interview me. I knew them all, we met regularly, but they never taught me in their courses. There's something rather peculiar about that. But I do now have, oh I don't know, some 20 essays written about me in various academic journals, and someone in Germany's trying to collect them, but again can't find a publisher in England. I know I've been put on American syllabuses for either feminist courses, though I'm not a feminist, or courses on this type of fiction, but certainly not in England. You see, I was very much better known when I wrote straightforward novels. Also, I was reviewing in the Sunday papers and so on, and perhaps I was better known because my name appeared regularly, which is not very flattering. But from the time I went to live in France – and I was very interested in the *nouveau roman*, and wrote critical articles about it – I was labelled as a mad Francophile and '*nouveau roman* in English', and lots of reviews would start: 'Miss Brooke-Rose lives in France…'. And so I probably did myself a lot of harm. But I don't regret it, because it really stretched my horizons. That's the price I have to pay for getting out of this slightly provincial English literary life, though it's getting better now.

*The novel of yours which seems to be most often cited in English
literary criticism today, generally in the context of literary theory, is
in fact* Thru. *In a sense, there is an attempt in England now to create
a theory-literate generation of students and it may be that you will
find a new audience there.*

Well, it is beginning. I appear in several books on postmodernism
and so on, but there is also – I hate to say this – a touch of unconscious 'machoism' in all this, a notion that women writers can be
very good, but they're imitating men, and they're very good at writing about themselves and their lives and love affairs and what-have-
you, but they can't create forms, a woman can't create. It's some sort
of mystique. And this is repeated quite a lot. And you find that the
American postmodern movement is very machoistic, even the novels
are extremely sexist, so in that sense, it's not postmodern at all, it's
oldfashioned. I'm beginning to pierce this now, in books on postmodernism, but I have to fight against that too. If you write a traditional novel, you're probably more successful as a woman than if you
experiment with form, because this is not supposed to be a woman's
domain, it's a man's domain. I'm not a rabid feminist, but on this
point I think the feminists are right. I remember when, shortly after
I arrived in Paris Hélène Cixous rang me up and asked me if I could
contribute an essay to a book she was editing on the difficulties I'd
had as a woman writer. Very naïvely, I said I hadn't had difficulties
as a woman writer, only the normal difficulties as a writer, could I
write about that? But she said, oh no, it had to be feminist. I was
against this sort of segregation. But later, and the more experimental
my books became, I realized that in fact there is that difficulty, there
is a certain resistance to the idea that a woman can extend the form
of a novel, can play with form. It's beginning to change, and I am
more and more mentioned but I don't pierce through to the general
public.

*As you've already suggested, science fiction is a mode you've used a
lot, in* Out *and* Such *and* Xorandor *and* Verbivore. *You've also written on it as a critic, very interestingly, in* A Rhetoric of the Unreal. *As
a novelist and critic, what interests you about science fiction?*

Well, I'm only interested in 'good' science fiction. There's a lot of
tripe in science fiction as in any other genre. I'm not interested in
imagined worlds on other planets, the adventure story type of science
fiction which is usually rather poor imaginatively. Broadly speaking,

there are two types of science fiction. One is, you're projected centuries into the future on an imagined world which is usually modelled on this one – obviously you can't invent a totally imagined world – and it's much more akin to medieval romance, the characters are types and so on; and then there's a type of science fiction which is this world – familiar, it often happens in an English village or somewhere quite ordinary – and then one parameter is changed, say an extraterrestrial appears. But the world described is totally familiar, it's today and now, and in *Xorandor* and *Verbivore* I choose that type. It interests me to reproduce this world, but minus something or plus something. But that's quite a classical genre: perhaps the parameters I choose are unusual. Now in *Out*, I did project a future world, but still it was very familiar, it's a place in some North African country or maybe the South of France, and the only parameter that has changed is that the colour bar is completely reversed, it's the whites who are considered shiftless, and they're all dying of some mysterious disease to which the coloured people have been immune, and I just tried to imagine what it's like to be excluded in that way. But it's not projected centuries ahead on another planet. And in *Such*, that was more metaphysical, because it's a story of a man who's died – I don't specify whether he's died for a long time or whether he's just had his heart massaged for three minutes – and it's his adventures in this psychic space of death, which is translated in terms of outer space. But it's not really science fiction, it's more a poetic fantasy. But in *Xorandor* and *Verbivore*, that's classical science fiction in the sense I describe.

What of your interest in the languages and concepts of various kinds of scientific discourse? You use biochemistry and molecular physics in Out, *astrophysics in* Such, *linguistics in* Thru, *computer science in* Xorandor *and* Verbivore. *What do you feel you're doing with those discourses?*

I'm always fascinated by jargon and discourse that human beings invent to protect their discipline and to keep the outsider out. That's one thing. But also, there's something extremely poetic about certain scientific discourses. If you use a scientific concept and you take it literally, it often becomes a metaphor. This is almost a schoolboy joke – if the science teacher says, 'Weight consists of the attraction of two bodies', they all giggle – and I just take that a step further. In *Such*, I use the laws of astrophysics which are actually the laws of communication, bouncing signals off the moon and so on, and as this man comes back to life, he sees the characters of his real life, his wife and her lover and other people, as the radio telescope sees the stars. So it's also about communication, but as a poetic concept. I'm interested in scientific discourse of all kinds, but in a way, I'm using it ignorantly. I'm not a scientist, and I'm fascinated by the fact that a scientific work, unless it's highly technical, can have another meaning when read by a layman. It becomes poetic.

Such is a remarkable work. Where did that novel come from? Can you speak about the process which generated it?

It was so long ago...*Out* I remember very well because I was extremely ill, and I thought I was going to die, and I wrote it literally one sentence a day falling back on the pillows, and then it became a paragraph, and then became several pages. So it's a very sick book in a way, because this man in the novel is sick, and I was exploring what it's like to be *out* because of sickness, but I just transmuted it into something else. With *Such*, perhaps it was a distant result of that. In more practical terms – I'll tell you exactly what happened, though it doesn't exactly answer your question – I was at a Congress of PEN in Oslo, and I had to read a paper which was slightly difficult; it was going to be translated by the simultaneous translator, and I went through it with him to make sure he got it right; I was absolutely fascinated by the man in the glass box, I could just hear his French, and I got this idea of the simultaneous translator. After that conference, we went – I was married then, and I went with my husband – to Portugal, and I started writing this novel about a simultaneous interpreter, and it just didn't go, the whole thing was dreadful, and I jettisoned it completely in despair. I bought another exercise book and started something else, but I had no idea where I was going. It started with a sentence which literally was the result of the hotel we were staying in. There was a notice which said 'Silence' on the stairs and the stairs were extremely noisy and creaked loudly. So I wrote: 'Silence says the notice on the stairs and the stairs creak'. Where do you go from there? That's a novel where I really didn't know where I was going. It led to the coffin lid opening with a creak, and then to these five moons peering in the way when you're ill you see all the doctors and surgeons and so on looking at you, so obviously it's a distant result of the sickness, but then it led to *Such*, gradually. And then I had to stop it because I didn't know anything about astrophysics. You see, I got the idea, but then I had to mug it up. I read popular books on astrophysics, got fascinated by this, wrote the novel, then went to Jodrell Bank on a visit and asked if I could be shown around. The second in command – called Graham-Smith, I think – was extremely nice, explained a lot of things, and said, if you like, I'll check your astrophysics. I sent it to him in typescript, and he wrote back to me and said, well, I'm glad you haven't asked me to act as a literary critic, but your astrophysics are correct, they're about the standard of a second-year student. I was absolutely bucked. But of course, one cheats, one takes what one wants, it's not actually astrophysics, it's just certain ideas that give you other ideas. I was using astrophysics poetically, metaphorically if you like, for the psychic space.

The following year we went on a long journey all around Eastern Europe, into Poland, Czechoslovakia, Hungary – it was in 1967 – Romania, Bulgaria, ended up in Turkey, the lot – and there I got all the material for *Between*, which I then wrote afterwards. I was collecting mineral water labels in all these different languages, all these signs in hotel rooms and so on. But you see, when I started it, I didn't have the experience, that's where I went wrong. Also, I had made my interpreter a man, and when I decided it had to be a woman, it suddenly worked, whether that's because – the idea comes back in the novel – an interpreter is just interpreting the ideas of other people and never has any ideas of her own, and that goes better with the cliché notion of woman…mysteriously it worked better once I'd made her a woman. With *Xorandor* and *Verbivore*, it's true I had the idea, but I didn't plan the novel. With *Such*, I had no idea, I started with a sentence and it became something and I didn't know where I was going and that's the chief pleasure of writing.

How do you feel the novelist and critic and theorist in you relate? Do you feel them to be in tension?

Well, it's a difficult relationship because in one way, and particularly if you study narratology, it spoils you. I find it very difficult to read what I call 'the average novel' because, oh dear yes, he's doing a flashback, and no, he's got this narrator like this and like that. It's a pity in a way, one is no longer a naïve reader, one reads technically, and that's also a block on writing. On the other hand, I think it does make you much more aware of what you're doing. It's self-conscious in a way, but it also increases your awareness, and you can play with narrative conventions and do things to the novel that you probably couldn't do without that knowledge. But it is difficult. I wrote *Thru* when this tension was at its height, because I'd gone to Paris, I was plunged into structuralism and poststructuralism, I had to teach it and so on, and it blocked me completely, I couldn't write for several years. Then I wrote _Thru_, but I had to write it four summers running before getting it right. It's a novel about the theory of the novel, it's a text about textuality, it's a fiction about the fictionality of fiction, it's the most postmodernist of my books, it really is the most self-reflexive. That cured me, it resolved the tension in a way. I had to write it, and I don't regret writing it, but I don't think it did me any good: I got this reputation as a difficult writer from then. Everything you do adds to your reputation or non-reputation or bad reputation, and that's the life of a writer.

Can I raise the question of mimesis as applied to your novels? What emerged from poststructuralism – I'm being fairly reductive here – was a notion that mimesis was a bad thing –

That was just a stage.

– and that it was very bad to read, say, a Robbe-Grillet novel in such a way as to recuperate or naturalize it for realism. Now it seems to me that if you look at, let's say, Out, _you could read that in two ways – you could read it mimetically, as a very powerful portrayal of disorientation and fragmentation in a post-catastrophe world, or, because of its repetitions, its variations, its hesitations, you could read it as a novel about textuality, a novel that's constantly drawing attention to how fiction constructs and then can deconstruct reality. And I wondered whether you have a preference for a particular kind of reading both in regard to_ Out, _but also in regard to_ Between, _which you could read as a polylogic sort of text, but which you could also read as a vivid representation of a specific consciousness._

There was a kind of revolt against the mimetic novel in the sense that it's true that the realistic novel – I'm talking about the great classical nineteenth-century realistic novel – had developed all sorts of techniques to capture the whole of reality. Once the structuralists had got going on that and showed that it's as unreal as anything else in fiction, that these are all techniques, that you can, not necessarily deconstruct, but pull to pieces and show how it works, there was a sort of demolition. But nevertheless, if they could show how the mimetic illusion was produced, it doesn't destroy the mimetic illusion – we still read these novels with great pleasure. After all, Oscar Wilde said that the nineteenth century as we know it is entirely the creation of Balzac; real history, the actual things as it were, tend to disappear. Historians come along and that's another kind of fiction, they impose their vision of it, but our idea of the nineteenth century is much more vivid through fiction than through history. And in the twentieth century realism went on, but in a very diluted way, so you get what I call the neo-realistic novel where a lot of these techniques have fallen apart and they're too transparent and rather irritating. So I can understand the reaction against the mimetic novel, that language isn't just a transparent window on the world. The idea was to make language disappear, so that you could think you were looking at the world, well no, you're looking at words, characters are just made of words, and so there was this movement towards the *signifiant*, the actual text, textuality, but language is itself representative and you cannot do without this representative function. A painter can perhaps produce a totally abstract painting, but even so, he's still reproducing forms that exist, he will put triangles and straight lines and curves, and these exist, he can't invent forms that don't exist, so even a non-representative painter is still representative. And it's more true with language, we can't get away from that function of language, because every word has a referent, here's a book, here's a table, and when we write any sentence we are in fact being mimetic. And just to try and jettison the mimetic function is nonsense. So gradually I too found that you can't write a novel without being mimetic. I think my recent novels are much more mimetic, but there is this extra dimension, of science fiction or something else, I'm nevertheless trying to show a world that is not the familiar world that many novelists write about. That doesn't interest me, just to reproduce my own little life and so on, that doesn't interest me at all.

One of the things that gave a great passion to poststructuralism in its really heady days, the days of Tel Quel *and Barthes and Sollers and Kristeva, was the idea that the subversion of the classic realist text, the production of the writerly rather than readerly text, was not only an aesthetically but a politically radical act. I can imagine a reading of your texts that would see them in that way. How would you feel about that?*

That's a difficult question. I don't think we should take that *Tel Quel* phase too seriously. Philippe Sollers, who was very much in on this, has gone back to writing completely mimetic novels – I mean, *Femmes* is all his women friends and mistresses and so on – and he's a bestseller. And Kristeva has just published *Les Samurai*, which can be read as a *roman à clef* about Paris literary life. *Tel Quel* was an interesting group because they kept shifting their political position. They were Communists, and then they were Maoists, and then they dropped that, and now they're practically pro-American or even interested in the Church. I don't think one should be too influenced by these fashions. I wasn't very influenced by that, but it's true that I became very interested in language, and in the fact that everything you write, every character, is a creation of words. In *Thru* I played a lot with it; I describe a scene, it's never clear who's telling it, there are two narrators but you don't know who they are, these two, this woman and this man who are inventing each other, and at one point it seems that the text is being written by Jacques le Fataliste's master, and they discuss it, and at another point, it's being written by students in a creative writing class. In other words, every time I create something with words, I uncreate it afterwards to show that it's just made with words. A lot of people have done that, but I was doing it in my own way. I've moved away from that because I think everybody accepts that now, that everything is created with words. Insofar as I play with narrative levels in *Verbivore*, I'm still in a way doing it, everyone knows that Decibel is an impossible character and so on. But I don't reject the mimetic function at all. As to the politics, I don't know if my work is politically radical. I mean, I'm centre-left, but I don't know whether this comes through in my novels. There are probably elements, if anyone did an analysis – this nostalgic element you mention – which might classify me as rather conservative and yearning for the good old days. One doesn't think of that when one's writing.

I want to ask more about influences on your work, or 'intertexts'. For example, when I read Between, *it related above all, for me, to* Finnegans Wake. *But I believe you hadn't read Joyce at the time?*

No, that doesn't mean anything. As Butor said, we're all influenced by Joyce, even if we've never read him. I don't actually like Joyce, so I can't really count him as an influence. My chief influence is Pound, because in many of my books, I use repetition, a sentence comes back but in a different context which gives it a different meaning, as in *The Cantos*. But also Beckett, and the *nouveau roman*, though less so than people think. Those are the three major influences. I acknowledge influences when they're conscious, but of course there are so many unconscious influences, it's not really for the author to say.

I think you mentioned at the time of Thru *the influence, in regard to the typography, for example, of a novelist whom you also discuss in* A Rhetoric of the Unreal –

Oh, Maurice Roche.

I don't think he's very well known in England.

No, though some of his books have been translated in America now – very difficult to translate because he does a lot of tricks with typography and so on. I like his work very much.

Would you acknowledge him, in fact, as an influence in relation to Thru?

For *Thru*, yes, not for the others. But you see, in *Thru*, I use so many things that Maurice Roche doesn't use, so it's an element, and one could say that it's also influenced by Apollinaire or some of the surrealists. No text just comes out *ex nihilo*, it always comes out of other texts.

In relation to the matter of intertextuality, can I put to you an interesting comment on Thru *made by Patricia Waugh in her book* Metafiction, *published in 1984? Waugh says: '*Thru *simply makes explicit the dialogic status of all novels. Christine Brooke-Rose takes the novel, and the metafictional novel, to their furthest extreme…* Thru *shows how all fiction is thus implicitly metafictional' (pp. 147-8). So in a way she's saying it's a kind of proto-novel, as Shlovsky said* Tristram Shandy *was. Would you accept that claim?*

For *Thru*, certainly. It is consciously intertextual and there are lots of quotations that people haven't picked up. At the end, I have this phony index. No-one's understood that, but it's actually a list of every author I quote in the book, but without page-references. It comes in after a class, these students are talking, and someone says, there are degrees of presence. This is a sentence from Genette, who says the narrator can be absent, and absence is absolute, but there are degrees of presence, there's the narrator who participates in the plot, there's the observer-narrator and so on. I turned that into an English pun, you give a degree for presence, and so authors are given alpha minuses and beta pluses and so on. I had to ask certain permissions when they were alive – everyone laughed. But you see, they're not according to my evaluations, it's the students who are doing this. So Barthes gets a beta plus simply because he appears quite a lot, and someone who is totally fictional appears also in this list, and some get a zero because they're not present at all. So it's a joke, it's the students attributing these degrees of presence but it's also an index. If anyone wants to chase up every time I quote something, it's all there.

Much of your work is very funny, but perhaps this doesn't come through in the way you're often described in criticism. You tend to be seen as someone more austere, more forbidding.

Very likely, yes. Well, that's my lot. I don't know why I get this label. I always think what I write is very simple, but – every time I'm told I'm difficult, so ...

Could I put to you a further point Patricia Waugh makes, which seems to accord with some of your own comments about mimesis earlier. She says: '[I]n its excessive self-referentiality ... Thru fails to provide, beyond itself, sufficient direction for the novel genre as a whole' and she suggests that 'the future of the novel will depend upon a transformation, not an abandonment, of the traditional conventions of fiction, though it may well be a transformation based on lessons learned from radical texts like Thru' (p. 148). I wondered how you felt about these remarks? And of course they raise that old, familiar question, which has perhaps come back in a different context at the beginning of the 1990s, of the future of the novel.

Well, I don't think *Thru* would necessarily lead to anything. That's not, certainly, why I wrote it. It's a thing, it's an object in itself. I mean, it might influence other people, but it might not. I have no illusions about that, and I may be totally forgotten in ten years. I'm not writing, as it were, for posterity, I'm writing for each book. But I agree that radical novels can then lead to something else, even indirectly. People always conceive of literature as a straight line of development, and when someone goes off at a tangent, it's called a dead end, nothing can come out of that. People said that about Joyce, you can't go further than Joyce. Well, Beckett went further than Joyce. It's as though the tangents then rejoin this imaginary straight line. As to the future of the novel, it's very much gone back to mimesis. And even my work, I no longer do what I did in *Thru*, I've abandoned that, and actually Maurice Roche has abandoned it too in more recent work.

The novels which are interesting today are completely different. The paper I'm going to be reading at Cambridge is called 'Palimpsest History' and it deals with Eco and Salman Rushdie and Carlos Fuentes and so on – people who write a sort of palimpsest history of the 'real' history – 'real' in quotes because history is itself partly a fiction. So you see, there are so many different modes, including science fiction: all sorts of ways the novel can go. And the notion that the novel is dead, perhaps I entertained it in my youth, but it's not true, there are always different transformations.

You've now retired from your Professorship at Vincennes, you've made, it seems to me, a creative comeback as a novelist, and you're possibly starting to acquire a new and perhaps younger audience. Your novels are very much concerned with futures: how do you see your own future as a novelist?

It's very difficult. One always thinks the last one is the best one. But – no, I can answer it to this extent, that *Amalgamemnon*, *Xorandor*, *Verbivore* and the one I'm working on now, which has nothing to do with computers, are part of a quartet – I think I'm going to call it *The Intercom Quartet*. Now in my head, that's going to be my last book, but one never knows, one always says that, and now I've got all the time in the world... It's true I've given up theory – I've got a critical book coming out from Cambridge University Press, *Stories, theories and things* which I worked on last winter, but that's the end, I'm not doing any more theory, and I just want to be totally free for novels. I may dry up even, who's to know? But I won't say more about the next one. As to the youthful readership, it would be nice if I were speaking to the young. Sometimes I'm made to feel an old has-been.

Frank Kermode

King's College, Cambridge
21 March 1990

NICOLAS TREDELL: *In the Prologue to your* Essays on Fiction 1971-82, *published in 1983, you call yourself 'a diachronic sort of person' (p. 5), and so perhaps we could trace your development through time, with some synchronic excursions. You were born and brought up in Douglas, on the Isle of Man – very much on the margin in terms of conventional concepts of 'England' – and you went to Douglas High School. You then came over to the English mainland, to Liverpool University, and took your Finals in 1940, in the shadow of war. Can you tell us about your literary and intellectual formation up to 1940, both inside and outside of formal education?*

FRANK KERMODE: Well, the Douglas of my youth was not a very bookish place, but there were people interested in books. I remember, for example, our local newsagent used to give me copies of *The Freethinker*, and things like Shaw's *Intelligent Woman's Guide to Socialism and Capitalism*, the two volumes in the Pelican series at 6d each, which I remember reading when I was about 16. There were bright people at school, of course. After all, I was a contemporary of Randolph Quirk's, and Randolph cannot be accused of not being bright. And there were good teachers, it was a good school in its way. My mother was sort of interested in poetry without knowing a lot about it. But it was very much provincial. And Liverpool, which was, as it were, the local university, the only one I could ever have afforded to go to, I think did well enough by us. The Professor there was a man called L.C. Martin who was known for his editions of Vaughan and Crashaw and later Herrick, rather than for criticism or any contribution to what is now called theory. I suppose most of the education that one gets is from contemporaries and I owed a great deal to Peter Ure, who was an exact contemporary of mine, and by my standards enormously learned. He had taken Classics at school and had read thousands of books that I'd never heard of, and I suppose the three years I spent close to him were very important to me. And of course we kept up that connection until his death. Right after university I went into the Navy, and that didn't afford me any examples of literary *cénacle* either. The war was really, from the point of view of any kind of career involving literature, a dead loss. Maybe it gave obscure benefits in other ways but not in any kind of professional way.

Do you feel the war affected your literary and cultural outlook?

I'm sure it did. You met different sorts of people. In fact, the Navy being what it is, you got a quite different impression of the world. I mean a ship, especially a warship, is a very sealed-off unit. I didn't know much about the world at all, and I didn't know that people like this existed. And then I came to think that they were in fact the world. Peter Ure constituted himself as a kind of one-man book club, he sent me a book every month or so, and so I had that kind of connection, but otherwise, that was unreal, that was out there, lost really. So one lived in this single-sex and, on the whole, extremely rough-tongued society for all those years. With intermissions – I spent some months in the United States and Australia and so on. And I wrote a lot of poems at that time. But it was not what you would call a good preparation for a literary life. I suppose I envied very much, or I daresay if I'd known about it more closely I would have envied, the kind of life people led in Fitzrovia, that kind of Tambimuttu circle. What fun it must have been not to have got involved in the war, except insofar as being in London was to be involved in the war. One did feel a lot of envy, I think, for those who were fortunate enough not to waste almost six years as I did in that way. And then, of course, the years immediately after the war were not exactly conducive to high-toned literary endeavour either. You had to scrape through: I remember I had a postgraduate scholarship which, I think, paid me £200 a year, or a bit less, so that I was always very poor. Anyway, everybody was poor in those days, or so we like to think now. The myth of the paradisal post-war period – it didn't feel like that at the time. So it was, I suppose, a rather unusual formation, if you want to use that posh word.

In The Sense of an Ending, *which came out in 1967, you discuss the paradox of the link between modernist radicalism in art and political*

*reaction, and you say: 'All who, in the 'thirties and 'forties, formed
their minds on the great moderns but spent their good years opposing fascism, must understand this paradox as in need of resolution'
(1968 edn, p. 111). I wondered if that was an oblique self-reference,
that you were one of those who formed your mind on the great moderns, and then went into the war and found this paradox pressing.*

I think that's true. I'd totally forgotten that remark, which I've probably made in other forms more recently. We were very keen, of
course, on Eliot, and we were also very keen on Auden. I suppose we
puzzled a bit about that paradox: there was the Pope of Russell
Square, a very, very right-wing figure, and he sponsored Auden, who
was, ostensibly at any rate, of the left: but he didn't stay there very
long, of course, he drifted over to the other side. So we were caught
in that, and I've written about that more recently in *History and
Value*: the difficulty that we now have in imagining what it felt like
at that time, when war was virtually certain, and all the things that
one really had emotional sympathy with were extremely left-wing. I
never joined the Party. And yet, as you say, our heroes included
people like Wyndham Lewis, writing anti-Semitic and pro-Hitler
materials, which he recanted. It was a very strange period, and that
was why it seemed worth reminding people that it was.

Yes indeed, and I'd like us to come back to History and Value *later
on. You've talked about the thirties and forties: how did you respond
to literary and cultural developments in 1950s England, to the
Movement, for example, insofar as there was a Movement?*

Well, I was, of course, very much on the fringes of all that. I was quite
close to John Wain, who had a lot to do with it, because he had his
radio programme *First Reading*, and he really had a lot to say in the
operation of that little press at Reading where these important little
books were hand-printed. I was much influenced, I suppose, by
Wain, whom I saw almost every day because we were working
together at Reading University, and who was and remains an
extremely attractive, funny man. I remember when he wrote that
piece about Empson, very important in the history of the Movement,
which appeared in the last issue of *Penguin New Writing* and which
he, of course, claimed closed down *Penguin New Writing*. All those
things were part of a quite deliberate attempt to steer a course for
English poetry which was away from Tambimuttu and things like
that, and it seemed fresh and clean, and a bit overstated maybe. And

then, with the publication of *Hurry on Down* in 1953, Wain could see his way to giving up teaching. *Hurry on Down* really was, in a sense, a pioneering work, although I think that particular aspect of the Movement ran out of steam very quickly. So did the use of very tight verse forms: it didn't really persist. So it wasn't an earthshaking affair but it was an interesting affair. We have these little movements now, some of them much smaller, like the Martians and so on, which are really much more quirky. This was a real attempt to put English writing on a new footing. It didn't really succeed, I suppose; it might have made some difference, though. But it was a bigger thing than just the latest flavour of the month. And it was quite interesting to be even very much on the margin of that. It was a question who was in and who wasn't: was Donald Davie a Movement poet or wasn't he? I remember that Donald Davie reviewed my *Romantic Image* in the *Twentieth Century* and endeared himself to me by carefully showing that a poem which he thought was by Blake was very superior to a poem which he thought was by Yeats, and getting them the wrong way round. The endearing thing was his apology: When I make a blunder, I really make it good. Of course, I've always been on amiable terms with Donald too. So I really do, in a way, belong to that time, though I moved off in quite different directions.

In the later fifties, you produced the book called Romantic Image. *That book, particularly if one puts it back in the context of its time – it appeared in 1957 – was intellectually very radical, in its questioning of certain ideas that were then very dominant: of a schism between Romantic and Modern poetry, of the autonomous, almost instantaneous image, and, of course, of the dissociation of sensibility. The main criticism that seems to have been made of it, both at the time – for example, by Donald Davie – and subsequently, is that, although in one way it seeks to return poetry to history, in another way, it's dehistoricizing, there's a very strong drive for identity: you produce from all these different texts the Romantic Image. How would you respond to that criticism?*

Well, I would, I suppose, accept it, for want of means to reject it. I don't remember a lot about the book. A year or so ago, I listened to a paper by John Stokes about it at Warwick University in which he made some quite severe criticisms of it; for example, there are passages in it about Wordsworth's 'Resolution and Independence', and he says that I simply didn't bother about the actual poverty of the figure, it was a kind of symbolic poverty I was interested in. And

I suppose that, in a way, was true, but I've always been interested in the idea of poverty as you get it in Wallace Stevens, for example, where there really is no difference between physical and metaphysical poverty. This may be deplorable in some ways, but it can also be very interesting and moving. As for the rest of the argument, of course there had been attacks on dissociation of sensibility before – Freddie Bateson did one, in *Essays in Criticism*, I remember, in which he showed that the expression itself was distorted from its original sense in Gourmont. And I suppose I was looking for someone to attack. *Romantic Image* was an odd book, in a way, because I didn't mean to write it. I was doing something else, I was very involved with English Renaissance literature at the time, and it came about simply because – I think it was Donald Gordon – had organized what here in Cambridge is called a circus, a series of lectures each on a particular poem, and I offered a paper on 'In Memory of Major Robert Gregory'. And then it was thinking about that, that the book sort of grew. I wrote it very quickly; it's the only time that's ever happened. Even so, it's got quite a lot of padding in it, as most of my books seem to have. Like all my books, I think it has two or three ideas, to cite Stevens again, and a good deal of it could be done away with. There's a lot of silly stuff towards the end, I remember.

I wouldn't have accused your books of being padded. They seem to me very compressed.

I think probably the parts that have got something in them are compressed. Perhaps it oughtn't to be so compressed, but expounded in a more leisurely way, and then drop the other stuff. I think that it is a fault of mine. I'm not a long-distance runner. Anyway, that's it, you can't rewrite everything after 30 years. *Romantic Image* had a success which surprised me. It was a little monograph which you'd expect those who were interested to digest in a year or two, and then it would be remaindered. However, it hasn't been, and it still gets mentioned. That's very pleasing, but perhaps not deserved.

Allowing for all the obvious differences, might one propose a link between Romantic Image *and Raymond Williams's* Culture and Society, *published in 1958? You're both attacking concepts which function, to some extent, to deny time and the possibility of rational communication. Would you see anything in such a link?*

Yes, I suppose I would. I remember reviewing *Culture and Society* in *Encounter* when it came out, with admiration but also with some reservations. I think it is, or was, an important book. I'm not sure now. I think Raymond himself moved away from that approach. This was, after all, the sort of Hoggart-Williams period, and my own background was very much like theirs, so I suppose a certain similarity of tint would be expected, though I've never had the precise kind of political interest – I mean, I was interested in politics, but it was something that somehow didn't seem to enter very directly into what I was doing. And of course Raymond in *Culture and Society* was already interested in the kind of process he later developed in *Keywords*, how concepts changed with use and so on. I always think that's a very interesting way to work, and in a very different sense, that's the way Empson sometimes worked, but I don't know that I did really. I think I've never had a method. You couldn't, nor should you, want to write an account of me which would be like an account of Raymond Williams, who had progressive, marked stages and so on. I'm too disorganized.

You've mentioned Wallace Stevens, who is a constant presence in your work. In 1960, at a time when he wasn't given much attention in England, you produced a study of him, which was reissued in 1989. Could you explore the nature of your interest in him?

I don't quite know how it started. Again, it's conceivably got something to do with John Wain. I remember we were sufficiently interested in Stevens to be shocked when he died, although there was no reason in particular to be shocked. But that was in 1955. The book was commissioned and written and published in 1960; there was some doubt on the part of the publishers as to whether they really could sell a book on Stevens. I don't think it sold fantastically well. It was written with great enthusiasm; I didn't know as much about Stevens as I know now, and of course, I didn't have access to the letters. In that sense, it's very much tied to the limitations of the moment. There's so much written about Stevens now. I've read a lot of it. It doesn't actually make much difference to the way I feel about Stevens. The biography and so on, it doesn't seem to me to make much difference. The letters, though, did; I was sorry not to have had access to those. He's always been important to me. I don't know how you know this. It's rather like being in love, isn't it? I mean, you couldn't exactly, you would not account for being in love with somebody by describing hair and lips. You might, that's a way of doing it, but…I feel a deep sympathy, also sometimes a lot of irritation, with Stevens, but he is, to me, a very important poet.

What irritates you about him?

Well, the fact that he rambles on when he really should have stopped. There's an awful period round about *Ideas of Order* when he just lost the capacity to distinguish between what should be thrown away and what should be kept. I don't think he ever did throw much away, and that makes him very bulky. Of course, a vast proportion of his work was written when he was quite old, over 60. That makes it interesting, but it also means that he did it when he was a) very good, b) very imperious in a way. So I think there is too much of it, in a funny kind of way, and yet I do so much admire those very late poems, which got no showing in my book at all, and which I haven't really come to terms with – things like 'The River of Rivers in Connecticut', a quite wonderful poem.

Stevens also figures in The Sense of an Ending, *your studies in the theory of fiction which came out in 1967. In the* Prologue *to* Essays on Fiction, *you say, of* The Sense of an Ending, *that the impact of structuralist and poststructuralist thinking about narrative made you feel 'rather dismally that quite a lot of work had gone into a book which became antediluvian almost on publication (1983 edn, p. 3). How do you feel about* The Sense of an Ending *today?*

It's got some good things in it, I think. One or two of the notions in it which have been taken up and are often cited are quite interesting, like the myth-fiction distinction and the *tick-tock* business and the idea of apocalypse as a fictive *tock*. But there are one or two things in it that were never taken up: the whole business about *aevum* fell flat, but that, I think, was actually rather a good idea: this idea of a fictive order of time, which after all has a long history, seems to me quite a useful way of talking about certain things in narrative. It didn't catch on, it was too bizarre really, the word itself was unappealing... I think it crops up in Iris Murdoch's novel *The Time of the Angels*, which is what *aevum* originally was, but I don't think she got that idea from me. But it is a fascinating idea which had a great influence on law and does reflect something that we do unconsciously, which is to re-order the sort of co-ordinates of time when we're reading a fiction. I was also involved at that time in a fairly friendly row with Joe Frank over 'spatial form'; all the business about the time of the angels and so on is really a way to try and get out of spatializing, to have temporal and not spatial co-ordinates, which probably caused various kinds of misleading formulations. But it is curious: *The Sense of an Ending* has got a tiny place, I suppose, in the big change that came over literary criticism in the later 1960s. Barthes was becoming a big name already, Derrida began to make an impact towards the end of the decade, and then we had really sophisticated stuff from people like Genette and Todorov. All that really did seem to give the subject a new appearance, and I think it has done, still is doing really.

In The Sense of an Ending, *you employ three major categories – fiction, reality and myth: and the privileged model of fiction seems to be literary fiction. But in your account, fiction seems to expand so that it might engulf the other two categories: myth becomes fiction misrecognized, or misread, and there's a very strong sense that our ideas of reality are shifting, liable to change, so 'reality' itself comes across as provisional, a construct that could fall under the sign of fiction. So there's a movement towards this all-embracing epistemological scepticism, which seems to have become more important in your later work and also much more widely in modern thought, with Rorty and Lyotard and so on. Would you feel that to be true of* The Sense of an Ending?

Yes, I think that's true. I was trying to remember as you were speaking, was there an obvious origin for my talk about it? I don't know that there was. I mean, I'd been reading Vaihinger's *The Philosophy of As If* with interest – he was totally unread at that time, no-one bothered about him, and I suppose... I don't know. I suppose I'm not really capable of coming up with any kind of truly radical philosophical ideas. I didn't know much about the kind of pragmatist tradition Rorty works in. I suppose I just blundered on something that other people have now taken very much further. I never, I think, want to go to the limit like some people. What I know about Lyotard, I don't care for.

What don't you care for in him?

In Lyotard? Well, I think the book about the postmodern condition is really a worthless book, frankly. I know it has a great following, but either the whole idea of the metanarrative, the *grand récit*, is so obvious that there's no point in making a fuss about it, or there aren't such things, and if there aren't now, then there never were. It seems to me that things are just hung on that notion. And also the kind of random attack on totality is really part of a contemporary assault on the whole notion of the aesthetic, which we're now getting from

Terry Eagleton's new book, *The Ideology of the Aesthetic*, which to my mind is far more impressive than anything Lyotard can say about it. Of course, Terry Eagleton does believe in a metanarrative, and he therefore very sensibly won't have to do with this war on totalities that is so popular now. It's a very, very difficult position to resist, and I suppose if there is a sense in which my notions about fictiveness were leading that way, then I wouldn't want to go along with it.

You've already mentioned the impact of structuralism and poststructuralism on literary studies, and your Prologue to Essays on Fiction *recalls the informal seminars which you held at University College London from 1967 to 1974, when you were Lord Northcliffe Professor, and which novelists, critics and theorists – including, on one occasion, Barthes himself – attended. You speak of the constant widening of horizons this produced, and say that no other phase of your academic life has given you so much pleasure and instruction. This must have been a fascinating period: can you reconstruct your response to these developments?*

Well, that was an interesting time. It came about partly by accident: all I began with was a quite ordinary kind of graduate seminar. Then people who were not strictly of the academy began to turn up, and then…I had very little to do with the success of it, except actually running it, because we used to get a regular contingent come from Cambridge: Stephen Heath, and Jonathan Culler who was here at Cambridge then, and his wife then, Veronica Forrest-Thomson, they all came. And there were some good graduate students like Christopher Norris, and there were other people about who were very sceptical, but who came – like Barbara Hardy – and so in the end, it became less of an academic occasion than something without walls, if you like. They were rather fatiguing: it was quite difficult to keep things going. I remember Christine Brooke-Rose, for example, coming, B.S. Johnson; they would come and give a paper and they would tend to come again when they weren't giving a paper. It was really quite an exciting time in that respect. I think proper credit should be given, if there's a question of dishing out credit, to Stephen Heath, who probably gave more papers than anybody else, papers which, as far as I know, he's never published and which were exceptionally brilliant. And Culler would do his more cautious stuff – he was then a structuralist, this was his pre-Derridean phase – but he was much quieter. Stephen was actually leading a revolution at the time, and he was willing to lead it in my office. Well, that was fine with me; I would simply resign the chair to him whenever he had something to say. So that was it. It was all full of goodwill; there was nobody there, I think, who was willing to say *a priori*, this is a lot of garbage, which is of course what happened in Cambridge. I remember Heath and MacCabe published a sort of cyclostyled volume, *Signs of the Times*, and that was the sort of thing people carried into the seminar with them. I don't remember that we had a lot of Derrida in that series. I think we must have done, on reflection, because I think Stephen was well into all that at the time, and I remember reading *De la grammatologie* on the recommendation of Paul de Man about then – about '71 or thereabouts. So anyway, there was a kind of great brew going on then. People were reading Jakobson, too, who still seemed very central in those days. I don't know whether he still does – probably not.

Yes, it was good, and yet it didn't seem discontinuous with the ordinary practice of literary criticism, somehow. It didn't seem – although Stephen, I daresay, didn't see it in this light – that we were doing something absolutely new; it was our kind of thing, only given a new and rather exciting dress, as it were. And now I see that's no longer a tenable view of it, because everything that we took for granted then, like notions of coherence, in fact everything that the notion of the aesthetic has trailed down the ages with us has now, of course, been discarded.

You came to Cambridge in 1974, as King Edward VII Professor of English Literature. What kind of intellectual atmosphere did you find here in literary studies?

Well, it's very difficult to assess atmospheres in a place like this, because for one thing, members of the Faculty of English meet only for administrative purposes, since they're scattered around the colleges and so on, so you first see them in the worst possible light really, that is, as kind of sea-lawyers, as I said in my unfortunate speech at Senate House, remarkable chiefly for vanity and vacuity. You see, of course there are people here for whom one has a lot of respect, and there's great variety here, but insofar as they functioned as a corporate body, they were philistine. And I think the treatment of Colin MacCabe was evidence of that. I would have very much liked there not to be a battle over MacCabe, especially as it had to be fought on false grounds really: people were put into a position of being either totally committed on his behalf, or against him, and no good ever comes of a situation like that. I think that whole episode was a disgrace, really, to everybody concerned, and it made the atmosphere unbearably unpleasant, which is really why I left.

And how did you find America in contrast?

Oh, polite and mild. Mind you, I wasn't there long, and I never really got into politics at Columbia. In literature at Columbia, there were some stars, like Edward Said, who had a lot at stake. I had nothing at stake at all. I just did my graduate seminar, my undergraduate class, graded papers, and kept my head down. I never really, in that sense, belonged at all. But here in Cambridge the difficulty was that you couldn't keep your head down, because if you had the number one job, you had certain responsibilities, but you had no power. You had a vote, like any temporary lecturer in a college, and I thought that was pretty intolerable too. I think the whole administrative system which is forced on this place really by the peculiar relation of the colleges to the university is very bad. It also tends to mean real power is not anywhere that you can see it, it's all in the Old Schools, a few administrators.

An important intellectual result of your engagement with structuralism and poststructuralism is your book The Classic *which first appeared in 1975. This rejects both the 'Imperial' classic of Eliot and Barthes's schism between the classic 'work' and the modern 'text'. Instead, it takes the idea of the plural text, and suggests that only this offers an adequate account of the classic: that the classic is the plural text, open to multiple and constantly multiplying interpretations. That seems to me a liberating and fertile idea. But one might ask whether plurality is in fact an adequate definition of the classic?*

No, of course it isn't, because there is a sense in which anything is open to plural interpretation. What's missing from that book is some notion of what I now think to be the most difficult question of all, of the way in which value is attributed to one text rather than to another. I think I rather missed that out, as if there were certain things which had, inherently, this capacity for fruitful plural interpretation, and of course, that's begging the whole question. The other argument, which you hear all the time now, is that these special values accorded to canonical texts are institutionally invented and imposed, and that you could do the same thing if you wanted for Zane Grey or whatever.

But isn't the tendency in many of your own arguments to suggest that value really comes from and is perpetuated by the institution?

Well, it is, it is, but you see, this is the crux of the whole argument. OK, if you set up an institution which says, let us demonstrate that Zane Grey is susceptible to endless, continuous, plural interpretation of a sort that the institution would approve, then the only way to do it is to give a demonstration. It's no use just going on saying that we can do for Zane Grey what they used to do for Milton. You've got to show it. And so there's another concept, a very, very vague concept of interest which comes in here, and interests who, well, interests what Fish calls the interpretive community. This is a really difficult question.

Yes, it's fascinating. For example, you have a very interesting discussion of E.C. Bentley's detective story, Trent's Last Case, *in your* Essays on Fiction, *and one could imagine somebody coming along to that and offering another interpretation and so on, and its plurality being brought out, and its becoming an object of institutional attention, valued by the institution. And if you apply this attention to film, as is done quite a lot now, you will create valued works: they already have been created to some extent.*

And you have canons of science fiction, of women's literature, black women's literature and so on. All that is true. I don't know where this question ends. If, for example – to move out of literature – you think about ethical values, it's easy to say these are contingent, there is no way in which you can define ethical standards. On the other hand, the people who talk like this actually tend to observe standards which may be, in fact, fictive, not simply because they're afraid of breaking the law, but because they prefer life that way. They prefer people not to regard rape as a morally neutral activity – that's obviously putting it very simply. Most people accept that, and most people would think that those who take a totally amoral disposition are, in fact, not members of civilization, community, society. Well, there must be something parallel in the idea of a literary community, though it might be very difficult to…Barbara Herrnstein Smith's book, *Contingencies of Value*, is the biggest treatment of that problem: but it's all very well to say value is wholly and in every case contingent – this applies not only to literary value, but to anything else – but then she will continue presumably to go on being a decent citizen. So the ethical implications are really quite serious. Value is a very, very difficult question, and it's a question which doesn't concern simply literature, it's much more general.

Can I ask you about the genesis of your book The Genesis of Secrecy, *published in 1979? How did you get interested in Biblical hermeneutics?*

Well, that was something I really owe to Cambridge, I suppose. I came here, to King's College, in 1974. My wife was working in London still, so I didn't buy anything here, I came and lived in the college. I found I had an amazing amount of time on my hands, and I'd always wanted to refurbish my Greek, such as it was, and read the New Testament in Greek. So I did this in the year of '74 to '75, and then I got very interested along the way, not only in the stories themselves, like Oscar Wilde – oh, do let me go on, I want to see how it ends – but in the scholarship too, which I'd known nothing about really. I began to read a great deal in Biblical scholarship, and I actually attended a very arduous lecture course in the Divinity School given by a man called John O'Neill, which I learned a great deal from. But this was a hobby. Then Harvard asked me in '76 to give the Norton Lectures, and there was no prospect of getting time off to write them – life here in term time is really very hectic – so I thought, I'd better give them on something that's in my head. And I boldly decided to do them about the Bible, about the Gospels. And then it came down to Mark more or less. That's how it happened, it happened just because I knew that the only way I could give those lectures was to give them on something that was occupying my mind at the time. It was a gamble. I wasn't even sure that people would be interested. But they were, and the lectures really came off quite well. They appear in the book much as they were delivered, I think, a bit longer, probably.

If one compares The Classic *with* The Genesis of Secrecy, *it seems to me there's quite an important shift from the idea of plurality to the idea of secrecy, though of course the two are bound up. And this difference could be compared to the difference between the idea that the parables were intended to teach and the idea that they were intended to exclude – the idea in Mark's gospel, which you discuss extensively in* The Genesis of Secrecy, *that 'for those outside everything is in parables; so that they may indeed see but not perceive, and may indeed hear but not understand; lest they should turn again, and be forgiven' (Mark 4:11-12). Plurality is, at least potentially, a democratic idea, whereas secrecy seems an esoteric, exclusive, élitist idea.*

But the proviso is that it always fails, isn't it? It never works. It's very interesting, that passage in Mark about the parables, because he goes on to say: If you don't understand this, you don't understand anything, so being inside doesn't help. I think the idea of secrecy is unwieldy in that book, just as the idea of plurality is in the other. I've no doubt that *The Genesis of Secrecy* is a much better book, but it needed a great deal of thinking about the whole idea. I think if I'd read Allon White's book, *The Uses of Obscurity*, before I wrote *The Genesis of Secrecy* – of course I couldn't, because it didn't exist – that would have helped, I think. It's such a pity he died – that was not the best book he was going to write, but it was very useful, this whole idea of symptomatic reading, the Althusserean notion. A whole range of ideas which are just locked up in that word 'secrecy' needed untying, setting out, which I perhaps wasn't capable of at the time.

There's a fascinating ambivalence in The Genesis of Secrecy *which seems to be more widely characteristic of your work. One might – and indeed some critics and theorists have done so – see this endless interpretative possibility, the sense that there's no end to interpretation, as a cause for rejoicing, but you, while enjoying it in one way, seem saddened by it in another. You cite Kafka's parable from* The Trial, *about the man who spends long years waiting for admittance to the Law and is told repeatedly that he cannot yet be admitted. When he grows old he sees an immortal radiance streaming from the door outside which he has stayed for so long and, as he dies, he asks the doorkeeper why he alone has come to this entrance seeking admittance. The reply is: 'this door was intended only for you. Now I am going to shut it'. This is an image of what you see and often refer to as the 'disappointment' of interpretation, and you eloquently conclude* The Genesis of Secrecy *by saying that, as interpreters, 'our sole hope and pleasure is in the perception of a momentary radiance, before the door of disappointment is finally shut on us' (p. 145). Is that ambivalence, between the desire to find some final interpretation and the sense that you never will, very much a part of your work?*

I was a bit carried away by that Kafka parable. Of course, it's true that if you're expecting certainties, you're not going to get them, so to that extent it's disappointing, you are *déçu* in both senses, you're disappointed and you're also in a way deceived. When I read Gadamer and so on and got into hermeneutics, I felt they were really on the right track about all this, because they have this creative idea of one horizon of interpretation melding into another, and the complexity of the relationship between the original horizon and the present one, and the questioning that interpretation requires, and the presence of tradition, all those things: I think maybe he doesn't get them exactly right, but they are extremely important. And of course, it disposes of the idea that anybody who's doing a bit of interpretation should ever expect it to be in some ways definitive, because it's contrary to the whole sense of the matter. There are questions that came up in the visit of Umberto Eco over here a couple of weeks ago: he gave a lecture called 'Over-Interpretation'. Eco believes that, in the end, you must be able to say some things are wrong, and of course the whole question, of who you are and what gives you the authority to say that, all comes up, it's a very difficult question. Who says that, of the endlessly plural interpretations, some are allowable and some are not? It's a question of authority here. But there is such a thing as a wrong interpretation, and I think once you admit that, and I think it's just common sense to admit it, then you are in a much more comfortable position.

Why do you think the idea of the interminability of interpretation has proved so unsettling? I'm thinking, for example, of Helen Gardner's response, in In Defence of the Imagination *to* The Genesis of Secrecy *– she was clearly emotionally distressed by your book, and one sees this much more widely. There's a very deeply held view that interpretation should have a fixed goal of the single, correct meaning. Why is that?*

Well, of course, it's a view that can be given a much more respectable sense than Helen Gardner was able to do. On the other hand, you see, it really comes of making too great a leap from the use of language in day-to-day situations where the whole purpose, usually – there are exceptions – of saying something is to get someone to accept it, or perhaps believe it. And that's why we go to such trouble to, as they say, disambiguate statements of that kind. When you move to a different use of language where there is no necessary interpretative disambiguation, then you are in a field where it becomes absurd to say that the purpose of using language in that way is to get someone to accept a message that's been sent by a sender. The whole subject drifts into problems raised by the Austin-John Searle kind of world. For Austin, all uses of language which we call literary are what he calls non-serious. He just rules out anything that can't be disambiguated. Searle is a bit more thoughtful about that, I think.

Let's move on to Forms of Attention, *published in 1985, because it seems to me this takes up, in a very elegant and compressed way, many of the matters we've already discussed.* Forms of Attention *suggests an awareness and acceptance of the mortality, the historicity, the necessary erroneousness of our interpretations, in the widest sense of the term – our systems, the ways we look at and order the world. But you also propose that we should go on generating them, that what Rorty calls the 'conversation' should continue, and you say: 'That the conversation, the game, must go on, I have no doubt at all, for it is the means by which the primary objects of my own attention have to be brought to the attention of another generation' (1987 edn, p. 88). But – and you're well aware of this yourself in the book – this reason seems to be undermined by your own arguments. Because if interpretations and orderings change, as of course they do, then one way in which they might change is to displace the primary objects of your attention, or anyone else's attention, to move them from the centre to the margin: so that, to use the example I mentioned earlier, the study of film could replace the study of literature, could become central. The 'forms of attention', the protocols and processes of interpretation, a kind of canonicity, might survive, but the primacy, the centrality of literature is surely by your own arguments, potentially transient?*

I daresay that's right. That is, of my books, the one I think best of, by the way, partly because it's the shortest and there's less padding, and partly because it does actually get outside literature, in the Botticelli material. I particularly liked writing it, because the chapter on *Hamlet* is, I think, a fairly good demonstration of what is conventionally thought of as its inexhaustibility. You can always say something new about *Hamlet*, and not only something new, but something that looks true, that actually is faithful to the text. I also tried to show the degree to which a single quasi-totality like *Hamlet* can be illuminated by another quasi-totality, namely, the whole Shakespeare canon, and so on. It's what's now called intertextuality, it stretches on and on. So I'm pleased with that. I don't know how to answer your charge that the sort of rhetorical attention I gave to, say, hendiadys in *Hamlet* wouldn't serve to perpetuate an interpretation of *Casablanca* – which came into my mind as a genuinely canonical work. I daresay it would. There seems probably a difference, if I could just dwell on that point. Eco has an interesting essay on *Casablanca* in which he points out that it really is almost entirely because *Casablanca* is a set of clichés that in fact it's so effective: the audience can know when the lines are coming up. There's a kind of deprecatory feel about what *Casablanca*'s fans say about it. Nobody ever says it's the greatest film ever made or anything like that, do they? It's like the song in it, 'As Time Goes By', which is total nonsense from beginning to end, just a random assemblage of clichés, and in a way the film is that too. I loved it, by the way – haven't seen it for many years, but I loved it, as everybody did.

But what I'm really getting at is that there are certain kinds of interpretation which make claims, not about canonicity, but about quality. And there are certain kinds which don't make claims about quality. I suppose there would be many other examples one could think of, cult movies and so on, *The Texas Chainsaw Massacre*, for example. They really become a kind of currency, a joke-currency that passes between a community of fans, which does seem in a way – I'm just thinking about this as I sit here – to make them a bit different from the kind of attention one gives, say, to the B Minor Mass or *Hamlet*.

That would be true of those kinds of films, but one might point to other films, some of the films of Orson Welles, for instance, that have acquired a more traditional kind of value.

Well, that's true if you're thinking of one or two of Welles's early films. I suppose *Citizen Kane* would be a case that you'd have to consider if you were going into this argument seriously. It could be regarded as a collection of cinematic tricks, couldn't it, yet it could be regarded as an important work with secrets and all the rest of it. So there will be borderline cases. The interesting thing about *Casablanca* is that no-one would dream of putting it near a borderline. We do recognize a limit here.

Yes, there are certain films we enjoy and in a sense cherish and watch repeatedly, but we don't value them in the same kind of way that we value a canonical literary text.

I think that's right, though this is another way of saying that the question of value is central here, and also extremely hard to get your fingers into.

The question of value is taken up again in the book of lectures you mentioned near the start of the interview, History and Value, *which came out in 1988. One notable feature of this book is that you engage much more directly than in your past work with the relation-ship between literature and politics, in your attempt to revalue the work of the politically concerned left-wing thirties writers whom you feel are the victims of a period myth. What prompted you to come out in this political way?*

I remember at one of those lectures, Terry Eagleton and Raymond Williams were sitting together. They both came up laughing after-wards and said: 'We didn't know you cared'. I think it was partly a kind of sentimental self-scrutiny. I remember thinking, I can now read books that I read 50 years ago, and it's quite an interesting thing to do, to look again. That's why I chose that book nobody could pos-sibly have remembered, Stephen Haggard's *Nya*, really as an exam-ple of something that wouldn't, on most criteria, have a lot of value, but which you could show had, consciously or not, certain merits. But I was really more interested in the kind of dismissal by Auden himself, and thereafter by most other people, of his more political poems written around the Spanish Civil War time. I'd always admired those poets, you see, and re-reading them made no differ-ence to that feeling. I admired people like Upward, who is a grossly underrated writer, and it seemed to me very strange that modern Marxist criticism has very little but contempt for the left-wing litera-ture of that period, it kind of patronizes it. In some ways, of course, it's very vulnerable, because – I try to make this point in the book – it's very difficult for us to recapture the extraordinary gap between young middle-class writers and the rest of the population, particu-larly in the 1930s: working people were exotics to them, and the idea of poverty was a novel one. But they did actually go and get killed in Spain. I think Caudwell, for example, is a far more interesting writer than Eagleton is willing to admit. It's true that their version of Marx-ism didn't have the benefits of Lukács and Adorno and Gramsci and Althusser and so on, all the phases that Marxist people go through. And it was relatively simple. There was a direct connection between what people were thinking about politics and what people saw around them in the Depression and in the war in Spain and so on. So to treat them, following Orwell's line, as silly Oxford dilettantes, is quite wrong. But it's only a model of how wrong we're likely to be when we're trying to get into the mind-set, as they say, of some other period. It just happens to be a period that I can remember, having been ten at the beginning of that decade, 20 at the end of it, impres-sionable, and, as you said earlier, having all this difficulty, rushing out to see the latest Yeats poem as it appeared in the *London Mercury*, and yet knowing that *On the Boiler* was an eugenicist fascist tract. But it was a time of genuine political excitement which penetrated everybody's life, as it doesn't now. We're fussing about the Poll Tax. Well, it's right to fuss about the Poll Tax, but it doesn't have quite the edge that the issues did in 1938 or 1939.

Another topic you tackle in History and Value *is postmodernism. And in a sense, your argument relates right back to* Romantic Image. *You argue for a necessary continuity: you say that the postmodernist elevation of the fragment depends on a concept of prior or co-existing totality. What would be your general view of postmodernism?*

I do think periodization can limit and reduce the possibilities of particular works. The other objection to postmodernism, I suppose, was that it's, as it were, a kind of fake category that's been got up by people. First of all, you get the category, then you fill it with as many things as you can, so that it becomes a political category, it becomes a historiographical category, it becomes something that actually affects the way people practise the arts, and I think this is the wrong way round. It's bad enough that expressions like 'baroque' should become such thought short-circuiters, but that was imposed *a posteriori*: postmodernism was not. We had concepts of the postmodern, as it were, before we had postmodernity, and I do think this is elevating fashion to the grand heights of historical change. But what was wrong with that chapter in the book, I suppose, is the idea that you can say to people, you stop this foolish excess. You can't stop it. It could die out: it could become a very ambiguous expression, like Mannerism. You don't know quite what Mannerism is meant to be. You might not know what postmodernism actually connotes, and how long it'll be useful. It might not be very useful very long at all. In fact, people are already speaking about it as an age which is past. The usual thing is that it starts off by being something fairly limited, like in architecture, but when it becomes a matter of describing a whole present state of the evolution of European civilization, of world civilization, it just can't help, it's a poor little word. And modernism is now something that's condemned by many as a sort of fascist phenomenon. Well, is Edward Upward a modernist? I don't know, these terms are so hazy, aren't they? And yet, in a way, you can see a need for them just because the historical data's so unmanageable.

Yes, you suggest in History and Value *that the concept of a period is*

necessary as a way of processing and selecting historical informa-
tion, but is also dangerous, perhaps – to go back to The Sense of an
Ending *– if it turns from an organizing fiction into a myth.*

Well, people have done a good deal of thinking about this, mostly in
terms of painting – Panofsky and Gombrich, for example. There's a
difference between a period description and a description of a movement, as Gombrich points out. I think the simple way of putting this
is that nobody in the Middle Ages thought they were living in the
Middle Ages, but people in the Renaissance did think they were living in the Renaissance, rightly or wrongly, and that makes a big difference. Modernism is a bit like the Middle Ages in that there's a
sense of hindsight about it. But postmodernism wasn't a movement,
it was a description that became a movement. But these are very, very
complicated questions. Only insofar as these terms actually restrict
freedom of intellect are they dangerous.

Can we consider the current state of literary criticism? In the Pro-
logue to your latest collection of essays, An Appetite for Poetry, *you*
say: 'this great efflorescence of literary theory seems to entail an
indifference to, and even a hostility toward, "literature",' and that
'[i]t is at least worth considering what it is that we are apparently
being asked or forced to give up in order to have the benefits of the
present critical revolution' (pp. 5, 6). What are we being asked or
forced to give up?

It's not absolutely general, as I pointed out in that Prologue. You
would not have got either of the two main theorists who have
affected Anglophone theory, de Man and Derrida, unequivocally to
admit this. But there is, no doubt, a programme for the abolition of
literature as a distinct category of writing. That's what we're being
asked to give up. And that seems to me a lot to give up without making any kind of enquiry. And there again, you run straight into the
question of value. People will tell you that the privileging, as they say,
of literature as a separate class of text is quite recent, the last 200
years or something like that, and it's never been perfect anyway. The
vicar's still likely to say that if you're interested in the jumble sale,
you'll find literature concerning it on your way out. But we know
what we're talking about, and so do these people, and they actually
don't want it. They regard literature, like the whole aesthetic ideology really, as a part of the bourgeois, racist system of oppression.
And it is a political issue in the end. So that's what that Prologue was

about, it's saying, OK, before we go along with this, let's have a look at what's being jettisoned and what's being put in its place. And it seems to me that a lot of people are quite glad to get rid of it, because it saves a lot of boring reading: one would rather be reading Toni Morrison than reading Homer. Fine. Most of us are in that position. We take down a new novel rather than *The Odyssey*. But people would like that to be a universal condition. There would be no constraints, no obligations on membership of the...That is what I meant: the abolition of literature is definitely on the agenda.

But couldn't one say that was one development of your own epistemological scepticism? Some of the questions you've raised could lead one to ask: OK, why not abolish literature?

Well, I suppose that's right. On the other hand, you see, I've never doubted the right that everybody has to treat *Hamlet* as a totality; this without prejudice to the idea that it exists in concentric circles of larger totalities which might stretch out, the way the New Historicists say it does, to any kind of document, to a kind of interchange of power between documents. I think that, in the end, one can reconcile epistemological scepticism with some sort of highly conditional aesthetic. Perhaps it needs doing. I haven't done it, but I hope it can be done. Whether it is done or whether it isn't, I don't think makes a tremendous lot of difference, because people will go on, in a sense, intuiting...mustn't use the word...the B Minor Mass. Of course, there's all sorts of senses in which it isn't a totality; you could put another bit of the Mass in, you can take one out, but that's a childish way to look at it, people will still think it's a totality. There it is, there are things that have been there for a very long time. Incidentally, this is why I object to the Oxford Editor dropping Hamlet's last soliloquy from the text of *Hamlet*. I mean, it may not belong to the *Hamlet* of 1623, but it belongs to my *Hamlet* and your *Hamlet* and everybody else's. I'm not like Hirsch who says, no, no, he didn't intend that, he intended a totality or whatever. But you've got to have a very relaxed view of these things. And what happens is that we get very extremely expressed views.

One argument that's been made for the value of literature is a kind of functional one, that it offers a mode of knowledge, of insight, that can help to make people better, to make society better. In your Bucknell Lectures in Literary Theory, published this year [1990] as Poetry, Narrative, History, *you discuss, in the lecture 'Poetry and*

History', Horace's 'Actium Ode', Marvell's 'Horatian Ode on Cromwell's Return from Ireland', and Auden's 'Spain, 1937', and you say, of these three poems: 'They make history strange and they are very private in their handling of the public themes. They can protect us from the familiar; they stand apart from opinion; they are a form of knowledge' (p. 67). Now that's a very interesting cognitive claim. Would you want to say that literature is a distinctive form of knowledge that cannot be achieved by other means? Because that might be one argument – a very difficult one, I know – for its retention and perpetuation.

I think the opposition that's at work in that expression is the opposition between knowledge and opinion, doxa. You can't reduce Horace's poem to further bits of evidence about how the Romans felt about Cleopatra. It constantly is, in fact, protecting itself against that kind of doxal reading. In that sense, it's a form of knowledge. Yes, I think very much I would accept the way you put it. I think we must take literature as serious, despite Austin, and that it is a form of knowledge. I think what I had in mind when I wrote those sentences was a simpler opposition between knowledge and opinion, but if you want to make it more general, I think I'd accept that. So that's an epistemological assertion which, as you say, might not come very well from me.

Your thought has always had a kind of doubleness: it's been both very radical and also recuperative; your explorations go to the limit and then come back again. In his Foreword to Forms of Attention, *Frank Lentricchia sees you as a performer 'on the theoretical highwire' (p. x), and there's very much a sense of this in that book, and in much of your other work. There's also a sense – and this relates to something we were talking about earlier – that your work has certain totalizing tendencies – one could imagine someone else, or you yourself with a different approach, producing a grand theory from it – but it's always being undermined by particularities and complexities. In* History and Value, *you cite Blanchot citing Friedrich Schlegel's epigram: 'To have a system, that is what is fatal for the mind; not to have one, this too is fatal. Whence the necessity to observe, while abandoning, the two requirements at once' (pp. 140-1). And it seems to me that all your work strives both to observe and to abandon the requirements of having and of not having a system and of being both radical and recuperative. Do you feel that to be the case?*

Yes I do, except that I think you put it in too eulogistic a sense. I've always thought that it was really a lack of the intellectual force to drive through to a conclusion. You see, when I read someone with an entirely different cast of mind from my own, very much more penetrating, someone like Bernard Williams for example, then I think, in a way, he ends up in similar *impasses*, but the way through them is very much more consciously explored than it is in me. I think that's the major difference. I've never really thought of myself as having much power of consecutive thought. Things occur to me rather than my pursuing things, and they often occur to me just as I'm sitting at a typewriter or a wordprocessor. But the capacity for that kind of very expert examination of all the stages along the way, or even less the power to burst through the *impasse* at the end, I don't have either of those. I'm very glad the aporia has been established as a good way to end an argument. To drive it into an aporia, that's what I usually do, but as Paul de Man remarked himself, in one of his rare moments of written humour – he was quite funny otherwise – it's a bit like getting stuck in a revolving door.

Karl Miller

University College, London
23 April 1990

NICOLAS TREDELL: *You're a man who's been much possessed, in your writing, by duality, above all in your fascinating book* Doubles, *published in 1985, but also in your earlier biography of Henry Cockburn, which came out in 1975, and in your recent collection of essays,* Authors, *which appeared in 1989. Can you tell us about the development of your interest in this theme?*

KARL MILLER: I kept this interest up over the years because it appeared to me that you could find things out by asking what was twofold and what was thought to be twofold in the world. I suppose it's also true that my interest in the subject dated from my growing-up in Scotland, where the subject has been rather prominent, in the literary culture and indeed elsewhere. Even people who didn't call themselves great readers spoke in terms of doubles and alter egos and inner conflict. This was, of course, a preoccupation, coming out of the ancient world, which was European, and worldwide, in the nineteenth century, and not at all restricted to Scotland: but Scotland was to leave its mark, with the activities of James Hogg, leading on to those of other writers, principally Stevenson. So Scotland was interested in that, and I was aware of it. I always took it with a grain of Scottish salt when I was young, feeling that it was a kind of *topos* or artifice in literature, an affectation or a style, rather than a rock-solid perception of something that you might think of as substantial and real. However, I had to modify that view somewhat in writing *Doubles*. Duality is the sort of thing which embarrasses academics. Colleagues look the other way when the word 'doubles' comes up. There is a tendency in English studies for the word to seem disreputable, as if it referred to contraceptives or betting slips. But no serious student of

nineteenth and twentieth-century literature lacks at least some
degree of lively interest in the subject.

*When I read what you write about duality, I start seeing doubles
everywhere. The question this provokes is whether the concept isn't
too elastic, whether, if you wanted, you couldn't find duality wherever you looked. Would you feel that to be the case?*

I think the elastic is often stretched, by commentators, and indeed by
human beings living their lives in the world we know. They tend to
see resemblance and duplication where it doesn't do much good to
see it. It's true that you have to use your head and your imagination
in posing yourself the question: does it matter that these two things
are alike? One thing you perceive when you start dealing with doubles is that doubles aren't always – in fact, they tend commonly not
to be – duplicates or the same: there's some difference, and that takes
you to the idea of conflict and tension in the field of psychology and
personal relations and literary relations – that's to say, the personal
relations which are expressed in literature. Wherever you look, it's
likely to be worth asking whether a perceived duality is merely trivial
or decorative. So I think you're quite right to say: am I seeing double,
does it matter, do these two things resemble each other? There's also
the question of whether replication involving difference as well as
sameness is necessarily conflict.

*How do you see the origins of duality? Sometimes in your work you
seem to suggest that it's a very ancient and perhaps even universal
phenomenon. At other times, you treat it much more as a cultural
product, emerging, for example, from the interfusion of German and
Scottish Romanticism.*

I think that it is universal, and it is certainly to be found in the ancient
literatures. When you come to consider the matter of origins, you are
bound to feel that it's not surprising that it appears in remote places,
in folklore and in early literature. Freud has an explanation for this
which talks about the prehistoric or the primordial and guesses how
the double may have signified in that setting: in fact he's only gues-
sing, and his guess is hardly any better than yours or mine, it seems
to me. But it's clear that the business of seeing resemblance in the
world will be greatly augmented by such things as reflections,
shadows, all these occurring in a world of animism or magic where
the soul can separate from the body. And the duality of body and

soul will be involved with the perceptions you make about the binariness of the environment and the twofold character of the body: two testicles, two feet, two brains. There's something twofold about everything, as Emerson said. And this is bound to induce certain ways of thinking, certain states of mind. Duality occurs in Latin literature, and it was derived by the Renaissance from the Classical past. Shakespeare doesn't richly use it, but he uses it, and others used it then. This was an awareness that had to be developed in me because I was too ignorant initially to know how spacious or how charged was the pre-nineteenth century dualistic heritage. I found that a lot of the dualistic preoccupations of Romanticism, the kind of thing you were talking about, the Scottish example allied with the German example, were reiterations of ancient, folkloric, Classical dispositions of mind and habits of speech. The idea of the 'strange compound' in matters of human psychology, for instance, goes back, first of all, to alchemy, but then it goes back, as alchemy does, into the deep and unassessable past. In *Doubles*, I took the Romantic period as a starting-point. In my recent collection of little essays and thoughts about authorship, I rather ruefully found that I couldn't forebear repeating my concern with the matter when I became better acquainted with what had been made of it in seventeenth and eighteenth-century texts.

In Authors, *as well as going back in time, you claim a wide range of recent writers for duality – Levi, Roth, Bellow, Martin Amis, Peter Ackroyd, Rushdie – and your claims often seem convincing. But I wonder if, in a sense, the age of duality – or at least the age in which duality was conceptualized as it was in the eighteenth and nineteenth and earlier twentieth centuries – isn't passing, because duality depends on the conception of a self that may be divided into two or more parts but is at least coherent enough to recognize that it's divided.*

I think that point is inadequately addressed in *Doubles*. It is taken here and there in the book, and in *Authors*, but I would have been glad to have pursued it more vigorously in *Doubles*. If there is a loss of confidence or faith in the integrity of the self, then the idea of there being two selves, or the idea of the self as possessed in some way or other, must recede, I think, to make way for what has proved to be an influential scepticism. You have people with the qualifications of a Philip Roth going on how the self won't do, just as his friend Saul Bellow had pronounced that the game of the self, the jig of the self, was up. So I have to add a *mea culpa*, a sackcloth note, an admission that I should have gone into that better than I did. However, I also have to say that I have my own doubts and predispositions on the subject of the self, and of whether there is one any more, which are such as to license some confidence that duality is not dead yet. You see, I think there *is* such a thing as the self. Those who suppose that I am influenced by my Scottish background in taking an interest in duality might also suspect that I am Scottishly forked and divided, tartanly cleft. But I don't feel that way at all. I'm not a stranger to conflict, and I've had various problems in my life which are, or could be seen as, binary in form, and I'm sure everybody is like that. But I have a very robust sense of having been one and the same from the start.

Now I don't know whether this is an illusion. I can only say that it is what I have to tell about myself. This is my news: that I have been one and am still one, and that I behave like Karl Miller all the time. In a way, I was exploring an alien mentality in *Doubles*, which is not, I imagine, what people might think. I am recalcitrant enough to believe, moreover, that I am in this book of mine, and that no author can produce a book which is separate from what he is. This doesn't mean that his book is in some way equivalent to an essential or definitive self. The self changes all the time; it's constantly being adapted. It is always on the move and different from what it was yesterday. At the same time, you can experience the self as being like that while also experiencing the idea of there being a self. You can think of it as mobile while continuing to think of it as unitary. These two ideas are not incompatible. In this book the orphan self is brought into relation with the dual self. I have always been given to thinking about what it is to be separate from other people. I happen to think that a lot of people are conscious of this: the difference in my case is that I *was* a kind of orphan, in that my parents separated at my birth and I was brought up by neither. I wasn't, however, an unhappy wretch. I was very fortunate in having a wonderful friend in my grandmother. I never felt greatly deprived, although we didn't have much money, and there were difficulties. I don't want to wring your heart: I'm only trying to suggest that this may have influenced the conception of duality propounded in the book. My name was uncertain, you see. I did have a name, but, for the reasons I've explained, I didn't live with a family who bore that name. When I went to school at the age of five, I didn't know who my father was, and I remember to this day queuing up in the village playground, and every other child had a mother or a fusspot with them for the registration. When

I came to be registered, I was by myself and unable to answer the questions. This is a thing that may have governed, not fully consciously, what I seemed to see happening in the literature of Romanticism: this harping on separation, exclusion, internal division, the wish to get out which can also be a wish to belong.

You yourself came out of Scotland in 1951, to go to Cambridge, to Downing College, a college then primarily associated, of course, with Leavis. What was your experience of Cambridge?

I was aware of Leavis before I went there, but there was more to Cambridge than Leavis. I had a good time, one way and another. There was just the being there with people one's own age, many of whom were interested in the same things as oneself. There were people like Thom Gunn there, who were interesting to talk to. I made many friends, and most of them have remained my friends. I found it rather a delightful, welcoming, almost Mediterranean place. Of course, when you reflect on it, Cambridge isn't very sunny, it's quite austere, and it can now look somewhat grim. I am putting, you understand, a youthful view. Leavis, though he wasn't youthful, was largely delightful. He had his enthusiasms, and his Cambridgeness, his local quality, which were diverting and attractive. He was injured by his experiences as a teacher and writer, and sometimes this led him into conduct which I believe was mistaken and painful to witness. Those of his adherents – and I suppose I'm an adherent too – who don't see this are missing something essential.

Leavis's great fame came later. He had enjoyed his supporters and coadjutors since the thirties and before, but his going to America and being fêted by Americans as someone very important in English studies, and his authority in the schools and universities of this country, were still in the future. But the lineaments of what he stood for, and what he had suffered, and what his mistakes were, were apparent in '52 or '53. I learned a lot from him. He was an exciting man to read – not so much to converse or argue with, because he wouldn't really listen, I think, to dissent. I did try a bit of dissent, but I think it's true to say that one didn't hold out much hope that he would discuss and share with you your sense of the issues. Through being brought up in Scotland and having made friends there – for example, I met Norman MacCaig and Hugh MacDiarmid when I was a boy – I was aware that literature was not exhausted by the image of Leavis's struggle. Leavis's refusal to countenance other people's struggles, and his inability to deal with the literature and ideas that had supervened since his youth, were depressing. Everybody who grows old experiences some estrangement. But he wouldn't admit that there was anything of estrangement about it in his own case: it always had to be that writers weren't as good as he thought they should be, the things they were doing were low things, and so on. And I think I always found this a deficiency in him.

You also met an American at Cambridge who was, to some extent, a follower of Leavis, and who was to become a notable critic of American literature – Marius Bewley. What did you think of him?

I was very fond of Bewley. He was a person who suffered from being constrained within the limits of an academic decorum and of the Leavisian enclave to which he devoted his Cambridge years. He was a talented writer who could have expressed himself more luxuriantly than he did. He liked Leavis, Leavis liked him, but they were temperamentally very different. Nevertheless, he was a very good critic, who saw the point of Leavis while managing to go his own way, both in Cambridge and later on in his native America.

How did you respond to the Movement in the 1950s?

I was on the young side for the Movement, but I suppose I joined it. At Cambridge, Thom Gunn was taken up by Movement writers like John Wain, who was also very encouraging to me. John Wain was an admirable man in that way. And I really was rather caught up in Movement thinking. I very quickly became an editor, after skirmishing or dallying with the BBC and the Treasury, and I published Larkin. It isn't evident to the world now that in those days to publish Larkin and Amis was like an act of arson or terrorism for some people. These writers were experienced as subversively young and working-class and left-wing, in contrast with their later reputations. Books are seen through different prisms, or a prism which shows them in different lights or whatever prisms do; their readers imprism them in successive jails. The jail in which I visited these two was the Movement jail, in which the relevant writers were usually expected to be socialists. We now expect them to have become knights.

In Authors, *you make the interesting remark that 'the Movement is not the only story that can be told of the Fifties, though it is the story that is currently preferred' (p. 171). What other stories might be told of the fifties?*

I say 'preferred' because you hear a lot about it in university class-rooms now, and I have been instrumental in calling attention to Movement works in these classrooms. But in the fifties we also had writers like Golding and Durrell, and along came Alan Sillitoe, to take his place among the many writers who could be considered romantically (or otherwise) remote from the Movement. There were various kinds of activity which pointed in quite different directions, and indeed at the time it was possible even for Movement people to wonder whether – to take only one strand – a phobic attitude to foreign writers was the right thing. That attitude arose for polemical reasons, I think, out of a dissatisfaction with the worshipping of foreign writers – of French and then of American writers – which had gone on before and which still goes on, and which is often, it seems to me, abject and debilitating for one's country. This was one reason for the partly joking, partly not-joking Larkin stress, which was also Amis's stress, on the awfulness of being a foreign writer. I remember trying to tell Amis that I had read the most amusing Amis-like book, as I thought then, *L'écornifleur* by Jules Renard. I wanted to interest him in that, but I could hardly get the words *L'écornifleur* out of my mouth without choking because I could see his face. As I embroider-ingly remember it, those intimidating eyes had become like the eyes of a wild animal when I mentioned Jules Renard. That was, as it were, the blind side of Movement values, and I think many people were conscious that there was such a side. Donald Davie was con-scious of it at an earlyish point, and someone like Gunn wanted to go to America very much as one might go to Paris in the twenties. He wanted out, and what he wanted out of included the Movement, probably, even though some of his earlier poems resonated quite well with Movement verse. There was also, at this time, Empson: the heart-lifting example of Empson, with his hurrying-on, as he put it, his wanting to explain things that people found difficult. These were writers that I was involved with in the fifties and sixties, some of whom I had to do with on the *New Statesman*, where I went from the *Spectator*. But I immediately left the *New Statesman* when Paul Johnson became editor: we didn't get on, and a great red-headed sigh of relief must have floated out from Great Turnstile when I left. Then I went to the *Listener* for five or six years. I used to read and write about the foreign writers who were known in those days as Com-monwealth writers – chiefly the novelists Dan Jacobson and V.S. Naipaul.

Naipaul and Jacobson, along with a wide range of other writers –

*from Amis to Achebe, from Waugh to Wesker—appear in a Penguin
anthology you edited called* Writing in England Today, *which came
out in the* annus mirabilis, *or* horribilis *depending on your viewpoint, of 1968. The anthology also includes Beatles and Pink Floyd
lyrics, as if seeking to register the broader cultural ferment of that
moment. How did you see the counter-culture of the sixties?*

It was thought in those days to be a good thing to go to pop or rock
lyrics if they were interesting. I thought they were quite interesting. I
wouldn't go to the end of the world in defence of the Pink Floyd lyric
that was included. I think I was really to one side of the counter-
culture. That book illustrates a failure of sympathy. I didn't take seriously a lot of what went on in the line of druggy poetry. I've never
been able to see the point of Ginsberg, for example, who is now William Blake and a classic. Clearly he is an interesting character, he has
charm, and ability, though he would hate the word 'ability': let's say
he has an interesting debility. But I didn't know or work with many
writers who could be called hippies. I suppose I've never lost a certain
mundaneness of taste. I think I'm not an intolerant person, I like a
wide range of writers: but I do have a tendency to prefer the common
touch and plainness of meaning, a concern with manners in the
novel, and a concern with intelligibility and sometimes even with the
didactic in poetry. At the same time, there should surely be a range
of styles on display in any complicated culture. If you only had the
one style, then there would be something queer about that, and a
hierarchy of styles, rigidly enforced, would be queer too. There were
more enforcers around 30 years ago than there are now. But they
were far from enforcing a single style.

Your introduction to Writing in England Today *showed some presci-
ence in identifying three kinds of writing that were starting to make
themselves felt and have since become more important. These are
what was then called Commonwealth writing; the work of poets
from the periphery of the British Isles; and feminist writing. How do
you feel those three kinds of writing have developed since 1968?*

The Commonwealth has disappeared, and the term 'Commonwealth writing' is no longer current, although there are scholars and
professors of it. The writers themselves, of course, still exist. It is
striking that some were magnetized to the metropolis or at any rate
to England, from the West Indies in the case of Naipaul and, in the
case of Jacobson, from South Africa. What do you call them? It

becomes invidious to call them Commonwealth writers all the time and to suggest that their merits relate in a very strong sense to their localities and to the emergence of literatures there. The problem of the periphery is complicated. There was once a joke about a Commonwealth writer, who shall have to be nameless on this occasion, meeting Vargas Llosa, many years before he was a Presidential candidate, and asking him: 'Where do you come from, Llosa?' Llosa said: 'I come from Peru.' 'And what do you do?' 'I'm a writer,' he replied. And the Commonwealth writer said: 'Ah, I didn't know there were any writers in Peru.' This was an aristocratic put-down, which raises the question of peripheries and centres, because Peru now has something like the look of a centre rather than a periphery: in a limited fashion, no doubt, but not in an entirely illusory one. And that reminds one of how foolish it is to be talking all the time about metropolitan centres, centres of excellence. It's true that some value inheres in highly developed institutions of learning where certain talents are encouraged – not necessarily the talents of the imaginative writer, but imaginative writers have often benefited from being in places where there are universities and so on. That can be accepted. But what also has to be accepted is that Peru could turn out to be more important than Paris, even if we were to withhold the description of it as a centre, just as Hawthorne turned out to be a more important writer than Thackeray for certain purposes or from certain points of view. So I don't feel it's wise to stress too much the origins of the Commonwealth writers, or even that they are Commonwealth writers, any more. It doesn't make much sense to be thinking of Jacobson or Naipaul in those terms.

What seems to be happening in Britain and Ireland is that certain onsets of talent and activity have occurred at the periphery – we call it that because we live elsewhere, but it's not the periphery to those writers who remain there and have something to write about. It has to be said *tout court* that Ulster writers have shown themselves to be very good, and that Scottish poets and dramatists have shown themselves to be live wires, liver than some English wires. But a magazine, the *Edinburgh Review*, came hurtling in here today, in which a Scottish writer declared that the English novel had died, it was a corpse, it was rotting, there was, or deserved to be, a mausoleum round it, a rather ugly one, I think she felt. She was saying that all the good writers were up in Edinburgh or Glasgow. Well, I don't go along with that sort of approach either. There's a dualistic aspect to all this. You can't give up the idea of there being centres. Equally, you can't give up the other idea, that centres are an illusion, or purely an oppression.

You wouldn't be able to describe what has been happening for so long except in terms of a tension or an undecidable element between centre and periphery.

And what of feminist writing?

I'm favourably disposed toward feminism and feminist writing. It's true that some of it is Amazonianly hostile, anxious to establish a stronghold and to bring down people who appear to be having too good a time of it. But my feeling is that despite the stronghold emphasis and the boastfulness of some feminists, this is a good cause and a new direction. To put it in simple terms, I'd want to say that the impetus within some feminist criticism has been to make problematical certain goals which have been thought distinctively male but which have at the same time been taken as natural and inalienable goals for any writer or thinker. These goals are to do with old notions of truth and utility and clarity. I don't want to disparage these goals, but I believe it can be said that feminist writers have been able to persuade people to think further about what rationality may mean, or may be made to mean.

You spoke earlier of the estrangement from new writing one may experience as one gets older. Do you feel this yourself in relation, for example, to contemporary poetry?

It has to be confessed that the middle-aged and elderly have a problem with younger writers. Some of their energy may have gone, and they're living in the past sometimes. In my case, I look at the poetry that's being written here and now, and I do see poets I like and admire. I am always excited when I see a poem by Heaney, and there are at least half-a-dozen other poets whom I admire. But I also see poets who have a name in this country but who seem to have little to interest one in what they write.

Would you like to identify some of those?

I'd be a little reluctant; I wouldn't get very much pleasure from naming a young writer whom I didn't think was quite up to his fame. Eliot once told F.T. Prince — this is to go back in time, of course, sidling away from the young — that 'not everything you write is very *interesting*'. And the word was appallingly underlined. There is, not a requirement, but a hope that poems will be interesting, and that hope is quite often not fulfilled. If you're on a magazine, you will know that through the mailbox every day comes a poem that says: I am beadily watching the grain in the wood before me, and I am fed up and I hardly know what condition I'm in, and yet the external world has a kind of dreary fascination for me. That's the burden of the poem. I think: well, I'm sure you're having a bad time, so am I, but why should I read your poem? Poems cannot be for that, they just can't. I don't think they'll survive if they're for that. It is surprising how much grousing and grieving, and beady looking at very little, goes on in the name of poetry. But now here I am making a complaint of my own, and probably over-exercising the common touch while I am about it.

In relation to the issue of being interesting, another statement of Eliot's comes to mind. He was actually talking about education, and he said that a part of education was 'to learn to interest ourselves in subjects for which we have no aptitude' (Selected Essays, 1951, p. 512). One might extend that by saying that a part of education is to make us take an interest in matters in which we might not spontaneously be interested. And perhaps one could suggest this is also a function of literary criticism, and ask how far a poem offers itself as immediately interesting and how far it's a question of a certain framework of critical attention that actually makes it interesting, or at least brings out its inherent interest. This relates to the problem of evaluation, particularly of new poetry.

Because there's no-one to tell you it's interesting. No-one to be interesting about its being interesting. That's right. But this being interesting about being interesting seems, in some degree, to be a thing of the past at this point. I think you're right that this is an office that criticism has discharged. And that's perfectly fine. There would even be something fairly fine, if not quite so fine, about an interesting critic making apparently interesting what in fact isn't very interesting in the field of poetry. That could happen. And indeed it has happened. There are poets that Donald Davie interestingly writes about whom I haven't been able to find interesting, and yet I have to say that there is an interest conferred by Davie's abilities. I don't want to sound grudging in relation to that, because I share your sense that it's a good thing to have discourse of this kind. What is also interesting to me is another aspect of interestingness which has to do with an interest being taken or solicited in the hard-to-understand, which may be in terms of a poem or of viewpoints or perceptions. At any rate, you have a discourse which is hard to follow and yet is interesting to people. I've been rather struck by the phenomenon of incomprehensibility. Nobody likes, do they, among the self-consciously educated, to say that they don't know what somebody or something means? Some of us will go to the stake rather than say we don't understand. And I suppose I can understand that. On the other hand, I believe that much that passes, and passes fairly plausibly, for being interesting is not understandable. Some degree of incomprehensibility is to be noticed in people who have been pronounced hellishly interesting in recent times.

Now Paul de Man – I don't touch on his, as it were, discrediting or disgracing, that's a separate issue altogether – but just picking up de Man and seeing him write about, I think it was Yeats's 'Among School Children', was, for me, to be staggered by how hard it was to know what he was saying. And since it's habitual for me to meet people who tell me how interesting they find Paul de Man, I am bound to wonder what they are finding interesting when they're finding him interesting. I myself have sometimes been interested in de Man's stuff, and I'm not saying it's all like that. But in this bravura passage of laden incomprehensibility, inspissated difficulty and allusion, and long words, several of which in a chain you had to look up in a dictionary before you could even start doing the syntax of his sentences, there are grounds for asking what these interested parties make of this interesting stuff. I believe that there must be some element of fake in all this, and that people turn to it as they turned to some of Dylan Thomas's poetry. They liked its being hard to follow, dark, because it made them different from people who didn't like its being dark and were shits and fools and clods who couldn't cope with 'Altarwise by owl-light' and other concatenations of words in Thomas. Meanwhile, tiptoeing past the clods are those persons who like not being too sure what the hell Dylan Thomas meant by 'Altarwise by owl-light'. I suppose that even those who are probably anxious not to be, as it were, overawed by pretentious utterances have been seduced by them. And I suppose that's true of me. I was seduced by the way that Dylan Thomas went on in the fifties, and found his poetry cherishable and memorable. That was very much a reason to fall out with Leavis's people. When I was an undergraduate, an oncoming disdainer of pretension wrote in *Scrutiny* a ferociously negative account of Thomas which, as it were, declared the battle lines. Here were people who wouldn't have Dylan Thomas's poetry, in which I had been interested before becoming interested in Leavis's criticism. Thomas was formerly a more commanding figure that it seems easy for people to understand now.

*But doesn't the example of Thomas suggest that one has to relativize
one's perception of incomprehensibility? Because, as you say, at a
certain point Thomas seemed comprehensible, or at least readable,
and then came to seem less comprehensible. And couldn't one
relativize one's perception of incomprehensibility in criticism, your
response to de Man, for instance? After all, people said Leavis was
incomprehensible.*

That's right. Leavis was claimed to be obscure and incomprehensible. This usually took second place to the claim that he was ugly
and clodhopping in his prose. But still it did go over into a claim as
to incomprehensibility. There was certainly a late Leavis who had
been tutored by Henry James in the matter of elaboration and intri-
cacy and disdain of coming to the point. I never found him very difficult to understand myself, but I was familiar with people saying
that he was, that he could be. I think he was often arduous to read
and cumbersome and not given to sacrificing to the Muses. But that
didn't trouble me very much, because I felt that he was comprehensible. This is why I was prepared to wrestle with it. But I would be
absolutely astonished and suicidally discredited if certain passages in
Paul de Man were ever to be generally considered plain sailing or
plain rewarding. What I'm nagging away at here is a case that is
designed to express my astonishment that we are so hospitable to
what can appear almost adversarially difficult. Americans are fright-
fully good at it. They take up with some foreign lore or specialism,
and they institutionalize and industrialize it, and the next thing you
know, there are 30,000 people speaking the words of the new industry and the new institutions, and outside of the institutions no-one
can follow them. The hospitality to difficulty is partly a function of
academic insularity, of the desire to set off the academic or intellectual as somebody who can read Paul de Man's hardest paragraph,
who can like and be interested by the darkest and knottiest writing
provided it has words in it like 'sexuality' and 'gender' and 'aporia'.
These are badges which suggest that the writing in question will take
you to a new or superior knowledge.

I remember, in the days when Barthes was knowledge, sitting in
this very room with students, very few of whom had read Barthes,
but who had gathered that Barthes was better than their stinking old
teachers, who, they supposed, didn't like Barthes. So we sat reading
some such text as *S/Z* and looking at one passage where I happened
to know that the word 'not' had been omitted from the edition. And
of course there was absolutely no way of telling that the statement

they had been examining and trying to untie had been negated by Barthes, that a 'not' had fallen out. The students couldn't be blamed for not catching that. My whole point is that there was no hope of being able to tell. Quite often, in fact, in the literature of the modern world, one can't tell. In darkest Henry James, so to speak, there are occasions when the absence of a 'not' would go richly unnoticed by the reader. You simply wouldn't know, in the course of one of his refined elaborations or distinctions, if a negative were to fall down one of his gerunds. This is not say that James was a *farceur* or not serious. What is it to say? That he loses control, or gets out of his depth?

A deconstructive explanation would be that he is entering into aporiae, into areas of undecidability.

Yes, because whether or not a 'not' is there may become, under dualistic examination, not a fault so much as a feature of interest. It would then be a matter of his being involved in the articulation of a dilemma rather than simply making a mistake. And indeed I suppose that is why the term 'dualistic' may sometimes be profitably applied to writing which is charged and complex and also worth having. It's true that it can break down and bore people, and be found interesting by the fraudulent. On the other hand, it just isn't the case that we want to give up a literature which taxes you in this way, which fools and deceives you even, because there's too much at stake, too much of value, there. My own discomfort in these areas, and my attraction to and enjoyment of them as well, have to do, I hope, with some notion of getting at the truth and speaking clearly. Empson thought that he wanted to explain clearly what needed explanation. He really did want to do that. And yet he was sometimes found unintelligible. And that's quite interesting in itself, because he was a man who had a fetish about plain meanings and being clear. I don't want to make an inescapable focus of the matter of difficulty, but it seemed to come up again the other day when I was thinking about Enright's poetry in comparison with a poem that was, let's say, not very rewardingly difficult. Now there was Enright, who believes in speaking of what is undecidable or insoluble or aporetic – he wouldn't use those terms, but he sometimes seems to have poems that establish the incomprehensibility of something. On the other hand, you read him always in the expectation that you will have a foothold and that if there are points where his irony is, in the end, unreadable or insoluble, nonetheless he knows that and he shares with you the ground on which you think you can try to assess the trajectory, and the limits, of the irony. But then that wouldn't lead one to say that there could be no good poet who had a lot of difficult stuff for one to encompass, because there just are poets who are like that. It is the case that, say, Thom Gunn and Philip Larkin are rarely insolubly difficult, no aporias in either. But take Les A. Murray, for instance, as a good example of a poet who is worth attending to, who is interesting, and who is at times quite difficult. Or Tony Harrison, who is a writer I admire, and who is also difficult at times, though not at all times. These are poets who we think are talented, that's the important point here: it's not at all that we're turning to people whom we think have failed. In fact, some of the people we know may well prefer Harrison and Murray to Gunn and Larkin, undeterred by the matter of the bafflement. I was defeated by the difficulty of a recent long Murray poem. I even rather lamely canvassed the possibility that there might be some Antipodean reason for it, that he was referring to things that I just didn't happen to have heard of before. But there was more to its taxingness than that.

Perhaps one needs to differentiate between difficulties. I'm thinking, for instance, of George Steiner's essay 'On Difficulty', where he distinguishes between contingent difficulties, which can be resolved, at least in principle, by looking things up, modal difficulties which are due to lack of empathy with an alien cultural context, tactical difficulties which aim to defamiliarize language, and ontological difficulties which press on the very possibility of authentic utterance (On Difficulty and Other Essays, 1978, 1980 edn, pp. 18-47).

Well, I suppose so. Or there could be difficulties which relate to malfunction or breakdown. I'm not trying to get at Murray here, whose work I enjoy, but we would have to say that there could be poets as interesting or as gifted as Murray whose difficulty might have the character of deficiency or limit.

You yourself have helped to disseminate difficult work – for example, in literary and cultural theory – in your role as editor of the London Review of Books. *Can we talk about your experience on that paper? First of all, how does it compare with your experience on the previous journals you've worked for – the* Spectator *and* New Statesman, *where you were literary editor, and the* Listener, *where you were editor?*

The *London Review* is, by and large, the most satisfactory of these journals, for me, because I have had, for the past ten years, the freest hand that I've had in journalism. You could virtually write about what you wanted. There were limits, there are always limits, and we weren't expecting, or weren't able, to discuss certain matters. But that said, we were very free. I think the *New Statesman* had some good issues over the six years or so I was on it. On the other hand, the *London Review* is more inventive and ranging and unexpected, and less hidebound. On the *New Statesman*, although I was younger, I was older in my response to what I took to be the decorum of how to conduct such a review. With the *London Review*, I'm part-time – because I'm a university teacher, I haven't been able to give as many hours to it – but this has been liberating, in a sense. I've been able to improvise and be more rash. It isn't all roses. There are certain features that alarm me. I can't give enough time to the discovery and development of writers and to thinking things up. Broadly speaking, though, over these ten years it has been very enjoyable. We have a simple format, and once we got it settled, which took a few issues, it served our purpose pretty well. My main regret is that we haven't been more inventive and found more new writers. The thing that exasperates me is journalism's habit of using the same writers all the time, with the big papers seizing writers who come up in the small papers, and running them into the ground. There are many writers who write constantly in the dailies and Sundays and who are no good, but they're there and they'll always be there, and that's it. It's true that I've not always developed my own writers. Sometimes I've used writers from other papers who were well-known. On the other hand, over the years I have found a lot of writers, and some of them have gone on to other papers, so that when I publish a writer from a paper like the *Observer* or the *Independent* in the shape, say, of Neal Ascherson, I'm working with someone whom I used to know when he was young and who has been associated with me as an editor in the distant past. But still, nobody can do without a dependence on other people's writers. I just think that you should always be looking for new people.

We too often print pieces that aren't good. But I'm old now and I'm reconciled to it. You just can't avoid it sometimes. But even now on occasion, despite this liberated sense that I have, I feel that I shouldn't have published something, and that's a bit of a knock. It's not pleasant to say to someone that you don't want to publish what they've written. It's very difficult, it takes a lot of energy out of you. Many people are too tired or too busy to face too much of that. On the kind of papers we're talking about, it's not standard to turn something down without good reason, or without thinking that you have some real reason, and to produce a real reason is to get into the area of difficulty and incomprehensibility, because my good reasons are not necessarily her good reasons or his good reasons. I have got on well with the people I've worked with in the editorial office, who have been very few in number. Over the years I've worked mainly with Susannah Clapp and Mary-Kay Wilmers, whom I've been with since we were on the *Listener* together.

One notable feature of the London Review *is that it has taken, or allowed its contributors to take, some vigorous political stands – for instance, on the Falklands, the miners' strike, the Middle East.*

But some people don't like that, of course.

But you yourself feel it's important?

Yes, I do. I would love it to be more bold, but then the political agenda is not exactly stocked with issues which require only one reaction or solution. The more one looks even at an issue that might be thought relatively clearcut, like the Trafalgar Square Poll Tax riot, the more one wonders what to say about it. If I had to write a piece about that, I'm sure people would find it aporetic, Jamesian, Leavisian, pointless, elaborate. I hated the sight of people poking sticks into the faces of policemen. At the same time, I didn't at all share the Home Secretary's purple-faced denunciatory approach, and it was soon to become clear that the police had exercised a strategy of aggression against the protestors, which they were later, with the consent of the media, to lie about.

But isn't it valuable to maintain that kind of undecidability in political discussion?

While also having at least a discernible point of view. We are, in fact, thought to have a point of view. We're attacked in the *Daily Telegraph* for being predictably left-wing and never having right-wing thinkers. This is quite untrue: we often have right-wing writers. Not that I minded the *Telegraph*'s attack. We *are* a left-wing journal after all, and want to be so discerned.

The political attitudes of the London Review *have been definite even if they've been expressed with a degree of complexity.*

Well, one hopes so. At the same time, there have been some changes of mind and of position.

For example?

I can't actually come up with a very strong example of the craven abandonment of a stance, unless you count our fairly early relinquishing of interest in the SDP. But I would be inclined to say that in the matter of speaking up for Welfare State-ism or Welfare State socialism – the National Health Service, a decent set of schools, matters like that – we haven't been anything like tough enough. We haven't published enough on these things and we haven't published effectively enough. We have had attempts. But I would like us to be more declaratory and less equivocal. On the other hand, it's true, I imagine, that there are literary people who would take the view that we are too crude and that we shouldn't have anything to do with politics. Larkin once denounced us, in Arts Council conclave, for publishing on political and economic matters: this meant that we couldn't be accounted a literary journal within the meaning of the Act.

How does your readership feel about it?

I think they want to have the mixture they have come to know. It's difficult to get a clear signal from the readership through the letters. You can't generalize from the ten or twenty letters you get for publication in each issue as to what they're thinking, but there is very little sign, though there is some sign, that they resent our paying attention to politics. And as a matter of fact the last two or three years have seen a tightening of our commitment to publishing on political matters which has been liked. It's not so much that there's more politics, but the politics are more prominent, there's a greater anxiety to have a say. And we've had some successes. A lot of people who are thought to be well-informed and authoritative in this field have spoken favourably about, for instance, the pieces by Ross McKibbin, who is a very good academic political historian. He's not the most driving and unequivocal of writers: *his* name is R.W. Johnson. Both Johnson and McKibbin have good approaches, but their approaches are different, Johnson being an immensely powerful polemical journalist. I only wish there were more of him. On the other hand, it's nice to have a repertoire of manners in the paper.

The London Review *has also been energetic, as we've said, in explicating and debating literary and cultural theory. You've felt this to be important as well?*

We've tried to keep up with it, and to offer contributions on the subject. Frank Kermode has done a great deal for us in that way. I'm probably the most interested in that area of those on the paper. We're in agreement, broadly speaking, about what we should and shouldn't chase. We're not tremendously interested in publishing long, highly technical, highly academic material addressed by one professional to other professionals. The idea of refereed journals in which your peers are addressed is poison to me. I'd prefer the odd barbaric outbreak to preserving a totally unrelieved, respectable, sectional, specialist composure.

In conclusion, let me ask you about your own plans for the future. You're retiring from your Chair here, at University College London, in a year. Are you going to do more writing yourself? An autobiography, perhaps? A very attractive feature of your writing is the portraits of people you know or knew – of Marius Bewley in Doubles, *for example.*

Maybe that's a thing I do better than the other things I attempt to do. It's something I like doing. I'd like to write an autobiography, but I don't seem to have any real impetus to start. It's not clear to me whether I should go on working at the *London Review* when I stop teaching. I am not as old as I may be implying, and I don't want to dive into the grave in a year's time, which has now been extended to two years' time, incidentally. I feel that, if anything, I'm a little better at editing than I used to be. But it has come to me that I may be deceiving myself in this respect, in respect of its being evident to others, and that my time may be up. We shall see.

A.S. Byatt

Franco's Restaurant, Jermyn Street, London
18 May 1990

NICOLAS TREDELL: *With its romance form and its partly Victorian setting, your latest novel,* Possession, *clearly differs in significant ways from your earlier fiction. How did* Possession *come about?*

A.S. BYATT: It came about really because I had the idea for the title. I'm putting together this collection of my essays, and the chap who was helping me discovered a review I did in 1974 of a book of essays by John Beer, and it said: 'I often think of writing a novel called *Possession*'. I'd had the idea when I was working on Coleridge in the British Library, and there was Kathleen Coburn working on him, and it came to me that possession worked both ways – she thought Coleridge's thoughts and his thoughts were entirely mediated by her. Then much later I got the ideas of the spiritualist mediums, possession in that sense, and sexual possession, if you had two poets rather than one, and economic possession. So, in a sense, it began quite differently from the other novels I've written. With, as it were, almost a witty concept, an idea. The people grew out of the idea and out of a sort of passion I had for Victorian poetry. And the modern characters are very secondary to the interest in the nineteenth century.

That sense of belatedness, of the modern characters as pale shadows compared to the Victorian titans who precede them, comes across very strongly in the novel. Were you happy to achieve that?

That was wholly intentional. It was partly a feeling, in reaction to the modern university situation, that critics are tiny people compared to writers: which is not a fashionable thing to say because all the critics are attempting to extrude. It's partly also to do with bits of my own intellectual history. My great friend Isobel Armstrong, to whom

Possession is dedicated, has had, during the whole of my acquaintance with her, a theory that the great Victorian poets have never been seen to be as great or as complex as they are, partly because Leavis and Empson chose to disparage them. And the more you read them, the more you realize that, for instance, *In Memoriam* is one of the absolute great poems in English literature. So it was partly a sense that these poets hadn't had justice done to them. Then there was a quite other starting point, which was my technical realization that John Fowles had pulled off *The French Lieutenant's Woman*, not because his knowledge of Victorian literature was vast, but because he had used a convention of illicit sexuality to make sexuality exciting again. About five years later, I had the thought that one of the reasons that sex isn't interesting now isn't because of the permissiveness of the novels, but because of the endless sexual analysis of everything done by theorists. So I started my satirical framework with all those things in mind. Then of course I realized I was actually allowed to be interested in plot. When I was starting to write at Cambridge in the fifties, what one admired was, say, Rosamond Lehmann's *Dusty Answer*, in which the heroine is sitting in a teashop, and the person she's waiting for doesn't come, and the whole of the future is indeterminate. Then later on you got all these multiple, variant narratives like the end of *The French Lieutenant's Woman*, or like Barthelme beginning his impossible narratives by saying that someone was dead then telling his life. So in a sense I was writing closure both in a highly theoretical way, and out of intense pleasure.

Yes, while Possession *is quite a plural text in some respects, the use of the conventions of the romance and of the Victorian novel do conduce to closure. You're unrepentant about that?*

I think closure is the really revolutionary narrative mode at the moment. Well, it must be, these things come in circles. I think part of the excitement about fairy tales, which increasingly people have got excited about, not only the feminists, is that they do have a beginning, a middle and an end, and I think people have a sort of huge hunger for this.

You don't feel that closure is an ideological imposition, as the poststructuralists argue?

I think they're confusing art with life when they say that. And ideas of the random, of the haphazardness and ungraspability of life, have been grossly exaggerated. When Virginia Woolf says that life hits us as a series of random impressions, it jolly well doesn't. It hits us as a series of narratives, though they may be mutually exclusive narratives. We may be hit by random impressions, but if we're intelligent we immediately put them into an order. Yet everybody accepts Virginia Woolf's remark quite uncritically, whereas if you say stories should have a beginning, a middle and an end, they say, no, no, no.

A potentially controversial aspect of Possession *is its treatment of feminism. The novel could seem to suggest, for example, that Maud's feminism is really very superficial, and she finds that the pressure of the past and of her desire for Roland goes far deeper. Is* Possession *an attempt to put feminism in its place?*

It's a double-edged weapon. Anybody who reads what Christabel says and what Blanche says should see that it's a very, very feminist book. It's about the right of a woman to be a great writer and to put her work first. Elaine Feinstein, in her review of the book, rightly saw the true point of contact between Maud and Christabel as the moment when Christabel gives a cry which I think is my cry throughout the book: you're taking away my autonomy, you're giving me something wonderful that I regard as secondary, my work is what matters: and nevertheless she falls heavily in love because she's a very powerful and passionate woman. And Maud has got Roland sitting in her room, and he doesn't know what to do, and she's trying to write an essay, and Elaine Feinstein quoted a passage that I'd forgotten that I'd written: 'If he went out of the room it would be grey and empty. If he did *not* go out of it, how could she concentrate?' (p. 430). I think Maud does hold her feminist views, but she hasn't solved, by holding them, the problem of how to behave, and she hasn't, which I think is purely comic, solved the problem of being very beautiful. I've known two or three very beautiful women and they've all had this problem of not being sure who they were. I know a very blonde woman who went to a feminist congress and was severely criticized because they assumed that she had dyed her hair. I think Christabel's feminism in the nineteenth century, which was partly instinctive, is a wonderful thing. And I've tried to reproduce the social circumstances which make her automatically abase herself as a poet before Randolph, though I think she secretly knows she might be better, but she only knows it intermittently. I really don't want, myself, to be ghettoized by modern feminists into writing about women's problems.

But does Possession *give feminism its due? In your earlier fiction – for instance, with Anna in* Shadow of a Sun, *and with Stephanie in* The Virgin in the Garden *and* Still Life *– you evoke with great power the enormous pressures women come under, from fathers, from lovers, from husbands, from children. It could be argued that what Anna and Stephanie lacked, in their day, was some kind of discourse of feminism that would have helped them to articulate and possibly to alter their situation.*

I think it's rather like George Eliot. The feminists in her own day accused her of not joining in, and yet the powerful images of what it was like to be a woman who couldn't use what she had got are those she produced in her creation of Dorothea in *Middlemarch*, not what they said. I honestly hope and believe that the existence of Stephanie and Anna is as strong a statement as any that I could theoretically make, and as much use. I read a very good article about descriptions of childbirth by women which assumes that my accounts of childbirth in the 1950s and '60s are informed by feminist perspectives, whereas in fact they are simply accurate memories of, for instance, the rage I felt at not being allowed to walk up and down when I was in labour. It's nothing to do with feminist theory having told me that, I observed it. I think in metaphors, not in propaganda. If Christabel's poetry is properly read, it contains all sorts of images which modern feminist scholarship has made available for me to see as the powerful guiding images of women's lot. For instance, the whole of Christabel's Melusina myth is constructed round a lecture I once heard Luce Irigaray not give on *Mélusine and le Chevalier au cygne* and then on the subsequent piece she published called 'Femmes Divines' about the dangers of female goddesses, all of which I transposed into Christabel's nineteenth century poem: so in a sense that runs forwards and backwards because it's a parody of both Irigaray and the feminist epic that was never written in the nineteenth century. I think I'm fighting a different theoretical battle, for the work of art not to be propaganda.

The argument today would be that your position is itself –

An ideological position. Of course it is. But is that the most interesting thing about it, having said that? I suppose I also think, when I really consider it, that the feminist movement, whatever its virtues, has not produced any satisfactory answer to what I see as the major biological/intellectual problem of women. Unless you choose doctrinaire lesbianism, which happens not to interest me either biologically or theoretically – people may if they wish, but it's not my line – this problem is what to do with the fact that you're a childbearing animal and that, whatever the feminists say, the nurturing of small children is a female thing. Men may join in, and this may be very desirable as a piece of social engineering, but damn it, one's instincts are there, you can't theorize them away. And this seems to me a more important problem than, say, Mary Jacobus trying to find a *prise* for feminist consciousness in reading *The Prelude*.

Possession also takes issue with poststructuralism, particularly with its challenge to notions of the substantial self and of character. But nonetheless, the way the novel is written, with its proliferation of putative texts and its range of linguistic registers, gives a greater sense than in your previous novels that the characters are, *in a way, textual products. They're not portrayed in the same way as the characters in, say,* The Virgin in the Garden.

No, they're not. *Possession* is a postmodernist, poststructuralist novel and it knows it is. It does present itself as a piece of Victorian melodrama, but of course it's no such thing. I don't believe it's possible to do that in good faith now. There's a marvellous bit in Bakhtin where, I think he's talking about the parodies of sonnets in Cervantes, and he says that they are, of course, perfectly formed sonnets, but the subject of the parody is always the sonnet. And because *Possession* is, in places, a parody of a Victorian poem and a Victorian novel and of an epistolary novel, the subject of the novel is, as in postmodernist fiction, the novel, the book. But within that, it is also a sort of passionate plea for readers to be allowed to identify with characters. I mean, you can do both. You can both feel the passion of Ash and Christabel, and do the standing-back and thinking. You don't have to cut one out. Most postmodernist fiction cuts out any emotion very much earlier on. It doesn't allow the reader any pleasure, except in the cleverness of the person constructing the postmodernist fiction. I think that's boring. I think you can have all the other pleasures as well.

You actually invented poets, rather than using real nineteenth-century ones. Was there any particular reason for that?

There were several reasons. I had originally thought of possibly doing it about the two Brownings, because they would bring in the sexual meaning of the keyword. Then I thought, you're in danger of a terrible libel action and you're actually very restricted in inventing your scholars if you do that. I also had this desire to have freedom of movement in inventing what happened to them and how they felt. And if I put real people into it, it could be much more anti-fictive, and since it was partly about the power of the fictive over the critical, it had to be fictive. Then I had the idea that I would do what Robertson Davies does in *The Lyre of Orpheus*; he invents a libretto for an opera without Orpheus, and for the lyrics he uses what he claims are the works of an obscure Victorian poet; I haven't checked, but I think it's all Thomas Lovell Beddoes. And I said to Dennis Enright – I really do owe him a huge debt – that I might do that, seize obscure bits of poetry. He looked at me robustly and drew himself up to his full height, and said: Nonsense, you write them yourself. I suddenly saw he was right, of course. The challenge was to create the poems as well as the people.

Did you find the poems difficult to write?

I thought I would find it awful, and then, when I started, something rather like possession actually did happen, and the whole of my passion for Victorian verse, and for blank verse as opposed to free verse, and for rhyming lyrics as opposed to delicate little half-lost lines which are again full of indeterminacy, came up, and all the poems somehow got written. The poems are part of the text, in the sense that they were all written at the place where they came in the text. The ordinary reader doesn't have to read it like that, but each poem should be read in its place and it's part of the metaphorical structure of the place it's in. For instance, when I got to the end of Sabina's diary, I knew I needed a poem by Christabel to show what Sabina couldn't fathom, which is what Christabel felt. I needed a poem that had to be a misleading clue as to what had happened to the child, and I suddenly realized I needed something blasphemous because Christabel had been studying Breton Christianity and looking at the granite Calvaries. All those little poems that Christabel wrote in Brittany came out of that, and those are the ones I'm best pleased with. And I remember thinking, of course, she would write a poem about spilt milk. Now that is a feminist poem at its deepest level. It really is a blasphemous feminist poem because it's set against the male Christ figure who in every icon pours forth blood and water from his side which feed the people, and here is a woman who has lost her child and is expressing this useless milk which any woman who has given birth to a child that has been taken away from her has got to do, and it's very painful. Two male editors have tried to take that out because they were worried by it, and I said it's because you haven't biologically imagined it. But a woman ought to. The poem says, this flow does not redeem, and Christabel feels herself excluded from the whole structure of Christianity. The first poem is about Mary, and it says Our Lady bore and bore, she bore what the Cross bears, which I like, because I think it's a jolly good Metaphysical pun. But her pain is not part of a redeeming icon and the male is at the centre of the religion. Christabel is actually inventing a whole feminist religion.

It's interesting that you use in Possession *the form of what one might call the literary detective story, in which the hunt for documents becomes a way of dramatizing and exploring all kinds of dubious human motives –* The Aspern Papers *is the classic example – and that you link this with the modern university world, the global campus. What drew you to that kind of story?*

It was partly – and one must tread carefully here – watching the greed of real scholars. It was partly, as you say, Henry James. There is a big joke in *Possession* about Adam Verver in *The Golden Bowl*, who bought Charlotte Stant and took her back to an American city; James sees this as the acquiring of people by profit, but also, I think, sees the American millionaire as a possible saviour as well as a possible destroyer. Mortimer Cropper's collection in my novel is called the Stant Collection, in memory of Adam Verver, and the whole poem about the Great Collector is actually a description of Adam Verver from *The Golden Bowl*. It goes into blank verse in my novel. I didn't have to change almost any of James's words or add any, except a little bit of Balzac and Swedenborg at the end. Also, when I was planning *Possession*, I read a book on realism which said that, in a sense, the plots of all fiction were like the archetypal detective story; you wanted to find out, and they wanted to find out, who the woman was. And I suddenly saw you could use this, because of course, in *Possession*, finding out who the woman was reveals who Ash was, and who the parent was, and so you're back again to modern critical theoretical concerns with the nature of origins, which is quite nice. I read detective stories, and I've observed that modern experimental novelists claim never to read realistic novels, but they do read detective stories. It's a strict form. I think I was terribly in need of strict form as opposed to me feeling out from inside realistically what was going to happen, as I did in the other novels.

You've spoken in the past, for example in your essay 'Nature morte' (Cross-References, *1986, pp. 91-102; reprinted in A.S. Byatt,* Passions of the Mind, *1991) of seeing the structure of your novels in terms of visual images. Did you have these images when you were writing* Possession?

Yes, I did. I don't think I drew it in quite the way I drew the others. And it wasn't as controlled by colour words: *The Virgin in the Garden* was red, white and green, and *Still Life* was purple and blue. I think the next one, *Babel Tower*, is probably red and black, but I haven't quite worked it out. But I saw *Possession* much more in terms of a series of different sorts of pictures. What did I see? I saw a kind of cat's cradle of patterns in which the linear narrative – I always have that pattern, which I got from reading Spenser really, in which there's a kind of linear narrative, and then an enclosed space which is a metaphor, or an object, or in this case a poem, which you interrogate differently, but which is part of the narrative movement; the line goes through it, it doesn't stop and start again. What colours did I see? I have a terribly clear visual image as I speak to you; it's something to do with a lot of different-coloured flowers on grass. It's very paradisal, and it's to do with the image of the tree and the serpent and the woman in the paradise garden, which comes from a wonderful book by John Armstrong, called *The Paradise Myth*. He says there is a sort of archetype, that he's found in paintings and myths and poems and everywhere, of a closed garden, which always contains a boundary, and a river crossing the boundary, and a figure like Hermes in the *Primavera* who is pointing out, and a figure of the woman and a figure of the serpent in some form. I saw *Possession* as a series of endless variations on this theme in totally different pictorial styles, some of them abstract. The worst moment was when they were trying to cut it, and I knew that the poem which ought to go was Randolph Ash's about the Garden of Persephone, and yet that was, in a sense, the central meaning of the novel. It starts with Vico's image of language and mythology as corn. It's exactly the same image as in *The Virgin in the Garden*: language is flowers, the flowers coming from the mouth of the Primavera. The reason I love North Yorkshire so is that for me language and the earth are really intertwined there. There are these wonderful words like the Boggle Hole, Jugger Howe, Ugglebarnby. It's a sort of image of a paradisal state as in our idea, Foucault's idea, of a sixteenth century in which words denote things. And of course, that's why I get so distressed by literary theories which say language is a self-supporting system that bears no relation to things. Because I don't experience it in that way. I don't have any naive vision of words and things being one-to-one equivalents, but they're woven, like a sort of great net of flowers on the top of the surface of things.

There's an interesting tension in your novels, certainly from The Virgin in the Garden *onwards, as to whether language is natural or artificial.*

And probably even *The Game* is about whether language is natural or unnatural. In that novel, Cassandra sees writing as artifice and Julia sees writing as natural, and Cassandra writes better than Julia. It's like Christabel in a way: Cassandra and Christabel are very close to each other. They're the woman closed in the tower who has given her soul for her writing but is also somehow destroyed. They're all the Lady of Shalott: that's another image which is so deep in my very early childhood. It's to do with the thing that all my books are about: the sensuous life, childbearing, therefore men, therefore danger, and making things by yourself of exquisite beauty which can be accused of being unreal. All my books are about the woman artist – in that sense, they're terribly feminist books – and they're about what language is. Because of course, if language is as much nature as childbearing, you're all right.

You spoke of your distress at literary theories which say language is a self-supporting system, but don't your own later novels, especially The Virgin in the Garden *and* Still Life, *tend to encourage that idea? You take such enormous pleasure in savouring words, almost for their own sake as it were, that words do start to escape from things.*

Well, Coleridge wonderfully said that he was sure that words were things like other things in the world. And the truth is that if you're standing on Jugger Howe or you're at the Boggle Hole, all those things are there together, the spiders and the stones and the sea and the words Boggle and Hole, and you're there and they're there and they're not separate systems. I know that Iris Murdoch is right and that Wittgenstein is right, to say that, however much we may try to get at what is under the net, we're only ever describing the net. But if you make the meshes fine enough, the net is so beautiful that all the bumps and humps of things under it are so, yes, so accessible, you can actually sort of see them under the net.

It's interesting that you use the verb 'see' again in this context, because vision is very important in your fiction, in a range of senses, from a very rich kind of everyday seeing, to a concern with disturbances of vision, to attempts to evoke the visionary – as with Henry's very primal kind of vision in Shadow of a Sun, *or Marcus's strange and intense visual experiences in* The Virgin in the Garden. *Could you explore the importance of vision in your novels?*

It goes back to very early childhood experiences. There are five or six childhood experiences which I always feel sort of made me what I am, and they're all solitary and they're all to do with light or dark. The very first thing I can remember is lying in a pram on the grass and seeing the edge of the pram hood and the shape of the wash-house roof and a piece of blue sky, and I do actually think I remember coming back from seeing these to realizing that I was there, in that, and thinking, here I am. And then I remember, when I was a small child, being frightened of shapes moving on the ceiling at night – there was a tree outside my bedroom – and thinking, do I think this is a bear, no I don't think this is a bear, but it means that there are things you can see and not see. And then I remember – I was a desperately unhappy child, it must be said – sitting up against a barred gate at my elementary school trying to get away from the other children, and I was sitting very very still so they wouldn't notice me. It was a very hot, beautiful day, and on the other side of the gate was a little strip of road and then there was a huge meadow full of buttercups – it always comes back in my books, it comes back in the epilogue to *Possession* – absolutely full of flowers, all of which were reflecting the light back. And I remember thinking, things are amazing, they're wonderful, if one could could see this instead of having to go back in there, it would be all right. When I first met Charles Rycroft, I mentioned that Helen Gardner had told me that if you haven't thought a thing out in words, you haven't thought it. I said to Charles Rycroft, it isn't true, I know that I know certain things and I know them in visual shapes, and the word may or may not come to be fitted to the pattern that I already know is there. And Rycroft said, of course, this is primary thought as opposed to secondary thought.

Isn't there a certain contradiction in relation to vision in your work? For example, there's a passage in Still Life *where Frederica goes to Provence: the authorial voice talks about our perceptions of Provence, and puts forward a complex argument. It begins by saying: we now see Provence the way Van Gogh saw it – he, like any other great*

painter, has influenced the way we see things. It then says, but he
himself saw these landscapes in a certain way, which was influenced
by his own previous knowledge of painting, It goes on to say that he
also had a vision of Provence all his own – 'he saw what no one had
yet seen, what was his to see' (1986 edn, p. 60). That suggests that
you want to retain the sense of a personal vision, of, not exactly an
unmediated seeing, but a kind of seeing that does escape, in a way,
the nets of linguistic or perceptual construction. Would that be so?

Yes, or inherited sets which you can put on things. One of my great
heroes is Gombrich, and one of the great moments in Gombrich is
when he says Giotto never drew a sheep, he saw other sheep that
people had drawn and corrected them against reality. I like painters
better than writers as an example of this. I was thinking in the bus
coming up – I think like mad in the bus – when we got to Hyde Park
Corner, all the houses on Park Lane at the top end are wrapped in
sort of plastic and scaffolding, and I thought that's interesting, why
is it interesting? Is it interesting as an image of the decay of inner London, and I thought, no it isn't, it's simply, purely, visually interesting
because of the flapping of the plastic. And then I thought, if I really
wanted to know that, I would have to know it like somebody who
intended to draw it. I would have to draw every flap and every curve
and then I would actually understand why the shape of those houses
is so moving. And I thought all that in words, but the actual experience was a desire to get every flap and every curve and the straight
lines of the scaffolding and the squashy greyness of the plastic. And
in some way that experience, which I think is a painter's experience,
always makes me want to write. It was then that I began to see how
to do my George Eliot and Michelet story, which had nothing to do
with that scaffolding at all. It sort of triggered something off, because
it wouldn't have been interesting without the scaffolding, which was
a perfectly regular grid representing form or structure, and what I
saw I had to look at was the flapping of the plastic between the grid,
because each flap was different, and if I'd had a pencil I could have
drawn both the regularity and difference of it by myself, on the bus.

Your novels explore, in their form and content, different ways of
structuring and ordering the world. In The Virgin in the Garden, *you*
draw a fascinating distinction between a kind of organic ordering –
the obverse of the dissociated sensibility, if you like – and the idea
Frederica has, after her day out in Goathland when the doll salesman
picks her up, of 'lamination' – of, as it were, dividing experience into

thin plates or layers which lie alongside each other but don't inter-
penetrate. Could you say more about that idea of 'lamination'?

Yes. I was about to say earlier that Frederica is not a visionary.
Stephanie is, Marcus is, but Frederica, I think, is in a way the modern
world. And of course she's going to be very unhappy in the sixties,
with all of the things that they stood for. I think the seventies and the
eighties do laminate. And I suppose I think of lamination in two ways
really. I remember thinking of it as a strategy for survival when I was
Frederica's age, in the sense that I thought you could possibly manage to be both at once, a passionate woman and a passionate intellectual, and efficient, if you could just switch gear and switch gear from
one to the other, but if you let them all run together organically,
something messy would occur and you would get overwhelmed. On
the other hand, I think I also have this desire to connect everything I
see to everything else I see, which you could take organically, in the
sense that everything is part of some monistic universe and that anyway it's all organic and connected because it's in my head, or which
you could take as purely mechanical. But lamination was related to
other things as well, like being in the middle of Goathland and knowing you ought not to be interested in the landscape because the
Wordsworthian vision is no longer accessible. You *know* that, even
while you're looking at the moors in an almost Wordsworthian way.
But if you laminate it, you can have the Wordsworthian feeling and
you can have the consciousness that you ought not to be having it. I
invented the doll salesman and I did him by instinct. He also, in a
sense, represents the modern world, because he makes dolls, not
people, he makes identical images quite a lot less well than women.
I felt that because he, who would never have been in Wordsworth,
was in that landscape, one was allowed to have the Wordsworthian
emotion back again even while saying you weren't allowed to have it.

You're talking, then, of a kind of modern consciousness which can
still, in a sense, have primal experiences, but only in a divided, self-
conscious way. There's no return to innocence?

No, but I'm not sure there ever was innocence, you see. I think it's a
misreading of Wordsworth and Coleridge to suppose that they
thought there was. The child in the 'Immortality Ode' is a fiction, and
the child Wordsworth in *The Prelude* who was part of the mountains
is a fiction. I don't want to go back, I never have wanted to go back.
But I also think that if one's spent the whole of one's life worrying

about T.S. Eliot and the dissociated sensibility, he must have said something that in some sense was true, or we wouldn't have been worrying about it. We would have just not understood what he was saying. And thinking back to the paradigm of oneself standing at the Boggle Hole with the words Boggle and Hole and all the light off the sea and the spiders and the ammonites: you think very fast about Lyell and time and geology and what you are and what you might write. It's all part of one thing really. And is it as immediate as the odour of a rose? I think it is. I think my thoughts are.

But it's the notion of 'immediacy', whether of thought or of sensuous experience, that has been a crucial target of poststructuralism and deconstruction.

I will tell you another story. Before I had the job at University College, I used to go to Frank Kermode's seminars on literary theory, and I enjoyed that. That was a wonderful and very formative experience. We made acquaintance with Barthes and structuralism – I don't think we got as far as deconstruction, I don't think it was in, in those days. But I used to come out of those seminars and write down lists of words rather as Roland writes them in *Possession* (p. 431), words that were not amenable to that theoretical language, words which were part of what I feel is the central and not peripheral work of what I call writing. I never call it anything other than writing now, I don't call it creative work, and I do it in a sort of mischievous way in order to claim it. When I say writing, I mean somebody making something which they think to be a work of art – though there are pieces of literary writing which call themselves criticism, like that Eliot essay on 'dissociation of sensibility', which actually are works of art. I think immediacy is an illusion, but I don't feel it. I mean, my actual consciousness denies it wholly. I think that most of the language in which this metaphysics of presence is talked about is an illusion; the word 'immediacy' is not the same as the odour of a rose. I feel it to be a language which, even if I learnt to handle it properly, wouldn't give me a great deal, whereas poetry does. And poets who have read some of that language and sensed some of those problems, they're all right. What I want to do in my novels is to describe varieties of human experience, like thinking very hard in abstract terms, which most novelists don't describe. And what I think I want to convey is that the experience of thinking very hard in abstract terms is just as immediate as the experience of standing next to a rosebush.

You've talked about Frederica in The Virgin and the Garden *and in* Still Life. *What is the significance of her sister Stephanie? Here's a brilliant woman who wins a scholarship to Cambridge, takes a Double First, then returns to her home town, teaches in her old school, marries Daniel, a dour but forceful clergyman, has two babies, and is electrocuted trying to rescue a bird trapped under her refrigerator. She seems to me almost a sacrificial figure.*

It's a rhyme originally. I think Stephanie is a sort of Persephone figure, and Daniel and the Church are gloomy Dis, which means, as somebody pointed out, that I have to resurrect her in some way, which I don't see how to do. And I think she also goes with Hermione in *The Winter's Tale*, and therefore she has a daughter, who has no character at all as yet. Stephanie also goes with the idea of female goddesses, which I don't think she consciously did when I wrote her. But the more I think about it the more I see that Frederica goes with a very early desire I had as a child to substitute female myths for Christianity, which I dislike. Frederica is the Virgin Queen and she goes with Athene, and she goes with Frances Yates's article on the paradox of Elizabeth's iconography as Cybele and Astarte, and with Diane of Ephesus who is fecund and yet virginal. Whereas Stephanie is the opposite: she must be like Demeter or Persephone. She is the earth-myth of the goddess who is maternal and therefore of course she goes to the Underworld. She also goes with the opposition between Queen Elizabeth and Mary Queen of Scots: Mary Queen of Scots got married and sank and indeed death took her. When I thought it out, I was only half-conscious of what I was doing. I was basically saying that marriage kills the imagination and separateness, and that lamination might save them. It gets more complicated in the next volume, but that may be a very depressed feminist message. Or at least both Frederica and Stephanie are rendered incomplete, because Frederica just isn't as intelligent as Stephanie. She makes greater play of her intelligence but I never felt that she actually understood any particular thing as well as Stephanie: she just talks a lot more. Stephanie has the Christian virtues of self-effacement and putting other people first. Frederica is the survivor. I think she is partly a very tiresome person. But she has a lot of energy and she sees what's going on and she tries to make sense of it. In a sense Frederica is a kind of puppet-master because her consciousness is too powerful and she tries to keep down her unconscious. She's due for her comeuppance.

Your portraits of women are very compelling. Your fiction also shows insight into men – for example, there's that passage in Still Life *where the narrator remarks on Frederica's discovery, by her third year at Cambridge, 'that women were not the only sex to have powerful fantasy lives. Men dreamed, or believed, they had a special relationship, an understanding, an intimacy on the most fragile bases, an intellectual confidence that could have been made to anyone who happened to be present, a goodnatured drunken kiss offered as payment for escort from a party, a childish scribbling of notes during a lecture on Mallarmé' (p. 291). How do you feel when you're writing about men?*

I like to feel that I can imagine that I am them. I watch them a lot when I'm with them, I watch the ones I know, and they give away quite a lot if you watch rather than just reacting and getting annoyed. And I was genuinely surprised at Cambridge, when I was Frederica's age, because I had this stereotyped vision of men as being brutal and casual in their relationships. I think that a lot of them felt they ought to be, but they were very romantic. When you're 17 and you find yourself being somebody's romantic vision in a way which bears some, but very little, relation to who you actually are, it's very difficult to deal with. But at the same time you can watch men, it's quite interesting. I would hate to be cut off from talking to men because it would make you into a bad novelist. I like to try and imagine what it's like to be in their skins, which is not all that easy, but it's not impossible.

You mentioned earlier the University College seminars, and you've been involved with the teaching of literature as a university lecturer and also through serving on the CNAA and the Kingman Committee on the National Curriculum. Has your service on those bodies changed your views about the way literature should be taught?

Sometimes I talk in a very alarmist way about how a culture of great complexity and beauty, which I value, is vanishing overnight, which I think is happening, and at other times I'm very excited by the new developments. I think the National Curriculum is possibly a very good thing, in the sense that all sorts of dotty educational theories will be curbed by it. All children will have to learn a body of knowledge. But then good teachers are going to be very inhibited by it, and I'm very deeply troubled, purely from the point of view of my own corner of the woods, by the disappearance of literature from most of the 'A' Level language subjects. I'm deeply troubled by the accusations of élitism that are levelled against anybody who really cares about the canon in the broadest sense as we have known it. Of course certain things have been taught that weren't actually worth bothering with, and certain things have not been taught that were marvellous, but to say everything must go out because it was once valued and that it's élitist to value things that everybody can't read, I find very frightening. I find the whole concept of élitism very frightening because I think it does down exactly the people it's meant to be helping. It's all right for postgraduates to study popular novels, but then they've got a real technical interest, and a big enough social knowledge to see what in society is being reflected by these things. But I really don't think little children who haven't read a good novel should be studying the form of a bad one. I'm frightened to death by the banishing of the literature of the past – I might say that fairly clearly for the record. On the other hand, I've seen wonderful things going on when I've gone round with the CNAA, and I've seen some wonderful teaching going on at schools when I went round with Kingman. And I think if you talk to schoolteachers, you feel that they're terribly battered people who actually once cared very deeply about literature and could again if – I think the whole profession has been bedevilled ever since the 1950s by turning the study of literature into a kind of huge piece of social engineering. I think Eliot was absolutely right that literature was being used as a substitute for religion, and it was then also used as a substitute for socialism. And the thing that went out of the window on both occasions was sensuous pleasure, without which, as Coleridge rightly said, there's no point at all. I mean, the primary purpose of literature, as Wordsworth and Coleridge knew, is pleasure. The thing is, the big people give you a much greater pleasure than Freddy Forsyth, whom I like reading, but who can't produce the kind of shiver that goes down your back when you realize that somebody's written something like 'that fair field / Of Enna, where Proserpine gathering flowers / Her self a fairer flower by gloomy Dis / Was gathered' (*Paradise Lost*, Book 4, ll. 268-71).

May I ask in conclusion about your future plans for your own fiction? You've mentioned that your next novel, continuing the series of The Virgin in the Garden *and* Still Life, *will be called* Babel Tower, *and it will presumably be coming up to the 1960s in terms of period. Can you tell us more about that?*

Babel Tower is about the cracking-up of language and the tearing-loose of language from the world. It ought not to be realistic in the way that *The Virgin in the Garden* and *Still Life* were, though they're both less classic realist novels than they look. What I want to do is to continue the note of the two previous novels, but I felt *Babel Tower* should be more fragmented up into a series of stylistic gestures and textures. I think I can write it as a cross between that and *Possession*. It's about voices as opposed to writing, and it and Volume Four move much more into different areas of visual art as a kind of para- digm. I thought that video art, for instance video portraits, which link up with Walter Benjamin and the work of art in the age of mechanical reproduction, would do very well for *Babel Tower*. It's different from the *Primavera* in *The Virgin in the Garden* and from Van Gogh in *Still Life*. I've got to get the beginning right. I want – in a sense, I want the Post Office Tower, because this novel is haunted by language towers, and the Post Office Tower is a sort of communi- cations tower, isn't it? Then I have stuck a thing called the language tower into the imaginary new University of North Yorkshire, and the students attack this tower. And I've got the trial of an obscene book and a divorce case, and both, as it were, produce a kind of degrada- tion of language, in the sense that the language of the court degrades the language both of the book and of the marriage. The novel also begins to be haunted by small children, the next generation arriving … *Babel Tower*'s got a big notebook written, but it's got far too much plot, far too many characters, far too many ideas. The next thing to do is the chronology, because I think some of the things don't happen in the right relation to each other, and I shall see what that is if I do the chronology. Then I hope to write it during the next year-and-a-half, and also another book of short stories. I've got another novel after that which is in many ways going to be the sort of pleasure that *Possession* was. It's about a sort of children's story writer and it's going to be called – let me get this right – *The Hedgehog, the White Goose and the Mad March Hare*. I'm quite pleased with that. You see, those are nice words, hedgehog and white goose. You can't have a theory about those.

George Steiner

NICOLAS TREDELL: *In your books, you've given some glimpses of your early life – of the 'polyglot matrix', as you call it in* After Babel *(1975 edn, p. 116), in which you were raised, of the influence of your father, of your schooling at* lycées *in Paris and New York, of the growing threat of Fascism. Could you give us an outline of your early cultural development?*

GEORGE STEINER: Yes. The first and central point is that it was physically very safe and privileged in Paris. Psychologically, my father had no doubt at all, from the late twenties on, that the catastrophe was coming, and among my earliest memories are those of Hitler's voice on the radio begin picked up by my parents with a sense of absolute and terrible certainty. So I was educated under the pressure of trying to get ready to move. My father saying, on a Monday you start packing your steamer trunk and on a Tuesday your hand baggage, stuck with me even before I quite understood it. And the polyglot matrix gave a kind of wonderful sense of not being afraid of being caught in any one place. Very systematically, my father suggested to me that the more languages you know, the more you learned of other cultures and other ways, the more you might have a chance of acting, of making a contribution, without necessarily being where you were as a child. I'd like to stress that this, far from introducing any particular sense of instability and schizophrenia, helped enormously – it took away a lot of fear. Another key moment was when I had been rushed home from school one day because of a fascist demonstration during one of the many anti-Blum uprisings and scandals in Paris. My mother very rightly began closing the windows and bringing down the blinds. I desperately wanted to see the mob in the street, as any little child would. My father came home and with extreme calm ordered my mother to open the windows and the blinds, stood next to me and said: 'Never be afraid, this is called history.' That was one of the real turning-points in my life. It placed what was happening in a fascinating and positive context.

So these were very important elements, together with being taught by my father to begin reading the classics at a very, very early age. He would take a Homer, look at some lines with me in English or in French, or in the great German Voss translation which he loved best, and we'd come to one of those unbearably exciting passages, the arrow, the spear, flying through the air, and I couldn't bear it any more, I was out of my mind with excitement. And he'd say, with tremendous regret, I don't know how to explain this, there is no translation of this passage, it's missing. And I'd almost shout for help, and he'd say, let's find out, and do the Greek words with me. And that simple device was, of course, tremendous. It gave me the idea that you had better learn to translate for yourself if you wanted to find out how the story went on. There was also the unashamed proud élitism of the French system, where the teacher says to the six-year old children who only partially understood him: You have walked this morning through the Rue de la Fontaine, Place Descartes, Place Victor Hugo and Square Pascal, and one in a million of you might one day contribute something worth preserving. I owe everything to that. And I have no grimmer sadness about what has happened to Western education than the fact that children are no longer allowed the great vision of eventual possibility, harsh as it is in one way, but in another way fantastically bracing and encouraging.

You then went to New York and to the lycée *there?*

In 1940, we were unable to get to England, where I was supposed to go. I had as a kind of unofficial godfather, because in Judaism you don't have official godfathers, Lewis Namier, who was a very close friend of my father. Namier, because he had some students there, put me down for Harrow. It is my humble conviction that, had I gone there, I don't think I would have found my way. Owing to Herr Hitler, I was unable to benefit from Lewis Namier's generous foresight and had to go to New York and to the *lycée* there in which some of those who were important figures in modern culture were earning their precarious living in exile, before they found university posts, by teaching little boys and girls. So I heard lectures by Maritain, by Gilson, by Lévi-Strauss, by Perrin the physicist. It was an extremely heady, complicated, stimulating atmosphere. The *lycée* was officially pro-Vichy, the students of course extremely Gaullist, and there is nothing healthier than to fear being beaten up by political opponents. It related again to what my father had said: Never be afraid, this is called history. I found history a very exciting business.

When you went to the University of Chicago, you switched for a time to the study of science. Why was that?

That had very special and bizarre reasons. Robert Hutchins, who was a great reformer in American education, a very, very Thomist, very fascinating figure, said that American undergraduate education was a complete waste of time for the literate. It was essentially designed for the semi-literate. So you had a system where you came and volunteered to sit any final exam in any of the fourteen basic subjects you had to take. If you got an alpha, you didn't need to take the course, a delightful idea. So I sat all 14 and got alphas in all but three, mathematics, physics and chemistry, which, coming out of a Greek-Latin French system, I failed with below gamma. So that's what I felt I had to study. I switched completely to science, and it was beautifully taught. Hutchins's rule was that the greater and more eminent you were as a man, the more you had to allow a little time for beginners. I learned physics from Enrico Fermi, who loved lecturing to idiots because physics itself was beginning again, so he wanted to know how you teach it. I had eminent teachers in chemistry and biology and worked day and night because I was so embarrassed, so ashamed. That led to a quite extraordinary ending of the whole matter. I did well on the Finals and rushed to see the science advisor of the university, a very distinguished man, saying I'd like to do science. He called in my papers, and he said: You got good marks, and you're an idiot. You learnt the maths by heart, and there isn't a spark of real insight in this. I was still in a period, 1948-9, when it was atoms or nothing. If you weren't good enough to do physics, particularly nuclear physics, in Chicago, you were called a bottlewasher. And of course I couldn't have coped even with the beginning of graduate work, because indeed my mathematics was learned by rote. I still remember the sense of shock, of numbing sadness, as I resigned myself to philosophy and literature. And let me say that the embarrassment about being so helpless in real mathematics has always stayed with me, and it may be that my passions for music and chess are, to do tuppenny psychoanalysis, vestiges of the sadness over the mathematics. We're meeting in a science college full of mathematicians, and I am unashamedly sad and in some ways envious as they pass by.

You went on to Harvard and to Oxford to do graduate work in liter-
ature, spent four years on The Economist *in London, and then, in*
1956, went to the Institute of Advanced Study in Princeton, where
you finished your first published book, Tolstoy or Dostoevsky. *That*
book, which came out in 1960, was written against what was then
still the dominant ideology in literary studies, the New Criticism.
What were your objections to the New Criticism?

The lack of a historical body and context, the autistic play with the
text, the lack above all of the possibility of intentionality. By then, I'd
come into close contact with Lukács in Budapest, I was beginning to
study Hegel and Marx intensely, I was reading Husserl a lot. The
New Criticism seemed to me a wonderful therapeutic, pedagogic
device, but finally false to the possibilities of the text. And its
incapacity to handle works like *The Brothers Karamazov* or *War
and Peace* or *The Death of Ivan Ilych* seemed to me palpable. I was
trying to see why the New Critical tools snap, like very thin metal
files which are not up to the job, when you have the real stone in front
of you. And *Real Presences*, 'The Grammars of Creation' which are
the Gifford Lectures I've just given, my fiction, everything I've written, they're all in *Tolstoy or Dostoevsky*, in the statement which
begins all my formal work, that true criticism is a debt of love, and
my sense that where the God-question is not fully admitted as a question, there are dimensions which are simply not accessible to style, to
discourse.

Developing that point, one particular anticipation of your future
work, and of your current quarrel with deconstruction in Real Presences, *occurs in this passage from* Tolstoy or Dostoevsky: *'The most*
stringent test of the aliveness of an imagined character – of its mys-
terious acquisition of a life of its own outside the book or play in
which it has been created and far exceeding the mortality of its
creator – is whether or not it can grow with time and preserve its
coherent individuality in an altered setting. Place Odysseus in
Dante's Inferno *or in Joyce's Dublin and he is Odysseus still...'*
(1980 edn, p. 104). Now the objection that would be made today is
that this continuity and coherence, even within a text, let alone bet-
ween texts, is a retrospective simplification, a construction, a synth-
etic act of the imagination which really leaves out all the differences
between, say, Homer's Odysseus and Joyce's Bloom.

I don't accept that. Because we start at different points of questioning.

Flaubert dies screaming – he was in pain – I'm dying like a dog and
cette putaine Emma Bovary will live. Deconstruction has nothing to
tell me about that scream, nothing whatever. The notion that Odysseus or Falstaff or Hamlet or Emma Bovary or Anna Karenina are
only semantic markers is entirely coherent. It cannot be disproved.
But I know it's rubbish. If that were so, more of us could have a crack
at creating those semantic markers. The survival of a fictional persona, the way it absorbs one's own life so that it is much more alive
than you and I – these figures have life infinitely beyond your and
mine, and a physical life strangely enough – all this entails a possible
analogy, and I'm using analogy in a strict, almost theological sense,
with the act of creation. Now that is another vocabulary, another
language game: let's be Wittgensteinian for a moment. Derrida has
his game. Nothing in Derrida's game is better than in my game. I
think mine accounts much more for one's actual experience of the
figure in the text. Indeed, if I ask myself why we lack, in our time,
epigones of this order of real presence, maybe the language game I'm
within at least offers hypotheses of a post-Nietzchean, post-Freudian
linguistic moment. The other can offer no hypotheses, it can merely
say hoorah. *And it may be right.* I do not say, as my teachers like
Maritain and Gilson, the great Thomists, could say: I am right. No,
I am saying that what I ask and what I suggest addresses itself more
to actual experiences than do the dances over the emptiness of Monsieur de Man and Monsieur Derrida. This is not to say either that
they aren't right or that there isn't only an emptiness to dance over.
I do not know. But I am accountable to the naive immediacy of my
experiences, when I read a major text, when a major melody enters
into me. Proust, dying, wants to see the yellow spot on the wall in
Vermeer's *View of Delft* because he says: to have seen that is to know
the essence of life. Now you can deconstruct that, and, by the way,
in so many more interesting ways than the deconstructionists. You
could make it a symptom of asthmatic decay. Very interesting. A
doctor might want to tell us something about that. You could deconstruct it in the name of dandyish aestheticism, of the religion of art
contra humanism, Maurice de Guérin and Baudelaire against
Matthew Arnold. And I wonder if what you have done is not to
wholly, wholly diminish it. In *A La Recherche*, on the night of the
death of the great writer Bergotte – and this is one of the last pages
Proust writes – his books are open in the *vitrines* of the Paris book-
stores in the silent city, and the narrator says the open books are the
wings of the death angels honouring the writer who will never die. If
that is the rhetoric of a language game, I would like to know why

there are many human beings who can, and indeed do, live and die by Proust. I wonder what book you have in your pocket when things go very, very wrong, or – an even harsher test in some ways – are ecstatically wonderful.

But aren't you moving towards using literature and art as a substitute for religion?

Certainly not as a substitute. At a certain range and reach, I see a continuum between art and religion. Plato teaches me in the *Phaedo* that the thirst for beauty is insatiable. It can never be slaked. That makes such obvious sense to me. When Baudelaire says that in and through the music, you will know what is on the other side of death, I'm sure I cannot paraphrase it, but it seems to me an imperative of common sense. When Lawrence says, you have to be so terribly religious to be an artist, the fire of God has gone through me this morning – as Blake would, of course – I don't think these men are mixing up art and religion, I don't think they're bluffing, I don't think they're deceiving themselves. They are reporting. All I can do is report on my thirst. My whole fifteen books have been a report on being very, very thirsty. And perhaps it would have been better if I could have had the Coca-Cola of complete relativism and playfulness.

  Please mark my prediction. Monsieur Sollers attacked me years ago when he was running a journal called *Tel Quel*: Monsieur Sollers is now a friend who, with Levinas, is editing an orthodox Jewish magazine called *L'Infini*. We've gone from *Tel Quel* to *L'Infini*. Monsieur Derrida will perhaps end in Jewish rabbinism, as Geoffrey Hartman has done. What a detour! A fine, exciting detour! But that's been clear from the start. Deconstruction is a thirst. Why is it so Jewish? Why has this country contributed almost nothing? Because it doesn't have a Jewish intellectual tradition? It's a complicated question. Why have all these people come out of the Talmudic tradition in order to mock it? They are thirsty. And it's almost embarrassing, the simplicity of the logic. If you begin with such craving, where else are you going to end but with *L'Infini*? I almost wish they'd stuck to their guns: if you are an anarchic, nihilistic dancer, don't for God's sake sit down! No, for me, there are very deep relations between art and religion, but art is not a substitute for religion. I fear the Arnoldian argument on substitution. Not a substitute, but an approach. Threshold. Door-handle.

Your next book, The Death of Tragedy, *which appeared in 1961, is very rich and wide-ranging, but perhaps also limiting – when you say, for instance: 'Tragedy speaks not of secular dilemmas which may be resolved by rational innovation, but of the unalterable bias toward inhumanity and destruction in the drift of the world' (1963 edn, p. 291). Isn't that too narrow a definition of tragedy?*

The book does not sufficiently distinguish between what I now call 'absolute tragedy' and the natural tragi-comic pulse which is there in most of the great plays that we call tragedies – namely, the act of trust in the world, in its continuation: that Cyprus will be better governed by Cassio after Othello's death, that Fortinbras will, though with less intellectual distinction, possibly be a decent king of Denmark: the great Shakespearean pulse of life. But there are a handful of absolute tragedies in which there is no upbeat – among them, the *Bacchae* of Euripides, the *Antigone* of Sophocles. *Timon of Athens*, which I now work on more and more, seems to me the only absolute tragedy in Shakespeare because it says, let language end. It is the only time in the whole Shakespearean canon that we do not even have the hope that language might persist. Timon's epitaph speaks of the end of language, which is the end of the Shakespearean universe. Absolute tragedies would also include *Woyzeck*, and certain plays of Racine where there is the vision that man is an unwelcome guest in the universe, hunted, harried, tortured and eliminated. We now assign to Theognis – but competent scholars tell me it may be much older – the famous saying which Sophocles and then endless others will quote: It is best not to have been born, and, saving that, to die young. The worst is to live. That famous triple statement, for me, defines the enactment of absolute tragedy. To look at a human situation in the light of that. I should have been much more rigorous in *The Death of Tragedy* and I should have made it clear that this tiny handful of tragedies are almost in the nature of experiments out of the night. They are testings of ultimate blackness. They can only be sustained for a very short period – though you might argue that the fact that you can write the play is a subversion of this absolute. I could add further recent examples of absolute tragedy – by Edward Bond, whom I admire enormously, and the last Beckett parables, the black mouth screaming, the extinction of the world and of speech within final sorrow. And let me say something more. You quoted this bias towards the inhuman. If you had told me that the world would not move a finger when Pol Pot was burying alive 100,000 men, women and children, and it was being reported to us, which was not true at the time of Auschwitz – sorry, I stick by that statement.

This leads on to a crucial, harrowing concern of your work, which you eloquently address in Language and Silence, *published in 1967, and elsewhere in your writings – the co-existence, and indeed the possible complicity, of culture and barbarism. Isn't that concern in tension with your desire to conserve high culture?*

In constant, unresolved tension. Had I only observed that one could torture in the morning and play Schubert at night, this would have been more or less valid. I ventured to go further and ask: what is it inside the playing of Schubert which may relate to the capacity to torture? That, to me, is the much more urgent question. Is it that people trained to imagine abstractly – and to abstract means to get out of, draw away from, separate, cut from – are made less human? That is what I keep asking, and I've never had anyone answering it. Does the cry in *Lear*, as it enters into me, silence the cry in the street? Or muffle it? Or make it messily boring? This creates a constant tension, and I have no answer to your question, I have a sense of bewilderment. My consequent position should have been an ultimately anti-cultural one. Mother Teresa does not need to read Shakespeare or Dostoevsky. One person – this is the later Wittgenstein torment – in a hospital taking care of the incontinent during the night is presumably, by my own convictions, nearer to God than is the greatest teacher or writer. And I cannot resolve that tension. I'm a mandarin. I was trained into this clerisy whose role is to pass on the excellence of the really creative, the really great; trained to be what Pushkin called the mailman, the courier bringing the mail from the great to others who may live by it and love it. I would give anything to be able to say that I now see a way through the antinomian contradiction. I do not see a way through. I see little clearings at the edge. For example, I think one can teach at risk and live one's loves at a certain risk. One can try to make imagining extremely concrete, and hope – it's a pious hope, perhaps something like what Trilling meant by the liberal imagination, what Leavis meant by his whole life-teaching, by life-enhancement – that the more scrupulous reader will not take for granted the barbarism around him.

A concern related to the co-existence of culture and barbarism, which you've taken up in, for instance, the essays 'Night Words' in Language and Silence, *and 'Eros and Idiom' in* On Difficulty, *which came out in 1978, is with, in Pound's phrase, 'frankness as never before', the new explicitness in literature in the twentieth century, and especially since the 1960s.*

I loathe that new explicitness, and let me quickly define the grounds. First of all, it makes it much more difficult to write well. That's a really mundane ground, but one which I could demonstrate without any difficulty. It has become much harder to say anything fresh or to educate the reader's imagination to work with, to collaborate with, the writer. There is more sexual charge in Casaubon and Dorothea's failed honeymoon in *Middlemarch* than in all of modern pornography and frank fiction. Secondly, the emptying-out of the ballast of the self, in psychoanalysis, in total confessional revelation, the making public of that which is your own strength, your own darkness, your own infirmity. Like many people who are slightly or otherwise handicapped, I have a cardinal, central sense of the privilege of wrestling alone. And that's how you make it or don't make it. I think we are defined by the weight of secrecy that we can carry, by that which is inviolably discreet within us. I have a deep distaste for psychoanalysis, for the pouring into another person's monied lap of one's aching, final secrets. The psychoanalytic, the revelatory, the confessional, harness the cheapest of human instincts, which is that of voyeurism.

I'll take a step further. The question of censorship seems to me an urgent and open one. If you were to ask me to balance between, on the one hand, the dissemination of child pornography, sado-masochistic literature in every window as it is now by the completely new instruments of video, and, on the other hand, the errors, the injustices, the corruptions which attach to any body that censors, ineluctably because it is a human interest body with its own power relations, I still opt for those errors which seem to me reparable, challengeable, reversible in a perfectly Miltonic and Millian sense. Nobody has tried to meet the argument of my work, which is a very simple one. If we are in deprivation, socially, physically, economically, explicit material is hot oil being dropped into dynamite. We do not have other escapes, we do not have ironic distances from this material. I want the argument to be looked at in terms of the power of images, of sounds, of words. Where does that power fall? The revolutions in Eastern Europe would not have happened without *Dallas*, without the soap operas that were beamed across the walls. People wanted to eat that way, to dress that way, they were ready to do almost anything so that they too could one day step into a car and drive off. This is being hailed as a triumph for free communication. If that is so, I have a right to ask what happens when images of the flogging and burning of the child can be bought in every video shop and shown on every screen. You can't have it both ways. If, as we know, the media of communication are the most powerful means of political suggestion open to man, then the whole question of what you're communicating and to whom is a fair question.

Aren't there, however, some novels which have benefited from, perhaps couldn't even have been written without, the new explicitness? I'm thinking, for instance, of a novel for which you've expressed your admiration, Doris Lessing's The Golden Notebook.

Very good point. First of all, would that we didn't have *Lady Chatterley*, which is a weak book. Or *Nana*. In most cases, the great moments of emancipation have been paid by for the quality of the work – which doesn't detract from the courage or martyrdom of the authors. I don't think of *The Golden Notebook* as necessarily a novel, but we do have the one important passage on the solitary practices of women, one of the first times when this is explored. And there are other books which indeed have benefited from the abolition of certain rather absurd taboos. By the way, those taboos are exaggerated. We now know that the Victorians were much tougher and franker than our textboooks would suggest to us. But nevertheless, there were absurd taboos, and there have been important emancipations. There have been some magnificent, I think oblique, realizations. I would not want Updike's best fiction to be impossible, Philip Roth's certainly not – one of the great comic artists of our time – nor Bellow, so restless, so classical. I suppose I would want Mailer's *Deer Park* to be available. There are not many. Great artists were able to say what they wanted before then. You're not going to tell me that we know more about sex than Dante or Shakespeare or Rabelais did. However, perhaps we can relax more with our readers in a shared pact of adultness. But compared to that, the servitudes, the number of writers under pressure who feel that they have to have orgasm when it isn't even within the reach or need of that particular book or of their way of feeling or of being. It is the blackmail of visceral totality which really worries me now and which is producing massive cruelty and trash.

Could we move on to that fecund and copious work, After Babel, *which is to appear this year in a new edition. A key aspect of the original book was your scepticism about Chomsky's postulate of universal deep structures of language. How do you feel about that today?*

More strongly than ever. I live among more and more languages, and, since 1974, in a totally polyglot society, Geneva, and I teach in it and dream in it and have my human relations in it. Are there any universal deep structures? We haven't come up with any concrete ones. I'm still waiting. But suppose there are: I still maintain that they are of the order of the fact that we need oxygen to breathe and cannot breathe carbon dioxide. Whether they can go much beyond that in concreteness, I do not know. Transformational generative grammars have nothing to say about the poem, and that, to me, is the tuning-fork test of linguistic theory.

There's a strong sense in After Babel *– and again this anticipates your quarrel with deconstruction – that translation – and, in that book, translation is, for you, the paradigm of all interpretation – involves the attempt to recover some kind of original meaning. Now it's the existence of any such meaning that deconstruction denies.*

Of course. Absolutely denies. I would like to say an original pre-sence. Almost a mute one. Let me move laterally here because you ask very difficult and central questions. Why am I a Racinian, perhaps more than a Shakespearean? Because there are moments where speech in Racine is the only thing left in the universe. Human beings are using very simple words that bring them to the edge and then to silence. If you had to put to me the famous *Desert Island Discs* situation, where you can take only one play with you, I would choose *Bérénice*. It captures the moment of utter desolation when you're standing in front of another human being whom you love more than anything in the universe and know it's the last time. No bears chasing you, no castles being stormed by moving woods, no hurricanoes spouting, no pother, no anything: language has ended quietly, calmly, with a word like *adieu,* and then a man and a woman are looking at each other. This is the kind of act of presence which may be more primary even than the most nakedly truthful speech. This act of presence involves a sense of the sacramental, and hence a sense of the theology of the Incarnation for which Shakespeare finds the words – bodying forth – an untranslatable two words. We could spend a lifetime pondering that phrase. The bodying forth of what? I think, of a real presence, which if you're that way inclined can be theological, but doesn't need to be. It can be immanent, the bodying forth of the other human being, of the other visage, of the other hand which you can no longer touch, which you will never touch again.

Why don't we give an example from, yes, from the realm of inspired kitsch which forms all of us. I was formed as a boy by a film called *Brief Encounter*. Did I see it four times, six times? I kept going in New York, drenched in tears of course. I can't put on the Rachmaninov to this day without having those tears come back. When they both know it's the last time, and there's the whistle of the train, and the smoke of the tea-kettle comes between them, and they will never touch hands again, it's nearer to Racine than almost anything English culture has produced. A Racinian film. So it can be the most humble of experiences: what it must be like when you see, for the last time, a child who is dying and who doesn't know it. It's not speech then, it is real presence, but speech is rooted in it, and the speech of supreme poetry more than any other.

There seems to be a certain equivocation in After Babel, *which very much relates to current debates between deconstructionists and liberal humanists, as to how far language shapes human beings and how far human beings shape language. What are your views on that?*

Heidegger's *die Sprache spricht*, language speaks us, and his sense that the poet is the one most open to this passage of language through him, was a flash of illumination that came to me very young – without full understanding, of course, but it seemed to me a revelation of what was happening, when a great poem, a great piece of meaning, which can also be music, passed through me. The idea that we are bespoken, we are uttered by, this. I know the full power of counter-arguments, which don't convince me. Nothing that men seem able to say about it makes any sense. The Rabbinic idea that language much precedes man, since God has been speaking to the universe before we appear on the sixth day, and that we are largely there so that, at a much lower level of form, the breath of speech which is *Ruah* can continue going on through man when God keeps quiet, which he does forever after the sixth day – this seems to me a marvellously reasonable hypothesis, compared to the notion that it's birdsong we imitate or that the larynx develops certain synaptic, cellular networks which, for reasons unbeknown to anybody, come out as syntax. Let the others do better and I shall most respectfully be taught and change my mind. They haven't done better so far and they don't help me with a poem at all, which is always the test.

With that quest in mind, could we focus on your desire – which you mention, for instance, in your contribution to a TLS *symposium on 'Modern literary theory: its place in teaching' (6 February 1981, p. 135) – to question Leavis's dictum that 'linguistics has nothing to contribute to our understanding of literature'. What do you think linguistics can contribute?*

The first books I like to give my students are Empson's. *Seven Types of Ambiguity* and more, to me, *The Structure of Complex Words* and some of the essays, show someone who smelt grammar like a palpable agency moving within the poem. When I heard Roman Jakobson, in a seminar, repeat to his students, do not come to tell me about the grammar of the poem if you do not know about the poetry of the grammar, it helped me enormously. And Jakobson could do it, he could take a Shakespeare sonnet and show that the grammar of poetry and the poetry of grammar are deeply congruent. Then there is Kenneth Burke on the grammar of rhetoric and of argument, and people who are less well-known in this country, like Contini and Timpanaro, who are highly alert to the interactions of linguistics and literature. Linguistics can tell us a lot about structure, about constraint. Take Chomsky's fascinating axiom that there can't be an endless sentence. It's very important, to the reader of *Finnegans Wake*, of Hölderlin, of late Proust, to understand what Chomsky is saying and what deep structural rule he's suggesting. I learnt much from Christine Brooke-Rose's *The Grammar of Metaphor*: it has behind it the lineaments of a trained linguistic awareness. And Donald Davie's early books *Purity of Diction in English Verse* and *Articulate Energy* mean a great deal to me, I teach them all the time. I do want my students, when they do, say, *Lycidas* with me, to show me they've learnt what a gerund is, what an ablative absolute is, what an anaphoric structure is, because they would not, I think, be allowed in a basic music class if they did not know there was a scale, a key, a dominant and a subdominant. And the idea that you can read literature from Milton to Geoffrey Hill, from Ovid to Robert Lowell, without knowing the lineaments of prosody and of grammar seems to me silly. In those respects, I'm sure Leavis is wrong. On the other hand, if we're told nonsense, such as, there will be a new generation of computers that will be able to give us a Shakespeare play or a Balzac novel, if we are told by Derrida that all texts are a pre-text of semiotic textuality, then I know Leavis is right. He didn't even need to see this kind of barbaric yawping. But a great deal can be learnt at the interface of linguistics and literary criticism.

You've brought up the topic of teaching, and I'd like to take issue with a comment you made in the 1976 essay 'Text and Context', which is collected in On Difficulty. *You say in that essay: 'The*

*attempt to impose "textual" habits or a transcendental convention
of the "classical" on a mass public, as it is now being made in many
of our universities, is a self-defeating hypocrisy' (1980 edn, p. 15).
I'd like to set against that another of your statements, made in 1974,
but to take the liberty, if I may, of altering one word. The statement
then runs: 'Is there even a shred of evidence to show that the capacity
for literary insight and enjoyment, up to a certain modest standard of
competence, is mysteriously or genetically specific? Or are we, actually, dealing with a long tradition of bad teaching, patronising sloth
and socially conditioned recalcitrance?'. Now I'm quoting, as you'll
recognize, from your address to the AGM of the Headmasters' Conference in October 1974 (published in* Conference, *vol. 12, no. 1,
February 1975, p. 9), and I've substituted 'literary' for 'mathematical'.*

Fine. You have every right to substitute one for the other. I was
speaking to headmasters and trying to prevent mass depression,
which I've sometimes been known to induce in generous audiences.
I don't know the answer. Could we, given ideal conditions, do much
better in bringing to far more young men and women and children
access to the best? Yes, we must, at some level, believe this. Yes, if we
have teachers almost capable of themselves creating something. It's
not infinitely elastic. I still think that, even under ideal conditions,
Shakespeare's *Sonnets*, Dante's *Paradiso*, Spinoza's *Ethics*, Bach's
Well-Tempered Clavier, are not infinitely 'bringable'. There were, at
the best scholarly estimates, nine people at the Crucifixion, *circa* 610
at the premiere of *Hamlet*, 1200 at the first performance of the *Missa
Solemnis* and a billion-and-a-half watching the World Cup Final.
Your and my brain cannot take in a billion-and-a-half. This is not a
statistical fact, it is a sociological fact of the most enormous importance. Eliot said human beings can stand very little reality. I'm not
sure that they can stand very much irreality – the mind-demanding
abstraction, demanding purity and intensity of meditation. The idea
which was inculcated in me, by my father, by the great French educational system, was that you sit alone on a chair in a quiet room – Pascal's formula – being neither afraid nor empty. Nothing in our culture now wants that. It even regards it as highly asocial and potentially dangerous. Those East European societies based on that Mes-
sianic heresy of Judaic élitism that was Marxism have now collapsed.
In those societies, the article on Hegel or the poem by Pasternak or
the next production of *Othello* or the next Shostakovitch quartet
were among the most important political issues, for which human

beings risked their lives. That was an enviable condition. And if that is gone, if there is no longer the pro-vocation, *provocare*, the summons, the calling – a beautiful word we don't use any more – the calling of that challenge to us in the West, then God help us. Then indeed there is a possibility that the best of liberal hopes and instincts will become the emporium of the McDonald hamburger and the fast food chain. And fast food is a formidable image, because, as we know, the idea of nurture has food in it, and the dialectic between humane nurture and fast food is the one we are now going to have to live.

Those Eastern European Communist orders emerged from a continent devastated by Fascism, and your most powerful exploration of the genesis of Fascism is your novel The Portage to San Cristobal of A.H., *published in book form in 1981. Relating that to your earlier point about the desirability of teachers being almost capable of creation, how do you see your own fiction?*

In a great creative artist, there is an innocence which I simply do not have. Such an artist has something which we don't have a terribly good word for, a supreme intelligence, an innocent necessity, of shaping. My fiction, which has had a very good run for it, and is now alive in many languages, comes out of an argument, out of an idea, out of what might have been an essay. I hope this is a little less true of some of the most controversial parts of *The Portage*. These are not things I could have said in any other form. The novel wrote itself in three days and three nights, at a moment of very deep personal crisis. So I've known a little whiff of the real thing. And of course if one could do the real thing all the time, one would. I hope I have never deflected from the statement near the beginning of *Tolstoy or Dostoevsky*, that no-one would write a book of criticism if he could write one sentence of *War and Peace* or *The Brothers Karamazov*. But the other job is infinitely worth doing. It's to be the pilot-fish in front of the master shark, or one of those wonderful birds that sit on the rhinoceros and go *pit-pit*, so that everybody knows the real one is coming. Ask a critic, a teacher, for whom he has helped to open the way. There are half-a-dozen major figures whose rhinoceros horns I've at least been lucky enough to chirp on. And that's exciting, that's what I look back on with pride. Figures like Benjamin, Adorno, Lévi-Strauss, Hermann Broch, are now available, and everyone uses them as if they'd always known about them. I hate those who close books. To be told you're mistaken, fine, but far better that error than the

English-English 'Come off it', the love of cutting-down which has crippled this insular culture. This is my deep difference with Leavis – the number of books he closed for others. That's unforgivable. You don't need to say you like them, you don't need to touch on them, but don't close them by fiat.

As well as introducing those modern masters, you've also sought to show – especially in Antigones, *which came out in 1984 – the rich afterlife of ancient classics in Western culture. A new Classics building opened here in Cambridge last month, Tony Harrison's translations of Greek drama circulate widely, Oliver Taplin's recent book* Greek Fire *and the related TV series, of which you were one of the presenters, have been successful. Do you see a general revival of interest in Classics?*

There is something of a revival. I don't know that we can be at all confident about it, however. What stands in its way is not only its élitist and formal character, but the fact that we're not in a pagan period at all. In order to have a strong Nietzchean paganism, you have to go around shouting that Christ was a crook and an impostor. If that's no longer an issue, then it's very difficult to return to the counter-statement of the immanent proliferation which is paganism. And as psychoanalysis ebbs, which it certainly is doing, something of the grip of classical mythology may ebb with it. Will this mean a greater catholicity of awareness of, say, African, Far Eastern, Amerindian myth, as Lévi-Strauss believes? It doesn't look that way. Few read the four volumes of Latin American and Amerindian myths which Lévi-Strauss hoped would be the new *mythologiques*, as Freud's Oedipus had been. But as the new Europe comes into difficult, confused existence, it looks as if certain classical authors and their afterlives, particularly Virgil and Homer, speak to the European condition as others have not. The *civilitas* of continuity may give us certain shared points of reference. There is a politics of the classical which has a new, though still marginal and preliminary, actuality. And the Victorian sense of being part of a Roman-Greek Hellenistic world would have made easier the entrance into Europe than what has happened since in this country. In that respect, the Victorians were more modern than we.

You suggested earlier in our conversation that you might be more of a Racinian than a Shakespearean, and you've expressed doubts elsewhere about this most exalted of English cultural icons, for

instance in your 1986 W.P. Ker lecture, 'A Reading Against Shakes-
peare'. Could you sum up your doubts about him?

There's a French fairy tale about Patapouf, who's big and furry and
rolls, and Fil de Fer, the iron thread who cuts. Shakespeare is Patapouf beyond Patapoufs: all the universe is in there. Racine is Fil de
Fer: he cuts and cuts and cuts, to essentialize, and that's a dangerous
Heideggerian term, to achieve a final, ultimate identity. I have problems, which are my problems, with an art that has so much waste and
contingency in it. This is the mark of a French and very classical
Greek-Aeschylean-Sophoclean education. I couldn't live a day without Shakespeare, of course. The *Sonnets* never leave me. They have
an intensity which is ultimate for me. I read Dante, the *Sonnets*, and
Proust, whenever I have the slightest doubt about human intelligence
and transcendence. But the doubts about Shakespeare of a Wittgenstein, of a Tolstoy, of a Lukács, of an Eliot, who is anti-Shakespeare,
who prefers Dante, do not seem to me trivial or not worth attending
to. And if they were more attended to, it would be even more exciting
to see the infinite gift to our language that is Shakespeare.

One could relate your uneasiness about the waste and contingency in
Shakespeare to the uneasiness about deconstructive dissemination
which has vividly emerged several times as we've talked, and which
is of course powerfully focused in Real Presences, *the book which*
appeared in 1989 and which has perhaps been implicitly present
throughout our discussion. But one might ask, given your stress in
After Babel *on linguistic plurality and proliferation: why not wel-*
come deconstruction? Doesn't deconstruction, after all, celebrate
that plurality and proliferation?

Could we first of all say of *Real Presences* that there is no recent book
which does not honour deconstruction more? I give the deconstructionists a glorious run for it and say how much we owe to them. But
finally they are guilty of an ethical, almost religious, breach of values.
They put the text below the commentary, they take away from us the
task of living a text by the abolition of the responding responsibility
of the reader. If that is all there is to reading – if, as de Man says,
every good reading is a misreading – then indeed I am in a world
which I am perhaps no longer brave enough or playful enough to live
with. Perhaps *Real Presences* is a certain cry of muddled despair at
my own incapacity to handle the possibility of nothingness. Paul
Celan I put above almost any other poet of this century. I've looked

at what Lacoue-Labarthe and Derrida do with Celan, and they can't really get anywhere because his work resists by saying: I come out of an order of experience which no playfulness has any purchase on. A Celan, a Walter Benjamin, should have written *Real Presences*. I certainly delight in plurality, in the richness of possible interpretations, but in this I am both with Blake's holiness of the minute particular and Leavis's 'Yes, but...'. After all, Leavis never denied that there could be plurality, but he thought that if we spoke to each other nakedly and patiently enough in front of the work, we would limit the disagreements to a fruitful area where they would have the dignity of promise. The deconstructionists and pragmatists would take that away from us. When a Rorty says anything goes, a Chesterton answers – and Chesterton is an out-of-fashion, anti-Semitic, hectoring writer, but he said one thing which haunts me a lot, which helps me as a teacher: when you stop believing, the trouble isn't that you believe nothing – that would be fine – it's that you'll believe anything. And that, I think, is a very strong point.

With this kind of playful irresponsibility, the inhuman is near. I have refrained from publishing a single word about Paul de Man, because I think we're too near the shock of the event and because I'm so involved in the Heidegger paradox. But I now have to review for the *TLS* these massive journals of Eliade, and it seems that Eliade was a Romanian Iron Guard sympathizer who made racist and anti-Jewish pronouncements (See *TLS*, 4 October 1990, pp. 1015-16). If deconstruction is right, this is of no interest whatsoever. It's a moment of one game contrasted with other games. I can't live by that. And by the way, Derrida doesn't either any more. Why should he bother to write so much in defence of de Man? It's a complete contradiction of his own doctrine. He's not deconstructing Paul: it's a long lovesong of aching sophistic agony. So we're all in a bit of trouble.

I hope that the Gifford Lectures which I've just completed, and which I hope to write up and publish as *The Grammars of Creation*, will mean that, in future, I'll be able to fail a little better in answering you and that my incomplete replies to your questions will be a little more worth disagreeing with. That is the Leavisian hope, that is the Arnoldian hope, that is the Platonic hope of the maieutic dialogue. What I try to do in the Gifford Lectures is to concentrate on a single question: why does the language invite, allow and solicit the sentence 'God created the universe' and refuse the sentence 'God invented the universe'? I have tried to think about creation and invention in art, philosophy and music, but also in society, in political institutions.

This seems to lead back to things right at the beginning of my work. And as I look around for help, I notice that there isn't much, that this question has scarcely been touched. The reason I mention it is the sense of boundless gratitude one has for the difficulty of what we have to think about. Never or rarely, I believe, has there been a period in which the fundamentals have become so daily again, so that it's not whether you get it right – you don't – but whether you get it wrong fruitfully. And of course the sentence 'to get it wrong fruitfully' does postulate logically the possibility of getting it right. And that's where the cut, the diacritical cut, in everything you've asked comes.

Bernard Bergonzi

Leamington Spa, Warwickshire
7 August 1990

NICOLAS TREDELL: *In the 'Anecdotal Introduction' to your latest book* Exploding English, *you offer a very interesting account of your development from leaving school early, in 1945, to becoming a mature student and then a university lecturer. Could you sum up that development for us?*

BERNARD BERGONZI: I had a lot of illness as a child and then again in my late teens. This was connected with TB, but into the bargain I had some quite disconnected things and, without wanting to be melodramatic, I nearly died two or three times before I was 21. And I think that gave me a certain sense of the contingency of experience. It made me wary, made me think that expectations are often likely to be disappointed. I have always felt life was a bit provisional and the more that you can get through without mishap, the better. In terms of intellectual development, being ill gives you a lot of time to read, but as I had not had very much formal training – I left school before I was 16 – I read in strangely undirected ways. I think it's the mark of the autodidact to be well-informed about very *recherché* and unknown works and have enormous gaps as far as the major canonical works go, and that sometimes gives a false impression of erudition. I was rather like that in my earlier twenties. So going to Oxford certainly put me through a more formal training. Although I'm very far from holding any great brief for the Oxford English School, there were some good things about it, and being told what to read rather than just wandering around picking up books was valuable – probably more valuable when one's 26 than a few years younger. I was a young enough mature student to feel a rapport with people who were about five years younger than myself, but I'd been around a bit and, having worked in offices, in blind-alley white-collar jobs, I was able to appreciate the extraordinary freedom of academic life to do what one wants all day. I still feel that to some extent.

Two of your poems were broadcast on the opening programme, in April 1953, of John Wain's radio series First Reading *— a series which was influential in promoting what came to be known as the Movement. How did you feel about the Movement in the fifties?*

That was rather exciting. People looking back at the fifties and the Movement now think what an incredibly tame bourgeois set-up it was. No doubt that is right in the long perspective of history but I was excited by the Movement and I felt in a small way I was part of it. I remember buying John Wain's *Hurry on Down* the day it was published in the Autumn of 1953: I bought it in Foyles and went and sat down in the foyer of the National Gallery and started reading it. People like Wain and Amis and Donald Davie were teaching in universities or had other connections with them, so that gave me all the more a sense that a university was a good place to be in from every point of view. You can write literary criticism, which I wanted to do, you can write poems, you can write novels. It all came apart after a very short time, but at that historical moment, from about 1953 to about 1956, I was excited by all that.

A volume of your poems, Descartes and the Animals, *was published in 1954. How would you characterize your poetry at that time?*

I think it tends to have the Movement qualities or — I don't know — possibly Movement virtues. At that time, the thing to do was to write in tight quatrains, which I did, to write villanelles, which I did, and occasional sonnets. I tended not to write in rhymed forms in later years, but I still write in what I think of as normal syntax. Donald Davie's book on syntax, *Articulate Energy*, made an impression on me when I read it and I still think it's a very fine book. The Movement virtues were clarity, crispness, coherence of structure, etc., etc. I realize that there are many things to be said against those qualities, but I suppose they are the ones which I still tend to feel at home with.

A further collection of your poems, Years, *came out in 1979. Do you still write poetry?*

It's like those people who carry Equity cards or have qualified for the Bar. I think, well, I can still do it occasionally. I haven't written a poem for a few years, but every so often one has these stirrings. Being a critic stops one from being a poet a lot of the time, but I'm perhaps unrealistically reluctant to say I am definitively an ex-poet.

Your first critical book, which appeared in 1961, was on the early H.G. Wells of the scientific romances. Wells was not a canonical author at the time. What led to your interest in him?

I can actually place the particular occasion. When I was an undergraduate at Oxford in 1956 – this takes us back a bit into the cultural history of that time – a chap called Colin Wilson, who I think is still functioning, wrote a book that was widely praised called *The Outsider*. I won't say any more about that because that was a curious chapter in intellectual history. But Colin Wilson came to Oxford to talk to a society that I was involved with and he was very pleasant and charming. He is in fact a very widely read man and he was talking at dinner about how good H.G. Wells's early romances were. That struck a chord with me – as a boy I had enjoyed the scientific romances very much – and he said why doesn't anybody ever write about these? That didn't do anything for me until a year or so later after I'd taken my Finals. I stayed on at Oxford to do research and I thought would it be possible – this remark of Wilson's had stuck in my mind – to make a study of these works? I was rather interested in the 1890s and it struck me that Wells, in his own way, was a man of the nineties but from a very different point of view. But in Oxford in the late fifties you were not supposed to work on modern authors – certainly not on living authors, and preferably not on modern authors at all. Helen Gardner was at that time a great dragoness in charge of postgraduate work and various people had been to see her and been thoroughly choked off: she wouldn't let them do what they wanted. So I went to see her in some trepidation and said I'd like to work on H.G. Wells. 'How refreshing!' she said. So I did this thesis on Wells and with a bit of revision it was turned into what became my first critical book. And I think it was actually the first book that anybody had written on that aspect of his work.

In that book, you make a very sharp distinction between Wells the imaginative artist and Wells the didacticist and propagandist. You say, for example: 'Wells, at the beginning of his career, was a genuine and original imaginative artist, who wrote several books of considerable literary importance, before dissipating his talents in directions which now seem more or less irrelevant' (p. 22). But is it as simple as that?

Certainly not as simple as that. That was a good fifties judgement. I had grown up with the New Criticism, which always made that kind of distinction between what was of literary merit, literary interest, what was imaginatively authentic, and practically everything else – any ideas or intellectual content whatever. So at that time it seemed a fair and natural sort of distinction to make. But if I say it's too simple, I'm not going to go so far as to say it has no validity, which a lot of people would like to say now, because I do think that there is something which one can call an aesthetic dimension in literature. It's not as easy to tease it out as one once thought, and I have come to think it's peculiarly difficult with novels.

Your next book, Heroes' Twilight, *published in 1965, is an absorbing and wide-ranging study of the literature of the First World War and one of its crucial concerns is a kind of dialectic, in that literature, between the mythologizing and demythologizing of war. What do you see as the relationship between mythology and war in the twentieth century – not only in relation to the First World War, but more widely?*

Whenever people write about war, they mythologize it. The Spanish Civil War was mythologized by poets and writers but also by lots of working men who were on the left and who went to fight in the International Brigade. An enormous myth about that came into existence. As Orwell sardonically commented, people who a few years before had been out-and-out pacifists were now writing about the Spanish Civil War as the *Daily Mail* would have written in 1918 about the British war effort. Orwell had the right to say that because he'd fought in the Spanish Civil War himself and been badly wounded. That mythology was in turn demythologized by people who, knowing the historical record, saw how much the volunteers had been exploited by Stalinists in Spain. Writing about war is always a matter of myth and counter-myth. Why that should be so is a large and fascinating question.

Could we broaden this matter of myth to consider, not only the relation of myth to war, but the value of myth in general. In both The Early H.G. Wells *and* Heroes' Twilight, *you very much value the mythopeic function, even while acknowledging, in the latter book, its potential for mendacity. In recent years, history has become the privileged term in literary criticism, and myth has been seen as reactionary and mystifying. What's your own view on that?*

I think that distinction between myth and history is totally false. When Marxists talk about History with a capital 'H', they invoke a great, Hegelian, dominating myth which is almost personified. Although one can get a lot of mileage out of saying, this writing's out of touch with History, I'm on the side of History, of what's real, there is no greater myth than the class struggle. I often feel mythic thinking is a concomitant of thinking at all, at least over and above thinking about where the next meal is coming from. Frank Kermode has explored that very well in *The Sense of an Ending*. But he thinks of myths as potentially sinister and dangerous, as against fictions. Fictions are what we use to live by, but once they start turning into myths – he instances Nazism and anti-Semitism and so on – then they're dangerous. Well, clearly some of them are very pernicious, but I would hesitate to say that dominating myths are necessarily dangerous. Democracy is a myth that directs our dealings in our kind of society and we don't like to think very hard about what an extraordinarily difficult system it is to run.

Another period which has produced much myth and counter-myth is the 1960s. You say in Exploding English *that you were 'peculiarly unsympathetic to the student revolts of the 1960s' (p. 5). Could you tell us more about your response to the ferments of that decade?*

I was extraordinarily divided about that. I was then in my thirties, I got married, I was becoming a family man and so I had that kind of commitment to, if you like, social stability and all the bourgeois virtues. But one did have this rather exciting sense of new ideas and new things coming along. I was very excited by Marshall McLuhan, partly because McLuhan did actually seem to be bringing into the study of popular culture, mass culture, certain symbolist or modernist insights, and that, I think, was valuable. But McLuhan became a tremendous cult figure at the time and this somehow blunted the edge of what he had to say. A lot of people were suprised to learn that McLuhan was a Catholic because he seemed to be so committed to a very materialist consumer-oriented society; but he always denied this and said he wasn't committed to that at all, he was simply showing people the way things were going. But I think he was very naive, so he tended perhaps to be used. I'm a Catholic, just as McLuhan was, and while my Catholicism has always been a fairly personal thing, it would have been at odds with much of what went on in the sixties in terms of ethical attitudes. But one also has to say that the Catholic Church had the Second Vatican Council from 1962 to '65, which was itself a very sixtyish phenomenon, and that did transform the Catholic Church in ways which were overall good – I won't say in all ways good. That too made it a rather exciting time to live through. You had Bob Dylan here and John XXIII there. But I have to say that the sixties increasingly tend to seem a rather anarchic and disagreeable period. I felt that student revolt in Britain had very little substance. In France in 1968 it perhaps had more substance and edge, and in fact it seemed indirectly to topple De Gaulle. And the Prague Spring was something else again: a real revolt against a totalitarian system. But British students were exceedingly privileged creatures compared with students in most other countries, certainly in the sixties.

Now they are less privileged and I feel more sorry for them under the stresses of an unsympathetic government. I think student revolt in the sixties had very bad long-term results for British universities, because many people now in the government and other positions of power and authority decided that all this had to change. So student rebels in the late sixties were responsible, perhaps directly, perhaps indirectly, for a very tangible hostility in the universities 20 years later. They sowed more than they bargained for, but it didn't affect them, it affected a subsequent generation.

In your own contribution to a volume of essays you edited called Innovations, *which appeared in 1968, you made the very interesting observation that '[w]e are facing now, not a mere survival of Romantic egoism, but an infinitely complex multiple concern with personality' (p. 197). Haven't we moved today towards a stress neither on impersonality nor personality but on the self as a psychological or ideological illusion – the poststructuralist idea of the 'self' as plural, dispersed, mobile, fragmentary?*

That certainly has been in the air for the last ten to fifteen years, but it takes one back to the great texts of modernism, to Lawrence saying you mustn't look in my novel for the old stable ego, or to Eliot in 'Tradition and the Individual Talent', resisting the idea of the unity of the personality, or to Rimbaud and '*Je Est un Autre*', fracturing French grammar to get that across. So it's a notion which has quite a lot of artistic mileage or artistic power, but it is an old notion. It tends to ignore the point that the self, the individual, is actually a legal and social entity. So you may be as protean as you like, but if you sign a cheque, or someone sends you a cheque with your name on it, then one of your personalities is actually a legal entity. Lots of people get money for writing articles saying there's no such thing as a self but they have little hesitation about paying it into a bank account with their name on. This is, of course, being cynical, but I think nevertheless there is a real point here. To be a self is to be a social and legal entity, however little you feel that you're one. If anybody said, I can't pay this cheque in because I don't know which of my selves it belongs to, this would be absurd. So I think there's an element of self-refutation when people who put their names on their books and their articles and receive cheques with their names on then argue that there is no such thing as a self.

But isn't the argument that, while the self as a legal and social entity may exist, what doesn't exist is the liberal idea of the self, of the sovereign, coherent, autonomous individual?

I tend to be fairly sympathetic to some aspects of that view. It may well be due to my own religious beliefs: yes, we are all members of one another, we are not isolated, fragmentary creatures in quite that sense. On the other hand, we are also individual consciences, consciousnesses, who are responsible for our actions. So it's a matter of balance between, on the one hand, the idea of the pure individual moral entity and, on the other, the sense that we are social beings, we are creatures who are continually interacting in families, in institutions and so on. It's a continually shifting emphasis which one's always trying to get right.

In relation to these questions about the idea of the individual, can we turn to the issue of character in the novel, which you discuss in The Situation of the Novel – *your exploration of postwar British and American fiction, which first came out in 1970 and, in a second edition, in 1979. In that book, you affirm 'the supremacy of character in the novel' and contend that 'a humanistic view of literature should enjoin both writer and reader to respect and even love the characters of a novel' – though you acknowledge that attitude to be 'historically conditioned' (1972 edn, p. 61). The idea of character in the novel, like the idea of the individual, has come under strong attack in recent years. What would your view of it be today?*

I think lots of people reading novels still like characters – even academics, although they keep quiet about it. That liking persists, although it may recur in different forms. The most fashionable critic at the moment – and I think it's right that he's taken very seriously –

is Bakhtin, who looked at one way tends to dissolve character into heteroglossic multiple discourses, a polyphony of voices, but looking at it another way, a voice comes out of a mouth, as it were, a voice is a human attribute, so much so that Derrida and his disciples have not liked the idea of voice, they want to reduce everything to inscription, to *écriture*. So although the notion of reading novels simply for the characters and nothing else is no longer tenable, something like the presentation of figures who are both individuals and types does persist. Character is perhaps the apotheosis of individuality seen in one way, but nevertheless you do apprehend it through certain cultural mediations.

One particular aspect of The Situation of the Novel *is your discussion of experimental writing in Britain in the sixties – in Doris Lessing's* The Golden Notebook, *for instance, or B.S. Johnson's work. In retrospect, what do you feel about that experimental moment in British fiction?*

It didn't seem to lead very far. Or to put it differently, I think that it became mannerist fairly soon, so that many a novel you read now includes self-reflexive commentary, the author appearing as a minor character in the text, and so on. I do think of B.S. Johnson, whom I knew a bit, as a chap who had enormous talent but was strangely dogmatic in his ideas, so rigid. And I suppose if you put him alongside Beckett, whom he greatly admired and who encouraged him, then it's a small talent. *The Golden Notebook* does seem to me to have survived really rather well. In 1988, when I was teaching in an American university, I spent time on it with students who were very fascinated by it. Of course, a lot of the interest in it is a feminist one – Lessing was ahead of her time in many ways – but, given that it is so fragmented, it is also a work of extraordinary solidity, strangely enough. The fragmentation has a kind of massiveness about it. So I think that book is probably the one that has really, to me, stood the test of time and actually seems more rewarding now than when it came out, when one didn't quite know what to make of it.

A very significant feature of The Situation of the Novel *is the contrasts you draw between postwar British and American writing. How would you see their relationship today?*

Probably less clear-cut now. At that time one did have this sense, which was rather encouraged by certain critics and indeed novelists, that English fiction was domestic and dull and commonplace and small-scale, whereas the Americans were going for the biggie and everything was up for grabs there. That was a kind of myth, if you like, a literary critical myth. So the English writers at the time that you mention were trying to pull away from that. But now there's much less of a clear distinction. For instance, Martin Amis's *Money* seems to me a most brilliant novel which has a great deal of American writing in it – Mailer, Burroughs and so on – but which is also a painfully sharply observed work of English social comedy: he's got them both going at the same time. We do now have novelists who are very metafictional and aware, like Julian Barnes and Peter Ackroyd, and if you take the unhappy Salman Rushdie, *Midnight's Children* is totally freewheeling. So English fiction is no longer just a matter of classic realist texts trundling on. It's perhaps learnt from North American fiction but it's also learnt from magic realism, Calvino, Borges, Márquez and so on. It is much more international than it was in the sixties. We are really in a more cosmopolitan scene.

Do you think in fact it makes sense any longer to talk of the English novel in a contemporary sense. Don't we have, as you suggest, a much more international kind of fiction in English?

Up to a point. It depends how you slice it, so to speak. There are still a great many novels coming out about adultery in Hampstead, etc., and in a way that has been given a new emphasis now by feminist work written from the woman's angle. The feminist movement in writing has actually enabled many writers to go back over old territory and illuminate it in quite different ways.

You have a very interesting discussion in The Situation of the Novel *of what you call 'the ideology of being English', and you talk then – in 1970 – about a crisis in English national identity. What do you think has happened to that ideology today?*

I think it's in a very interesting state of division and crisis. There are many factors in that. The impact of Margaret Thatcher, whom I suppose I dislike as much as anybody else, has nevertheless, one must admit, changed all sorts of English attitudes, in trying to make people a bit more like the Americans or possibly the South Koreans. It hasn't been an absolute success but at least something has been shifted in British modes of thinking. And there is also the impact of Europe, which is something that even now is dividing people, but most people now think, yes, it is going to come – and as far as I'm concerned, a good thing too. What's paradoxical with Mrs Thatcher is that she has changed British attitudes but is quite clearly anti-European in her bones. But these things are undermining the so-called English ideology; the insularity has broken down. On the other hand, I think there are features of the climate and topography and so forth which are still there. This country is a particular sort of landscape, it is a particular sort of milieu, and living in it does give people a certain kind of consciousness. The English are still partly made by where they are.

Could we talk some more about poetry? In your book on T.S. Eliot, published in 1972, you say 'the present decline in Eliot's reputation may be both inevitable and salutary' and that 'when the cultural idol has been displaced the voice of the poet may be heard more clearly' (p. 192). Eliot is still under fire from some quarters: what do you think his reputation is today?

Eliot's reputation is under fire, but it's a living reputation. You only attack what you feel to be important. Leavis is a great instance of this. Leavis began as an Eliot disciple and his rewriting of literary history followed Eliot's hints. And then, right at the end of his life, he had that extraordinary kind of revulsion from Eliot in *The Living Principle*, where he went back over the *Four Quartets* and said, not that they weren't great poetry, but that it was a malign greatness. Leavis made Eliot into, as it were, a satanic figure, but he couldn't leave him alone. One couldn't imagine saying, well, I used to read Eliot, but now I find him dull and boring. Eliot has always meant an enormous amount to me. When I was a young man, back in those days before I went to university, I used to read Eliot's poetry, when I was about 17, and a little later I got on to his criticism, and Eliot's essays gave me the idea of what criticism was. But I think some of his writings are better than others, and that he was a strange and difficult personality in many ways. There are all sorts of unpopular aspects to Eliot – his anti-Semitism, however deep and far it went, his attitudes to women. And his religious dimension is one that a lot of people find difficult to deal with. There was a time, a few years after he died, when nobody seemed to say a good word for him, but I think he's come back from that. On the one hand, the vogue of deconstruction has given new insights into what sort of poem *The Waste Land* is, and on the other hand, he's now seen to be a much more personal poet than we once thought him to be. There are plenty of people who say, I don't like any of his attitudes, but I do like the poetry, it comes across. Eliot does seem to have a capacity for having more and more new things said about him. That slim collection of poetry does have a remarkable ability to renew itself in all sorts of ways.

In your Introduction to the Casebook *on* Four Quartets *which you edited and which came out in 1969, you suggest 'that with the passing of time Eliot's earlier poetry is likely to endure rather better than the* Quartets' *(p. 20). Would you still hold to that view?*

With many more qualifications than I made then. I still enjoy 'Prufrock' and 'Portrait of a Lady' and *The Waste Land* the most. Someone I've been reading recently pointed out that they've got more jokes in, more wit and irony: they are funny. When you come on to *Four Quartets*, it's a much more solemn world. I think there are passages in the *Quartets* which are not very good. Somehow, because of the peculiar way in which that sequence was constructed, the intensity of inspiration did falter in places. He was really writing against the grain of his own method by repeating a pattern that he'd already established some years before. There are these curious descents into flatness. Now that's not quite the end of the argument, because one wants to say that if the *Quartets* is a sort of polyphonic work, then maybe the flatness is to contrast with the elevated passages. But there are still things where one thinks, well, he could have done that a bit better. At the same time, I find much more in the *Quartets* than I used to. Overall, it is a pretty powerful work; in Bakhtinian terms, a great mass of voices interacting. And I suppose when you start getting on in years, Eliot's reflections on old age and death and so on come across with rather more resonance.

How do you feel about Pound?

The *Cantos* is a splendid anthology of good lines and passages. I believe it's said of C.S. Lewis that when he'd finished reading *Don Juan*, which he didn't like at all, he wrote at the end of it: 'Never again'. I feel like that about the *Cantos*; I've been through once. The problem is now that Pound, like Joyce, is so much caught up by an academic industry that you can make a whole career explicating the *Cantos*, or a few cantos of the *Cantos*, and never ask yourself the question: Is this any good as poetry? The earlier critics did ask that question, even if they were explicating as well, and would still say, this seems to me very flat. Whereas latter-day academic explicators will say that what seems flat to you has its own very subtle richness, etc. It's analogous to the problem with *Four Quartets*, but on an enormously larger scale. I like to dip into the *Cantos*. The Malatesta sequence is very fine. Pound did have that capacity to make history seem very here-and-now. Certainly bits of the *Pisan Cantos* are good, and there are good fragments right through to the end. But it is a matter of fragments, really.

What of another poet of whom you've written a full-length study, Gerard Manley Hopkins? How do you feel about him today?

The interest holds up, very much so. There is such a strange intensity and curious originality about Hopkins. This was a man who could say, of whatever context he was in – poetry, ideas about literature, his religious life: I did it my way. I do still read Hopkins with great admiration and pleasure. There are places where the poetry seems to get too twisted, too contorted, and this is a revelation of a very strange but impressive personality. But it's a personality revealing itself always in relation to God, rather than in a simple romantic act of exaltation. Hopkins was pretty much of an egotist in his way, and he knew it, and this caused struggle and tension, but it's a struggle with God, as we get it in the terrible sonnets.

How do you feel younger people now respond to him?

Very well. Increasingly in schools they tend, alas, not to study poetry at 'A' Level but only fiction. But the minority who do study poetry are often given Hopkins and they always seem to enjoy it. Of course, it's a kind of poetry that fits well in the New Critical modernist context because it's short and intense and you can get a lot of mileage out of those sonnets, as they mostly are. But it's not only that: they've also got a balance of intellectual complexity and emotional intensity, as in Donne, whom students also enjoy.

Do you think younger people still respond to the religious element in Hopkins?

Yes. I think people don't know very much about God, but they know a bit. I've also found this with Eliot. I don't know how many people actually regard themselves as real believers, but probably at least as many as would call themselves out-and-out atheists. God knows what religious emotion is, but there is perhaps something that people can feel. At least the idea of God is still a fairly meaningful one and all the ideas that go with it, prayer and aspiration and so on. At least it's a working fiction for them, either with Hopkins or with the *Four Quartets*.

One of the things that you mention in Exploding English *is that in recent years in literary criticism there has been a strong drive towards a materialist approach to literature. George Steiner has suggested that a renewed religious hunger may emerge in the 1990s among readers and critics of literature. Do you yourself feel that this is likely? Will there be a reaction against the emphasis on a materialist poetics?*

I would have thought it's quite likely. I think a materialist poetics is a self-contradictory term, in fact. It's very curious, this notion of people calling themselves materialists. I take it it's really a development of Marxist dialectical materialism; you drop 'dialectical', the grand Hegelian notion of the huge struggles going on through history to eventually produce the great synthesis of the classless society. I don't quite know what it means when people say that they are materialists, period. At least it must beg a great many philosophical questions. I'm sure that there are materialist ethics, based perhaps on utilitarian concerns – the greatest good of the greatest number – but the closest you come to a materialist poetics is Richards's *Principles of Literary Criticism*. He felt, not that God's in his Heaven, all's right with the world, but that if the human nervous system is lined up properly, all's right with the world, and that poetry could help to achieve this. That neurological aspect of Richards is not one that has lasted very well. I'm prepared to assume that human beings need transcendence, which may or may not take an overtly religious form.

What do you feel to be the relationship between your own religious beliefs and your literary criticism?

I don't think there's a direct one, at all. If people dig deep enough it may emerge that I have this sense of the need for transcendence and that insofar as I have expressed an emphasis on the individual, it isn't quite a conventional liberal emphasis, but may well be a Christian sense of the individual worth. It has also perhaps led me to write about certain religious authors like Hopkins and Eliot. But for me, religion is important but somewhat private. Many of my evangelizing co-religionists may think it's a bit too private, but that's up to me. A lot of the time, I suppose I think and feel like my agnostic colleagues and contemporaries. This is not a very deep answer to the question because I'm not sure that I know the answer. The one thing I have never felt impelled to do is to say that I have got to write as a Catholic critic, whatever that is, sorting out positive and negative values and all the rest of it. That may be because I was a cradle Catholic. Catholicism was just something I grew up with and it seemed to be very much a part of life, rather than something which I chose in later life. I suppose there is a sense in which even a cradle Catholic, if he remains in the Church, makes a kind of choice, but it was not, for me, a single dramatic moment. It was remaining on a certain path rather than stepping off it.

Could we ask about your novel The Roman Persuasion, *which came out in 1981, and which explores some of the tensions in a part of the English Catholic community in the 1930s. How did that novel come about?*

Partly because I wanted to have a go at writing a novel. I was trying to write novels in my teens, and I did actually write one in my mid-twenties and another in my early thirties. These were not published, and that was just as well. So I gave up all that. But then having written a lot about novels – it was some kind of mid-life crisis – I thought I would like to try and write a novel again. But I also had a subject, which was an aspect of the English Catholic community in the 1930s. This was partly a spin-off from having written a book on the thirties, *Reading the Thirties*, but less directly it was a spin-off from the Hopkins book, which had made me interested in the English Catholics. But there was also, much more immediately, the family of my first wife, Gabriel – we were married in 1960 and she died in 1984. She came from a literary Catholic family; her great-grandmother was Alice Meynell, the poet, and her father was Bernard Wall, who was a Catholic man of letters in the 1930s, and her mother, who is still alive, was a novelist, who wrote as Barbara Lucas. So through that family, which I had become very close to, I had a sense of the way in which the literary people of the English Catholic community lived as part of a minority – not a totally isolated minority, but they had their own ideas and attitudes and values which made them different from the surrounding culture. So all of these things came together.

I was also very interested in sort of reversing the myth – if I could get back to that word – of the Spanish Civil War as a struggle of light against darkness, with Franco as the ally of Hitler and Mussolini, destroying an elected government. If you say that in the early days of the war, 6,000 priests and several bishops were killed on the Republican side, people dismiss this, saying, well, the Church was corrupt, it was bad. But it's interesting that when Auden went to Republican Spain in 1937, he was very struck by the closure of churches and the persecution of the clergy, and this seems to have started him on his return journey to Christianity. In no way did I try to make a propagandist book, simply to say there was another way of looking at this. The English Catholics at the time found themselves in a difficult position, because they were democrats, they weren't fascists, but they were very struck by these anti-religious atrocities, which were difficult to ignore, just as the persecution of Jews that was going on in Germany at that time was difficult to ignore. You could be pro-Franco for purely religious reasons, at one end of the scale, and at the other end of the scale, you were an out-and-out fascist. I was trying to explore that spectrum of ideas in the book, but a lot of people found it so unfamiliar and strange that they couldn't hook into it at all. *The Roman Persuasion* didn't make a lot of impact, but at least I'd done it, I'd proved I could write fiction. But it's rather hard work. I'm not sure I'll do another one.

If we come up-to-date with your latest book, Exploding English, *that has an interesting subtext, which occasionally surfaces, about how your attitudes changed while you were writing it. Could you tell us about that?*

Round about 1970, one was aware of all the new ideas coming into literary studies – Marxist, structuralist, etc. – so one felt much more vulnerable when one said, this is a good poem, you can see it's a good poem, everybody knows it's a good poem, and that's it. Because somebody would say something like: this is simply an example of a kind of bourgeois mystification. That was disturbing, though also rather interesting and challenging. I began in the late seventies thinking: let's make a case for good humanist literary value against all this stuff. I was planning the book and working on it as though there was still a system in place to be defended. So it had an embattled tone. But I was writing away in 1985 and not really getting where I wanted to go; I wrote about 30,000 words and thought, this isn't right. Then the point came to me: the system has collapsed. There's no longer a system to be defended. It was certainly a very interesting shift of perspective on my part, which I think occurred in the course of 1986. And then when I had some leave I really ploughed into it and I wrote the final version quite fast and finished it in the summer of '88. The ideas seemed to cohere then. So I think it was realizing that what one feared might happen had already happened and that there was still life after that had happened. That's what really gave the book its direction. But there are still traces – probably much more than traces – of my earlier defensive attitude in it.

In Exploding English, *you identify an emerging consensus that cultural studies should replace literary studies and you make a very radical proposal: that cultural studies should be left to go its own way, taking with it much of what had previously seemed to belong to literary studies – including prose fiction – and that a degree in poetry should be offered. Could you sum up your reasons for that proposal?*

It's a combination of pragmatic and theoretical considerations. The arguments of people who want to engage in cultural studies are quite good ones, and there are plenty of good precedents in the work of Raymond Williams and others. Cultural history is very important and very interesting, but it's not the same as literary criticism because it's got a different concept of value. A bus ticket is interesting to a cultural historian, but it's of no use to a literary critic, I take it, if one preserves that distinction. So I think, given that the traditional system seems to have collapsed, then one might come to an accommodation with cultural studies. Why let them have the novel? This is the element of my proposal that's caused some *angst*, and I suppose I was being provocative there. But having written a lot about novels, and written one myself, and having taught novel courses for 30-odd years, I've come to the conclusion that the novel's practically impossible to teach. In *Exploding English*, I quote from Fredric Jameson's book on Wyndham Lewis, where he says that there is a secret which nobody wants to let out: that there is no corridor between the stylistic investigation of passages from novels and the analysis of narrative structure. With poetry – and yes, all right, we're back to the New Critical model – you can look at a poem on a page and you've got something to talk about, and it is intense experience, whereas, with the best will in the world, the novel is a diffuse experience. A problem of course comes, not with short poems like those of Donne and Hopkins and early Eliot, but with long poems like *The Prelude*. Even so, that presents fewer problems than, say, *War and Peace*. So my proposal springs partly from pragmatic, pedagogic considerations. But it springs also from my sense that poetry is, in some way, the most intensive form of literary experience. And whilst acknowledging that there is quite a lot to be said for cultural studies, I still want to preserve an aesthetic approach in which you do not read bus tickets, you read poems said to be of merit, and what you're reading them for is some sort of poetic or aesthetic experience, always intermixed of course with other things.

David Caute

Hammersmith, London
12 October 1990

NICOLAS TREDELL: *Your first novel,* At Fever Pitch, *set in an African colony as it moves into independence, was published in 1959, to great acclaim, when you were still an undergraduate at Oxford. Can you tell us how the novel came about?*

DAVID CAUTE: Mainly the long-term urge to write – since the age of, let's say, seven. During my childhood and adolescence my stories, little novels, plays, were ferociously derivative. Not only in form but in content. My response to a radio play about Francois Villon would be a play about a romantic/tragic medieval poet. My own life never entered into it; it was only a candidate life, an apprentice life, I had no instinct for translating my own experiences into words. I was entirely mimetic, entirely responsive to the big adult themes I absorbed. I suppose National Service produced the necessary transition – I'd gone through 18 months without reading a book (so to speak), just living and observing, a dramatic change of scene, and I emerged, for the first time, with my own *cahier,* my own personal literary project (heavily adapted and rearranged by literary influences, one must emphasize). I'd had a 'good' National Service in a rather different sense from the officer who's had a 'good war'. That usually means heroism, achievement; in my case it was a matter of being pitched out of the potential boredom of regimental maneouvres in Germany into the highly exotic world of the Gold Coast. There were palm trees outside the mess; then the sea; and the politics of the country coming to the boil, on the eve of Independence. The Nkrumah era. An army of white officers, though some black, and of black soldiers, tribally affiliated – very interesting. We travelled a lot: I saw not only the Gold Coast (Ghana) but also French West Africa and Nigeria. At one stage a Brigadier took me on as his personal 'liaison officer' – he probably fancied me, but it stayed at the intellectual level, and I never fancied my own black army servant, or 'boy', as the young hero of *At Fever Pitch*, Michael Glyn does – that was fictional invention, though perhaps effectively done. I knew about homosexual impulses from public school – I mention this because it looms large in the novel – but all my drives were towards girls. In the novel, Michael Glyn is both predator and victim, and I was using homosexuality as a metaphor for power, for authority, for submission. For the hierarchies I'd grown up with. This was probably subconscious or instinctive.

But this is only half the answer to your question – how the first novel got written and published six months before I took my Finals. I took time off from my studies without telling anyone, wrote the story to an ending (for the first time), re-wrote it, day and night, with obsession. Getting to the end may seem self-evident, but it's what separates most published writers from many very talented unpublished ones, who never cease to refine and agonise over their first chapters. It has never occurred to me that I could know what I ultimately wanted out of a first chapter until I'd written the last. The whole dictates the parts.

At Fever Pitch is notable for its rich variety of technical devices – you tell the story in a wide range of ways. What led you to do that?

I shudder to think. I was still intensely imitative, a thief of the literary Baghdad. When the novel won a couple of prizes I was asked who'd influenced me, and I gave answers which were quite touchingly (in retrospect) honest and, less touchingly, pretentious. But Greene, Mailer, Patrick White, even Joyce, still come to mind. I had no literary training or education; I'd read avariciously, eclectically, whatever was to hand, but I was entirely self-taught and therefore not taught at all. Everything was regurgitated undigested. Jumping from one literary style or device to the next was like a child rummaging through a bag of coloured sweets, then throwing them about to attract attention. I don't mean I was insincere.

Were you conscious with At Fever Pitch *of trying to write a politically committed novel?*

Yes, 'committed' with a capital 'C'. I was a little ball-breaker. I saw myself as exposing colonialism – and African nationalism, its avowed enemy – for what they were. But the primary impulse was to dramatize the interplay of private and public life, as I'd experienced it in West Africa. But not, of course, as I'd experienced it; as I'd romanticised it, dramatized it, injected it with a voltage in excess of the reality. When the novel came out – Blackwell's filled all their big windows with *Dr Zhivago* and my offering – my history tutor at Wadham, Lawrence Stone, decided to read it and to discover what I'd really been doing with my time instead of sitting in the Bodleian. He was very kind about it but pointed out that I evidently thought that what made the world turn is sex, whereas what really made the world turn was money. I've often 'rehearsed', in the retrospective sense, the riposte I'd give now: neither sex, nor money – but power. Power is the black hole at the heart of Marxism. For Marx power is merely the mechanical, and transitional, executive pursuit of class interest – one of the bigger errors. Marx knew nothing of the ego, though he had a huge one; he had no psychology of power, which must be the first consideration of a novelist.

So you published At Fever Pitch, *you got a First in History, and you became a Fellow of All Souls. Did you think of yourself at that time primarily as a novelist or as a historian? Or didn't you make that kind of division?*

It was very much in my mind. When I went for my interview at All Souls, after the written papers, Charles Monteith, one of the non-academic Fellows and a senior editor at Faber, kindly said he'd liked my novel and wondered whether, if elected, I intended to spend my time writing some more. I said I thought I would – was that a problem? As it turned out, it was my problem alone, the balance between academic and literary work – one had a great deal of freedom. So, within six months of going to All Souls, I set aside my work on my doctoral thesis to write *Comrade Jacob*, which was not directly related to the nineteenth and twentieth century history I was then studying and teaching, but came out of my undergraduate work with Stone and Christopher Hill on the English Revolution, the Commonwealth and Protectorate. I sat in the Codrington Library reading all I could about Gerrard Winstanley and his Diggers, and then I wrote *Comrade Jacob*.

Did you find that your imagination fired easily despite the fact that Comrade Jacob *was based so much on historical research?*

I was moved by the story, and probably moved about myself being so moved. (I thought well of myself). One started with a real event, or story, but with huge gaps in it, for lack of evidence. The Diggers established a kind of 'communist' colony on St George's Hill, in Surrey, and they lasted a year. Certain incidents are well documented: how soldiers came from the New Model Army to disperse them, but went away; how the local landowners reacted to the chopping of wood and the tilling of common land; the counter-revolutionary movement led by Parson Platt; the bad winter, the failure of the crops. And we have Winstanley's writings, an astonishing mixture of Puritan attachment to the Old Testament, a notion of the Norman Yoke as the foundation of the class system, and, finally, a very modern utopian-anarchist plea for communitarian socialism. But one man, or two, does not make a novel. We also have these long lists of the Diggers, men without histories or faces, Will Starr, Henry Bickerstaffe, Tom Hayden. They had to be turned into 'characters', with personal histories and personalities. This one staunchly reliable, this one inclined to make trouble in the village. Yet still this is not enough. The bare outlines of a narrative do not make the human interactions essential to a novel, or my quite traditional conception of one. So you create complicating subplots, for example Winstanley himself having an illicit desire for the young wife of his most devoted disciple. This is partly my instinct for 'contradiction', for a clash between values and behaviour. Winstanley also gets a bit above himself; he comes to regard the colony as 'his'; I was keen to 'find' the hidden ego in the idealist. It always comes back to self-scrutiny and integrity.

What did you feel at the time to be the relationship between fictional writing and historical writing?

At that time – 1960 – the prevailing historiography that I absorbed was 'scientific', sociological, materialist, analytically rigorous, 'objective'. My teachers and tutors were dismissive of the 'literary' historians whose emphasis was on personalities and evocation: C.V. Wedgwood, Arthur Bryant, and most of the biographers. I was learning a very dry, reified language, very explicit. I suppose fiction is implicit. The more that the 'real action' lies between the lines, the better. The language of good fiction is tactile, sensuous, sly, indirect – percolating its points through personality. I can say only that my early novels suffer from the categorical habits of thought and language I was absorbing as a historian.

I associate the writing of fiction with guilt, the sense of playing truant, of setting aside the stern and proper tasks for the frivolity of invention, of making things up. I remember Isaiah Berlin saying that, in the last judgement, he'd choose Tolstoy over Spinoza and Hegel because it's the great artist who provides the extra, sublime invention. If I'd asked him how he would weigh a third-rate novel against a third-rate article in the *Journal of Philosophy*, he would probably have said that the novel did less harm.

Of course historiography has moved on, the imagination is back in fashion, the gap with fiction has narrowed. In my experience there are forms of journalism which also bring together the imagination and analysis, evocation and categorization, the sights, sounds and smells of the tactile universe with the wider view.

Can I go back to this business of guilt? A historian starts from given material – his research – and that, in a way, validates his enterprise. Invention is by contrast arbitrary, you can begin anywhere, which in a way is presumptuous. I used to compensate by preparing for a novel by filling notebooks about real events, which is valid in a way, but dangerous. It means you start your fiction from the outside and then search for characters to carry this external load. My fictional notebooks nowadays are more impressionistic, more concerned to catch the oddities of *l'expérience vécue* – just as many writers keep a notebook at their bedside to write down their dreams. Instead of fishing for characters in the great ocean of actuality, I prefer now to find the characters first, and then push them out into the bath, to see when and where the dinghy will sink. But, of course, all these distinctions and dichotomies are schematic, and the actual process of invention is so complex, so moment-by-moment, that it can only be falsely summarised.

In The Decline of the West, *which came out in 1966, you do try to bring fiction and history together in the sense that you seek to set the individual invented stories in a kind of grand historical and political perspective.*

The Decline of the West is the perfect example of overloaded notebooks in search of a narrative and characters. It has a huge sweep, a vast embrace, geographical and cultural. No doubt the ambition and energy behind it are admirable, it carried the reader along through every imaginable crisis – colonialism, civil war, armed rebellion, weaving a vast cast into the tapestry. Commercially, it was my most successful novel – but not critically. The American reviewers were generous, but the English ones pounced on mixed metaphors or florid language – and I think they hated the book's politics, though they never say that, the execution is always in literary terms. I'll always remember the anger I felt when I read Angus Wilson's put-down in the *Observer*. However, in the course of writing *The Decline*, my third novel, I discovered – an almost mystical experience – control over narrative time. What does this mean? It depends on the writer. Take Pinter's screenplays, for example, or his play *Betrayal*. Narrative time is a reordering of actual time (itself a much-challenged notion), perhaps in terms of the relation of sub-narratives to the main narrative, perhaps in terms of a narrator's self-serving manipulation of events.

With regard to the political dimension of The Decline of the West *did you say to yourself when you were writing it: I'm writing a Marxist novel? Was it that kind of consciousness?*

The Decline was certainly received as a Marxist novel, but when you're writing you don't keep a notice on your desk: 'Remember! You're a Marxist.' It was anti-imperialist, anti-fascist – I was influenced by Sartre and the possibilities of linking a commitment to human liberation to a narrative which offers protagonists a genuine choice – although in some cases cultural or personality factors dictate the decisions taken, which are therefore not choices or decisions at all. *The Decline* was largely about those who retained the capacity to choose – this might be called 'conscience' or 'consciousness' – and about those whose allegiances and actions are pre-determined. We're talking about Western soldiers and mercenaries of various backgrounds in an African country, partly Algeria, partly the Belgian Congo, at the moment of crisis and chaos.

Can we pursue the question of the influence of Sartre? At an ICA discussion in 1986, you made the interesting remark that you'd been influenced in your fiction, not so much by Sartre the novelist as by Sartre the political writer and philosopher. Would that be the case?

Yes, Sartre is the writer to whom I owe the most, but much more in his capacity as philosopher, critic, journalist and guru, than as a novelist or playwright. His novels and plays are fascinating, but intellectually rather than artistically. He's not a great artist like Brecht. For me Sartre is above all the master cartographer of false consciousness and 'bad faith'. One can't judge one's own work, but it's my impression that all my fiction is about false consciousness. Not merely in Marx's rather narrow, class-bound sense – much wider. As a historian, too, I've been mainly concerned with why people – groups, individuals – see things as they do, how they reorganize reality to suit their own chosen causes, to service their fears, to prop up their own positions. Even confronted with colonial memsahibs or know-nothing Rhodesians, that's interesting, because they don't really know nothing, indeed their intelligence may be acute in some directions. False consciousness becomes even more interesting when people – or one's fictional characters – tend to be aware, alert, self-scrutinising, well-read, even tortured by guilt. This must, I believe, finally carry one back to oneself. Oneself as the only person to whom one has free and total access (though I expect that's psychologically naive). In a certain sense, the author himself is the only model he has for every human being he portrays – which is why Hitler is a feasible fictional target, and Christ not at all – unless debunked. The author as manipulator, fixer, deceiver. Does this culminate in downright narcissism? I don't think so – particularly if you are generally trying to relate private lives to public issues.

The Decline of the West *is notable for its graphic accounts of violence, torture and death. It could be said that it panders to a kind of voyeurism. How would you feel about such a charge?*

What you say could also be applied, in slightly different terms, to *The Occupation*, the novel that followed. There's always a fine line betwen 'revealing' or 'exposing' violence, and somehow exploiting it, retailing it as a commodity. A very clear example of this is found in those *marxisant* films where we end up revelling in the decadent decor of the dying bourgeoisie, et cetera. In *The Decline of the West* one was dealing with a number of documented horrors, crimes, which occur in time of war, particularly race war, when fear and loathing result in 'de-humanization' of both victim and violator. On the other hand, there are passages in the novel where violence is viewed, perhaps pornographically, from the perspective of the transgressor. I've always enjoyed pornography. If that's a reflection of a badly disturbed or deranged imagination, then I've got one. Was there, also, an element of commercial calculation? Probably, I can't remember, or don't want to. I'd much enjoyed Jean Genet's *The Balcony* and maybe the big scene with Commandant Laval in the brothel was derivative of that. Being concerned with power, I'm bound to be interested in the overlap between, or symbiosis of, its sexual and political dimensions. One can overdo it and fall into the trap of exploitation or, as you say, voyeurism – though what is all art, if not legitimated voyeurism? In that case you're inviting the reader to enjoy what he is supposed to deplore. The problem with *The Decline* is its lack of authorial alienation; it's written in the realist convention and invites total empathy. You can do many of the things I've been discussing much better if you find a fictional mode which draws the reader's attention to what is happening between 'the product' and its consumer. That may be why *The Occupation* was a step forward.

By the time The Decline of the West *appeared, you'd resigned from* All Souls, *after the failure of a reform movement, which you had strongly supported, that had aimed to persuade the College to use some of its large revenues to finance a scheme to admit graduate students. How do you look back on that decision from a distance of 25 years?*

It depends on whether one views one's actions in the context of history, or in the context of a novel. I did both, starting with an article in *Encounter*, 'Crisis in All Souls', a well-informed indictment, plenty of documentation, but, of course, polemical and entirely self-righteous. A few years later I briefly resumed the experience in a novel, *The Occupation*, with rather different results! In retrospect I think I was right about All Souls – a rotten borough, stinking rich, jealous of its unjustifiable privileges. I also think – should I say this? – that resigning was quite a courageous gesture. I was giving up a lot, I had two children, I felt that after all those years of comfort I had to face myself. We had battled for genuine reform, we had lost. It's all very well to be radical on paper, as a writer, but when you find yourself involved – well, think of Mathieu in Sartre's *The Age of Reason*, always finding a reason for backing off by abdicating responsibility. No doubt I saw myself as a bit of a hero, but I'm still basically in agreement with myself about what I did.

So we're coming into the later sixties and those extraordinary events which culminate in '68. What were your feelings about, and indeed involvement in, all that?

I was a child of the Old Left. That meant good causes. Marching from Aldermaston. The New Left came as a shock. I was by then a university teacher – a year after leaving All Souls I was teaching at New York University and Columbia, then I moved to Brunel. Vietnam was an issue which united us all, but the New Left was not content to march and demonstrate, it carried its existential rebellion into the campus, challenging everything. Politics, suddenly, was not 'out there' but wherever you are. So you set essays, reading assignments, and they didn't get written or read because of LBJ, because of patriarchal authoritarianism, and so on. The kids would sit in the corridor, interlacing their legs, to block one's path to the lecture theatre – nothing personal. I came to that in *The Occupation* and, later, in *News from Nowhere*. The thought was inescapable: no-one likes to write an essay. You're lazy and self-regarding and ignorant and full of slogans – so read the books and write your essay. Some of the interlaced legs in the lecture theatre were well-shaped; my first marriage was ended and there I was in New York, a radical professor – everyone's a professor – with a nice accent and some money of my own. Sex and intellect, desire and authority, a life both principled and hedonistic, a year living in Greenwich Village. That's all part of the novel.

Your experience in the later sixties flowed into your Confrontation *trilogy, of which your novel,* The Occupation, *published in 1971, formed one part. How did that trilogy develop?*

I didn't set out to write a trilogy. I started with a play, *The Demonstration*, which Stuart Burge directed at Nottingham, and later it was done at the Unity and in Hamburg. It was about a Professor of Drama of the Old Left confronted by drama students of the New – where is the frontier between 'reality' and 'art'? I'd spent a year at New York University with Conor Cruise O'Brien, George Steiner and John Arden, and for the first time I'd had an opportunity to study and teach the interaction between literature and politics, form and content, modernism and Marxism. For the first time I was reading literary criticism – though actually I think my first essays about Lucien Goldmann were produced earlier, under the patronage of John Willett at the *Times Literary Supplement*. A lot of that came out in the book-length essay which comprises the second volume of the trilogy, *The Illusion*. But I also discovered the need to write a novel overlapping with the play and the essay – the interweaving was so complex that I have no inclination to describe it here. I happened to be having a bit of a breakdown when I first wrote the novel, *The Occupation*, and I put it away as a hopeless failure, self-pitying, awful. Some months later I read Philip Roth's *Portnoy's Complaint* and that did the trick. The world of Portnoy had nothing to do with the world of my novel but it's like finding the right musical key, in

this case a certain kind of humour, or 'voice'. *The Occupation* was
my first comic novel.

Were you conscious, with The Occupation, *of a break from the
realistic fiction you'd written previously?*

Yes, but these things, these 'breaks', tend to be clearer in retrospect.
Later you can stand outside the 'you' and convert 'I' into 'you'. Previously 'form' had been a matter of craft, as with the *pièce bien faite*
– call it crafting the illusion. Writing the trilogy – the play, the essay,
the novel – I found myself dis-assembling the realist-illusionist
image. This is only to say that I had come to modernism, but not to
'art for art's sake', not to the élitist disdain for politics displayed, for
example, by certain French writers in the post-Sartrean reaction. For
instance, I much admire John Berger and his novel *G*. When you use
alienation techniques you can gain more technical control over what
you're doing because you no longer believe a word you write.

After The Occupation, *why did eleven years pass before you produced another novel?*

I regret it. When I published *The K-Factor* in 1983, a new generation
of reviewers tended to take it as a case of a historian and journalist
who was trying his hand at fiction. After leaving Brunel in 1978 I
took on several large, time-consuming non-fiction projects involving
years of research: *The Fellow-Travellers*; *The Great Fear: The Anti-
Communist Purge under Truman and Eisenhower*, and – later –
Under the Skin: the Death of White Rhodesia. But that may not be
the whole answer because I remember that soon after I published the
trilogy in 1971 there was a novel I very much wanted to write, and
tried to write, and failed to write because I couldn't find the voice, the
key, to make it work. Trying to write something new and coming to
a dead end was a new experience, it may have shaken my confidence.
There were other diversions: involvement in the Writers Guild,
drafting the Minimum Terms Agreement, declaring war on publishers, and then editing the literary and arts pages of the *New Statesman*. I wrote a couple of 'upmarket' thrillers, under a pseudonym, to
make some money. Very enjoyable. It occurred to me that if I wrote
a third I might never do anything else.

*You said you were interested in Rhodesia, and when you began to
write fiction again, it was about Rhodesia. What drew you there?*

In Rhodesia/Zimbabwe I found and explored an almost self-contained 'other' world, set in a strange time-warp during the Ian Smith years – you know the joke about re-setting your watch, twenty years back, when arriving at Salisbury airport. That world had, as they say, 'everything', and it was also a tough shell to crack, tightly controlled, the Special Branch on your tail, clandestine meetings with guerillas in adrenalin-raising circumstances. It involved also, on one's own part, a certain amount of indispensable deception. You couldn't turn up at a white tobacco farm, virtually besieged by ZANLA guerillas, and announce cheerfully, 'I'm from the *New Statesman'*. A moment of unguarded frankness with some ZIPRA guerillas almost turned nasty. I fell in love with journalism. Not the day-by-day stuff, you understand, but the life of a roving correspondent writing longer reports.

Why did three books emerge from your Rhodesian experiences – Under the Skin *in 1983, and the two novels,* The K-Factor *in the same year and* News from Nowhere *in 1986?*

When you're face to face with a drama as intense as the one in Rhodesia/Zimbabwe, there seems no need to invent anything – I mean no need to write a novel. But after I'd delivered the big narrative in *Under the Skin*, the fictional impulse returned in the shape of *The K-Factor*. The point is, the real people I knew in Rhodesia I knew only partly; in theory a fictional character is wholly yours. As for *News from Nowhere*, that was essentially about something else, it was an attempt to reconsider my own recent life, and in no way did it, seminally, emerge from Rhodesia – but, two-thirds of the way through the story, I sent the protagonist, Richard Stern, to Rhodesia, to explore, not the country, but his relationship – or mine – to it. Obsessions are fertile – I wouldn't censure Tom Sharpe for biting the South African cherry again and again, nor Athol Fugard. As a matter of fact, there was also half of a fourth book with a Zimbabwean derivation, 'Marechera and the Colonel' in *The Espionage of the Saints*. I may like that more than anything I've written because its form is fluid between the categories of journalism and fiction.

With The K-Factor *and* News from Nowhere, *how far were you still trying to realize the anti-mimetic project you'd outlined in* The Illusion?

Tentatively in *The K-Factor*, and flat-out in *News*. As I said in *The*

Illusion, alienation or 'dialectical' writing is more obviously achieved in the theatre than in the novel. The big trap for novelists is to write novels about novelists writing novels. I object to that on, I suppose, moral grounds. It's narcissistic. And it usually subscribes to the romantic myth of agonized creativity. I mean, who really cares whether I failed to write that novel I mentioned? Recently I was sent a questionnaire about whether I used a pencil or a word-processor, whether I drank tea or coffee or 'other' while working – balls to that. I'm digressing. To achieve alienation in the novel one must, I think, discover a certain displacement appropriate to the story and characters: look at *Don Quixote*; or *The French Lieutenant's Woman*. This displacement must come from inside the narrative, from its engine room. By 'displacement' I mean creating cracks in the illusion, subverting empathy without abandoning it. In effect you're partly suspending the suspension of disbelief (if that isn't a mouthful), but not meretriciously, not a box of tricks; really you're adding layers of understanding and awareness in the reader. I'd hate to be an Experimental Writer, in capitals – they tend to be impenetrable. Language, artistic forms, cultural conventions – the lines of communication – move quite slowly, and a century after the birth of modernism the most-read authors still write, essentially, like those of Dickens's day, though in shorter paragraphs.

I embark on a novel on conventional lines, anchoring it in reality; the subversion begins when you discover what you're doing. Picasso could knock the human face about so successfully because he was already master of conventional perspective. Beckett could unpunctuate to brilliant effect because he knew where every missing comma should be. A bird that can't walk can't fly. I think you may find that in the best modernist writing, the really crucial moments keep coming back, but from different angles, and so it is in one's own life. The realist novelists endowed their characters with memories, with recall, nostalgia, but the event that broke the heroine's heart is fixed and defined (even if a tragic misunderstanding made good many years later), like a date in the calendar. We learn relativity by variable repetition.

Moving on to your novel Veronica or the Two Nations, *which came out in 1989, could I take up a very interesting remark you made about the novel when you said: 'The "Thatcherism" dimension of* Veronica *is both serious and a private joke. I think the "joke" is also serious. The reader is invited to notice and lament Michael's capacity for self-deception and "false consciousness" – but not to notice that*

Michael at least builds an ideology in conformity with his own needs and personal conduct – a contrast with the affluent, careerist lives of some of us who imagine ourselves to be progressive' (personal letter, 18 September 1989). Can you say more about this?

It's rewarding if readers 'notice' everything, but you haven't necessarily failed if they don't because it depends at what level of recognition this 'noticing' takes place. In paintings, for example, or in the cinema, the spectator may be affected – his overall impression – by elements that don't isolate themselves, announce themselves, to his eye. Tom Keating's television series brought that out – the layers of paint which are apparently beneath the surface picture but which affect it. A ship at anchor in the Thames, part of it shrouded in mist; but if the artist had not first painted the whole ship, before misting out the upper rigging, the effect would be less authentic. In both *News from Nowhere* and *Veronica* there are sub-texts so misted out as to be virtually unidentifiable, but their presence may not be without effect – one could call this the 'subliminal rigging'.

Veronica's sub-title, after Disraeli's *Sybil*, refers to the two nations, and at first glance there are two narratives, each representing one of Britain's nations. They work by point, counter-point, covering the same story but by reverse chronology. In fact, Michael Parsons's narrative is quite obviously altered by a third metanarrative, his occasional 'John Ford' commentaries on the theme of sibling incest in literature. At the end, with Michael dead, the journalist, Bert Frame, 'tidies up' by publishing all three narratives within the covers of one book. But this neat knot is of course both convenient and false – tying knots which cannot be tied. Indeed the novel offers many clues that the three narratives are really one, by the same hand – I'm not making the banal point that my name is on the title page. If this is so, if three independent narratives are really one, we may wonder whether the Thatcher Home Secretary, Michael Parsons, is really revealing, in a manner both intelligent and vulnerable, how his great and jealous passion for his sister led him to his present political philosophy.

Yes, he is, but his controlled narrative is also a text outside of his control, saying something different. Your question mentioned a 'private joke', but that word's a bit unfortunate, as if suggesting I wanted to mislead the reader like a detective author who sows totally misleading clues everywhere. The point is: to place your central character in Mrs Thatcher's Cabinet is to offer most 'liberal' readers an escape-hatch – Thatcherism being the non-kosher face of possessive individualism. I think this is the answer to the last words of your question. Michael is a man who's peculiarly honest about adopting an ideology which meets his own needs and ambitions. Of how many of us can that be said? I was talking earlier of the false consciousness of the self-aware; so the key subtext of *Veronica* is: why is Michael Parsons, whom we're invited to deplore, so honest? Notice that Bert Frame can reveal nothing about him that Michael himself doesn't reveal – Frame can only expose him publicly.

One interesting aspect of Veronica *is that the character of Veronica herself is more sympathetically portrayed than the main female characters in much of your previous fiction. This raises the general question of the representation of women in your work. In* The Occupation, *for example, you have, on the one hand, the bitch-goddesses like Eva and Miriam, and on the other, the faithful but sexually dull Tania. And even acknowledging that these can be seen, at least in part, as generated from Steven's disturbed mind, isn't there a great sense of hostility towards women in that novel?*

Yeah. Hear my snarl. Sartre's Kean remarks that the women one doesn't love always arrive on time. The corollary is obvious. Sex is always about power – and genuine love doesn't preclude that because the best answer to the question 'What is power?' is 'Two or more'. I think this is my answer to your reference to *The Occupation* – it's not a question of what women are like, but how they are viewed from the other side in the heat of passion and battle. The women you badly want but can't get or keep, destroy you, they are malign demons – even if they're nothing of the sort.

We know that authors can cross the gender boundary, like an impartial referee, but my novels have tended to preserve their male subjectivity because it's the dominant force in lived experience. But the central character of *The K-Factor* is a woman, and things are often seen from her viewpoint. Esther in *News from Nowhere* is a heroine on a Joan-of-Arc scale, and we are invited to feel disillusion about her at the end only as a reflection of Richard Stern's thwarted love. In my next novel, *The Women's Hour*, this theme is dominant – a ferocious battle of the sexes in which the author is an even-handed referee who never blows the whistle or calls 'foul'.

What about the treatment of feminism in News from Nowhere? *Whilst one recognizes that Stern's attitudes aren't necessarily your own, and that, as with Steven in* The Occupation, *the women can be seen partly as Stern's own phantasms, isn't your portrayal of feminism caricatural?*

A good novel isn't a health food store. It's a butcher's shop. Any ideology is a bundle of contradictions, modern feminism not least. I'd better get this out of the way, but I'm totally supportive of any practical measure to advance the status, dignity, rights, self-confidence, security and career opportunities of women. Including reverse discrimination and quotas. Modern feminism is about many things, however, some of them retrograde, locking women into their ancient gender-prison rather than releasing them. As a novelist I'm interested in exploring how individuals who classify themselves as members of an oppressed category – women, blacks, Irish – may use that macro-scenario to evade micro-responsibility, to evade the specific. It's 'the K-Factor' in reverse. This can be more widely applied to the Left in general – you didn't ask whether the radical students depicted in *The Occupation* were also 'caricatures'. Self-righteous progressive piety can be as blinkered as your time-warped white Rhodies. 'Hundreds of Fascist Mercenaries Die' announces *Liberation News*. Happily the dead included no people. The individual sheltering under a group identity is the rule rather than the exception – so flush him out with the aid of a mirror.

You spoke of 'caricature', which, like its cousin, satire, is a dangerous weapon – *The Women's Hour* is also about that, about the nature of caricature and how to deconstruct it. Caricature is not merely a distorted exaggeration on the page, a cartoon, but also a mode of seeing and not-seeing we practise every day. A building-site worker who wolf-whistles a mini-skirt, oblivious to the uncertain person wearing it, is engaged in caricature – which means distorting the parts in relation to the whole. I hope I've successfully evaded your question.

Terry Eagleton

Oxford
24 October 1990

NICOLAS TREDELL: *Could you start by telling us about your early life and cultural development?*

TERRY EAGLETON: Yes. I was born in Salford in Lancashire. My parents were first generation English and my grandparents were all Irish immigrants. My two grandfathers, quite coincidentally, both worked in the gas works in Salford, my father was an engineering worker in what was then, I think, the largest engineering plant in the country, in Manchester, and my mother was a shorthand typist. They were part of enormous Irish immigrant families who had little formal education themselves but were ambitious for their children. So that was the background I came from. It was to some extent a Catholic ghetto, in the sense that one was aware early on, in some mysterious way, that one was different from other people. One of the more positive sides of it, however, was that I was educated by the De La Salle brothers who had, whatever else one might say about them, a fairly good track record in Ireland in getting the sons of poor peasants out of the bog and into something else. That was really what they were doing, and so I was astonished to find that, despite this rather rigorous and scholastic mode of education, it made ultimately for the kind of systematic thought which is of value to the Left. In other words, I would say that one advantage of a Catholic education, from a left-wing point of view, is that you don't have to take a detour through liberalism.

How did you find coming to Cambridge?

That was a fairly traumatic experience. In those days – this was the early sixties – Cambridge and, I suppose, Oxford were much more

obviously upper-class in ethos and in, as it were, external signification. Everybody seemed to be about six-foot-five tall and to address
each other like public meetings. There were, of course, very few
women. All the appurtenances of a certain confident and dominative
upper-class style were much in evidence, and I think to be a working-
class student in that milieu was particularly tough. By some utter
accident I ended up at Trinity, the most aristocratic of the colleges,
and learnt extremely little, formally speaking, from the supervision
system. But then, I think in my second or third year, I encountered
Raymond Williams, who had come back to Cambridge in the same
year that I arrived. He seemed to be somebody who was speaking of
literature in a language which I found at once familiar in a certain
sense, and something I could understand. So things really changed
from there.

*Was there a moment when your political attitudes crystallized into
Marxism, or was it a more gradual development?*

I certainly wouldn't have regarded myself as a Marxist when I was a
student, although there were other students at that time, some of
them close friends of mine, who saw themselves as Marxists – they
were mainly of public school background. I then got involved, in the
early sixties, in the project of the Catholic Left. Just at the point
where any normally sensitive and decent young intellectual would
have left the Catholic Church in disgust, the Vatican Council broke
out with *éclat* and left a shower of debris around the place which
looked interesting to somebody who was already of left-wing views.
It provided a set of reasons why one might, for a while at least, stay
on in some kind of loose affiliation with the Church, do some kinds
of radical work. That resulted in the journal *Slant*, which ran from
1964 to 1970. When we got into *Slant*, we wouldn't have regarded
ourselves as Marxists – early New Leftists would be the nearest kind
of identity. As socially radical currents developed in general over the
sixties, we moved with them, and I think I can say that by the time we
emerged from the *Slant* enterprise in 1970, I certainly would have
been, for a while, calling myself a Marxist.

Would you have called yourself a Catholic Marxist?

I suppose I would. It sounded like a hell of a lot of belief. But that was
the position we'd come to. Looking back, though, I think that while
Slant and the Catholic Left did an enormous amount of pioneering

intellectual work, there was a sense in which it was condemned to be intellectualist. I would now say that whether it meant much to be a Christian Marxist really depended on where you were. For example, the whole liberation theology phenomenon postdated the British Catholic Left movement, but one can see in that phenomenon, in the Third World, how it makes a kind of practical sense to call oneself a Christian Marxist, whereas we were cobbling together a kind of intellectual synthesis, of a certain elegance and subtlety, but one that was very hard to cash in political terms.

What would you now see as the possible relationship between Christian commitment and the project of human emancipation to which you're committed?

As a kind of cultural milieu, Christianity has remained important to me. I think that the kind of Christianity which is properly rejected by a lot of the agnostic Left is probably a straw target. It seems to me that nobody in their right mind would accept some of the caricatures of Christianity that are regularly promulgated. What my training in *Slant* gave me was an understanding of a possible version of Christianity which had something going for it, which made some kind of human and political sense, so that if one rejected that, at least one knew what one was rejecting. I would still have sympathy with those sorts of Christian liberationist projects. It seems to me a much more interesting and plausible version of the Gospel than, say, Margaret Thatcher's. I think in the end the *Slant* project foundered on the question of what did being a Marxist add to being a Christian? It was the relations there that we found it hard to get straight. The other important factor was that as a socialist, particularly in the Left climate of the nineteen sixties and early seventies, it became increasingly offensive and distasteful to be aligned to the more reactionary aspects of the Christian institution, so that even to refuse the label 'Christian' had a certain politically strategic importance. But certainly I would still count among my friends theologians and others who date from that period and who, as Christians, would hold political views that I would regard as very close to mine.

If we come on to your early works of literary criticism – Shakespeare and Society, *published in 1967, and* Exiles and Emigrés: Studies in Modern Literature, *which came out in 1970 – one notable feature, from today's perspective, is that you very much stay with the syllabus authors, the canonical texts. Did it occur to you, with* Exiles and

Emigrés for example, to write about, say, working-class writers, or about those middle-class writers, like Edward Upward, who had very definite Left commitments?

No it didn't, and I'm sorry it didn't. I was much too well-trained in the lit-crit stable; I'd had my head well and truly fixed. The criticism that I've dealt largely with canonical writers, not only in that early work but also later with Richardson and so on, is absolutely right. The defence I would make is that it's not the Left who calls the tune as far as the selection of authors and texts goes. One can't simply ignore the canon as an illusion. It has been there first. It is the patch upon which, as it were, battle is joined. These are the chosen terrains of the literary institution, and I think there would be a kind of ultra-leftism in simply pretending that didn't exist. The task of salvaging and proclaiming the non-canonical is vital, but it seems to me that one shouldn't give it an exaggerated importance, in this sense: one could just about imagine a canon consisting entirely of working-class and women writers which was processed in a critically conservative way. One can see that happening in institutions like Oxford, where gradually and grudgingly new kinds of writing will be admitted to the official structures, but the views and methods and attitudes don't change. But I've moved at the moment into beginning what would be a pretty big project on Irish history and culture where I think a lot of the names and texts would not be canonical, even in Irish, let alone British, terms. I've begun to explore what you might call a non-canonical history, the history of a colonized people.

Ideas of the canon are bound up with ideas of literary value, and Criticism and Ideology, *which appeared in 1976, does, for all its iconoclasm, hold on to the concept of literary value and affirms that '[t]he task of Marxist criticism is to provide a materialist* explanation *of the bases of literary value (1978 edn, p. 162). Would you still see that as an important task for Marxist criticism?*

Yes, I think so, if only in the sense that, whatever the intellectuals might want to say about the problematical nature of value, value is part of common social life. People will go on valuing this and that willy-nilly, and not only in a literary sense. I always thought the question of evaluation was important and that the fundamental problem was not one of scrapping over this or that normative judgement but of trying to throw some light on the hidden criteria, the hidden institutional forces, which were guiding it. On that, as in *Literary*

Theory, I'm prepared to go a very long way down the relativist road, to say that value is a transitive phenomenon in the sense that it involved particular people in particular circumstances. But to relativize value historically and ideologically in that way doesn't mean to deny its importance. It never meant that for me. One of the choicest comments on literary value I've read recently was in a footnote added to an obituary of Graham Hough in one of the newspapers, in which a former student recalled Hough's remark that when you're in a Japanese prisoner-of-war camp, as Hough had been, with the *Collected Poems* of W.B. Yeats and with dysentery, you very quickly find out which are the great poems.

Would you still want to pursue the theory of literary value that you outline in Criticism and Ideology *— the idea that a work's value is proportionate to its achievement of a kind of internal, distantiation from the ideology which it produces?*

No, I'd want to qualify it now. It was too Machereyan, too Althusserean, although I think that there's something in it and that it works as an account of a certain literary history. It assumed too readily that distantiation is always productive. There might, for example, be ways in which, by establishing a distance from its own ideology, a work might confirm rather than interrogate that ideology. It's a kind of Russian Formalist argument and it perhaps too easily assumes that any effective literary work is somehow radical — that would be the logic of the case, but it then makes certain literary phenomena difficult to understand. I think also that the argument in *Criticism and Ideology* concentrated, as far as value went, too much on the moment of production. Quite soon after that, the argument shifted, usefully I think, to the question of reception. I would still want to see some relation between moments of production and reception as far as the value question goes, but I think my account in *Criticism and Ideology* is at once too productivist and in a certain sense too formalist.

Your next book, on Walter Benjamin, published in 1981, five years after Criticism and Ideology, *is in many ways different from your earlier work — there's both a great loosening up and, in some respects, a sharpening.*

Yes, that's my own epistemological break, you might say, somewhere between *Criticism and Ideology* and the book on Benjamin.

It was a moment of political transition both for me and more generally, as a certain wave of early 1970s Left confidence began to subside. It was post-oil crisis, Thatcher had just come to power, the political climate was altering rapidly, and new kinds of political and theoretical developments such as feminism were rapidly making their mark. Benjamin attracted me in that context because he seemed to be somebody who had been in one sense a resolutely committed Marxist – not always, but during his political period – but who had nevertheless been able to take the pressure of forms of thought which were really very distant from, alien to, Marxism. That appealed to me. I suppose I found a kind of echo of that in the work of Raymond Williams, which was a continuing influence on me, because Williams, different though he is as a thinker from Benjamin, seemed to combine, and more so as he got older, an even more resolute Left commitment with a kind of openness which I think was there in his work from the start. The other change with the Benjamin book was more in my own style of writing perhaps than simply in political position. *Criticism and Ideology* belongs very much to the Althusserean school in its style and form. Although the relations between comedy and politics had always intrigued me, I hadn't found a way to bring them together myself. That reflected something of my own split education; if, on the one hand, I'd been trained as a formal English academic, on the other the Irish milieu from which I come and which had in fact imprinted me much more deeply than I'd realized, was much more, as I remember from my childhood, one of wit and anecdote and humour. It took me a long time to find some outlet for that in my own work, or some way of combining it with the more obviously academic qualities. *Walter Benjamin* was what you might call a more broken-backed kind of book which was bringing critical and creative writing closer together, whereas previously one had made a sharper dichotomy between them. In a sense, the now rather fashionable deconstruction of the distinction between creative and critical writing was one that I'd felt from the outset. Writing criticism has always been most enjoyable to me and when I come to write 'creatively', I don't actually feel, as an experience, that it's very different. I think that probably, in Barthes's sense, I'm just a writer, and what I write is sometimes rather subsidiary to that end.

One of the most provocative arguments of Literary Theory, *which appeared two years after the Benjamin book, in 1983, is that 'literature' doesn't exist as a distinct and stable category, so that the study of texts transitorily designated as literary should be inserted into the*

study of the whole range of signifying practices. The question which
then arises is how to give the study of the whole range of signifying
practices some kind of direction and coherence. You propose that
what should shape its priorities is a political goal, 'the strategic goal
of human emancipation, the production of "better people" through
the socialist transformation of society' (p. 211). A difficulty there, it
seems to me – and this appears to have been borne out to some extent
by what has happened since – is that the kind of iconoclastic scepti-
cism you apply to the category of literature can also be applied, for
example, to the category of politics and to the political goals that you
posit. And indeed, the postmodernist, postmarxist kind of critique
does this, it deconstructs Marxism, it deconstructs socialism, it
points out that these aren't stable or bounded categories either. How
would you argue against an extension of that scepticism to politics in
general and to socialism and Marxism in particular?

I'd still retain the scepticism about the category of literature, though
in the book I was perhaps a little too cavalier about the undoubted
practical efficacy of that category. It's one thing to argue, as it were,
ontologically against the stability or identity of the category. It's
another thing to ignore or pass too lightly over the fact that it
indubitably exists as a social power, as a history, as an institution.
The question of how far you push the scepticism and the possible
effects of that on one's politics is the kind of question I've been
exploring in terms of the relationship between, to borrow from the
title of my Field Day Theatre Company pamphlet, irony and commitment. I don't think there is a final way of closing on that question.
If postmarxists, postmodernists and others are sceptical about what
I would regard as utterly serious political goals, then you have to
argue that out with them, while recognizing that those political goals
are complex and capacious in their definition and therefore accommodate a good deal of plurality – this is why, in *Literary Theory*, I
talked about political emancipation without specifying that more.
All the arguments can then begin with the sceptic, the conservative,
the liberal, or whatever, on that terrain. The problem of Marxism, as
I've written before, is that it has to move under the sign of irony,
under the awareness that it is no lasting definition. Now it seems
simplistic to assume that irony is not combinable with seriousness. It
seems to be the case that it is. This may appear a problem when one
poses it at a rather abstract level – if one's trying to combine the brit-
tle cynicism of a certain kind of postmodernism with certain kinds of
political commitment, there's no way one can do so. But within the

socialist or the radical tradition itself, that ability to be ironically self-relexive about one's position, to see its limitations, and to see that its whole identity is exhausted in realizing itself has been, I think, very valuable.

Literary Theory also advocated, and helped to promote, a shift from literary studies to cultural studies which has gathered force in the last eight years. This is often presented as a kind of revolution from below – for instance, as a response to students entering higher education from different social and cultural backgrounds. But it can also seem like a revolution from above – coming from the top down, through the existing power structures of education. Do you feel that to be the case?

I think that it's probably inevitable, in the institutional situation at the moment, that the demand for cultural studies is going to flow, at least in part, from people already ensconced in a respectable academic field. But that's been no detriment to the fact that it's also coming, if you like, from below and that, in my experience as a teacher, it makes a good deal more sense to students. In the end, I would want to argue for the shift from literary to cultural studies, not only because of what I regard as the intrinsic value of such cultural studies, but also because I think that literary studies are really now poised at a crossroads. They have the choice of making themselves socially relevant in some way or their future is very grim. I don't want to make this sound as though cultural studies is the way of rescuing traditional literary studies, but I do think that there's a logical momentum there which, as I argue in *The Function of Criticism*, would, in a sense, restore literary criticism to what it began by being, as a discourse with a sense of responsibility to society as a whole. It's in a certain way a creative movement back as well as forwards.

In both Walter Benjamin *and* Literary Theory, *you offer feminism as a paradigm of what a politicized cultural studies would be. But your use of feminism – perhaps most notably in* The Rape of Clarissa, *published in 1982 – has been criticized by some feminists as a* macho, *patriarchal appropriation. How do you feel about that?*

I was somewhat surprised that the book on Richardson was received as a piece of feminist criticism. Clearly feminism, gender, were among its concerns, but it was really much more of an experiment in bringing together different kinds of critical discourses. In that way, it's perhaps my most pluralistic work, in that it deals with feminism, psychoanalysis, Marxism and poststructuralism. It's not that I wasn't interested in Samuel Richardson – I was intensely, still am – but he also seemed to provide a space in which one could watch those discourses interact. Feminism was one of them, and not particularly, to my mind, the dominant one. If the book is taken as a straight feminist work, then of course it has various limitations, but it was never quite intended to be that in the first place. There are, of course, broader and more specific definitions of feminism. It seems to me that male radical critics can perhaps best be influenced by rather broader notions of feminism – for instance, going back to the Benjamin book, those that would try to deconstruct certain very male forms of intellectual earnestness and uprightness. I think that's a perfectly valid sense of feminism which is different from writing specific gender criticism.

Doesn't a macho *earnestness and uprightness recur in* The Rape of Clarissa, *though? Take your verdict on Lovelace: 'Thoroughly narcissistic and regressive, Lovelace's "rakishness", for all its virile panache, is nothing less than a crippling incapacity for adult sexual relationship. His misogyny and infantile sadism achieve their appropriate expression in the virulently anti-sexual act of rape. It is this pathetic character who has been celebrated by the critics as Byronic hero, Satanic vitalist or post-modernist artist' (p. 63). In effect what you're saying here is: Lovelace isn't a man – and the male reader, presumably, is. And doesn't this lessen the radical force of the presentation of Lovelace, since arguably, rather than being a pathetic deviation from a straight male sexuality, he is, in fact, an extension of that sexuality?*

Yes, as an American friend of mine said, 'Give the rake a break'. That passage is a dreadful lapse into Leavisian moralism among other things, a resurgence of early Cambridge. As you say, it's a defensive way of identifying Lovelace as somehow deviant and therefore separable from normal male sexuality. In defence of it, though I wouldn't ultimately want to defend it, I was actually writing the book partly against what I thought was a very bad book on Richardson which celebrates Lovelace as the great exponent of *jouissance*, poststructuralism, postmodernism in general, passing over such little deviations as rape as a mere afterthought. So perhaps my schoolmasterly tone was countering the somewhat too laid-back tone of the other critic. The more general issue there, in terms of *macho* forms of writing, is an issue of authority – that is to say, of authoritative writing, of a certain kind of rhetoric. In my own case, that inescapably carries suggestions of a certain sort of mastery which is very much open to a feminist critique. So it's a matter of style as much as anything else. In my own case I'm always reminded of Eliot's comment, which I quote in *The Rape of Clarissa*, about the *braggadocio* of the mild-mannered man safely entrenched behind his typewriter. Maybe I saw something of myself in Richardson and the way his style functioned as defence or displacement. But it's a more serious problem than that, it's more than just biographical. I don't want to reject the words 'authority' or 'authoritative', to write them off as irredeemably masculinist vices. I think that there are kinds of authority, the kinds won from political experience and conflict, for example, which should be listened to. One thinks again of critics like Williams whose authority was very much paid for by his own political experience. If the authority has a certain currency behind it, then it might be more acceptable than if it's simply a kind of rhetorical gesture.

Could we broaden out this question of macho *rhetoric, because it seems to me that the qualities you sometimes tend to scorn as complicit with capitalism and exploitation – qualities of moderation and compromise and caution and quiescence – are qualities which have tended to be displayed – not for any essentialist biological reason – by women in many situations, and which perhaps have a more positive value than you allow. What place do you feel there is for, say, gentler and more compassionate virtues which might not always be confrontational and thus might indeed run the risk of becoming, at certain points, complicit with oppression?*

I would want to claim, as a socialist, that the virtues and the values represented by socialism are as compassionate as we can now envisage historically, and that the unavoidable contradiction is that, actually to realize those values and to bring about a society where they could be active, demands conflict and confrontation and polemic. It's another version of the irony and commitment paradox I was speaking of earlier, which interests me a lot. What I object to in certain forms of liberal humanism is not the undoubted sensitivity and compassion and concern and respect for the autonomy of others, which I don't in fact see as particularly feminine, but their failure, as I see it, fully to grasp that kind of contradiction and try to live awkwardly in the midst of it. One of Raymond Williams's novels, *Second Generation*, finally offers a very stark choice between, on the one hand, trying now, in the present, to nurture those virtues and thus risking a false kind of political prematurity, and, on the other hand, stressing the virtues of combat and polemic and confrontation but finding that, in the process, those values might themselves be jeopardized. As Williams puts it, we people who have fought for the change may not necessarily be the ones who represent what should come through on the other side of that change. That does seem to me an irresolvable contradiction in class society, or when faced with any kind of oppressive structure. I would want to hold to what I see as the absolutely inescapable virtues of conflict and contention and confrontation, and to my mind not only much liberal humanist work, but even some work that would regard itself as radical, has been insufficiently combative in that way. In other words, I don't want to make any excuse for that combativeness. When one thinks of the direness and urgency of the political situation confronting us, it would be hard to imagine, in my view, that one could have too little of it. In that situation, somebody's as it were critical bad manners seem to me a minor vice. The question of the reconcilability of confrontation with certain forms of value is one that can be lived, but I don't think it can be theoretically resolved. And the fact that it can't be resolved is an index of what has to be changed.

Could we turn to another of your cultural interventions, the novel Saints and Scholars, *which came out in 1987. How did that novel come about?*

The origins of a book are always, for me, buried in the mists of time. I usually find out retrospectively, so many years later, what it was all about, which is hardly ever what it seemed to be about. As I said before, the experience of writing criticism and theory has always been, for me, a creative one, and it therefore seemed logical to move on to fiction more directly. I've always felt that I've worked in a number of different styles in writing my academic work, and, perhaps under the influence of a certain Bakhtinian concept of fiction, it seemed to me that the novel was a place where that medley of discourses could be best developed. There are a number of different languages within *Saints and Scholars* and therefore, to some degree, it flows out of that sort of theoretical background, those reflections on language. I was also perhaps then beginning to get interested in what later emerged as *The Ideology of the Aesthetic*, and I suppose that again in some sense spurred on my interest in writing in that vein myself. *The Ideology of the Aesthetic* appeared almost simultaneously with the play about Oscar Wilde, the aesthete *par excellence*, so perhaps now, rather than, as earlier, exploring the relations between comedy and politics, I was looking at relations between the aesthetic and politics, either trying to think about them, as in *The Ideology of the Aesthetic*, or trying to do it in practice.

How did the play about Wilde, Saint Oscar, *published in 1989, develop?*

Certainly I felt the pressure to write somehow on Wilde building up. The idea of a play was very late. I really began by trying my hand at a few Wildean epigrams – or sub-Wildean epigrams, as some of the critics said – and even then it wasn't necessarily a play, but it sort of built up from there. I can see pretty clearly, looking back, the sorts of political and biographical reasons that were leading me towards Wilde, and I try to lay these out in the Preface to the published version of the play. In a sense, Wilde became my figure for the late eighties as, say, Benjamin had been for the late seventies and, to some extent, represented similar kinds of concern. But I think the move to writing a play was more important than the novel in that it led me into a world of cultural production. Because of the collective and practical nature of the theatre itself, I was much involved with that whole process from beginning to end, and perhaps therefore the play more than the novel was my real break from the critical to the cultural.

As well as fiction and drama, you also, I know, write songs – do you write poetry as well? You included a poem about Benjamin in your book on him, for instance.

That's probably the last poem I wrote, which now makes it about a decade ago. I used to write a lot of poetry when I was a student and actually published some in *Granta*. I never quite abandoned it, but I largely gave it up because it was extremely difficult, which is perhaps a better reason than its extreme facility. I think I just did find writing poetry quite a sweated labour. But again, in a way, the kinds of impulses which that was satisfying could equally be fulfilled in writing criticism. I never really felt any disabling gap between the two. As long as I was writing, the poetic impulse was somehow accommodated.

If we move on to The Ideology of the Aesthetic, *which came out in*

1990, you set up, in the Introduction to that book, a dichotomy: on the one hand, those ideas about the aesthetic which you examine in the book, and, on the other hand, actual works of art, particular artefacts, which you don't examine there but which you have, of course, examined elsewhere. But couldn't one say there was a vital intermediate zone between those two categories which one might call that of aesthetic practices – not only abstract aesthetic ideas nor simply particular artefacts, but those practices of the definition and production and reception of art, from concepts of art to specific technical procedures – the way a brush is applied to a canvas, say – to modes of response, where, arguably, the aesthetic is at its most powerful and its political and social imbrication most intricate?

I think that would be the more important project to follow out. I don't regard *The Ideology of the Aesthetic* as anything like my politically most relevant work. It's an abstruse book that moves at a high level of abstraction from, as you say, specific aesthetic practices, which I think are very important to examine. One reason for that, however, is because I want to take a definition of the aesthetic which is, as it were, abstract and wide enough to encompass a lot of other kinds of ideas which I think are rather more politically relevant than just the aesthetic itself. So in any oblique way, it has a political relevance, but only by dint of widening out that concept of the aesthetic to the point where it then takes away from any more materialist examination of those kinds of practices. I followed up *The Ideology of the Aesthetic*, as I did some of my earlier books, with a more popularizing book, a little study of ideology that is going to be published by Verso. That is again, in the style of *Literary Theory*, a more concrete and polemical kind of book, and I tend to find my work dividing in that way.

And what about the book you adumbrate in the Introduction to The Ideology of the Aesthetic, *on the literary culture of Ireland – will that be the study of Irish history and culture you mentioned earlier in our conversation?*

I don't as yet know. It will be something like it. Whether it will be exactly the coupling of concerns that I give there remains to be seen. I want to write on Ireland partly for biographical reasons, in that I'm now continually re-exploring my own cultural roots in that way, and partly also because I think that if you look at colonial and postcolonial history, there's a certain sense in which it saves you having to argue for the connections between culture and politics in the way that one more commonly finds oneself doing in more advanced societies where, as it were, the privilege of culture has meant that connection can afford to be suppressed. It's right out in the open in Ireland or, I'm sure, in equivalent societies, where culture tends to mean less individual artefacts than certain kinds of politico-cultural currents and movements. Part of the experience of playing *Saint Oscar* around Ireland, and other involvements with the Field Day Theatre Company, is that there is so much that can be taken for granted – not in an indolent way, but there are certain arguments you don't need to make. The reception of the artefact is automatically in a wider cultural context. Those connections are expected. So a lot of the preliminary groundwork that the Left finds itself having to make on the issues here can be assumed and you can get on with something else. The other reason I want to write about Ireland is not because it hasn't been sufficiently well-trodden as a literary patch already – of course it has – but I don't think it's been particularly looked at from the viewpoint of contemporary theory. The book would be something of a conjuncture in that way.

One of the aspects of The Ideology of the Aesthetic *that I found most intriguing – though it was, perhaps necessarily, an unformed aspect – was your suggestion of a possibility, which you see as inherent in Marxism, of closing the gap between fact and value and of generating a morality from the labouring and desiring body. But at the same time there seems to be a reluctance, which is also evident in your earlier work, to take this too far for fear of playing the game of bourgeois morality or moralism. But shouldn't socialists and Marxists try to produce a socialist morality that could perhaps win conviction from others?*

Yes, I'm sure of that, and I'm sure also that it is as yet an unfinished project. It is something I sketch out but I don't carry it through – I don't think at the moment I've got the resources to do that. It's an area I was opening. I've never been frightened in my cradle by the idea that value or indeed morality was somehow bourgeois. I've never accepted that at all. As I argue in the book, I think that what commonly passes as middle-class morality – personal values, personal relationships and so on – is, from a Marxist viewpoint, so abstracted from the whole context of the making of our values that it's really a very deformed kind of morality. My claim is quite a bold one: that in the classical sense of morality, Marxism is a morality, but exactly one that tries to combat idealist notions of the moral. I'm trying to show in the book that this is intrinsic to Marxism itself, not some regrettable lapse on my part back into a Papist past. But Marx lays the materialist foundations for an adequate morality without himself following that through. I raise certain criticisms of him in that respect. I certainly don't think that I've got some instant solution to the fact/values problem, but I do think that looking at it in a materialist perspective is a way of resituating it and sketching a project then to be carried out. And although I say it's an unfinished one, there is a growing and absorbing body of work on Marxism and morality.

In the last chapter of The Ideology of the Aesthetic, *you mount a swingeing attack on postmodernism. Why do you think postmodernism has become so attractive to a substantial proportion of young and not-so-young radical intellectuals?*

Postmodernism is so durable and pervasive in that way that I think some sort of explanation like Fredric Jameson's, in terms of prevailing material and political conditions, must almost intuitively be right, whatever disagreements one might have with him here and there. It wouldn't have the tenacity it has unless it was somehow clued into that wider design. Postmodernism does seem to answer very immediately and spontaneously as a set of doctrines to a set of lived experiences in advanced capitalism. This bond is what secures its power and, argue theoretically with it as you may, it's there, it's a whole cultural milieu, and you're not going to disperse it in purely intellectual terms. One has to look, as David Harvey has done in *The Condition of Postmodernity*, which I think is the best book on the topic so far, at the material infrastructure, at the way that postmodernist theories themselves mime important changes in advanced capitalism, and therefore important changes in subjectivity, in people's sense or lack of sense of themselves, in the problems of orientating and coordinating oneself within that space. And if one then adds to that all the theoretical and practical reasons why it seems that Marxism is discredited, it's not hard to see why some people might want to scramble into those postmodernist positions, not least because they seem to keep a certain kind of radicalism warm, as poststructuralism had previously appeared to promise a radicalism which was often very difficult to identify in concrete political terms. To that extent, postmodernism doesn't seem a wholly negative phenomenon, any more that poststructuralism did. It does seem to preserve, in however muddled and mystified a way, certain impulses that could otherwise be put to good political use.

What still guarantees for you, or at least suggests, the privileged status of Marxism as a metanarrative? Because your argument against postmodernism, that it is a product of, and complicit with, capitalism, is of course also the argument that postmodernists use against Marxism.

I think the difference is that we're willing to admit it and they're not. In other words, I think it would be very hard for radically inclined postmodernist theorists to take the pressure of Jameson's sweeping analysis – which is not an indictment, but an analysis – of the complicities and still feel politically chirpy and confident. Whereas when Foucault says that Marxism swims like a fish in the sea of the nineteenth century, my response is: Yes, of course. Of course Marxism understands itself as a specific historical interrogation of capitalism, with which it must share a certain terrain. To some extent, the so-called radicalism of postmodernism, as opposed to Marxism, then stands convicted of a kind of ultra-leftism: the belief that it can even now catapult itself on to some entirely different terrain, that it's left behind all the junk of history and so on. Whereas Marxism understands a certain dialectical relationship between itself and capitalism, postmodernist theory disastrously, I think, abandons the very concept of dialectical thinking and thus leaves itself in a somewhat naive political position, in that it can't really figure out its own inevitable relations to what it's simultaneously opposing.

Could we focus more directly on the future of Marxism and socialism? Because socialism, especially of a revolutionary Marxist kind, is now beleaguered in a wide range of ways – by macrotheoretical doubts about its cognitive status, like those raised by postmodernism, by specific doubts about crucial concepts such as the labour theory of value, by widespread intellectual defections, by the collapse of 'actually existing socialism' in Eastern Europe and the USSR, by the repression in China, by the stagnation in Cuba, and by the great difficulties that states born of Marxist national liberation movements, like Zimbabwe, now experience. Has Marxism had its day?

The obituary notices issued for Marxism have normally proved remarkably premature and my hunch is that this one will too. They've always been vigorous controversies within Marxist theory and they carry on. The more important phenomenon, of course, is Eastern Europe. I suppose those of us – and they form quite a large body within the English Marxist community – who have never regarded Eastern Europe as being in any sense socialist are not then put in the embarrassing position of those who nailed their colours to that particular mast. I think the English revolutionary Left was right to insist that democracy is not an optional extra to socialism but of its very essence. What perhaps irritates us is that some of us are indebted to quite mainstream movements in the Marxist tradition which have been saying these kinds of things for 70 years. We've not just been saying it since Tiananmen Square. What has happened in Eastern Europe – rather belatedly, but happened nevertheless – is exactly what, for example, the Trotskyist tradition within Marxism has continually called for, and in continually calling for the revolutionary popular overthrow of the Stalinist bureaucracy, it has always simultaneously warned of the dangers of a reversion to capitalism. So the scenario is not, in principle, an unfamiliar one for a long tradition of anti-Stalinist Marxists and socialists. And I think one can be more blunt than that and say that Marxism was always intended to be a theory and practice of how you might emancipate yourself in an advanced society. If you try it on, for understandable reasons, in a chronically backward society and try then to catapult yourself into the twentieth century, you are in grave danger of Stalinism. Now the downfall of Stalinism is unequivocally to be welcomed by socialists everywhere. It's a *sine qua non* of the construction of socialism. But of course it is occurring with a reversion to capitalism which is not to be unequivocally celebrated, in my view. If those societies do then end up as the banana republics of Europe, if they do undergo, not only the traumatic effects of shifting from a centralized to a market economy, which will happen anyway, but also the effects of being overshadowed and exploited by their far more advanced capitalist neighbours, I think socialism will be all the more necessary and all the more on the agenda. So we've not seen the end of the process yet.

Aren't you making too clean a distinction between Marxism and Stalinism?

Marx's claim that the ultimate goal of communism is the free development of each in terms of the free development of all, which I quote in *The Ideology of the Aesthetic*, is radically incompatible with Stalinism and demands participatory and democratic institutions far beyond the meagre parodies of them we have in bourgeois society. I don't know of any deeper or richer ethic than that of Marx, and that remains, for me, what has to be realized, politically. But to realize that politically demands certain material preconditions which were not there in the case of the societies which took the Stalinist road. But to make that point is not, in a certain sense, to disclaim responsibility for Stalinism. Stalinism after all, whatever it's a monstrous parody of, is probably a monstrous parody of socialism. Stalinism has ensured that the values of socialism stink in the nostrils of millions of men and women, not only in Eastern Europe, but also in capitalist societies. That has been one of its most invisible crimes, as opposed to some of its more dramatic crimes. Responsibility therefore, yes, not in the sense, for me, that in any way Stalinism springs from Marxism, but it does spring from a gross deformation of a Marxist tradition to which, however falsely, it aligns itself, and the political effects of that have then to be honestly dealt with by Marxists. They can't simply shut that off.

In The Significance of Theory *you say – and it's a statement you've made before, in the Benjamin book, for example – 'the only good reason for being a socialist, in my opinion, is that one cannot quite overcome one's amazement that the fate of the vast majority of men and women who have ever lived and died has been, and still is today, one of fruitless, unremitting labour' (p. 33. Cf. Walter Benjamin, p. 112). I'd like to link that with a newspaper report of a debate in 1918 in which Mikhail Bakhtin took part, as quoted by David Lodge in his* After Bakhtin: *'At some points Bakhtin did recognize, and even expressed appreciation of socialism, but he complained of, and worried about, the fact that socialism had no care for the dead' (p. 2). Millions of people have, as you say, died after lives of fruitless toil; many of them, in this and the last century, have been socialists. Even if socialism were successfully achieved one day, what could it possibly offer the dead?*

I think that is a non-negotiable tragedy: that the dead are dead, and, as Marx says at the beginning of *The Eighteenth Brumaire*, let the dead bury their dead. On the other hand, James Connolly, in *Saints and Scholars*, says that although the dead can't be resurrected, they can be given a different meaning; there is the notion there of retrospective meaning. I think I would certainly die rather more happily if I thought I was part of a narrative to which, in some small way, I might have contributed, and which would mean a more general emancipation. So the future can alter the past in that sense. It's a very limited sense, and it shouldn't be overplayed to the point where one loses grip on the reality of absolute loss. It's only in revolutionary imagination that the dead can be recycled in that way.

In conclusion, can I put to you the last question you yourself put to Raymond Williams when you interviewed him in 1987, about six months before his death: 'History, as Walter Benjamin might have put it, is more barbarism than progress; what you and I might consider moral and political virtue has never ruled any social order, other than briefly and untypically. The real historical record is one of wretchedness and unremitting toil; and "culture" – your and my speciality – has its dubious roots in this. How then are we to undo such a history with the very contaminated instruments it has handed us? Is socialism, in other words, anything more than a wishful thinking which runs quite against the historical grain?' (New Statesman, vol. 114, no. 2941, 7 August 1987, p. 21). How would you answer your own question?

A thought inspired by that question if I'm the recipient of it is: Why is it that history has been like that? In a way, I want to turn that question back on the liberal humanist and say: if there's some good and some bad around the place, then surely, by the law of averages, it wouldn't have worked out that the bad had so durably dominated. The rather complacent liberal humanist notion of the inextricable mixedness of things should surely apply to history, but there's no doubt what the balance or imbalance has been in history as far as moral and political vice and virtue goes. There must be something more at stake here. That's one very central reason why I'm a materialist, because I think you can only explain it in terms of certain kinds of material conditions, unless you attribute some utter monstrosity to the majority of people, which would not itself be a radical argument. There must be conditions of scarcity and artificially induced scarcity which twist social relations into those forms of violence and domination. There must be some way of accounting for that and of saying that, at least in principle, history could have been or could now be different. If you say there are no real material determinants here, that it's just a matter of who won out, then of course it's simply wishful thinking to say it could be different in the future: you have no historical evidence for that at all. What you can say in a materialist argument is that if it is to be different in the future, these different material conditions will have to prevail. Now clearly that's not to say that forms of virtue flow magically and spontaneously from certain kinds of material conditions. It's certainly not to say that they flow spontaneously from prosperity. But it is to say that virtue has a chance to flourish when, for example, people don't literally have to fight each other for survival. Without *that* kind of explanation, one would either be nonplussed to explain this strange predominance of vice over virtue, or one couldn't explain it in a way that would tell you how to change it.

Roger Scruton

London
26 November 1990

NICOLAS TREDELL: *Could you first of all tell us about your cultural and intellectual development through home and school and university?*

ROGER SCRUTON: I come from a poor lower middle-class background, my father being a primary school teacher. It was not a highly cultivated background; there were elements of musicality in the family, and a certain interest in ideas, but there were very few books in the house. I was, however, one of those lucky people who got to grammar school, before the grammar schools were destroyed, and this was the first major intellectual influence on me. My school was extremely energetic and intellectually active, so that although I did sciences at 'A' Level, I spent much time reading and talking with fellow pupils about music, art and literature. There was a Leavisite English master, whom I never met, but whose influence spread through the school. All pupils of any intellectual awareness came to believe the fundamental axiom of Leavisism, which is that literature is a moral force, and that it really matters what things you read and what things you like. I'm sure many people of my generation came under such an influence. The result was that by the time I left grammar school, I already saw literary criticism as a fundamental intellectual pursuit and one of immense importance to the nation. This perception was picked up by osmosis, and I couldn't have provided any theory to justify it.

When I was about 15, we moved to a house which had belonged to a librarian, and who had left many of his books behind. These books had a great impact on me. Mostly poets, especially Dante and Rilke (there was a lot of Rilke in the house) but also Bernard Shaw's *The Intelligent Woman's Guide to Socialism and Capitalism*. That was the first political book I read. It awoke me to the realities, as I saw them, of the capitalist system and to the nobility of the socialist alternative. I began to agree with my father's vision, which he derived from the old Labour Party, of social harmony produced by the equalizing machine of socialist policy. I did not realize at that time that I had benefited from the competitive, rather than the equalizing, element in the British system.

I went to Cambridge on a Natural Science scholarship and after a couple of days I changed to philosophy. I wanted at first to read English, but my tutor persuaded me that English was not a sufficient discipline for the mind. I didn't like analytical philosophy, but after a year I determined to make a go of it, and as I proceeded I came to value the discipline more and more. It was useful to have had a scientific background, which made formal logic easy; but my interests were still in the arts. So that when I later came to consider whether I would go on with philosophy, it was because of aesthetics.

Nor had the interest in literary criticism waned. I discussed all those questions again with my old circle of friends from school, who were at Cambridge with me, and also with people reading English. It was in the twilight days of the Leavisite era, and the questions that had been going around for a decade or more were still alive in Cambridge, where they mattered very much, as the questions of theology must have mattered to those Irish monks, surrounded in their monasteries and cut off from a godless world. Eliot meant more than anybody else to our generation; and, through the influence of people like Michael Tanner, the meaning of music and drama, the significance of Wagner and Nietzsche, and the ideals of German philosophy, were added to the old Leavisite agenda. All those ideas took me a long way away from analytical philosophy, and I have tried to amend my philosophy in a literary direction so as to take account of them.

Were you politically active at that time?

I was not political at Cambridge. Insofar as I had political views, they were soft middle-of-the-road leftist. I was always fairly rebellious, but not against anything in particular. Then I left; I decided not to do research, being fed up with the dryness of academic philosophy. I had ambitions to be a writer, and thought I should go away and try it. I got a job as Lecteur in a university in France from 1965 to 1966, and that was another formative experience: first French language and French literature; secondly, becoming acquainted with a French university and its vacuousness compared with Cambridge. I realized for the first time that there are places that call themselves universities in which there is no intellectual debate.

Would you apply that to the whole of the French university system?

No. I can only judge from the little college of the University of Bordeaux in Pau, which is where I was. But I made friends in the rest of the country and got to know the Sorbonne during the run-up to 1968. I had my first encounter with Marxism, student Marxism that is, and I was absolutely appalled by its fatuousness, its aggression, and its hostility to the ideals of culture and traditional order which I had absorbed through my Cambridge education, and which I had come to love, even without confessing to this love. *That* is what made me politically aware.

Was there a moment when your conservative commitments crystallized, or was it a more gradual development?

It was a gradual thing. The first stage was revulsion against French Marxism and against the threat that it seemed to pose to the culture of France and to European values. I also began to acquire an emotional attachment to the Catholic Church – an attachment which received an enormous blow at Vatican II. For a while after returning home I had to care for my mother while she was dying, and after her death I went to Italy to finish a novel which I never published (and which is indeed unpublishable). I was lonely, grieving, and uncertain of the future; naturally I didn't succeed in writing the great novel which my adolescent aspirations envisaged. But I saw more of another adolescent aspiration – the Marxism that was beginning to dominate the intellectual life of continental Europe. In Italy, Marxism went hand-in-hand with the Philistine politics of the Italian Communist Party and of the Mafia that surrounds it. Rather like George Orwell in Spain, I sniffed, from a distance, some of the smell of Soviet Communism; only I picked it up without interpreting it and by a kind of gut reaction. I knew in any case that it was a threat not just to political order but to all the social and cultural values that were beginning to matter to me. I didn't have anything to put in the place of it. But it prompted the decision to go back to Cambridge and to do research.

I realized that my education was incomplete and that I should try at least to understand that part of philosophy which had begun to interest me, the philosophy of art. I wanted to grasp the meaning of this great activity, about which I was always fruitlessly speculating. In my period as a research student, I met a new kind of Cambridge person: John Casey, an outspoken right-wing don, and Maurice Cowling, a very different instance of the same genus. After two years I was awarded a Research Fellowship to go to Peterhouse, where I fell in with many more such people. As always happens when you are beginning to think in a certain direction, your first worry is: Is it permitted? When I saw that it was not only permitted but actually done, within weeks I no longer had any worries. I saw that there was an alternative to the various brands of socialism that I had been hitherto acquainted with. But what this alternative was, in precise, concrete terms, remained elusive. High Table discussions did nothing to define it; besides, in Cambridge conservatism was very much wrapped up with the donnish way of life, for which, although I approve of it, I had no taste. In fact, to be honest, it repelled me, so that I gave up my Fellowship and went to London, to Birkbeck College. By then, I had become actively interested in politics and in the possibility of a conservative political philosophy. But my main work was still in aesthetics, which remained my principal academic interest until about 1980.

You began to edit the Salisbury Review *in 1982. What were your aims when you started that journal?*

Let me go back a little if I may. When I first moved to London in 1971, it was in the aftermath of '68. The universities were dominated by the radicals: the whole ethos of the place was repugnant to me. So I decided to take up a profession where a reactionary would be more at home, and read for the Bar. Far from being a professional training, this turned out to be another enormous intellectual adventure. Law made me realize that the political philosophy which was being taught in my college, was a complete nonsense, since it was entirely divorced from jurisprudence, and therefore from the real content of political decision-making. Its airy-fairy Marxism had lost all contact with English life, and in particular with the real historical grounds of our national system of politics. I therefore renewed my interest in philosophy. I also became interested in practical politics and, together with three friends – John Casey, the late Hugh Fraser, and Jonathan Aitken – started the Conservative Philosophy Group. This was at the time when the Conservative Party was floundering, not knowing where it was or what it believed. Ours was a discussion group for MPs and academics, the intention being to reach some self-understanding, to discover what we stood for, and to answer the question, if it could be answered, as to how our beliefs might be translated into policies. One of the strengths of socialism is that it is able to pass directly from an underlying philosophy to both political doctrine and practical policy. Conservatism has tended to distance itself from philosophical speculation, regarding policy as a matter of day-to-day adjustment, in the face of largely unforeseeable change. That may be a sensible view, but it too has a philosophy behind it, and I became interested – as much intellectually as practically – in examining it.

Then another important experience occurred – the experience of Eastern Europe. I went to Poland in '79 and from there to Czecho-slovakia, where I tried to give a private seminar in Prague, but was prevented by the Secret Police. I was shaken by this experience. It was my first encounter with the reality of the thing that I had sensed in 1968, but believed to be more an intellectual than a physical menace. I realized that I had overlooked a whole area of modern experience, and turned a blind eye to tyranny, as had almost everybody else.

I had already written *The Meaning of Conservatism*, which was a sort of statement of position, when somebody – Maurice Cowling, I think it was – asked me to join the Salisbury Group. This I did, and when the *Review* was founded, the group asked me to be its editor. I agreed – reluctantly at first, because there was no money attached to the post. My idea was to draw on my own experience, and to encourage my friends to 'come out'. This was after the invasion of Afghanistan, when the Soviet Union had launched a peace offensive and the peace movement had become a powerful – or at any rate, eye-catching – force in European politics. I had begun to travel fre-quently to Eastern Europe to help those who were setting up the underground universities; I was alarmed by what I saw there and by what people told me. And I was disturbed in consequence by the peace movement. Nobody among Western intellectuals seemed to be truly aware of the Soviet threat. If you mentioned it, you were scorned as a Cold Warrior. One of the aims of the *Salisbury Review* was to point out the reality of Soviet Communism and the dire condi-tion of the occupied half of Europe. We therefore started off with a column called 'In Search of Central Europe', which contained anonymous contributions from the Eastern bloc. But that was one component only of the *Review*. We also hoped to express some of the root ideas of conservatism and to continue discussions of policy at every level, so that conservatives might become self-confident intel-lectually and not just practically.

How successful do you think that has been?

Conservatives should not claim success, but only dignified failure. As failures go, however, the *Review* has been quite influential. Many of the conceptions that we were ridiculed for defending are now common currency. People accept the market economy as the only possibility, however qualified. They accept the rule of law and many of the theoretical conceptions by which we have defended it. They accept our vision of what was happening in Eastern Europe and they accept the need for some kind of social continuity and traditional order, or at least for institutions outside the control of the State. All this is now common property of Left and Right. It would be wrong to say this happened because of the *Salisbury Review*; nevertheless the existence of a radical reaffirmation of those principles has been useful. It is always safer to be right-wing when there's someone further to the right of you. I think we have therefore helped to make the world safe for conservative thinking.

Why do you think that you and the Salisbury Review *have aroused such hostility? You say, for example, in the Introduction to* Conservative Thoughts, *a collection of essays from the* Review, *that you 'can no longer speak publicly at British universities without running the risk of heckling, intimidation and violence' (p. 8). You've become a hated man in some quarters. Why is that?*

Intellectual life has been regarded as the preserve of the Left. Hence if you speak out against left-wing views from within the intellectual enclave, you are regarded as a traitor. Moreover people on the Left characteristically believe that they are morally right and that those who disagree with them are morally wrong. Whereas we believe that socialists are mistaken, socialists believe that we are evil. It is also true that we have published provocative articles like Ray Honeyford's. However, since the Rushdie affair, anybody who read Honeyford's article would see that what he was saying is true. If you say what is true but inconvenient, you are committing a far greater political sin than if you say what is false but comfortable.

Could I put to you some remarks from a recent issue of New Left Review, *made by a Marxist you've written about in* Thinkers of the New Left, *Perry Anderson. He says:*
   Limited in size, the new Right made up in leverage. Variously locked into the backlands of company finance, the counsels of the

Conservative leadership, and the service of the Press tycoons – the worlds of [Michael] Ivens and Digby Anderson, Ferdinand Mount and Hugh Thomas, John Vincent and Roger Scruton – its contribution to the ideological momentum of the Thatcher regime was considerable.

But the political prominence of this sector was never proportionate to its more strictly intellectual impact. Not large in numbers, it depended for much of its sound on the amplifiers to which it was wired... The new Right had always been relatively weak in the academy, and lacked the cadres to impose its vision at large. The great bulk of the British intellectual establishment held fast to its moderate liberal verities, indifferent or hostile to creeds of either Left or Right ('A Culture in Contraflow – I', New Left Review 180 p. 45).
How would you respond to those remarks?

I would say that whole passage is mythopoeic. It tells a story about our influence and power, for Anderson's own benefit and for the benefit of his friends. But the story is false. If he means by the New Right people like myself and John Vincent, then he is making a great mistake in thinking that we have anything to do with industry or with the great leverage exercised by the Conservative Party. On the contrary, we are regarded by the Conservative establishment as marginal. The *Salisbury Review* has never had any funding from industry. It has survived on its own subscriptions, something that it is able to do only because its editor and contributors are unpaid. The Conservative Party keeps us at arm's length; for its concern is to appear middle-of-the-road (which is of course understandable). As for the ability to amplify our voices in the media, it just so happens that some of us, like Digby Anderson and John Vincent, write things that people like to read. But the same is true of Edward Pearce, of Martin Jacques, and of Perry Anderson himself.

The question of intellectual impact is more serious. I would say that the universities – Anderson is quite right – do suppose themselves to adhere to a middle-of-the-road left-liberal position. (He says liberal, but in fact left-liberal is more accurate.) The same is true of the whole education system. This is a necessary part of the self-image of the British intellectual, but it does not follow that he has not changed his mind. On the contrary, we now find among the tenets of this middle-of-the-road left-liberalism the market economy, the need for social continuity in the face of disturbing changes, the belief in a rule of law, and a condemnation of communism, even of Marxism itself. In other words, the actual influence is there. But it cannot be confessed to. Only after another 20 years could it be acknowledged without loss of face. The same happened with the New Left in the sixties and seventies: the New Left changed the curriculum, and put on the agenda all those ghastly frauds like Althusser and Foucault. You will see in due course that we have succeeded in taking them off the agenda; and in five years' time you will find that Hayek, Popper, Polanyi and Oakeshott are back on the curriculum in departments of political science.

What do you feel to be the proper role of intellectuals in relation to politics? There seems to be some ambivalence in your work – at times you deplore their role, while at other times you assert their importance – for instance, you say in The Meaning of Conservatism *that 'it is by intellectuals that modern politics is made' (1984 edn, p. 12).*

When I said that in *The Meaning of Conservatism*, I wasn't recording a fact of which I approve, I was referring to one of the lamentable legacies of the French Revolution. Let me put it in a different way. Since the rise of Marxism, modern politics has been within the grasp of intellectuals; they have had a system which reduced the complex facts of politics into something within their mental compass – into something which could be captured by *l'esprit de géométrie*, as Pascal called it, as opposed to *l'esprit de la finesse* which is the spirit of the true politician. The entrance of the intellectual into politics is always accompanied by enormous danger, for the reason that his theories are not only wrong, but a mask for passions born of failure and anxiety. When one thinks of the major intellectuals in modern politics, those that stand out as having really succeeded, like Lenin, Stalin, Mussolini, Hitler, Mao and Ho Chi Minh, one can scarcely feel reassured. In England, in fact, our political process has never been subjected to the ideas of intellectuals. Indeed we have not actually had the concept of the intellectual. Historically we have thought instead of the educated person, who may enter politics, but who gains, in doing so, no credentials for his education. His education may help him to communicate and to understand the history of his country. But it does not prescribe any special code of behaviour – still less the massive exemption from the claims of ordinary morality that is assumed by intellectuals in the continental mode. He doesn't have a scheme or a plan for re-making the world. On the contrary, his education makes him more hesitant in the face of political complexities, rather than less.

Educated men like Gladstone and Disraeli made an enormous difference and kept the ship of state afloat in a brilliant way. Salisbury
was the same. In fact most of our leaders have been highly educated.
Even Mrs Thatcher is genuinely educated, though painted up in
other colours by her foes.

Could we turn to your book Sexual Desire, *which came out in 1986.
Reading that book, one can see how the topic of sexual desire is a
focus for a whole range of your concerns, but can you yourself tell us
how you came to write it?*

I grew up during the last days of sexual constraint. I was taught to
believe that sexual relations must be tempered by institutions like
marriage and that they were not to be freely engaged in – although
of course I was introduced to the Lawrencian literature, with its
glorification of sexual union. After that last twilight came the sudden
blaze of liberation, under whose withering light all our certainties
perished. Nobody knows how to return to that lost sense of orderli-
ness in the sexual life of the adult human, though few now approve
of the ethic of liberation. My historical position caused me to think
about the nature of the sexual bond and about why it has always
been moralized. The question of sexual desire goes to the heart of
what distinguishes man from the animals and touches on the essence
of our social relations. I came to the conclusion that the philosophy
of sexual liberation was founded on a false description of sexual
desire. People had accepted the picture of desire as an animal
instinct, which could only do damage by being dammed up and
which must be allowed to find release through whatever channels it
was aching against. That image of desire is, I believe, completely
wrong. It derives from a hasty assimilation of the human to the animal, not recognizing what has been apparent since Plato, that in sexual desire both the subject and the object are persons and see themselves as such. Desire does not aim to connect two parts of two
organisms but to establish a relation between two people. I went into
the phenomenology of this experience and concluded that, while
there is no easy way back to the old sexual morality, its underlying
philosophy of human nature was much nearer to the truth than the
philosophy implied by the ethic of liberation. This proved to be a
fruitful ground from which to explore my general philosophical position.

One of the most controversial questions you take up in Sexual Desire

is that of homosexuality. The argument against homosexuality you
propose is that the homosexual relationship lacks that dimension of
otherness which can only be found in an encounter with the other-
ness, the mystery, of the desire of a person of a different gender. So
the homosexual encounters in his partner not a different structure of
desire, but a simulacrum of his own desire. But it seems to me that,
even within your own terms, two people in a homosexual relation-
ship could achieve as fully as a heterosexual couple that reciprocal
and responsible recognition of each other as desiring, mysterious,
inviolable persons which seems to be, for you in that book, the fun-
damental constituent of sexual morality. The recognition of each
other as persons could still occur even without what is arguably a
superadded element, the encounter with the structure of desire of a
person of another gender. How would you feel about that?

My criticisms of homosexuality in *Sexual Desire* are fairly muted. I
was trying to identify what people think to be threatened by the
homosexual relationship: what it is in the heterosexual relationship
that is undermined by this 'cheap competitor'. In the heterosexual
relationship there is a diffidence between the partners which comes
from the fact that they can wound each other and bind each other in
ways that they do not and cannot fully understand. A complex
negotiation has to go on before and through the sexual act, a negotiation which tends to leave the partners indissolubly joined. They
may break apart, but that will be because of some outside impact on
their relation, and not from the relation itself. This diffidence-creating mechanism does not exist between a homosexual and his partner.
For the homosexual act is narcissistic: the desire that you arouse is
the desire that you feel, and is focused in exactly the same way. Between men, homosexual desire becomes phallic: the anatomical fact
comes to dominate and finally to eclipse, the life of the emotions.
There are ways in which the diffidence-creating mechanism is reconstructed between homosexuals by role-playing, by modelling themselves on the marital unions by which they are surrounded – as between Benjamin Britten and Peter Pears. But such role-playing
requires a background idea of sexual normality. By recognizing the
normality of a sexual desire disciplined by gender difference, homosexuals may recreate the commitment that arises between man and
woman.

Would you want objections to homosexuality to be embodied in
legislation of any kind?

The concept of the sexually normal goes much deeper than the ethos of liberation will allow. When all is permitted, the concept of normality has no place. I think, however, that the concept of the normal is a vital component in the building of social relations, and in securing the stability of family life and the commitment to children. To that extent it is a prime candidate for legal protection. It does not follow that you have to punish deviations; but you certainly might want to protect people from being enticed into deviant relations prematurely. Such legislation indeed exists in Britain. The age of consent for homosexual relations is higher than that for heterosexual relations, offences like the corruption of minors are treated extremely seriously, and there are legislative measures against campaigning for homosexuality in schools. I regard these as perfectly natural and acceptable pieces of legislation. They are not genuine interferences in human freedom; they constrain our conduct only in the interests of responsibility.

Another minefield you enter in Sexual Desire *is that of feminism. Could you sum up your differences with feminism?*

In *Sexual Desire*, I was really concerned with a particular kind of feminist philosophy, according to which gender is both an arbitrary social construct, and at the same time one of the ways in which personality finds expression. I'm prepared to accept that there are two kinds of persons, the male and the female, and that this division in kind, while being rooted in biology, is not merely a biological one. It is also cultural and moral; as in all moral distinctions between people, it fixes the terms of negotiation. Being a man, being a woman, will enter into any relations that are negotiated between them. It is inevitable therefore that there will be distinctions between men and women in society. To complain against this fact is to throw away the one great insight the feminists have, which is that being a woman is a non-accidental part of your make-up. Accepting this insight, you might use it to articulate ways in which women have been badly treated by men. But you should also be aware of the complexities of human experience, so as to recognize the ways in which men have been badly treated by women, and to recognize too the fact that the relations between men and women are the outcome of centuries of negotiation and not merely the result of *force majeure*.

Could we move on to a matter which you certainly discuss in Sexual Desire *but which has much more general implications, and seems to*

be one area in which your thought comes very close to some radical
thinking on the Left. This is your idea that the person, or self, is an
artefact that is fashioned by society, and that self-consciousness
comes about as a result of public linguistic practices. That is not too
far from the Left idea, widely current today, that the self is a con-
struction and could therefore be reconstructed. What then are, or
what should be, the constraints upon the kinds of selves that could be
fashioned or constructed?

This is a deep point, and I agree with you that this is something that
I share with many Left-wing thinkers. My own conservatism has its
philosophical roots in Hegel and Wittgenstein. It takes from Wittgenstein the view that I am to a great extent the product of the social
practices in which I engage, and it takes from Hegel the notion of the
self or the person as created through its own objectification – in
institutions, in history and in the workings of the will. That is what
I mean by saying the person is an artefact. It does not follow from
that, however, that you can freely make yourself according to your
own recipe. On the contrary, if you take seriously the Wittgensteinian position, you will recognize that you are not an artefact of your
own devising, but a product of the whole society of which you are a
part. To entertain the thought that you can remake your personality
according to your own prescription is extremely dangerous. In order
to do that you would have to pull down society without knowing
what will come in place of it. The human person is an artefact; but
the thing which creates it is an artefact of the thing it creates. Society
is the result of transactions between individuals who are created by
society. There is no vicious circle here: it is a circle of mutual support.
Rather than seeing in this an opportunity to remake everything in the
image of some new-favoured human being, one should recognize, on
the contrary, that it lays on us an enormous obligation to treat the
social organism for the delicate thing that it is – to make small adjust-
ments perhaps, but to beware of destroying the whole. That is why
it leads me in a direction which is the polar opposite of the direction
in which it leads a man like Foucault.

But haven't massive reconstructions of selves occurred, as with the
Industrial Revolution, which have involved very great transforma-
tions in the social order?

I don't say that great changes have not occurred. But some of the
greatest changes that have occurred – the Industrial Revolution, for

example – were not the product of design. They arose by an invisible hand from a million tiny transactions. Those changes are the ones that, in my view, have done the least damage. Changes which have been initiated by an idea of the new self – the new socialist man, the *übermensch*, the blond beast, etc. – have done enormous damage to the human soul. Indeed, as our Eastern European friends constantly remind us, they have destroyed civil society itself. Havel is very good on this subject. He writes about the new consciousness of the self which is produced by the totalitarian order, in which a person is complicitous in his own enslavement. This is absolutely right. The attempt to make a new man has produced not only the greatest piece of social engineering but also the greatest social disaster that Europe has seen. When changes occur by an invisible hand, however, they become absorbed into the ongoing history of the human psyche and are not ultimately destructive.

The issues of change and continuity bring us to another crucial concern of your work, which is with tradition. I'd like first of all to take up your affirmation. in a lecture collected in your latest book The Philosopher on Dover Beach, *which appeared this year, that one major task for the conservative 'is to give up this breast-beating, guilt-ridden desire to throw away our inheritance' (p. 282). But isn't that guilt, that desire, part of our inheritance, a vital component of that tradition in which Western intellectuals are born and bred? Aren't we therefore, in seeking to give it up, seeking to give up part of our inheritance?*

I would say that there is a healthy form of it, which is certainly part of our inheritance: this is the practice of confessing to our faults and taking responsibility for them. That is not the same as what I was talking about in that lecture. For there is a morbid guilt-feeling too – the disposition to confess to faults that do not exist and to repudiate all in ourselves that gives us the strength to assume responsibility. I do agree with you, however, that one of the greatest achievements of Western civilization is to have founded not only the moral life but also the political life on the practice of self-criticism. No other society apart from the Athenian ever managed this.

Much of your work seems like an attempt to gather and bind together fragments of tradition. But isn't the crucial problem that in any complex modern society, tradition will never again be unified and given – if it ever was – but will be fragmented, contradictory, self-conscious? So we can only have the illusion of tradition by what you call a process of 'endarkening' rather than 'enlightening', and that process is not likely to be sustainable for very long in modern society. Isn't your project in that sense an impossible one?

If it were merely that, then I would agree with you. Certainly Wittgenstein is right that the attempt to restore tradition is like the attempt to repair a spider's web with your bare hands. But matters are not so simple as you imply. It is not that one wishes to repair something that has been broken. I think of it much more as an attempt to discover those things which are still living and to create the space in which they will grow again. Many things are dead, but in Britain we have often stood back from ourselves, so as to assess what we are and to allow those things which are genuinely living to grow. This way we re-establish the continuities which matter to us. We did this in Elizabethan times, at the Restoration, at the Glorious Revolution in 1832, and throughout the last century – Disraeli did it and so did Salisbury. I do not regard this as a hopeless task; nor is it peculiarly British to embark on it. Look at the founding of Alexandria and what Alexander achieved. Of course he did not perpetuate the culture of Athens, but he did perpetuate something which was an enormous landmark and without which the world would never have inherited what it did inherit from Athens. So let us not despair.

Aesthetics, as you've indicated earlier, has always been one of your absorbing interests, and you've been Professor of Aesthetics at Birkbeck College since 1985. In your inaugural lecture 'Modern philosophy and the neglect of aesthetics', collected in The Philosopher on Dover Beach, *you say: 'In our post-Enlightenment world, it is natural that we should look elsewhere than towards religion for the "sense" of our actions. And Kant was in a way right to single out the aesthetic as, so to speak, next in line to the Eucharist, as the source of meaning' (p. 110). Now the function you propose, or at least imply, for the aesthetic in that lecture seems open to two objections which come, on the one hand, from a conservative religious viewpoint, and, on the other hand, from a radical Left viewpoint. The first objection would derive from T.S. Eliot and would say that what you're doing is putting forward the aesthetic as a substitute for religion, and that it cannot be an effective substitute, because while it may offer moments in which thought and immediate experience are, or seem to be, fused, it can't locate them in a comprehensive system of consolation and redemption in the way religion can. What would you say to that objection?*

I would agree with what T.S. Eliot says entirely. There is of course the danger of making the aesthetic into a substitute for religion. Art cannot provide the consolation that religion provides: the best it can do is to cause you to look for consolation in a place where it cannot be found. I do not mean that the aesthetic provides a substitute for religion. I mean just what I say: that it is, for many people, the nearest that we have to what religion gave us. It is therefore a way to understand what religion was. This is why, since the Romantic movement, people have seen art as something holy, as the occupation of a priesthood. My intellectual purpose in that essay was to point out the deep similarity between the aesthetic and the religious experience. This similarity is often overlooked; and especially by people like structuralists and deconstructionists who entirely fail to identify the real sources of the aesthetic experience, and the depth to which we can be, and must be, moved by art.

What about the problem that religion is, or was, available to everybody, whereas aesthetic experience is only for a few?

People are wrong to think that aesthetic experience *must* be available only to a few, although it becomes like that in our rarefied conditions. Just look at the Athenian drama, and you find something there that not only was available to everyone but whose distinctness from a religious rite was barely perceivable.

Do you think it is possible then to envisage a situation in which art would be widely available in that way again, or is that quite unthinkable in the modern world?

I don't know. I would not rule out the possibility. Popular taste is, of course, extremely depraved. The nearest you would have is the soap opera. On the other hand, the growing appeal of true opera suggests something in the order of a religious revival. It has a most extraordinary effect on people, and a growing effect, and its audience is now vast.

Let me put the second, Left-wing objection to the function for the aesthetic that you suggest. This objection would be that the aesthetic is being used to perform a covert political function – of compensating for and concealing social divisions – which it can't adequately perform, any more than it can adequately perform the functions of traditional religion. Moreover, this objection would run, when the aesthetic is used in this way, a vital but potentially subversive aspect of it has to be suppressed – a Utopian element which offers an implicit criticism of the present and an intimation of some better future order. How would you respond to that objection?

For somebody of a Marxist persuasion, the aesthetic, as introduced by Kant and his followers, involves taking up a particular attitude of disinterestedness towards the world. This also involves, by its nature, an attempt to perceive the world as harmonious. To that extent, aesthetic experience has an ideological function. It encourages the acceptance of things which ought, in fact, to be criticized. So identified, moreover, the aesthetic attitude is merely a historical option. It is not part of the human condition: we did not have to have it. It did not occur until the eighteenth century, let's say, or until the so-called *bourgeois* era, and its persistence is merely an offshoot of the political order which it helps to sustain. That is the Marxist theory. And I think it is wrong through and through. In my view, it is part of being rational, in other words part of human nature, that we should have these redundant experiences, that our interest in the world should not be exhausted by our practical and theoretical urgencies, that we should sometimes stand and contemplate. Maybe there is an evolutionary explanation of this strange fact. I don't know. But it is an obvious fact, and was obvious to Plato and Aristotle. They did not use the word 'aesthetic' to describe it; but they used equivalent language. In Aristotle's *Poetics*, you find all the elements of the aesthetic, as this was described by Kant. It is part of our rational nature to contemplate the world, to look for things which are intrinsically ordered, and to find meaning in them, even in suffering and tragedy. Whatever the surrounding social order, this has been the case. The Utopian element in the human imagination is only one small part of this. The capacity imaginatively to perceive and understand the world and to find rest in that act is, I think, intrinsic and intrinsically valuable.

So if one takes, for instance, Kant's idea of aesthetic experience as offering 'purposiveness without purpose', you would see any suggestion that such an idea anticipates some future and better society as superadded to the aesthetic rather than an essential part of it?

No, I would not quite say that. The aesthetic experience is essentially imaginative. It always leads one both to look intensely at what is and to see it in terms of imaginative possibilities. The Utopian imagination is naturally part of this. But the Utopian imagination, untempered by actual observation of reality, is an extremely dangerous thing. The great virtue of art is that it inspires our Utopian impulses and at the same time tempers them. One of the wisest things Freud said is that art offers the passage from fantasy back to reality. That is what you see happening before your eyes in Aeschylus, and also in Shakespeare.

You spoke near the beginning of our conversation about your early ambition to be a novelist, and your first published novel, Fortnight's Anger, *appeared in 1981. How did that novel develop?*

As I said, I wrote a novel in my youth which I put on one side. Then, in the troubled period when I was thinking of leaving the university and reading for the Bar, I wrote the draft of a second novel which suggested itself to me. The characters are all fictional; but it came out of the feelings of unreality that I had after my mother's death. I began by trying to capture that experience and to embody it in characters who would represent to me the emotional and moral complexities of modern England. It was an incredibly ambitious thing to do, so not surprisingly the novel creaks rather, although it has passages which I still like. Then I wrote other things for a while, before recently returning to fiction. A third novel, *Francesca*, is about to appear, and a book of stories is due out later this year. In these I try to reconcile my literary and philosophical interests. I have written a collection of four Xanthippic dialogues, as I call them, which are partly commentaries on Plato, but with women taking the leading parts: Xanthippe, Plato's mother Perictione and so on. My philosophical ideas are here given fictional form, and in the last of the dialogues – 'Phryne's Symposium' – I try to justify the arguments of *Sexual Desire*, in a work that is halfway between a novel and a philosophical essay.

What would you say the relationship was between your fiction and your philosophy?

My philosophy, especially the social side of it, aims at giving an objective account of modern experience and discovering the posture that will bring consolation and acceptance to the ordinary person. I have the desire for such a philosophy, indeed the need for it, because of my own subjective position, having suffered experiences of loss and felt the inner disorientation of modernity. At the same time as aiming for that calm and collected thing, therefore, I have tried to express the opposite, and this is what I attempt in fiction. There is a Kafkaesque part of my make-up, a sense of being utterly at a loss in the remnants of society which surround me. My ambition has been to capture that subjective experience, to give it objective form, and to bring it back towards the thing that will console it. My desire is to reconcile the ideal of objectivity with the dishevelled subjectivity of my own experience. This is a philosophical task, and also a dramatic one. Whether I can manage it, I doubt. But one thing is certain: academic philosophy, as it now is, contains no tools that would permit a writer even to begin such an enterprise.

Robert Hewison

Fetter Lane, London
17 June 1991

NICOLAS TREDELL: *You're active in a variety of cultural fields – as a Ruskin scholar, as the author of a trilogy on postwar British culture, as a contemporary cultural analyst in books such as* The Heritage Industry *and* Future Tense, *as a* Sunday Times *theatre critic, and as a presenter of the Radio 3 programme* Third Ear. *You said recently, when you were interviewing Terry Eagleton, that you had come through 'the standard bourgeois upper-middle-class training' (*Third Ear, Radio 3, 5 June 1991*). Could you tell us first of all about your background and education?*

ROBERT HEWISON: You could say that I come from the administrative class. My father was a senior Civil Servant with some literary talents – he used to set the competitions for the *New Statesman*, he has four limericks in the *Faber Book of Limericks*, and he wrote pastiches for *Punch*. He also translated some of Simenon's novels. I was sent to public school which I detested and I then went to Oxford which I loved. I did very little work at Oxford. Much more important to me was confirming an interest in the theatre in a very practical sense. Michael Palin and I very quickly teamed up as a cabaret duo and so I had three very enjoyable years at University writing and performing in the post-satirical age. One of the most useful things I did was to be in a University production called *Hang Down Your Head and Die* at the Comedy Theatre in the West End. This cured me completely of ever wanting to be an actor but I do believe the experience helps when it comes to being a theatre critic. I got a very mediocre degree in History and I really thought that I was destined for television in those days. Indeed after leaving University I worked briefly for Southern Television as a graduate trainee. But in fact I disliked television, or rather I disliked commercial television in a provincial city, after the mythical golden years at Oxford. So a year later I went to Ravensbourne College of Art and Design, from 1966-67, and I had a very good time supposedly learning television technique, writing and directing programmes I wanted to make.

At the end of that year, I was commissioned by the BBC to do a half-hour drama documentary on a topic which I'd suggested, the Ruskin-Whistler trial. I remembered the trial from the book that had influenced me most as a teenager – William Gaunt's *The Aesthetic Adventure*, which I know is a fairly lightweight cultural history but which recreates the nineteenth century in a very pleasing and intriguing way. I went into my research for the programme thinking that Ruskin was a Victorian fuddy-duddy and that Whistler was the ultimate sort of sixties radical. I came out thinking that Ruskin was the most fascinating and complex personality I'd ever encountered and Whistler was really rather superficial. As a result of that, and because I'm a perpetual student, I returned to Oxford to do a thesis on Ruskin from 1969 to 1972.

You suggest, at the end of Too Much, *the last of your trilogy on post-war British culture, published in 1986, that your approach to cultural history derives from Ruskin (1988 edn, p. 306). What do you feel you learnt from Ruskin?*

The point about Ruskin was that he existed before any of the disciplines of the twentieth century developed and that he existed as a kind of totality. He didn't know that he was doing art history or cultural history or economics; it didn't bother him. He had the arrogance of genius to see everything as a whole. And really the theme of Ruskin's work in whatever field is that the health of society relates to the health of art and the health of art relates to the health of society. My view of Ruskin has changed in that, in those days, I think a lot of us bought the myth that Ruskin was somehow the founding father of the Labour Party whereas, as I subsequently argued in an essay which revises some of what I said in my book on Ruskin, *The Argument of the Eye*, he was in fact an ultra-Tory. But what was important to me was the practical experience of having to handle Ruskin's holism – the way that he connects art, economics, sculpture, dancing, museums, everything, into some sense of what we now call cultural history. In those days I think it was quite difficult to call oneself a cultural historian but one nonetheless had to be a cultural historian in order to try to make sense of what Ruskin was saying.

After your book on Ruskin, The Argument of the Eye, *which came out in 1976, you went on to write the first book of the trilogy,* Under Siege, *which appeared in 1977. This was a study of literary life in London from 1939-1945 that focused on the myth and reality of Fitzrovia. What drew you to that period and milieu?*

One reason is pretty autobiographical. When I was with Southern Television as a totally miserable graduate trainee, I discovered the public library, and I read a book by Julian Maclaren-Ross called *Memoirs of the Forties* which is all about Fitzrovia. This book delighted me, as I was living a completely anti-literary life in South-ampton at the time. Maclaren-Ross was of course perpetuating the myth of café society, and I got interested in this because I had become interested in French café society and indeed in the idea of a Bohemia, which is one of the themes of Gaunt's *Aesthetic Adventure*. There's also the fact that I was born in 1943 and therefore the War is very important to me as an experience that I have had, but not witnessed. I discovered that I was very interested in the topic of Fitzrovia and that no-one had written a book about it. I was fascinated by this little experiment. This is where many of the sort of things that happened in the broad sweep of the nineteenth century, and in Ruskin's life, all focused, between 1939 and 1945. It all happens at the same time in the same place. It wasn't until the end of the book that I realized that there was more to the story than that and so what had originally been conceived as a single volume later acquired volume two, on the fif-ties, and volume three, on the sixties and early seventies. I still in fact think, though, that the most fascinating period is 1945 to 1951 and the imaginative failures, the *trahison des clercs*, which took place during those years.

How would you sum up those failures?

I think that people like John Lehmann and Cyril Connolly and Stephen Spender, who had sustained the struggle for the idea of a literary culture during the war, had got so exhausted by about 1944-5 that when the opportunities of the peace came, they let them slip through their fingers and began the massive cultural regression which, apart from a few very brief years in the sixties, we've been going through ever since.

Would you also see the failures of those years as political?

Yes, I'm afraid to say that I would. The books of the trilogy were not conceived in a critical spirit, in the sense that they were not there to evaluate and to say 'this is good, this is bad'; they were more concerned to be a kind of preliminary survey. Raymond Williams actually reviewed *In Anger* and he said this book is the point from which discussion can reasonably begin. Now some may say that means no more than, 'he's laid out the materials', but I regard it as a compliment because that is precisely what I wanted to do. In a sense, my work since then has been, and is certainly going to be, the discussion which follows from the survey of the materials of those years. I think my views have hardened. In a way I've moved more self-consciously to the Left, culturally speaking, since writing the trilogy and therefore I feel that, in its original form, the trilogy is less politically and culturally critical than it might have been, though when I transferred the trilogy from Weidenfelds to Methuen, and Methuen reissued them in paperback, I was invited to write new introductions, which are actually slightly sharper, and indeed *In Anger* has been slightly rearranged to make, I feel, better sense of the period.

How did the shift to a more culturally and political critical kind of writing come about?

What gave me the confidence to become more polemical was, curiously, selling out to the capitalist press. Having totally failed to get any work as an academic, I found myself being, *faute de mieux*, a kind of man of letters, and as a man of letters, you have to earn your living somehow – you certainly don't earn it from writing books. So I sustained myself by working for the BBC, mainly in the African and World Services but, as these things happen, that dried up rather. I wrote for the *TLS*, and then I started writing for the *Sunday Times* as a theatre critic, and what was interesting about that, after the BBC, was the way in which you really were astonishingly encouraged to have your own opinions rather than the Corporation's. You didn't have a producer sitting beside you when you went to see a play. Writing that kind of criticism on a regular basis, where you were expected primarily to report your own experience of the event and your own critical response to it, simply showed me that it wasn't necessary to hide behind the third-person conventions of ordinary academic discourse. So by the time that I was finishing *Too Much* I realized that I wanted to make an intervention, which is why I deliberately made the rather dramatic gesture of switching to the first person for the Epilogue to that book. Since then I have wanted not just to be a historian, or a contemporary cultural historian, I've wanted to be a contemporary cultural *critic*, which I know is an arrogant thing to be. And when I wrote *The Heritage Industry*, which I suppose is the one book which has had an impact outside the narrow specialisms of literature and art history, I had no idea whether I was going to disappear without trace or not. I just thought the timing of the book was interesting. It had to be written very quickly because a general election was coming and I and my publisher felt that there was a need for the old kind of publishing in which people actually wrote books which made a noise and rattled the cages a bit. And I suppose it's true to say that intervention worked in that I'm still being rung up by people and asked to take part in the discourse on 'the heritage industry' – indeed you could say that I had coined the phrase 'the heritage industry'.

The Heritage Industry, published in 1987, is a very hard-hitting attack on the way in which, as you see it, the past, in 1980s England, has been converted into a profitable consumer spectacle. How did that book develop?

I think it is true to say that *The Heritage Industry* grew out of having conducted a survey of British cultural life from '39 to '75; it was only in the course of writing the trilogy that I began to see that there was a kind of creeping nostalgia spreading over English culture and that we may have an ever-improving past and an ever-declining future. Indeed, as I admitted in the Epilogue to *Too Much*, there was a kind of nostalgia attached to my own idea of writing about the myth of the Blitz and 1940 and all that, as I did in *Under Siege*. And it seemed to me that we have to sharpen ourselves up and we have to look much more critically at the whole heritage industry as it developed from about 1975 – though it is the result of a nostalgia that goes back to the eighteenth century or earlier, in terms of the pastoral myth and so on. We actually have to conduct some kind of cultural revolution – that very unfashionable phrase – and we need to be producing something new in terms of physical objects and of a cultural life to go with them.

Despite your attack on nostalgia and the heritage industry, you've emphasized that you don't reject the past – indeed your work as a cultural historian is very much concerned with at least the recent past. What would you say our proper relationship to the past should be?

We need a *critical* connection with the past. We don't know where we are unless we know where we've been and we don't know where we're going unless we know where we are. I think that history is too important to be exploited in the way it is by the heritage industry. It seems to me that most of the heritage projects in this country are to do with rewriting the past into some saccharine parody which is there to deny the one thing that is certain, which is change. We live in constant change, and all they're trying to do – by 'they' I mean the administrative class and the commercial interests which govern this country – is somehow to freeze a totally false image of the past in aspic in order to deny change in the present. I think there is, or has been, a political project to say that things were better then and there-fore to conduct a kind of cultural counter-revolution, a turning-back. I think we have to understand the past in terms of change and in terms of competing discourses, of competing powers really, and until we understand that, we won't understand the extent to which we continue to exist in competing discourses with competing pow-ers. And I suppose the objective then would be to ensure that one's own particular set of discourses and powers won.

The Heritage Industry *is also strongly critical of the Arts Council in the 1980s. What kind of public funding would you like to see for the arts?*

I'm an old-fashioned socialist in the sense that I believe that the wel-fare state, the welfare settlement, was the right direction in which to go, and that public support of the arts is a social duty. How it should be done is another matter. I think the history of British cultural poli-tics since the War has been one of consistent obfuscation and failure – in fact, pusillanimous, to quote Jimmy Porter. I've come round to the view now that the Arts Council in the last ten years has become so politicized at a simple bureaucratic level that we might as well have a proper Ministry of Culture and that we could certainly dis-pense with the taste, attitudes and influence of the members of the Great and the Good who are responsible for the arts in this country. I think it might be possible to break up the Arts Council and try to create a series of competing institutes which were financed by a Sink-ing Fund so they were not dependent on annual grants – rather like the National Heritage Memorial Fund which was originally created out of the Land Fund that was a residue of the sale of surplus World War Two materials. You could then have, say, an Institute for the Promotion of Literature and an Institute for the Promotion of

Contemporary Art, which would be much smaller but much more focused and committed. They would be, if you like, competing bureaucracies rather than the monolithic bureaucracy they've become.

You've examined the history of censorship in postwar Britain in the trilogy, and you've also offered a case-study of the workings of censorship in your book on Monty Python, Irreverence, scurrility, profanity, vilification and licentious abuse, *which came out in 1981. In that book, you say: 'Some form of protection for the young seems necessary, to shield them from images of violence and sex which adults may deliberately seek out, whether they are forbidden or not. Adults must be free to choose' (p. 93). Perhaps I could put two objections from different viewpoints. The first comes from George Steiner. When I interviewed him, he said that he thought '[t]he question of censorship [was] an urgent and open one' and that there might be a strong case for censoring, let's say, sadistic child pornography. He also made the point that explicit material may have different effects on differently circumstanced people – that, as he put it, '[i]f we are in deprivation, socially, physically, economically, explicit material is hot oil being dropped into dynamite' (see above, p. 83) – whereas your opposition to censorship seems to be based on a liberal model in which all adults, whatever their situation or background, have the same capacity to choose. How would you respond to that kind of objection?*

Child pornography, because it exploits the child who is the subject of this pornographic imagery for a start, is something which I'm perfectly happy to see banned. But it's certainly true that I take a liberal view of the issue of censorship, and, as I say somewhere in *Irreverence, scurrility, profanity, vilification and licentious abuse*, censorship is always a question of where you define the line, and where you define the line defines the enlargements of the society you are in. Now I think that Steiner, as a mandarin, would define the boundaries of society rather more narrowly than I would. He has less faith in human kind than I do, and perhaps, coming from Central Europe, he has a right to have less faith in human kind than I do. I'm practical and pragmatic and I can see that there are forms of censorship which have to be in existence. But I certainly think that we can afford to be as liberal as we have become.

From another viewpoint, there is now a growth of, what one might call, on the analogy with positive discrimination, positive censorship, which aims, for example, to promote less degrading images of women or ethnic minorities. How would you feel about that?

I think you have to take it on a case-by-case basis. The new fashion for PC, political correctness, as reported from America, does seem to me absurd, though of course you don't know that the reports that you're getting are not, rather like the reminders that de Man was once a Nazi, a means of attacking, not the radical extremists, but the liberals who allow radical extremists their legitimate space. Now I believe that radicals should have their legitimate space. A radical might reply, well of course you're the worst kind of person because you're actually being oppressively tolerant. If you like, I'm oppressively tolerant.

The book that you wrote after The Heritage Industry, Future Tense, *which appeared in 1990, focuses on postmodernism – a term which is difficult to define, but which has come to be the term around which debate about our present cultural condition is conducted. How would you assess postmodernism?*

You can distinguish three different kinds of postmodernism – a progressive postmodernism, an oppositional postmodernism, and a reactionary postmodernism – but what they all reflect is a total discontent with today, and that discontent is a product of the very word 'post', meaning 'after'. It appears that our contemporary cultural situation is only defined by coming after something which, by implication, was rather better. In a sense, it's a modernist version of heritage. But modernism genuinely held ideas of social progress: it had faith in democratic planning and in the possibilities for production, for design and for the amelioration of society, and indeed it had a very strong place for the arts. All those things make me a modernist rather than a postmodernist. In many ways, postmodernism doesn't mean anything, or add up to a consistent set of ideas: it is merely a state of mind, a condition of society, in which all meanings are slippery, all values come on a sliding scale, and we live in an age of complete relativism. Yet overarching this strange and slippery condition are those key notions like 'surface' and 'screen' and 'fragment' and 'crack' that are always turning up in books on postmodernism. Postmodernism is characterized, I believe, by the transcendence of capitalism: that is to say, we can no longer identify the operations of capital as being located in a single place, like the factory or the shop.

They are everywhere: they are whizzing through the air with the speed of light of the information industry, and the fact that information itself has become the key commodity is very much part of the postmodern condition. The effect on the arts is that the arts themselves become much more of a commodity.

You identify yourself as a modernist but there is one aspect of postmodernism which you do seem to endorse – which is postmodernism's assault on the division between high and low culture that modernism in fact sustained and elaborated. That division you have, at least partly, rejected, and you welcome what you call in Too Much *'the long front of culture'.*

The long front of culture is not specifically tied to the postmodern condition. It's a feature of the social revolution which took place in the latter half of the twentieth century. The problem with the long front of culture within postmodernism is that it simply becomes the supermarket of culture, a series of style choices – although the condition of postmodernism may be limited to the eighties when there was an inflationary bubble upon which style, graphic design, clothes – literally superficial imagery – appeared to matter. With the second recession of the current Conservative government, that bubble appears to have burst and it may be that cyclically we're going to move on to something else. 'The long front of culture' was a phrase which emerged in the debate about Pop Art in the 1960s, and I think it relates to the democratization of culture, which I don't regard as being anything less than a good thing. You see, what is interesting – and this is something I'm working on at the moment – is that there are, it seems to me, two ways of looking at culture. There is the production theory of culture, which is to say that there are people like George Steiner and Virginia Woolf who make culture, which the rest of us come along, admire, and are influenced and in some way dominated by; but there is also the consumption theory of culture, which says that people make their own identities, they construct their own identities, from a series of cultural choices, so that if you read the critical works of George Steiner and the novels of Virginia Woolf you construct, out of that act of consumption, a particular kind of identity – in this case, a rather mandarin identity. I think the consumption theory of culture goes too far when it argues that people who spend their lives selecting new kinds of Reebok trainers and rushing about on skateboards are engaging in forms of culture as valid as those of the people who read Virginia Woolf and George Steiner.

I think there is a qualitative difference, though not an absolute one, between one form of culture and another.

But there is something to be said for the consumption theory of culture in that it hands the idea of cultural control and choice to the selectors rather than the self-elected. I think, in the end, I still tend towards the production rather than the consumption theory of culture, but I like the idea, not of text, but of intertext, I like the idea of participation, and certainly I question the idea of there being some holy grail called 'culture'. Some people think there is a holy grail called culture but what is actually contained in this holy grail is cultural domination. What I would like to see is a workable pluralism. How we achieve that, I'm quite honestly still not sure, but that is what I would like us to work towards, a long front of culture literally, abandoning the old hierarchical models. There's been a rearguard action to maintain hierarchies of taste. One of the Arts Council's problems is that it's still working with an almost eighteenth-century definition of what culture is. It has never been able to surmount the old academic divisions between painting, sculpture, dance, music. And in fact where the most interesting work is being done formally is precisely between the disciplines. And what I enjoy particularly and want to do now as a theatre critic is to look not just at West End theatre but at dance, mime, performance art, installation work and so on, because I think that is where artists are finding the most interesting work formally.

You said that postmodernism was characterized by the transcendence of capitalism, and the idea that we are living in an era of transcendent capitalism is one that you stress in Future Tense. *That sounds rather close to Fredric Jameson's Marxist position, as expressed in his essays which have been collected and developed in his recent book* Postmodernism, or, The Cultural Logic of Late Capitalism. *How would you differentiate your position from his?*

Jameson follows the mistake of Ernst Mandel and talks about late capitalism. Frankly, I see nothing late about contemporary capitalism. I cannot make the imaginative leap to the point where we don't have a capitalism of some kind. I can see the ways in which the market, however distorted, does allow for a certain individual choice, provided you a) have the means to exercise the choice and b) have things to choose from. There is a kind of transcendent capitalism – we know that the tendency of capitalism is towards monopoly and we see with Sky and BSB a classic example of what capitalism leads to – but postwar capitalism in Britain is modified and modulated by the Welfare State or what shreds of it remain.

Would you agree with Jameson when he talks about the need, in the conditions of postmodern culture, for what he calls cognitive mapping – the need to chart the cultural and political territory and to locate oneself on that chart?

Isn't that what a cultural historian tries to do? When I set out to write the trilogy I knew that I had to do a long march from 1939. I always keep a journal when I'm writing a book and the metaphor of the survey recurs throughout my own account of what I'm doing. The books of the trilogy are surveys in the sense that they're trying to establish trig points, if you like, from which discussion can reasonably begin.

In Future Tense, *there seems to be an imbalance between your perception of transcendent capitalism sweeping through everything and invading the minutest spaces of personal identity, and the kinds of cultural activity you bring in as a possible remedy for its ills – because it appears, in terms of your own argument, that those cultural activities are not powerful enough to effect any real change in global capitalism, and that in any case they are, given capitalism's transcendence, already the product of capitalism anyway, and have, in effect, been assimilated in advance. So the cultural means you call on to ameliorate the political and cultural problem you identify seem inadequate to the task. Do you feel that to be the case?*

Yes, I accept that. The reason that *Future Tense* has not been as well received as *The Heritage Industry*, insofar as anybody's noticed it at all, is precisely because it is doing something more difficult than *The Heritage Industry*, which was largely critical and destructive. *Future Tense* is trying to assert something positive. But the interesting dilemma in the way we look at culture is that, ever since Arnold, culture and society have always been opposed. They are held to have opposing values. In many ways I can see why that is so and indeed agree with that view. Nonetheless at the same time we have to recognize, if we are materialists, that culture is a product of society. Now somehow or other we have to work out a way of resolving that paradox, that contradiction. With *Future Tense*, is it not bound to be the case that on the one hand I'm presenting a vast generality which happens to express itself in some rather glamorous specifics like the Saatchi collection, and setting over against this the series of small individual acts by artists which are seen, probably, by very, very few people, although they do get through. And of course that is why *Future Tense* is very deliberately constructed on a series of images. It is consciously: so that you start with the reflective surfaces, the blinding mirror, of postmodernism, and then you discover that it is cracked and that within those cracks are areas of possibility. The metaphor of the crack, the fracture, does suggest that some alternative forms are growing and indeed it was, in a sense, a reference to cognitive mapping – by which I suggested that it might be that if all the cracks joined up we might emerge with a different pattern. But of course this is pure rhetoric.

In Future Tense, *you strongly advocate the development of a critical culture, which would look searchingly at both past and present. A crucial difficulty with that idea, particularly in a postmodernist context, is: where does criticism stop? Because there are kinds of postmodernism, or of modern American pragmatism – one thinks, most notably, of Richard Rorty – which say, in effect, that there is no solid and enduring basis for values and that although we do, in practice, stop somewhere at any given moment, we really needn't stop anywhere, so that criticism rests on nothing and could end by devouring itself. Thus the critical culture you advocate could subvert the values – liberal values, if you like – that you want to conserve and affirm, showing them to be relative, provisional, and implicated in structures of domination? What would be your response to that difficulty?*

I think you have to be a materialist in this and you have to look at the relationship between culture and economics and institutions and at the conscious and unconscious ideologies which construct our culture. To do all those things, you have to exercise your critical faculties in some way and you have to realize that you're living within a dynamic, a dialectic, you're living with change, and not be too worried by whether or not you're matching some absolute standard, because when you actually look at what people have done, if you're a historian rather than a literary critic, you can see that people's ideas, images and values have changed the whole time, so whether you like it or not we live in a shifting world. Obviously my values derive from being a member of the administrative class, having gone to public school and Oxford, and being white, male, middle-class and heterosexual. There's no doubt that I am a member of the Coleridgean self-appointed clerisy and I recognize that. I'm always tripping myself up on my own ideological assumptions. But the first step, I suppose, towards a critical culture is that you have to have a self-critical culture and have to recognize and admit the extent to which your views still respond to Leavisite, even Reithian ideas, and criticize and contest them. I think part of the problem in discussing cultural values is that we're talking about culture as an object: but the point is culture isn't an object, it's a mode of transmission which uses objects, representations, as modes of transmission. The problem in Anglo-Saxon culture is that we've always interpreted culture in terms of paintings and performances and so on, whereas these are merely the particular forms in which certain ideas are transmitted. Now those ideas originate in the social; they come out of society, they find certain forms of representation within a theatre or a football stadium, and the particular forms of representation contribute to the way that message is transmitted, in fact they shape it in many ways, so that *Daniel Deronda* as a novel and *Daniel Deronda* as a television series are not the same thing. They each modulate or, if you like, add a different kind of interference to the message, but the message returns to the social. And this is where I'm trying to evolve a theory of culture which is both a production theory and a consumption theory: the transmission theory. The questions the cultural historian first of all asks are: where does the message come from, how is it transmitted, and how is it received; and the critic in a sense actually criticizes the mode of transmission, and then asks: what is the value of this message to the society in which it is being transmitted and received. That is the critical judgement and that, if you like, can be a moral judgement. You could say that the bedrock of my cultural criticism is my commitment to the idea that there are certain injustices in the world which need to be eradicated. That doesn't make me a practising Marxist but it does give some sense of moral value, and certainly when I have to judge a play in a hundred words or fewer, at least a couple of those words will be devoted in some way to the truth of the experience which is being presented to me.

You've said that we don't know where we are unless we know where we've been and we don't know where we're going unless we know where we are. You've written about where we've been in your trilogy on postwar English culture and you've written about where we are, and how we should develop, in The Heritage Industry *and* Future Tense. *Could I ask, as we move into the 1990s, where you think we are going now?*

Since 1945 we have had, as it were, the thesis of welfare socialism and we then had the antithesis of welfare capitalism. It seems to me that, whatever happens, we're not now going to go back to the position of the Welfare State settlement. Whatever government gets in next, the commodification of culture, the pressure on the arts – particularly the performing arts, but in fact any kind of art – to earn their keep through the box office and business sponsorship and so on, will continue. It seems to me that one result of the profound cultural revolution that Mrs Thatcher has managed to achieve in this country has been the treatment of the arts as an extension of the public relations industry. I fear that's going to take a long time to change. We're not going to go back to some notional ideal of the Arts Council. I think that we will continue to see the arts, in relation to public subsidy, being used for instrumental purposes; that is to say, they will be used, as they are being and have been used in Glasgow and as they're being used in Birmingham, as a means of economic and cultural regeneration. I know that the Labour Party is proposing a Ministry of Culture and Media and that a small Arts Council would survive, but there would be much more emphasis on the regions and the new regional arts boards. But even though local authority arts funding and so on will improve a great deal if we have a Labour Government, there won't in fact be the money to sustain the sort of change that Jack Lang has achieved in France. That's what I believe is going to happen in terms of cultural affairs.

In terms of what artists are going to be doing, and by artists I mean all kinds of creative people, I do think that identity is going to be a major issue and, in particular, that masculinity is going to be a very important theme, not simply because we've done feminism and we've done gay rights, but because there is now the recognition of a much more pluralistic sexuality. Masculinity will be under pressure and challenge. But it's not just a question of individual identity: national identity is being dissolved by transcendent capitalism and also by the emergence of concepts like European unity, and I think we're going to see a corresponding resurgence of regional identities and regional link-ups – Birmingham to Barcelona – and of various kinds of nationalism. Now the real problem – and of course this is already happening in Eastern Europe – is: are these new national and regional identities going to be, on the whole, benevolent, or are they going to be fissiparous? What is interesting is that identity is formed and expressed through the arts, through culture, from your choice of shoes to what kind of plays you produce and what interpretation you put on those plays and those productions. So I think that in developed society culture, meaning more than just the fine arts though less possibly than the whole way of life, is going to be increasingly important.

Stephen Heath

Jesus College, Cambridge
12 July 1991

NICOLAS TREDELL: *Could you tell me about your family background and education prior to going to university?*

STEPHEN HEATH: I was born in Haringay, North London, of a family none of whose members over the generations had ever continued in education beyond the age of fourteen at most, so my background was not academic in any way. After the 'eleven-plus', I went to Enfield Grammar School which was very successfully committed to winning university places for its pupils, preferably Oxbridge places. Largely due to the school and the strength of that commitment – I didn't show any particular academic aptitude during my time there – I was carried along into the Sixth Form and then got into Cambridge by the skin of my teeth.

What was your experience of Cambridge?

My experience of Cambridge was one of complete shock, in rather the standard forms that someone coming from that kind of background would have and which have been recorded many times. It seemed like a mistake that I had been accepted and I spent a lot of my time in Cambridge nervously disliking it, since in any but the most formal senses 'acceptance' was indeed the problem. I felt socially inept and culturally out of things, though I suspect that the Cambridge of those days, thanks to the existence of grammar schools such as the one I went to, was taking in more people from different backgrounds than it does now. One of the features of Cambridge today is the regain in the imbalance between the state and the private sectors, the degree to which it appears quite literally to be a possession of the upper middle classes, part of their education system.

In the Preface to your book The Nouveau Roman, *published in 1972, you say that 'the teaching of Raymond Williams and Terry Eagleton gave meaning' to the time you spent as an undergraduate here (p. 12). Could you say more about that?*

I think I was too nervous and unsure when I was here as a student even to be given meaning to. That said, the presence and teaching of Raymond Williams and Terry Eagleton in the college I came to gave me a strong sense of what to do and why it would be worth doing. I remember working through very systematically on my own the reading Raymond must have done in order to write *Culture and Society* and attempting to understand in detail the whole history of which that book and *The Long Revolution* were themselves so much a part. From Terry, who did a great deal of the weekly supervising, I learnt much about the critical-historical analysis of writing and about the politics of such analysis. The academic work was for him, as for Raymond, fully alive: what you studied and the arguments you could have around it, all this was shown to be of real significance, which gave me an awareness that what I was doing would mean something eventually, despite all the difficulties I was having.

How did your turn towards French culture come about?

It would be hard to overestimate the extent of Raymond Williams's intellectual and political influence in the late sixties when I was reading English here. As I have already suggested, much of my student work was done in terms of thinking through the issues he had raised, the material he had used, the kind of cultural analysis and understanding of literature and writing he was proposing. The turn to what was going on in France was not in opposition to that but began to run alongside it, without me quite knowing how to put the two areas of work together for a while. In fact, it was unknowingly prompted by Williams himself, who set some topics for a college essay competition one of which was 'the anti-novel'. Now I had no idea whatsoever what that might be, and I never went in for the competition, but I did decide to try to find out about it; which led me to the *nouveau roman*, since I discovered that 'anti-novel' was a term that had been used by Sartre in connection with the work of Nathalie Sarraute. So the intellectual interest grew from there, from studying the contemporary French experimental novel, as I was able to do in my last year at Cambridge, very much on my own, finding out as much as I could about the theoretical context (it was more or less completely absent from the official teaching, though George Steiner was once or twice graciously allowed, by the Faculty that refused him a job, to give a mind-opening lecture). Hence I encountered the work of Roland Barthes and moved from his essays on Robbe-Grillet to the book on Racine which I tried to incorporate into my preparation for the exam paper on tragedy I had to take. The turn to French writing and thought happened that way, developing a little while I was an undergraduate without me having much of a hold on it and trying to accommodate it as best I could into what I needed to do for the Cambridge English course.

Had you learnt French at school?

Yes, in the way that everyone used to learn French at school, but that was about it. The relation to French, to the language, came later through excitement at the ideas and the theoretical and literary work I was discovering. There came a point at which I just fell in love with it all, and this brought the language on. I fell into that too. When I went to live and work in Paris after taking my degree, I had an experience of changing languages that was really quite complex for me. As I said, I didn't come from a background that was at ease with academic or intellectual speech and this, coupled with my naturally quite pronounced North London accent, made me feel very uneasy in language in Cambridge – the fear of not speaking 'properly' still haunts me, of not having control over the right language and not knowing where I am, being in a kind of constant linguistic dissociation, a constant social displacement. Turning to France was deeply liberating, both intellectually and linguistically – the two went together. To change language was the possibility of thinking differently and also of feeling at home, of resolving the conflicts I had in English; all of which fed into and ran out of the literary-theoretical emphases that were so much part of the work in France at that time, the whole stress on language indeed and the concern with the terms of subject-positioning in discourse. There was a pleasure in language which came easily for me in French but which Cambridge blocked for me in English. Philippe Sollers had a statement in one of his novels of that time about the need 'to change language in language'; for me, the change was also *from* a language. I wrote a piece about this all for *Le Magazine littéraire* in 1975, called inevitably enough 'Changer de langue'. Of course there then remained the problem of coming back into English.

What was the impact of Paris and of Barthes at that time – because this was really, wasn't it, the high semiotic moment?

It was even, still, the moment of approach to those heights. The impact for me was immediately, and always thereafter first and foremost, Barthes. I went to the seminar he was then giving, the seminar that subsequently became *S/Z*, and was held by the sheer intelligence in play, the intellectual fineness of the particular analyses and the general developments coming out of his reading of the Balzac story. I'd been brought up on practical criticism, an exercise for which I retain a certain respect and which I believe to have educational value, but nothing had prepared me for this relation of cultural-ideological analysis to linguistic and textual analysis that Barthes was inventing week by week. With it too went that presence of intelligence that Barthes produced, a kind of unemphatically strong, highly sensuous ethics of reading and reflection.

What do you think Barthes's standing is today? It's my impression that he's now far less cited and discussed than, say, Derrida.

It's true that Derrida has produced a specific school of criticism in a way that Barthes has not: whatever Derrida's misgivings and disclaimers, whatever the insistence on the need always to unsettle any given theoretical or critical confidence, deconstruction has itself been settled into a standard critical procedure and a powerfully influential body of theory ('deconstruction', indeed, has become something of a synonym for 'modern literary theory'). Barthes, it seems to me, is increasingly read as the great writer he was; at the same time that specific books and articles of his are cited and used in a whole variety of different contexts. There's a diversity in Barthes – an extraordinary range of concerns, procedures, insights – that has no parallel in Derrida, in whose work you find a level of repetition as deconstruction is ceaselessly deployed and redeployed (which possibility of repetition is one reason why he has produced a school – you can *do* deconstruction, *be* a deconstructionist). With Barthes, it's not an analytic system but an ethics of writing that moves around with signs and meanings, entering into questions of value, turning aside the hold of the stereotypical, interrogating power in language, envisioning utopias of 'meaning in peace' (no 'scenes'), exploring new forms of individualism through fictions of the subject, versions of the imaginary, incidences of the body... It's in that writing, I think, that his 'standing' must be seen today.

Obviously though, as I've already suggested, specific books and articles remain decisively influential, constantly helpful. *Mythologies*, with its development of semiotics to give a cultural-ideological analysis of the everyday, is a good example. It's an example too of something by Barthes that has passed into people's perceptions, become so much part of our seeing that we most often no longer refer to the book itself – Barthes, as it were, is *thinking in us*. A lot of his work now exists like that: the book on love, or the analysis of the Balzac story in *S/Z* which has changed our ways of thinking about fiction and narrative. Depending on what you're doing, at any moment, this or that from Barthes will come back.

You wrote a book about Barthes in French, Vertige du déplacement, *which came out in 1974, and you became involved, through Barthes, with Philippe Sollers and Julia Kristeva, and with the journal* Tel Quel *at the period of its greatest influence. What was it like to be involved with* Tel Quel *at that time?*

It was exciting. *Tel Quel* must count as one of the great avant-garde literary reviews of the twentieth century in its influence and the quality of its writing. To be involved with it, even in a modest way, had a significance for me that preparing a thesis for Cambridge – which is what I was probably supposed to be doing at that point – simply couldn't. The basic *Tel Quel* premise was that revolution in language and revolution in social structure were necessarily interdependent and in some sense simultaneous. This was not a new position – it's one that can be found in one form or another in many twentieth-century avant-garde movements – but in the immediate context of 1968 it had very powerful and practical effects. It made political sense of literature as the mode of the accomplishment of the revolution in language; it gave a programme of intellectual work (evaluating texts in relation to their practice of writing, elaborating theoretical understanding of the politics of language and its poetic transformation); it offered urgency and value to a cultural work of critique and opposition in the politically confused post-1968 moment when the old versions of politics were deadeningly reasserting themselves. Much was achieved in those terms, but there was also a kind of literalization of the idea of the simultaneity of linguistic and social revolutions at points which produced very unlikely and damaging accounts of things. Julia Kristeva's *La Révolution du langage poétique*, published in 1974, which I reviewed at that time in a long piece for *Critique* entitled 'Théâtre du langage', can be read as the most thorough and far-reaching theoretical treatment of what the linguistic and social-political independence might mean, of the specificity of 'poetic revolution', of how we need to understand the relations of the subject in language, and so on. Ironically, with hindsight, we can see that Kristeva's book came at the moment when *Tel Quel* would begin to move away from its radical political impetus.

Why do you think the Tel Quel *project which you outline – that of combining the idea of political revolution with the idea of revolution in language – broke down?*

I think it was largely the kind of romantic Maoism to which the project became attached, the whole self-confirming investment in China and the cultural revolution. One can see something of the rationale for this (if 'rationale' is the right word) in the French context of the time. You had a powerful and sclerotic Communist Party deeply entrenched in dogmatic reference to the Soviet Union, quite unlike its counterparts in Western Europe. Maoism, the cultural revolution, were taken over as the grounds for a euphoric vision of revolution and transformation, outside of the Soviet reference, in direct opposition to the French CP. Though more than simply a strategy, *Tel Quel*'s Maoism had a very strategic function as the expression of that opposition and the violence of this was extreme – it can be seen in the little bulletin *Tel Quel Informations* which was brought out a few times in virulent attack on the PCF, its leaders, its press, its writers (Aragon especially). Of course, there was a limit to the amount of sublimation of what was really happening in China that you could manage, and the *Tel Quel* trip to China in 1974, although the responses were muted in the immediate aftermath, shifted the perception of things: the militant Maoist image could no longer hold.

Much of Tel Quel's *work, and your own work at that time, was linked with the* nouveau roman, *on which you wrote the book that appeared in 1972. Could I ask how you see the status of the* nouveau roman *today, particularly in the light of some remarks on Fredric Jameson's recent book on postmodernism. He places it as a distinct retro-mode by saying '[s]ome will remember what reading a* nouveau roman *felt like' and raises a number of questions – for example, '[i]f the* nouveau roman *is over, can it have been a fad and still have literary or aesthetic value today?', and '[c]an certain books have become unreadable since feminism?' – I suppose Robbe-Grillet is the most obvious reference here (*Postmodernism, or, The Cultural Logic of

Late Capitalism, pp. 131-2). So the general question arises: what would you feel to be the value of reading the nouveau roman *today other than perhaps that of trying to recover a certain historical moment when those works did indeed seem – and this comes across strongly in your book – tremendously exciting and radical?*

Firstly, I think that the *nouveau roman* and *Tel Quel* were different. *Tel Quel* was informed by the kinds of questioning and disruption of the novel, of its assumptions of representation, that the *nouveau roman* had produced; at the same time, it was already reading the latter as a practice of writing without a politics of writing, as not engaging with the matter of subjectivity and meaning. The *nouveau roman*, in other words, was an important part of contemporary writing but was blocked in a literary formalism, as distinct from the semiotic/symbolic revolutionary exploration of language that was *Tel Quel*'s project. Secondly, Robbe-Grillet hadn't at that point moved into – or was only just beginning to move into – his subsequently characteristic postmodernist use and exploitation of the detritus of contemporary cultural pornography. If one looks back now at the early works, one can see the elements of the later development; but at the time, novels such as *Les Gommes* or *La Jalousie* were very powerful explorations of the terms of representation, realism, reality, perception, fiction, reading... They stand as classics, with an impact when they appeared such as Jameson suggests but also with continuing impact and value today. Similarly for, say, Sarraute's work – *Tropismes, Portrait d'un inconnu*, these retain the possibility of the new literary experience they were, even if the possibility is inevitably realized differently today, without the same excitement. That later development of Robbe-Grillet, though, is another kettle of fish: much of the work has become unreadable since feminism, rightly so.

What about the Sollers texts of that period? Do you think they are read today?

Probably not, except academically, in order to understand the history. Texts like *Drame* or *Nombres* were theoretical fictions, powerful attempts to hollow away all the traditional contents of the novel and come close to the dramas of the subject in process in language, in the orders and disorders of meaning and meanings. They were purposeful inscriptions of key themes of writing and history, with scriptural gestures at other economies of signification. Which brings us back to China, with Sollers's use of Chinese references, Chinese characters physically there on the page. There's an interesting piece to be written one day – perhaps it has been – on the importance of Chinese language and script, their *appeal*, at certain key avant-garde moments in the twentieth century; think of Pound, Eisenstein, Brecht ... (we should include too the kinds of reference to Chinese and other non-alphabetic writings generally in, for example, Freud, Wittgenstein...). Sollers's work had its evident relation to this tradition and the political-visionary Maoism had its point of juncture with avant-garde literary practice ready to hand in that appeal to and of Chinese writing. So Sollers's texts of the time have their status as theoretical fictions; they can be read now in the same sense that one could go back and read the issues of *Tel Quel* from the same period – texts and journal run into each other.

One important result of the developments around Tel Quel *and the* nouveau roman *was that it offered new and fruitful ways of reading* Joyce's work, especially Finnegans Wake. *You yourself wrote about Joyce in* Tel Quel – *for example, in the essay 'Ambiviolences' (*Tel Quel *no. 50, Summer 1972, pp. 24-43 and no. 51, Autumn 1972, pp. 64-76; English translation in D. Attridge and D. Ferrer, eds,* Post-Structuralist Joyce, *Cambridge 1974, pp. 31-68). Could you tell us about your engagement with Joyce's work at that time?*

Although Joyce had lived and been published in France, his work by then seemed to have lost whatever existence it had had there; certainly, it lacked any effective contemporary literary and literary-theoretical presence. Cixous had written her huge thesis on Joyce, but it was mostly in conventional academic terms, notwithstanding a few Derridean-oriented pages at the end. Derrida himself had gestured towards Joyce in a wonderful footnote in his introduction to Husserl's *Origin of Geometry*, just some lines on *Ulysses*. That was about it, and no one, of course, seemed to have read *Finnegans Wake*, to have any particular idea of what to do with it, me included. At which point Sollers said to me something along the lines of 'Joyce has got to be important, we need something in *Tel Quel*, write it'. So surrounded by the writing going on, the theoretical work being produced, I read and re-read in Joyce's work, especially *Finnegans Wake* of which I'd only read this or that brief run of pages before and which had clearly now become an available contemporary text in a way it hadn't previously been, and everything came together, resulting in the long piece you mention. Lots of interest then began to get focused on Joyce. Sollers himself became deeply involved and I spent two or three mornings a week with him reading the *Wake*, translating bits, which was a great experience for me, being in contact with Joyce's text through Sollers's brilliance, his extraordinary perceptions of language. The tangible result was the translation of fragments of the last section, which appeared in *Tel Quel* in 1974 and for which I wrote an introduction dealing with the *Wake*'s recasting of questions of language, sexuality, and origins.

Could we come back to England now, and talk first of all about Frank Kermode's University College London seminars, which seem to have been very important in disseminating structuralist and post-structuralist ideas into English intellectual life and in which, according to Kermode, you played a leading role (see pp. 24-5 above). What was your own view of those seminars?

I think Frank is being really kind, or else discreetly saying I was unbearable. But there's no doubt that those seminars were important, to the extent that such things can be important. They decisively influenced a number of people's intellectual lives; though for me the decisive influence had come directly from Barthes and the work I was doing for him. What the seminars did give me was a context, a space in which issues could be explored that seemed unavailable anywhere else in England. They could provoke the same kind of intellectual excitement to be found in Barthes's seminar at the Ecole Pratique or Derrida's course at the Ecole Normale. Kermode had the gift of getting together a range of interesting – and diversely interested – people to confront the theories and texts that were being produced in France, this along with a range of other ideas, different versions of things. The main focus was, broadly, the poetics of fiction; it caught up and extended Kermode's own central concerns, took *The Sense of an Ending* towards the subsequent major work on narrative and interpretation, fiction and history.

You were also very much involved with the journal Screen *during its period of greatest influence, when it tried, drawing on psycho-analysis and poststructuralism, to find new terms for the analysis of cinema in the context of a much broader social and political and aesthetic critique. You were on the editorial board from 1973, and you contributed a number of major essays which are still widely cited (for example, 'Film and System: Terms of Analysis',* Screen *vol. 16 no. 1, Spring 1975, pp. 7-77 and vol. 16 no. 2, Summer 1975, pp.*

91-113, and 'Difference', Screen vol. 19 no. 3, Autumn 1978, pp. 51-112). What was it like working on Screen at that time?

For me, it was a tremendous learning process, however tiring the continual intellectual and political questioning and battling could be. I have instant physical memories of long evening hours spent in the office we had in Old Compton Street, with Soho lights and street noise as backdrop to the intensity of our debates. There was a sense of inventing a cultural politics around education and the media, of thinking about what the critique and transformation of film and then television might be. *Screen* had a marginal institutional position as a subsidiary part of the Society for Education in Film and Television which was itself an outpost of the British Film Institute; at the same time, it interconnected in various ways with the educational sector, with various cultural and radical bodies, with a number of independent film-making groups, and so on. These interconnections were often difficult, contradictory, and tense, which was the point, the impetus in the working through of the issues. More than a journal, *Screen* was also meetings, weekend schools, interventions in different kinds of event, a whole educational process sharply centred on matters of cultural-political analysis. How do you think about, analyse, understand, effectively criticize and change such powerful and widely received social productions of meaning as film and television?

A major criticism of Screen, both at the time and subsequently. is that, in pursuing its exploration of film, it overvalued psychoanalysis and took it as offering a transhistorical, universal account of the functioning of mechanisms of identification that were activated by cinema. What would you say to that criticism?

The question, as I said, was that of understanding how film and television functioned to produce meaning; and at different levels: not just this film is about this or that, but equally this form of narrative fiction film involves these terms of representation, this kind of construction and conjunction of images and sounds brings these ways of making and limiting sense, with these effects... An important aspect of the project thus became looking at the specific institutions of cinema· and television as we know them, as they have been developed. What's at stake in going to 'the cinema' or watching 'television'? Part of an answer to that question involves exploring the psychological mechanisms utilized, the terms of the subjectivity set by our cinema and television. This was where psychoanalysis entered the picture, where we got into considerations of fetishism, voyeurism, fantasy, and so on – the positioning of the viewer as subject in the instituted forms of these 'media'. The subsequent account of cinema – our initial work was centred on film – did not say that there was only one possible subject-positioning; it said that historically there was a development of film into this dominant cinema, *this* institution, which is a matter not just of economic and technological factors but of their cultural configuration in specific possibilities of subject-meaning production: their configuration as '*cinema*'. Now, every film is *in* cinema, within or in relation to this dominant and defining institution, but it is always also *more than* cinema, is an operation of cinema that has its own particular material complexity, that realizes, redeploys, recasts the institutional terms. So simultaneous with the analysis of 'cinema', there developed, too, a use of psychoanalysis to read individual films, to think about their particular narrative strategies and representations, moving back from there to cinema, to how films brought with them the repetition of certain forms of articulation and closure, how that realization-redeployment-recasting of the cinematic apparatus *worked*. The feeling was that if we were going to understand film and cinema culturally and ideologically, then we were going to have to get beyond analysing 'contents', or 'structures' even. There was no political value to be got out of some formalist structural analysis (old styles of content analysis were more useful and necessary than that); what had to be looked at was the subjectivity the film invokes, how it sets the viewer up as viewer, positions you, moves you along. It's not that this is totally, monolithically determining of your relation to the film; the point is rather that there are grounds of subject-positioning that the film, in cinema, involves you in even as you take your distances. The aim was to arrive at a mode of analysis that would neither collapse a text or a cultural form into being absolutely determining (imposing the one reading on a passive viewer) nor simply push it out of the sphere of critique by saying that it didn't determine at all (an active viewer who would simply make up his or her own individual reading). We were trying to negotiate an analysis that brought determination and indetermination together. The point was the historical nature of the production of meaning, of 'readings', with that history including the specific terms of subjectivity realized in the institution of cinema, the conventions of filmic narrative, filmic genres, and so on. From which you could then think more effectively about possibilities of transformation, alternative images, different practices.

There were times, however, when we put the weight so heavily on describing the subjectivity constructed that we could be, and were, criticized for giving a deterministic account. But whatever the failings, the criticisms that have sometimes rightly been made, *Screen* played a large part in putting questions of subjectivity in new and important ways into cultural analysis, cultural studies, and produced work which is fundamental to people's conceptions today, work that people build on – think only of Laura Mulvey's essay on 'Visual Pleasure and Narrative Cinema'.

You'd worked with Barthes and Tel Quel *and you were working on* Screen, *but you were also, in the 1970s, teaching in Cambridge and involved in the movement for reform of the English Tripos here. What kind of reforms would you have liked to have seen in Cambridge?*

It has to be said that the Cambridge English Faculty in the mid-1970s, however unbelievable this now seems, looked as though it might be an arena for lively intellectual development. Kermode had just arrived from London to take up the Regius Professorship, Williams was here, there was a range of interesting younger people, even the new appointment of Christopher Ricks could be seen positively, as the arrival of someone able to enter debates from a more traditional position in literary studies with a competence that we'd hitherto badly missed here. The situation as regards the English course itself was basically that it was the same course that I'd taken a few years earlier, that Terry Eagleton had taken before me, and, quite frankly, that Raymond Williams had taken in the period of World War Two. 1968 and its aftermath had produced – it's difficult now to recapture this and it was, and will be, denied very powerfully – extraordinary panic and fear; 'extraordinary' because we're not talking about much more in Cambridge than some small-scale student sit-ins and some general agitation. As far as the English Faculty was concerned, the panic and fear translated into a response to demands for change that came down to maintaining what was there while simultaneously saying we'll add on this or that and then this or that, in a kind of self-protective collapse. There was, that is, little, if any, attempt to rethink the bases of the course, to reconstruct a course that would be educationally responsible and effective for the present.

In the mid-seventies a group of us thought that the moment had come to approach this task of rethinking and reconstructing, to provide a better context for students to learn and work in. A big problem was – it still is – that the first two years are spent doing this massive sweep of English literature from 1350 to the present day, in the name of 'coverage', an indicatively dampening word. The result is that students feel they are rushed from author to author week by week, and with no particular rationale of study, just 'English literature'. There is more literature now (the growth of academic studies has extended the field), no self-evident tradition to follow, and the common educational level of incoming students is no longer what it might once have been assumed to be (range of cultural knowledge, linguistic skills, etc. are different). We believed that there must be some way of reorganizing things so that the student could get an educational base in the first year, a foundation year, and then move on to a two-year Part II course that would have more flexibility, allowing individuals realistically to build up something of their own course. That Part II, as well as the Part I, would include current concerns around critical theory, gender and identity, minority and colonial discourses, and so on, but integrally, not just added on as a 'special paper'. The proposals, in fact, were rather conservative: we didn't propose that we go out and teach 'Theory' (none of us had any interest in that); we said, simply, let's get some coherence, let's give people the conditions they need for doing English now, educationally, intellectually.

Why then do you think the proposals of the group with which you were involved aroused the degree of hostility that culminated in the MacCabe affair and the crushing of the reform movement?

If you go back to the 1950s, Leavis, though in some senses marginal, and certainly dependent for his self-presentation on an idea of marginality, was in fact dominantly influential in what the study of English was and what it was about. I don't mean that everyone in the Cambridge English Faculty was 'a Leavisite' – not at all – but there was agreement as to what was to be studied and as to the values it embodied, at least as to the terms of the critical discussion of values. Something like practical criticism, which was a central part of Cambridge English and was so powerful in schools and other universities, was dependent on a consensual version of what was at stake and you could have critical discussions on that consensual basis. Now, for a whole number of reasons – which include the expansion of the universities, the increased numbers and diversity of the student body (even if not that much in Cambridge), the professionalization and massive growth of English studies (especially in the US), pressures against the accepted and defining tradition of English literature from newly identified groupings of readers – the consensual centre has given way: there's less and less certainty about central values. The academic result in Cambridge, as often elsewhere, was the exacerbation of a defensive complementarity: on the one hand, the appeal to scholarship – we've got the facts, we can get on with our literary history and research; on the other, the appeal to the value of literature as a question of personal response and fulfilment – the poem just speaks to you. But there was no way of holding these things together in the way that Leavis held together a literary history and a question of responsive – 'mature' – reading.

I remember a lecture at the time of the MacCabe affair in which a member of the Faculty Board made a lengthy plea for the undefined importance of studying the equally undefined 'facts', before briefly turning at the end to a demonstration of 'what we are here for' which consisted in the reading aloud of a poem by, we were merely told, 'a girl from Hong Kong': nothing between the facts, the specialist's bread-and-butter that nourishes professional status and claims to neutrality, and the naked response, the instantaneous assent to the poem, 'the literary experience' which turns out not to need any of those facts. It was the absence of centre that made the existence of a group of people who looked as though they might be about to propose one seem so dangerous: it was fine as long as a few youngsters were following their individual quirks but the perception that there might be some coherent proposal, involving Williams and Kermode, was very threatening. The reaction was latched on to, quite ludicrously, a fear of 'foreign theory', provoking the aggressive assertion of a mission 'to protect English' (remember that all this took place in the heady first years of Thatcherism). The theory supposedly involved was said to bring imposed meanings ('Marxism', this directed at Williams), no meanings at all ('Deconstruction', this directed at Kermode), plus the suppression of literature (directed at me, possibly because I taught a course on film). Since this was all a bit difficult, 'Structuralism' surfaced as the key, ignorant, catch-all word; it meant 'everything we don't like'.

Could we move on to your book The Sexual Fix *which appeared in 1982. Your argument in that book is that 'what we have experienced and are experiencing is the fabrication of a "sexuality"...through a set of representations...that make up this sexuality to which we are then referred and held in our lives, a whole* sexual fix *precisely; the much-vaunted "liberation" of sexuality…is thus not a liberation but a myth, an ideology, the definition of a new mode of conformity (that can be understood, moreover, in relation to the capitalist system, the production of a commodity "sexuality")'. The Sexual Fix is a very forceful and funny book, but isn't it, in a sense, undialectical or undialogical? You say, at the outset, that the contradictions of your argument should equally be stressed, and that '[t]o say that liberation is the definition of a new mode of conformity has to be accompanied by the recognition nevertheless of what has been in many respects a truly liberating progress: we do, clearly, live in a dramatically improved sexual freedom when compared with our Victorian ancestors' (p. 3). But it seems to me that in the insistent polemic of the book, that sense of contradiction, the sense that the stress on sexuality is both liberating and coercive, tends to get lost. Would you feel that to be the case?*

It's a valid point, there is a question of emphasis, and perhaps I would do it differently now. At the time, I think it had to be that way. There was no problem then about the liberation bit, that was screamed at you from the pages of every magazine you picked up – you were always being invited to congratulate yourself on its achievement and learn to live up to it. *The Sexual Fix* was written against the grain of that. I think I do state, as in the passage you read out, the contradictory nature of liberation here: sexual liberation brought with it real advances, new possibilities, at the same time that it was welded into a compulsory, narrowly-conceived, male-defined heterosexuality. There was a whole conformism of sexual standards and imperatives; that's what I was interested in analyzing. The silly version of your point was that of all those people who got off on saying that *The Sexual Fix* was 'puritan' – a predictable response straight out of the ethos I was describing.

Could we focus on one question in particular that arises from The Sexual Fix *– the question of censorship. In the dialogue at the end of the book, 'Y' says 'I don't see how from the left there can be anything but sustained political and ethical opposition to pornography': when 'X' challenges '[s]o then it's censorship', 'Y' responds that '[t]he challenge for a left practice…is to speak and act in relation to all this without falling into the terms of the right-wing moral opposition movements, the terms of Lord Longford or Mary Whitehouse or David Holbrook. And those terms include censorship. What we need, in the struggle within this existing society, is to find new and*

*original and educative ways of protest and resistance' (pp. 163-4). So
'Y' seems to reject censorship there. But isn't opposition to pornography, and, more widely, to certain kinds of, say, sexist representations going to mean, within this existing society, censorship of some
kind – even if not of a formal or legal kind? From the perspective of
'Y', won't the nettle of censorship have to be grasped – positive censorship, if you like, on the analogy with positive discrimination, but
censorship nonetheless? And if you're going to have censorship, isn't
it better, as George Steiner has suggested, that it be of a public and
formal kind because it can then be challenged (see p. 83 above)?*

It's a big question, one that I don't know how to answer. I have contradictory views which I believe have to be held together in thinking
about this, at least for the moment. There's been a glorification – an
'extra-specialization' – of sexuality in our societies, leading people,
who are willing to accede to arguments about censorship in an area
such as racism, categorically to refuse any discussion of them when
it comes to pornography, to anything that seems to involve sexuality.
So I think that there's an important initial stage which is saying sexuality is not something special in the ways that it is assertively presented as being, which is insisting that we need to look at what is at
stake in this 'sexuality' that is taken as so special, *and for whom.*
Then we always need too, concomitantly, to refuse to accept any
suggestion of some assumed self-evident relation between pornography and the free expression of sexuality. What's important is not
to start from a position of assent to exactly the system of sexuality
that I was concerned with in *The Sexual Fix.* From there, I can only
go on to say that I feel that there should be censorship of pornography at the same time that I have or see problems with censorship
in its classic forms. We need, therefore, to imagine new forms of censorship ('censorship' may then be the wrong word).

What should they be? Well, I believe that in relation to the dominant industry of pornography, from porno movies to the mass-dis-
tribution magazine pornography you find in newsagents, there's one
simple measure to be thought about: divorcing pornography from
profit. One way of answering the difficulties that people have, that I
have, is to say in relation to pornography, not that this or that is banned, that it can't be produced, but that it cannot be done for profit,
that all profit arising will be socially redistributed, preferably chan-
nelled into educational projects around issues of sexual violence and
homophobia. It's a paradox to use the profits of oppression to help
work against the oppression, but it seems to me an acceptable form

of censorship to curtail profit from pornography – and, of course, it could, would, remove levels of oppression in its 'industry', the exploitation of the people hired or coerced for the making of pornography. There are other forms of censorship one can think about, such as changing the terms of its distribution so that its reception is subject to certain conditions – making it carry social health warnings detailing its offensiveness to large numbers of people and the climate of sexual harassment it creates; stipulating forms of educational display about arguments around pornography in places where films, say, are exhibited...I can imagine all sorts of ways in which one could, without any traditional censorship of pornography, significantly change the terms of its social reality. But I'll always come back to the matter of profit and of recasting the ownership and control of the means of production. Let's not say pornography can't be made; let's change how and why it's made. This could be tried out in our societies without any substantial infringement of freedom of expression and we could then see what would happen.

It's not in itself an adequate answer, it still doesn't alter facts of the relations between pornography and sexism and the climate of social-sexual violence. But then, if one did try such a censorship, it's possible that the nature of the pornography would change. If the ownership of the means of production were in the hands of those caught up in its production, if there's no profit, how do we know what we'd get? So I can see possible strategies for accommodating my desire for censorship with my distress at censorship, strategies that would be as eminently 'public' as the mode of censorship George Steiner is referring to. Let me add, finally, that I feel a good deal more serious attention should be paid to the work of Catharine MacKinnon and others in the United States which is seeking to arrive at a feminist jurisprudence on this issue; one concern, for example, is to establish grounds on which actions could be brought against pornography for sex discrimination, incitement to violence against women, etc. Note that this again would not be a matter of *ante-facto* censorship.

Could we pursue a broader issue which leads on from the question of censorship and indeed has implications beyond sex and gender. The Sexual Fix *is a strongly anti-normative work. It's against the setting and fixing of gender identity and sexual practice and experience. Nonetheless it seems to me that a kind of norm does begin to emerge in the book, a non-normative norm if you like, in which gender and sexual and personal identity are not fixed and rigid but constantly mobile and displaced and dispersed. In other words, what you seem*

to be working towards is a norm or ethic of difference. Would you
feel that to be the case?

I feel that to be the case and I'm happy with some ways in which difference can be used as an expectation of what things might be like, of
what can be worked for from today. There's a phrase going through
my mind that I think must be a condensed expression of something I
got very powerfully from Barthes, though he may never have said it
in quite this form; a phrase to the effect that fundamental to our politics should be a utopian vision of a world exclusively of differences
such that no difference is exclusive. In that sense of ambition for a
world of difference in which there is then – by definition – no difference which is one of exclusion, I'm in agreement with your formulations. I'm less happy, though, with the 'everything-is-a-play-of-dif-
ferences' school of theory; and much less happy again when that
theory does service for thinking about anything in particular,
becomes a means of not thinking to any concretely political-ethical
purpose. There are politically pressing issues of identity and identifications, subjectivity and its social constructions and interactions,
that the theoretical language of 'differences' can quickly obscure and
avoid.

You imply a distinction between the idea of difference as a utopian
intimation – the Barthesean idea – and the idea of difference that
appears in some forms of postmodernism – in Baudrillard, for exam-
ple – where it's a matter of an endless play of differences that dis-
perses any utopian or emancipatory critique. It seems to me that
there is a great difficulty now in making a distinction between what
one might call valid kinds of difference and kinds of difference that
are in a sense products and reinforcements of the kind of society we
have, that are really modes of indifference and conformity. One
could argue that contemporary Western society is now into a differ-
ence fix. In order to distinguish between differences, don't we have
to reintroduce the notion of normative criteria?

For me it would be a matter of what I take to be an important area
for thought and work today, an area that needs to be recovered: that
of what I've called the *political-ethical*. The translation of this into
'the reintroduction of normative criteria' is exactly the kind of
automatic response we need to learn to move on and away from. If
'normative' means the imposition of oppressive, anti-human, so-
called 'standards' of behaviour, then this is clearly not what is at

stake. But the opposition to norms in those terms does not put paid to the need to make judgements, to use a fashionably unfashionable word. One of the things I believe now to be essential is establishing the terms and working out the possibilities of making such distinctions, distinctions that are non-oppressive *and themselves creative and protective of non-oppression*. Current modes of liberalism have produced a kind of paralysing fear of evaluation and judgement, while postmodernism has been set up as the alibi for white intellectuals to abandon responsibility and bliss out in the consumerist relativization of cultures, meanings, values, in an apolitical surface-world of simulacra that, precisely, they can afford. Hence the need to recover the political-ethical dimension, to face the difficult matters of distinction, evaluation, judgement – human 'criteria', if you like. That's what's needed, for example, with pornography.

A lot of issues that are important in this context, acutely important for the nineties, come together for me around the question of *representation*. Here we are in a situation in which we have demands on and critiques of representation by various groups concerned with the inadequacies of existing political representational systems. We also have a critique of representation by high theory which undermines the grounds of any representation or, the same thing, converts everything into representation (there is nothing that representation represents, there are only other representations, endlessly reflecting one another); this in societies that are, indeed, saturated with representations, permeated with media culture. The result of which – the Baudrillardian analysis, itself a kind of condensed development of the commonplaces of this culture and its producers – is that the idea of representation is anachronistic.

The saturation is such that we have passed into a new age of simulation: there is no longer any identifiable representation, no identity to represent; we are in 'the screen-stage', everything is just tele-existent. All the old political realities 'disappear'; there are no social signifiers to give sense to any political signifiers. Don't talk of emancipation, alienation, or whatever, it's not cool, it plunges you back – oh, horror! – into matters of representation. So there's a struggle for and around representation, which, of course, is a central notion and aspiration in the modern history of the West; and outside that history too, in the democratic ideals that can be derived from it and used in political struggles in non-Western societies. Of course, it was always a notion that was in crisis, from the moment it appeared, since it's bound up with notions of likeness and identity, and the process of a group's coming into representative identity is immediately challenged by the exclusion of other identities which historically, on the basis of this very notion and the project of recognition it suggests, then make their own claims to be represented (think simply of the representational history in nineteenth-century Britain of the middle classes, working classes, women). It's a crisis term too in epistemology, in thinking about knowledge and the nature of its relation to the world outside the mind. It solves the problem – knowledge is a representation of the world – at the same time that it becomes itself the problem: that of the grounds of correspondence with how things really are, of securing the status and faithfulness of representations. And it's then also an aesthetically important term, bound up with the development of realism which, in turn, involves critical questions as to what counts as significantly real, representatively identifiable. Representation has that political, epistemological, and aesthetic history, and today is this crucial site of struggle and theory and cultural production. What I see as going to be central over the next few years are the terms of identity and their relation to representation (across all its fields), the reassessment of representation as an adequate political concept and goal, and the urge to find new modes of representing that recognize likeness or representativeness *without constraints*, something in the order of a non-representative representation – neither old immobility nor postmodern superficiality, but necessary *processes of identification*. That's one necessarily paradoxical way of talking about the political-ethical without returning to an oppressive version of the normative yet retaining the necessity of questions of value, which for me is primordial. I can't imagine a socialism that does not involve the negotiation of human values; and this involves the constant risk of transcendence – if one can no longer stay with the old, fixed Western universals, neither can one give up to some crude cultural relativism.

Isn't there a crucial contradiction between your desire for humanly transcendent values and your desire, in your writing and teaching, to produce a critical consciousness of the ways in which values are never simply given, but constructed in particular cultures? Won't a consciousness that one's values are the constructs of a particular culture always threaten to subvert any attempt to construct transcendent transcultural values?

I can first of all agree that the transcultural is always going to be raised, posited, worked to, from the cultural – you're within some culture. Let me then add, though, that there's a dangerous tendency to think of culture and cultures as unified entities, coherent blocks of identity (the history of the word itself, with its connotations of organic growth, and reductionist anthropological visions of 'other cultures', have not been helpful). Being in a culture is more like being in a mesh of interacting – sometimes connecting, sometimes disconnecting – areas of meaning and knowledge and custom and so on. So that the transcultural isn't to be imagined as a person held in some unified culture and then stepping out of it into a realm of non-culture. It's not about the negotiation of values somehow from outside culture that are then brought back in and also imposed elsewhere. On the contrary, to talk about the transcultural is to indicate values which can be derived from and seen to permeate across cultures; values of which some cultures in a given instance will offer a realization, while others in certain of their practices may be a shocking denial. Producing a critical consciousness, which is what I take education to be fundamentally concerned with, is for me partly a matter of calling into question things that are taken for granted, things we assume culturally, but it is equally about the derivation from cultures, ours included, of critical values – 'critical' in the sense of the values from which one makes criticism and in the senses of values which are *critical*: they're *critically* the basis of what, across and through cultures, we can produce as the definition and recognition of the human, of human being. We only ever define and recognize the human in relation to culture, so the deconstructionist critique of grounds will always be possible, necessary indeed; but who ever thought that grounds could only be the kind of rigid, blind-spot, foundational bedrock that deconstruction is so taken with? Producing critical consciousness is for me more profitably about calling into question ideas of the unity of culture, about examining the claims and the realities of culture as the expression of an identity, about seeing ways in which the practices of people, as 'culture', can be split up, looked at differently, in their actual processes. Political-ethical intervention depends on this critical cultural thinking and has as its pivotal point the appeal to values which cannot be conceived as merely cultural; one is going to have to say – and I think socialism has its grounds in this – that there are terms of respect, non-violence, non-constraint, and so on which are fundamental and not – in that simple, limiting, relativist sense – cultural. There's no way for me of avoiding a discourse and a project of emancipation (once again, in whose interest is it to avoid them?) and that includes, finally, emancipation from some fixed cultural identity, even if the construction and assertion of some identifying unity of culture may be an essential part for a specific group at a specific conjuncture of political struggle for emancipation.

Brian Cox

University of Manchester
20 August 1991

NICOLAS TREDELL: *Could I start by asking about your cultural and educational background prior to university?*

BRIAN COX: Reading mattered from the very earliest days. We had very few books in the house – my father bought H.G Wells's *Outline of History* in monthly instalments, and that and an encyclopaedia was all we had, so the Grimsby public library was important. I was very fortunate in that I went to a working class housing estate elementary school that was known to be about the best academically in Grimsby – and this was the 1930s, when such schools could be very good indeed. I then got a scholarship in 1939 to a co-educational school in Grimsby, so I was there during the war. I'm rather proud of the fact that it wasn't even called a grammar school because it didn't become one until the 1944 Act. I think the co-educational side of the school was very important in my development. The atmosphere in the school was excellent, but academically it was not a very good school and I learnt a lot about the difficulties, I think, of that kind of school. The grades that I got in what is now called 'A' Level are lower than those required for entrance to my English department, and I was very lucky really because in my second year in the sixth form I applied for London University and was rejected, but in those days you could get a period of exemption from the Army to take Oxbridge entrance. So I did that and got a scholarship to Cambridge.

What was Cambridge like for you?

I went up in 1949 and I think in a way I was unlucky in that this was before people like Donald Davie and John Holloway arrived. The lecturers were people like Joan Bennett, and I don't want to be unkind, but by and large she was giving the same lectures in 1949 as in her book on the Metaphysicals of the 1930s. Leavis dominated, and I went to his seminar for one term. At the time, and for many years afterwards, I thought that I was in reaction against him, but I think retrospectively one realizes that a great deal of the ambience was dominated by him. When Dylan Thomas came to read his verse in Cambridge I didn't go, and I feel very ashamed of that. One had contempt for his poetry, one was almost taught to have contempt. I think I was very lucky not to be at Downing because under Matthew Hodgart at Pembroke, one kept sufficiently separate, whereas many of the people that went from Downing disappeared without trace because of Leavis's influence. The major thing that happened to me was that at school I wrote verse, and in the Army – I was a conscript in the Education Corps for two years – I wrote a novel – a bad one, only half-completed – but when I arrived at Cambridge and came under the influence of Leavis I stopped writing. That's a very common experience, of course, and I think it took me a long time, almost until I began to edit *Critical Quarterly* and see a great deal of minor verse, to get back the confidence to write. In that way, Leavis did much harm.

What were the ways in which you dissented from Leavis?

I suppose it's fundamentally the narrowness of his concept of the great tradition. I prefer a much more generous view. I love minor poetry, wandering through the eighteenth century, and all kinds of things of that sort which I think are crucial really to one's sense of language and possibilities. I think Leavis imposed – this has been said often enough, hasn't it – this strong puritanical view, and obviously he was very much against the twentieth century as well in his writings. It led to a kind of pomposity I think we indulged in. My thesis, which was a disaster, was called 'Moral Implications in the Fiction of Henry James', and what can sound more pompous than that?

What did you take from Leavis in a positive sense?

I think I would still accept many of his basic assumptions. The kind of arguments that I felt I was having with his influence are now seen as minor. I still believe, very much so, in a great tradition, but in a much wider and more generous concept than his. I still believe that the canon, which is so central to the Cox Report, needs to include great writers like Shakespeare and Dickens, and I still believe in the good old-fashioned idea that the study of great literature is a way of achieving wisdom. All those old ideas I still believe just as strongly as I did in those days and they're all part of the Leavisite inheritance.

Could I ask about your book The Free Spirit, *published in 1963, which is an exploration of the liberal tradition as it manifests itself in fiction and also, by implication, in the wider society. It seems, from that book, that you obviously admire the liberal imagination, but you're also very critical of it in some ways – of how, for example, an awareness of many sides to an issue can paralyse action. How would you locate yourself in relation to the liberal tradition, both at the time of* The Free Spirit *and subsequently?*

I go on thinking about that almost every day and my view at the present is that I'm still very uncertain on the issue. I have great admiration for the argument that E.M. Forster's greatness is partly due to the fact that he couldn't solve these problems and that the dramatic tensions in his work are created because he couldn't solve them. I'd like to think that I'm very much in that kind of mould. I was brought up as a Methodist and for many years really I wanted to make a relationship with the Christian Church and tried very hard, attended and all sorts of things for a long time, including the time when I wrote that book. Since then I've found it quite impossible to go along with belief in the resurrection and many other things about the modern church. So I was trying to relate liberalism, with which I have great sympathy, with that kind of Christian belief. Today I think I'm probably even more in sympathy with the liberal side and I recognize this more and more. On the other hand I am fascinated with this problem, which Lionel Trilling dealt with throughout his career, of the paralysis of the liberal imagination, and I would say that a great deal of the work that I have done in administration, say through helping to run *Critical Quarterly*, through the university and then through being involved with the National Curriculum, has been an attempt really to commit myself to making decisions, to being active in the political world in order to bring about those liberal beliefs in practice. I'm very critical of many university people who, on the bylines, are rude about politicians, for example. It's very easy to do and it seems to me that one has to be involved and recognize all the problems of compromise and of how to win battles and the rest of it. I've been heavily engaged in that kind of activity for over twenty years now, so in a way that has been all part of that kind of thinking – that I would like liberalism to be active and positive.

*The attacks that have been made on liberal humanism in recent
years, within literary studies for example, have charged that it is inef-
fectual and sanctions quiescence and withdrawal. You recognize in*
The Free Spirit *that it can have those consequences, but you are arguing now, it seems, for a different vision of a much more active and
committed liberalism.*

I disagree with those attacks on liberal humanism very strongly.
Terry Eagleton writes about the way in which the tendency to univer-
salize, the sort of thing that I do, makes Chaucer's meanings similar
to those of T.S. Eliot and gives the impression that the hierarchy is
stable and unchanging and that revolution is impossible. It seems to
me, as a leading activist in the area of culture and education, that's
one of the last things you can say about me. Tony Dyson is crucial
here as well, because Tony not only was involved with me in the
Black Papers but also was the initiator really of the homosexual law
reform society and very instrumental in the change of the law about
homosexuality. He's a liberal too. So to say that people like us have
been quiescent seems to me absurd.

*Let's come on to one particular activity of which you and Tony
Dyson were the prime movers – the magazine* Critical Quarterly
*which you co-founded and edited and which first appeared in 1959.
You didn't open the magazine with a manifesto statement but I wondered if you could reconstruct what your hopes and desires for the
magazine were?*

I think they were very simple, and perhaps different from those of
lots of people who start magazines with a manifesto. That's why
there wasn't one. The simple aim – and it goes right down to the present day in all my work as a teacher, to which I feel very emotionally
committed – is to help more people to understand and enjoy literature. And the aim of the journal – which is very important and again
leads one right down to our problems today – was to create a widely
available language for talking about literature. In the editorial of the
tenth anniversary issue, we quote Northrop Frye on making literature 'accessible to any student with goodwill' and preventing it from
'stagnating among groups of mutually unintelligible elites' (*CQ*,
10:1-2, p. 6). We were not in the least bothered about committing
ourselves to one view. We published Eagleton when he first started
writing, we published Empson, we published Helen Gardner, with
whom I don't agree. It was intended to be that kind of open journal.

What would you say was the major achievement of Critical Quarterly?

In those first ten years, I think that we did a great deal to give enjoyment and understanding of literature to the large audience we built up. One of the crucial points about *Critical Quarterly*, which had a very large sale – it was 5,200 plus for those 10 years – was that it was not a magazine selling only to university teachers of English: at its peak in the mid-sixties, we sold to over half the grammar schools in the country – this is in the pre-comprehensive school days – and we ran huge sixth form conferences and created really a large community and audience of sixth form teachers of English. And the magazine was actually read. I think we were very fortunate at that time in that a number of poets who were readily available to a wide audience were writing some of their best work, and we published by and large some of the best poems of Ted Hughes, Philip Larkin, Thom Gunn, Sylvia Plath and of many other people, and of American poets I like such as Louis Simpson and Gary Snyder. So in my view the achievement of *Critical Quarterly* is in these educational terms and in creating a community that really knew a great deal about recent literature. I think lots of things have gone wrong since then.

Critical Quarterly *began by opposing what, for example, you call the 'myth of a culture in decline' that 'has dominated much* Scrutiny *thinking' (CQ, 3:4, Winter 1961, p. 291). But there was a sense by the end of the 1960s, and certainly by the 1970s, that* Critical Quarterly *had itself come, to some extent, to subscribe to that myth, or rather to see it, not as a myth but a reality and to repeat* Scrutiny's *sense of being under siege – when you say, for instance, in a 1971 editorial: 'The existence of the humanities, of verbal culture itself, is under attack. The traditional belief that study of great literature releases us from the debased myths of the present, that it ennobles and civilizes, needs to be fought for both at the level of theory and at mundane discussions of curriculum development' (CQ, 13:3, Autumn 1971, p. 197). Would you yourself see the trajectory of* Critical Quarterly *in those terms?*

I think I would make a distinction. From the beginning we were opposed to these myths of culture in decline particularly in terms of what was being done by writers and artists. I think that there are many new writers and new forms and that this goes on right down to the present day. The idea that, in terms of art, the post-1945 period has been purely a culture in decline is wrong. That's the first point, which we made very strongly, and that was a very anti-Leavis view at the time. It's with regard to the question of readership that the anxieties and worries about cultural decline come in and I would feel that there are great shifts, particularly in responses to the written word, which alarm me a great deal. I think probably one became more conscious of those in the sixties, for a number of reasons with which the Black Papers deal.

Could I ask more generally about your own response to the 1960s? There is a sense, earlier in the sixties, of a readiness if not to welcome, at least to be open to, new and even potentially threatening developments – I'm thinking, for instance, of the well-known article by you and A.R. Jones, 'After the Tranquilized Fifties: Notes on Sylvia Plath and James Baldwin' (CQ, 6:2, Summer 1964, pp. 107-122), or of the delighted initial response to the USA, and your liberal support for students 'canvassing for political, cultural and religious groups' whom the university authorities moved away from the campus entrance at Berkeley, which you expressed in the Autumn 1964 editorial (CQ, 6:3, p. 195). But you also, for example in your Winter 1962 editorial, expressed uneasiness about '[t]he more violent kind of satire' of, for instance, That was the week that was (CQ, 4:4, p. 292), and, in your Winter 1968 editorial, you deprecate ' "pop" verse' (CQ 10:4, p. 307). There seems to be a growing sense of rejection and uneasiness, not only in the magazine but also in yourself, so that the sense of things opening up which you shared at the beginning of the decade turns into a kind of closure towards the end. Would you feel that to be the case?

Listening to that summary, I would have thought that it is in many ways, is it not, an account of many people of my generation. I think that many such people really did have a sense of openness and possibility and that there is a sense of closure, an anxiety that grows in the 1960s. Why that happened is difficult to answer very briefly. I suppose that basic to the beliefs behind *Critical Quarterly* – and this comes from Leavis – was a concept of quality. You mention *That was the week that was* and it seemed that a good deal of the satiric force of that period had no controlling set of values and was anarchic. I think that's what we felt very powerfully indeed and that view of course was to some extent supported by my experiences at Berkeley, which were very formative in my career. I think I learnt a great deal by the ways in which the Free Speech movement which began in

Berkeley went wrong. It's so relevant to what's happening in Russia for example at the present moment: the movement towards freedom in many ways gets out of hand and leads off into violence as it did in Berkeley. After the Free Speech movement, where I think the students were completely in the right in that they were denied the privilege of touting for support at the entrance to the university for everything, politics and religion and so on, we had the Filthy Speech movement where they used four letter words etc. etc. in public because black people do that and therefore we must overcome racial discrimination. One of my students read *Lady Chatterley* in a public place and was arrested. I think one of the interesting things at Berkeley, and it amazed me at the time, was that the Jews who were professors, many of whom had of course escaped from Germany, were opposed to the Free Speech movement from the beginning and they said that this kind of demonstration and breaking of the law leads inevitably to a reaction. I would have thought that they were right. Ronald Reagan became Governor of California, did he not, as a result of all this. I think I learnt that from watching things go very wrong at Berkeley.

Could we come on then to the Black Papers and ask what led you and Tony Dyson to launch them?

In summer 1968 we decided that we had to raise the subscription for our Critical Quarterly Society and that therefore we would announce it in March 1969 in our other journal, *Critical Survey*, with an issue which would be so good that all our subscribers would have to resubscribe even though we'd put a lot more money on to the subscription. So after some thought we decided we'd do a special issue on education and make it very lively. That's how it started, for economic reasons. But at that time we felt very strongly in opposition to student rebellion in this country. In my case it was having watched what had happened at Berkeley. I felt that in this country, I welcomed student participation in the evaluation of teaching or in the running of halls of residence; but the crucial arguments of the Black Papers were that only those who know the canon can decide on changes in the canon. One of the key arguments in the Black Papers, put forward by people like Imre Lakatos, was that if you allow student power in universities, then you can offer no rational defence against the imposition of government power. One felt very strongly that the autonomy of the universities, as Lakatos said, is a fragile autonomy and it's almost a rare thing in this country, the freedom that universities had in the fifties and sixties. We now see in the nineties, I think, that the Conservative Party in the last eleven or so years has more and more interfered with that kind of freedom. In my view we are at a period of great crisis at the present moment, with the growing emphasis on the utilitarian and the vocational and I would see all that as coming from the student dissent here which really in this country, as opposed to America where you had a civil rights problem, had no great warrant. Students in this country in universities have been extremely fortunate, they still are, and to see them as browbeaten oppressed people seems an absurdity.

We also felt very powerfully in 1968 that immense damage was being done to the image of the university and that, I think, was true and goes right down to the present day. It's one of the reasons why today the Conservative Party still doesn't need to attend to us because we do not have the goodwill of the majority of the public in the way that we did, say, in the mid-sixties before all this happened. But our intention in the first Black Paper was only to address this issue, and then we decided for various reasons to put in one or two articles about comprehensive schools and progressive education and those were the ones which of course created such a furore. So the second Black Paper tried to deal properly with those issues.

You say in the 1977 Black Paper that another reason why you began your campaign in 1969 was 'personal contact with schools of this kind' – and you're talking about schools like William Tyndale. (Black Paper 1977, p. 4). Was that a very important factor at the outset?

Oh yes. I had seen schools of that kind and I'm very proud of the fact that the Black Papers, I believe, did a great deal to stop that particular development which I think everyone now agrees was completely over the top at the time. There was the belief that children really developed naturally, that they grew like a tree, all the Summerhill business – I find it almost difficult to explain these ideas because they seem so ridiculous now. People deny this, but there were in fact schools, and I visited them, where children were allowed to choose their own activities all day for the whole week. And the press in that period – say in 1968 – when we were thinking of the Black Papers were completely dominated by arguments in favour of this kind of progressive education. It was a huge bandwagon. It's been said, and it was definitely true, that promotion in schools depended upon being in tune with that. So that became increasingly at the centre of the Black Paper campaign.

You feel that the Black Papers contributed to stopping the excesses of progressive education in schools. What other positive achievements do you think they had?

I think if we're talking in large general terms that was probably the only one. I think that is a very big one and that in the 1970s we helped to swing the whole of public opinion behind a return to a more structured concept of education so that I could quote to you leading members of the Labour Party in the late eighties saying, where did we go wrong, obviously children, particularly children from poorer homes, need structure etc. etc. I think we were largely responsible because it wasn't just the Black Papers themselves, there was a massive campaign of course as soon as one realized that the thing was so important and so powerful. It was discussed in the House of Commons and all that kind of thing, and I was going round the country for many years speaking to all sorts of groups and writing pamphlets and articles. I discovered the power of pressure group activity, which worries me a great deal. It's not difficult to apply group pressure, it really is very easy in this country, and it's very frightening. I believe that you and I, if we could agree upon it, could change significant things in this community; we'd need about ten more people and we'd need to know what we were doing and we'd issue statements to the press and write letters and so on. For example, the recent great argument over reading which started in the summer of 1990, is in my view absurdly out of touch with what was really going on in schools and I think the number of people that started that is very small. It's probably only about six or seven people. This happens again and again and we did that with the Black Papers, and of course the great worry is the responsibility when you're involved in that because there's no doubt in a massive campaign of that kind that some of the things you do are wrong.

So it wouldn't be inaccurate to say that the Black Paper campaign had some consequences which you found unwelcome?

I'm very happy to agree with that. I've had a problem for twenty years now in that I like to think of myself as a liberal but I'm supposed to appear on television as the Enoch Powell of education. You see, the problem is that university people like to write books and get good reviews and then move on to the next publication. But once you're involved in political, educational controversies of this kind, you have to accept that you take a whole series of decisions and actions and, as with running this university, you win some and occasionally you lose, and not only lose but also you do things which weeks later you realize were wrong. I think that the Black Papers did harm to the status of the teaching profession; that's the thing that has worried me most and that I've been trying to put right for many years now. I think the teaching profession was culpable in that in the 1960s it allowed itself to be taken over by this progressive bandwagon. On the other hand I think that as the years have gone by – and it's going on to the present day – the Black Paper campaign has been far too successful in encouraging extreme right-wing groups who are very much anti-teacher and I've given a lot of speeches and written a lot of articles in newspapers over the last five years trying to put that right.

Couldn't it be said in fact that the Black Papers contributed to a cultural climate in which it was more difficult for the Cox Report to find acceptance?

Yes, absolutely. It's one of the problems at the present moment. The joke is that the *Evening Standard* in the last two years has been attacking me quite often in exactly the terms in which we were attacking the progressive establishment. They're using my rhetoric to attack me. As a result partly of the Black Paper campaign, quite a number of right-wing groups have prospered, and in fact the split between my group and those groups I could date precisely. It was in 1980 when I went to a meeting of the Centre for Policy Studies where Sir Alfred Sherman was present – I'd not met him before – and as a result I resigned because I found the kind of right-wing dogmatism for which he stood repugnant. So I have been conscious of that for a long time, but once you're involved in this kind of pressure group and cultural activity it's very difficult to control it. Once something becomes as powerful as the Black Paper campaign then it attracts a large number of people. I'd like to think the Cox Report itself is a major blow against those right-wing groups and one goes on fighting because I feel that they are still far too powerful politically at the present moment.

While you were involved in the Black Paper campaign, you also, in 1974, produced a book on Conrad in which you argue that he exemplifies 'a basic element in the modern imagination' in his ' "stoical recognition of the precarious status of mind"' (Joseph Conrad: The Modern Imagination, p. 12). Could you say more about how you developed that kind of interest in Conrad at that time?

I went through quite a black period at that time, partly because of the Black Papers. The shock to me personally over the Black Papers was considerable and I think in a way that relates to what we saying before about the question of committing oneself to positive action in society. It seemed to me that's the kind of question that Conrad asks in the most profound way, particularly, say, in *Nostromo*. I don't altogether agree with my book now, looking back. I feel perhaps I was too sympathetic to Conrad. But it seems to me that Conrad was addressing a growing scepticism, and by that time in my own life, in the early 1970s, I'd given up having anything to do with the Christian Church, and I was trying to see what kind of positive values might emerge when one accepts the kind of darkness which is so central to Conrad's imagination.

You mentioned that you stopped writing poetry at Cambridge under the influence of Leavis but since then you have written poems and indeed published two collections – Every Common Sight in 1981 and Two-Headed Monster in 1985. How would you characterize yourself as a poet?

I think I base almost all my poems on personal experience, though by and large the poems are fiction. I feel it's quite proper, in order to try and say something, to change actual experience slightly, so often a poem will bring two experiences together into one and things of that kind. I now find verse immensely helpful in trying as honestly as I can to understand what's happening to me. My problem in writing verse, because I depend upon personal experience, is to get ideas. That's why travel is often quite helpful and the cultural clashes that one sees. Once I've got an idea then it may take me three months to write the poem. It takes me a great deal of time to write an individual poem and I'm obsessive about changing individual words, but once I've got the idea, I know I'll make it one day. I think my poetry is very much in the Larkin tradition, and I'm also very much influenced by Lowell, particularly by *Life Studies*. Lowell very much admired Larkin, and though their poetry is different, a lot of Lowell's work, I would have thought, is, like Larkin's, an attempt to understand personal experience.

Could we raise the question of the Arts Council, which I discussed when I interviewed Robert Hewison (see above, pp. 169-70)? In an Arts Council lecture you gave, with Raymond Williams, in 1981, you very strongly supported public funding for the arts (See The Arts

Council: Politics and Policies *(1981). The Arts Council has been under all kinds of pressures and been through all kinds of transitions in the 1980s. What would you think would be the best form of public arts funding and provision in England for the next decade?*

I am in favour of power at the centre. Obviously this is a matter of balance; I'm very happy for the regions to have some power but I do think the centre should have a great deal of power and that relates, of course, to my concept of artistic worth. I think it's very important that the Arts Council should be helping to promote the very best, and there's a great danger, when financial power goes out to the regions, that lots of very trivial things of one kind or another are subsidised. I accept the need to subsidise young people and that seems to me essential, in terms of the vitality of the community. But I'm a believer in parliamentary democracy, if you like, as opposed to participatory democracy, and that means that we appoint the members of parliament who then do a good job which may not always be exactly what the majority of the community want. And as far as arts provision goes that job involves understanding the immense importance of the arts to the total cultural life. I think that relates to my liberalism because the way in which language has been perverted and corrupted by the media does seem to me deeply worrying – this is Leavis again, and matters are worse now than they were in his day. From these points of view, the role of the Arts Council seems very important.

Let's come on then to the Cox Report, English from ages 5 to 16. Could I ask first of all why Kenneth Baker disliked it?

I think that Kenneth Baker was most anxious that Mrs Thatcher, the Prime Minister, should be enthusiastic about what he was doing, that he was under great pressure from the Centre for Policy Studies, and that he wanted a simple curriculum with great emphasis on spelling and grammar and utilitarian values. I do not think he knew very much about all the problems of teaching literature and language and I think he learnt quite a lot during the process. But he wanted something he could sell to parents and sell to right-wing people like Mrs Thatcher herself, and that's not what the Report is. I was mainly concerned with producing a document in which I believed completely, but also one that would be welcome to the best of the teaching profession, and I'd like to think that's its major achievement. It's been very popular with the teaching profession. I would argue, and I think there's a lot of agreement with this, that the situation in 1989-90 is completely different from what it was when the Black Papers were coming out. I think that the battle in favour of some kind of structured education has long been won, although we may disagree about the nature of the structure and the kind of emphases etc. etc., but those are very productive debates.

You stress in the Report that the need to teach Standard English should not result in the devaluation of other forms of language – dialect, pupils' home speech, other languages in the case of bilingual pupils. It seems to me that in terms of actual teaching this poses a great problem, since it could be very difficult to avoid at least implying that, say, a certain dialect was in some ways limited and inferior because it was not the language of power, the language that matters. Would you feel that to be so?

I think that you are addressing a very major difficulty in the classroom and that this difficulty is central to the cultural identity of England – when I say England, I mean England particularly, Wales and Scotland and Ireland have different problems. Standard English is the language of power and also – the Report does not say this strongly enough but I think I do in my book – Standard English is superior to the other dialects. It needn't have been, originally it was only another dialect as we know, but it has been elaborated, and therefore as Gillian Brown says, in her article in *Critical Quarterly* which I quote in my book on the Report, *Cox on Cox*, the languages of school subjects such as geography, chemistry or English literature are those of Standard English. They are not available in dialect and you can't expect a working-class child who comes from a home where dialect is spoken to cope with school subjects without Standard English. I put this rather strongly to you because I have been very much attacked by some militant left-wing people who say that the Report should not have taken this position. I think they are very wrong and that they, to use the jargon, ghettoize the people they're trying to protect, that they themselves would never dream of allowing their own children to speak dialect, and that they are a most malicious influence and do great harm – they're very powerful in many ways. But the point the Report makes about the relationship between Standard English and other forms of language is perhaps just as important. It does seem to me that we must have a kind of balance between a common national identity and language, so that you and I and everybody else understand each other as much as we can, and a recognition and respect for diversity. That seems the kind of balance which we need to achieve in, to use a cliché again, our multicultural society. It is going to be frighteningly difficult to achieve and it will, going back to your question, be particularly difficult to put into practice in individual classrooms. But I'm proud that we addressed the problem. And one thing I've said many many times in public is that this report was prepared in thirteen months and I wouldn't like to see it written in stone. It must be reconsidered and I'm sure that, at the very least, some of the emphases will need to be corrected.

I'd like to put to you one point in particular which Colin MacCabe makes in his article in the special issue of Critical Quarterly *on the Cox Report (CQ, 32:4, pp. 7-13). Before the Cox Report, it was still possible to maintain that Standard English was correct English. But your Report in effect undermines that position by recognizing that while Standard English may be a* superior *form of English in terms of its greater elaboration, it is not the* correct *form – it is just the form that happens to be dominant. MacCabe suggests that there is thus a profoundly subversive movement in the Report. Would you say that was the case?*

Yes. I think MacCabe's article is brilliant. Again it goes back to your point about how difficult it is to put into practice the Report's emphasis on the need to teach Standard English while also promoting a recognition of and respect for linguistic diversity, because a teacher needs to say to Johnny 'you are wrong' and it's very difficult to say to him 'you are wrong in certain social contexts'. But it does seem to me that the absolute concept of correctness which I was taught is linguistically wrong, that certainly as children get older they need to be alive to that, and that a good deal of the stagnation of thinking and language that you find, particularly from essays by older public school products, is because they have been given this very pure concept of what is correct. I'm an admirer of Toni Morrison and it seems to me that kind of English from an American black writer is immensely enriching. But on the other hand one has to accept the existence of the kind of language which *Critical Quarterly* intended to give power to when it first started and that is the general educated Standard English which you and I are trying to use at the present moment. And I think it's incredibly important that all children should have access to that language to the fullest possible extent.

Perhaps the most crucial question in the Report is that of national identity and the Report itself, and certainly Cox on Cox, gives a sense of the kind of national identity which you would like to see emerge and which might indeed be called a liberal vision – you advocate, for example, 'a new cultural awareness' in order 'to promote true peace and co-operation in British society' (Cox on Cox, p. 19). Would you see the proposals of the Report as an attempt to perform a social and political function – that of helping to bind together an increasingly divided society – which it will be very difficult to discharge?

I quite agree that the proposals of the Cox Report would indeed perform a social and political function and imply certain ideals which will not be capable of complete implementation. On the other hand it seems to me, as a teacher, that any teacher must have such ideals which they spend their lives trying to achieve and will never completely succeed in achieving. With regard to the question of national identity, it is true that in certain ways the society is dividing and I think one has to accept in the future that there will be radical differences between religious cultures, for example. I think the Report comes out very strongly for the possibility of certain common values and that these are absolutely crucial to a national educational system. The use of Standard English has lots of implications in this respect. We also, for example, say that all children should read some English literature written before 1900, including Shakespeare, and that is part of the concept of national identity. I suppose that the Report by implication does address the more difficult political issues because I believe that it implies tolerance, and it does seem to me – for example, if you take the Rushdie affair, which we very sensibly did not mention in that Report because it raises all kinds of other issues – that it's going to be very difficult to have any kind of cohesion in our society if we don't have toleration of dissent and that means dissent from Islam and also from Christianity – I take the point that Christians need reforming too. But I think there is a concept of toleration and the sentence you've quoted is to do with that. The more children understand and learn to respect different languages and different ways, the more this will help to produce tolerance in the future, though one realizes that we are already, are we not, in a period of such division that it inevitably produces conflict.

Could we come finally to the Cox Report's arguments for placing the study of literature at the centre of the National Curriculum. In the chapter of Cox on Cox where you discuss this you quote in bold type

*a passage from the Report which says '[a]n active involvement with
literature enables pupils to share the experience of others. They will
encounter and come to understand a wide range of feelings and
relationships by entering vicariously the worlds of others, and in
consequence are likely to understand more of themselves' (Cox on
Cox, p. 76, quoted from* English from ages 5 to 16, *7:3). You talk, for
example, just a couple of paragraphs earlier in the actual Report
about literature's 'unique relationship to human experience' (7:1) –
which is an Arnoldian or a Leavisian kind of perspective – but the
questions that then arise are: is it unique, and even if it, is is its
uniqueness any longer of a kind that justifies the claim for its centrality? How would you answer those who would say that you can
encounter and come to understand a wide range of feelings and
relationships and enter vicariously the world of others through all
kinds of cultural forms and certainly not just through something
called literature.*

I wouldn't like to suggest that I have an easy answer to that question,
which obviously is one that I've thought about for a long time. First
of all I would agree that other forms can be just as enabling, and if it's
done properly I have every sympathy with the development of media
studies and I think that children should indeed study film and that for
many of them – that's why in the report we strongly emphasize drama
– Shakespeare is best taught almost entirely through drama. You surprised me a little with the emphasis you gave to the word 'unique'
and if I'd done that when I was revising it in draft I'd have crossed it
out. But I do believe that language has its own kinds of distinctions
and subtleties and tones, and I think film has a very different kind of
rhetoric. And one is worried that the kind of language which, for
example, *PN Review* takes for granted is now becoming a small
minority form of awareness – that if one talks about all sorts of quite
important English writers, there are very few people in this country
now who would recognize the names. So from the point of view of
the classroom and the universities at the present moment, should one
just say this is happening and we abandon the field? Probably the
danger of this kind of debate is that one simplifies it. Although there
are great shifts in the way that young people read, they still are doing
a great deal of reading, and maybe unfortunately they won't know
much about Milton, but I think that as we move on in these conflicts,
literature still remains unique and that my students – and there are
large numbers of them – still have great passions, though the passions
may be changing a bit and the canon may have to change as a result.

Catherine Belsey

University College of Wales, Cardiff
21 February 1992

NICOLAS TREDELL: *Could you begin by telling us about your development through home, school and university?*

CATHERINE BELSEY: All through my childhood I encountered a disjunction between what I was being encouraged to believe by a very respectable school about the world I lived in and the values my father subscribed to. At school we had prayers every morning, and over the washing up my father fulminated against religion. He was a socialist and very resistant to the minor forms of social snobbery that were part of secondary education for girls in those days. I went on to Oxford, where I was on the whole fairly conventional, and afterwards I got a job as a casual labourer at the London Zoo, where I worked with people on the margins of respectability in a number of ways. This was another fairly radical disjunction. I was very naive, and the experience made me reconsider some of the values I had begun to take for granted. After a year at the Zoo, I got a job in publishing, but it turned out that the firm was on the verge of bankruptcy, so we had to publish pornography – well, very soft pornography by today's standards – in order to survive. Probably none of this would seem very startling now, but I'd lived a sheltered life, and each time my horizons expanded, I found myself having to interrogate my existing assumptions all over again. Research at Warwick in the sixties was as different from Oxford as it could have been. Then a job at Cambridge, followed by Cardiff. Cardiff was a shock in a quite unexpected way, because when I arrived in 1975 it was more Leavisite than Cambridge was, and probably more than Cambridge had ever been. I think it was Cardiff that made me question at a fundamental level what I was doing as a teacher of English, and why

I was doing it. That led directly to *Critical Practice* and an attempt to answer those questions.

Could you reconstruct the intellectual stages you went through on the road to Critical Practice?

I wasn't very self-conscious about any of them. As an undergraduate I'd discovered New Criticism in a library somewhere – I don't think anybody really led me to it, but I had to write an essay on Donne and I found Cleanth Brooks. At that time I found his way of reading very exciting. And so I read everything I could find of what we would now call New Criticism – I'd no idea then that it was called that. This was close reading of the texts in order to make them say something that you didn't quite expect them to have said, and I think in a way I'm still doing something rather like that. I don't want to be recorded as still doing New Criticism but I still find it thrilling to discover that a text, if you look at it closely enough, doesn't just say the obvious things that you first supposed it said. It can be read as saying something quite different. So I still have a high regard for close textual analysis and I'm sorry in a sense that, in America particularly, having been so fashionable, New Criticism became totally unfashionable, so that now there's a reaction against close reading. I think I've been doing close reading all along. I hope the way I've been doing it has changed fundamentally since then, but I think I retain the project of attending very closely to a text.

I've also consistently been accused of being a Leavisite in wolf's clothing, and I think that probably, although I studied at Oxford, there was a certain amount of the Leavisite tradition around at that moment. I don't think I'm a Leavisite and I don't think I ever shared Leavis's commitment to the moral values of the text, but what I perhaps retained from that epoch was taking texts seriously. I think what Leavis was saying passionately was that literature matters, that it matters what we read and how we read. I don't mind so much what we read but I think it does matter how we read. In other words, literary criticism is not just playing, it's not just a sort of aesthetic activity, it's not just an end in itself. Insofar as Leavis was arguing, from a quite different perspective, that what we read influences the way we understand the world, I think I believe that too. My feeling, however, is we need to be very sceptical about it: that's why we need to read texts so closely: to see what set of values they are inviting us to subscribe to. Leavis would say that you choose the works with the right values and go for them; I would say be very aware of what it is that

you're committing yourself to if you say you think this text is 'good'
or is 'great art'.

*When you became interested in New Criticism, what kind of rela-
tionship, if any, did you then see between literary criticism and political commitment?*

Probably not a lot in explicit terms. I think the politics came later. As
I indicated, I was brought up to be critical of the regime, on the left,
but in a fairly unspecified way. I'd already read Roland Barthes
before I discovered Marxism in the late seventies, and as far as I was
concerned then, Marxism was a very rigorous, very sophisticated
theory of society. I was always prone to be critical, but it wasn't
really until I got to Cardiff that the accumulated heritage of asking
what I was doing began to seem to demand clear and specific
answers. At Warwick I did historical research, and I was supervised
by G.K. Hunter, who is a great scholar. He taught me that you
checked your sources twice and that if you were talking about a historical period you represented it as accurately as you could – I don't
any longer believe we can have this kind of accuracy but I do still
believe in the rigour to which he subscribed. So I think at that stage
I was probably preoccupied by constructing an argument and sub-
stantiating it was well as I could. But I remember at the end of that
period – and this is where the quasi-Leavisite heritage comes in – saying to George Hunter, OK, I've done this thesis and I hope it's all
right, but what use is it? And it was at this point that I discovered
Roland Barthes. I finished my thesis in 1973 and in 1974 I read *S/Z*.
I don't think I understood its implications, I don't think I had any
idea what it would lead to, but I did think, this is telling me, but in a
totally new way, that fiction and the world are in some way connected, that fiction matters in terms of understanding the world it
comes from and the world we inhabit, and I want to go on with this
kind of analysis. But of course in those days it was quite hard to go
on with it; there were no obvious authorities, no feet I could go and
sit at. So it was a question of reading – of reading *Screen* which, with
Stephen Heath and Colin MacCabe, was the main theoretical influence in Britain in those days, and it was brilliant; of picking up anything that appeared – mostly I waited for the translations if I could,
but I read *S/Z* in French and Macherey in French, and very difficult
they were too – but then they were not much less difficult in English:
the language barrier was not the problem.
    By now it had become clear to me that the only way I could really

make sense of anything was to write about it. I don't know what I think till I see what I write, and *Critical Practice* was very much a voyage of discovery. It was an attempt to write down what these new ideas seemed to amount to. Cardiff was good at that time: Chris Norris and Margaret Atack and John Hartley were here then, Terry Hawkes of course, and we had reading groups on Lacan and Althusser where we read them and said, what in the world do you make of this? It was very collective, we pooled our resources, we had no experts and we argued about it all but in a friendly way. I just made as much contact as I could with anybody who was doing theory and *Critical Practice* shows the marks of all that. It's very experimental, it's very exploratory, a certain amount of it is wrong, but it was as much as I knew at the time.

In your contribution to PN Review 48, *you ranked yourself among those 'who went straight from C.S. Lewis to Roland Barthes' (p.26). Could you explore that particular connection?*

That was obviously a bit reductive, but I was attempting to say that I'd never been through a stage of believing that literature told moral truths about life. I'd never thought literature was 'good for you'. Hunter and C.S. Lewis can't be conflated, but my research training was historical, and Lewis was historical in that kind of way. I think *The Allegory of Love* is a great book and I still draw on it. Lewis was trying there to establish a cultural difference between that moment and this and to locate the founding moment of the modern world in the sixteenth century. When I read the sixteenth century, that's exactly what I'm trying to do. I'm not doing it the way C.S. Lewis did; I don't share his project of installing the Church of England as a moral authority. But nevertheless I think he was interested in establishing the difference between the Middle Ages and the modern world, and so am I. So I still have that heritage of an approach to history as difference. What I left out in that reductive jump from Lewis to Barthes was the close reading which I've mentioned. But I don't think I ever thought that literature was true, and I think that's what Leavis did think and that's my overriding disagreement with him. He looked for great truths about life in a diminishing number of texts. This is the second problem with Leavisism; if you can only endorse what you agree with or what seems to you to contain some sort of universal truth, then you inevitably end up with only a handful of writers – in this case the Famous Five, Austen, Eliot, Conrad, James and Lawrence. My quarrel with Leavis was that in the end his followers

were able to read only a selection of writers and then only a selection
of their work, and that seems to me narrowing and exclusive. I think
we should read everything and I think we should read it all in order
to make cultural history out of it, to make cultural difference out of
it, and to see its own instabilities and precariousness. I'd never shared
the view that literature told the truth about life and that seemed to
me a dangerous belief.

*The question of whether literature can tell the truth about life, as
Leavis thought, or whether it can't, as you argue, relates to the more
general question of the relationship of language and reality – a question which has been very important to your project and to that of
poststructuralism generally. Whereas the old idea was, to put it simply, that language and literature express reality, the idea is now that
language and literature construct the reality they seem to express. I'd
like to quote a particular passage from* Critical Practice *– acknowledging your earlier point that* Critical Practice *was experimental
and that you would not stand by it all now – and then develop a more
general question. You say 'colour terms, like language itself, form a
system of differences, readily experienced as natural, given, but in
reality constructed by the language itself' (pp. 39-40). Two responses
which that statement invites are: why should language want to construct a system of colour differences and how does it have the power
to do so? In your work, language seems to be both personified and
deified: that is, it is given human attributes and it is also given a priority and a power that in a more traditional perspective might be
reserved for God: language is a universal mode of production, it's
pervasive and constructive and to quite a large extent – though not
wholly, as you stress – it's directive and determining. In* Critical
Practice, *it seems that language simply is: it has this power, we don't
know why it has it, but we have to recognize it and let our hubris, as
liberal humanist subjects say, be suitably humbled by it. Isn't this linguistic stress a metaphysics rather than a materialism?*

If by materiality we mean the economy, I think language is something other than the economy. What legitimated this stress on language was Althusser's Marxism, which analysed the social in terms of
three instances: the economic, the political, and the ideological as he
would call it and as I called it in *Critical Practice* – now I would call
it culture. His argument was that each of these three levels was the
condition of possibility of the other two: the economy was determining in the last instance, and the rest of his work agonized over what

that might mean, but since we're never in the last instance, in practice each of these levels makes possible development in the others. Now the economy is doing its important economic thing; I'm in an English department, so what can I be expected to know about the economy?; but language is my job and what Althusser legitimated was the analysis of language as a material practice, and that analysis as a serious proposition, because if culture was material, in the sense that it made people act in certain ways or legitimated certain models of society or identified as objectives particular social goals, then language was crucially important. So for the first time really, from a left-wing point of view as opposed to a Leavisite point of view, English departments had an important job to do.

So there's a sense in which Leavis meets Althusser – Leavis without the content but with the conviction that what we do is important, and Althusser's argument that the educational apparatus is the central ideological apparatus: it's reproducing the values of a culture and society but it's also the location of resistances. I don't wish to make language determining, not even in the last instance, though I can see that a lot of what I've done might make it look as if I do. I don't want to isolate language as the single cause, but insofar as the way things are is overdetermined, has a multiplicity of causes, one of those causes is language, and it seemed to me that we had tended – and Leavis would be particularly culpable in this respect – to treat language as a means, a nomenclature. Think of Leavis's word 'plainly' which recurs in his work – 'plainly x is the case', and then a quotation, and if you can't see it you can't see it, and you're stupid. 'Plainly' suggests exactly that language is a transparent access to something beyond it. That's what I would call metaphysics: the idea that there's something beyond language which language labels, and I would say that to identify language as *a* material practice – not the only material practice – is precisely to break with metaphysics. Language is important, certainly, but it's not the fundamental determining cause, which I think is what would make my position metaphysical. The little human animal learns *in* language to think and speak, but language doesn't bring children into existence (though it commonly plays a part even in that process). It does, however, pre-exist the individual child, and it's in that sense that language seems to have a life, or at least a history, of its own.

There is then a problem, if you have an emancipatory project, of working out the relationships between language and those other areas of possible determination about which you talk, so that one has some sense, in any given instance, of how to intervene in order to have a good chance of changing things for the better. In other words, you have to say at a certain point that what counts most here is changing the economy, or changing subjectivity, or changing these relationships between the economy and subjectivity, or whatever. It doesn't seem to me that those relationships actually have been worked out by radical cultural and literary critics: rather, they have – perhaps because, as you suggest, it provides them with a sense of mission – laid a great stress on language, which perhaps they regard in theory as only one determining factor but which becomes in practice their major preoccupation.

There is another possible point of view, which is, as it were, less global. The Enlightenment project is to produce a complete map of the world and to understand exactly the relation between the economy and culture, let's say, or the economy and the political and then start getting in and doing something about it. That's the model you've indicated.

Isn't that the Marxist model?

It probably is the Marxist model, because Marxism is an Enlightenment project. But there's another more modest possibility which is that, rather than standing on a high mountain and viewing the kingdoms of the world, you think what can I do – what difference can *I* make – as a contribution to a collective project, in the position that I'm in. And I think this is probably where Foucault comes in, because Foucault, with his despair of any kind of macro-politics – there are no great ruptures, he says, or very rarely, and certainly we don't look as if we're heading for one now – offers the alternative that you work in the institution, the location, in which you find yourself in order to make a little contribution to – I don't even want to say a jigsaw because a jigsaw sounds as if it could be complete, and I don't think that kind of complete global knowledge is possible now. But you can try to contribute a fragment of analysis in the hope that it's useful, that it can be picked up and if necessary modified and adapted to the circumstances. I think my project is this more modest one: it is to see if we can't do something with this institution of English, which I regard still as so important and so formative, and whether we can't make it ask questions instead of proclaiming truths, problematize our culture rather than reaffirm certainties. I don't think I ever had, but I certainly don't have now, any idea that *I* am going to change the world. I don't even know that *we* are going to change it in any very dramatic way, but I think you can make little differences and I'm still interested in doing that. But you make them on the whole where you are rather than by producing huge pronouncements about how everything relates to everything else.

How far then does that idea of small-scale activity differ from the old liberal humanist idea that you do your little bit to try and improve things? It sounds like an enormous renunciation of the emancipatory hopes of liberation raised both by the Englightenment and by Marxism, and indeed even by the 1960s.

I think recent history makes those global and utopian dreams seem pretty imaginary. What would differentiate my position from a liberal humanist one would be the content of the little contributions you might make. My great optimism insofar as I am still optimistic, and I am – I think things can change, but not in a global way, not overnight – is precisely the effect of the postmodern condition. Julia Kristeva, in her 1977 book on Chinese women, makes a little observation, just in passing, to the effect that we live in a society where we have to learn to do not only without God but also without man. That seems to me a brilliant synopsis of the postmodern condition. In other words we live not only in a secular society but in a society which can no longer have the old Enlightenment protagonist, 'man'. Now 'man' has been extremely important and extremely oppressive in my view, and this would probably be the point at which I would differ from those liberal humanists who share my view that you can only work piecemeal. 'Man' has meant that there is a single universal narrative and a single universal truth of the progressive emancipation of 'the rational or working subject', as Lyotard says, thus condensing liberalism and Marxism into five words. I think we can't have 'man' any longer. Kristeva's reason why we can't have 'man' is that she's encountered the otherness of the Chinese. We probably no longer subscribe to the account she gives of Maoist China. But if you now read that book as a fictional utopia rather than as a journalistic account of China, what you see is an encounter between the West and a cultural difference that is so great that this figure of 'man', who is the representative type of all human beings, can no longer hold. 'Man' was white, heterosexual, masculine whether we like it or not, Western, probably liberal, knowing and mastering. Recently groups of people who are none of those things have begun to make a lot of noise: women – not just women as one solid bloc opposing men as a binary opposite, but different kinds of women, black women, lesbian women; gay men, black people, the Third World in its difference – Brazil is not the same as India. All of these groups have begun to say, I have a story to tell, listen to me, and the stories can't any longer be conflated and collapsed under one great narrative, under one great universal truth. They contradict each other, they don't sit easily side by side.

So now we have a world of conflicting interests and of separate narratives, and I think it's imperative that we listen to these narratives in our own interest as well as theirs if we are to survive. South Africa's learning this, fast, and I think the whole world is probably going to have to learn it. So the content of my political analysis, my political optimism, is not a liberal one. It isn't about tolerance, it isn't about getting closer and closer to universal truths, it isn't about changing it when you can never be certain you understand it correctly. But changing it on the basis of interests now, seeing where the interests of these many groups can coincide and where they separate and choosing a position over and over again. Now that's hard. That's not a question of easy piecemeal analysis. It doesn't allow us easily to denounce or to reject or to condemn. It means we've got to listen closely to unfamiliar narratives. I don't know if liberalism is quite such hard work, because liberals always possess the truth and can measure the stories they hear according to it and discard a good many of them. For example, liberals always say that Salman Rushdie is right and the Islamic fundamentalists are wrong. I don't know that for sure. I don't want them to kill Salman Rushdie, but I'm not sure I can so easily just take sides. The relationship between Islam and the West has a history. Of course, we have to defend Rushdie's life, but we also need to attend to the reasons why it's in danger.

But it could be argued that the dissolution of 'man' and the dissolution of the individual subject which postmodernism promotes and celebrates is not, as you imply, liberating, but is rather, to a large extent, precisely what contemporary capitalism needs. It needs precisely a world in which identities are not fixed, in which people are mobile, in which different interests are allowed as long as they don't join together in some big unified claim that would really threaten the sites of power in that way that, to some extent, the Enlightenment did in the French Revolution, or in the way that Marxism did. How far do you think these notions of the dissolution of 'man', the dissolution of the individual subject, are in fact presenting a real challenge, or are, as Fredric Jameson puts it in Postmodernism, or, The Cultural

Logic of Late Capitalism, *'a description of the way we live now, rather than its rebuke or subversion' (p. 339)?*

I can see Jameson's point, but I would say that we need to differentiate the postmodern condition. Insofar as its representative is Baudrillard, for example, and its argument is that there's nothing but style, I have no sympathy with it at all, and it seems to me that it's that version that capitalism needs. Capitalism needs a fragmented culture in which everybody is concerned about style and nobody is busy challenging anything that matters – the challenge is at the level of dress or something of that kind. If, however, the representative of the postmodern were to be Lyotard, I would say that there's a really very radical and fundamental challenge going on there. It's not, for Lyotard, just a matter of style. It's a matter of recognition of the connection between knowledge and power, a recognition that knowledge, in the Enlightenment sense, is no longer a possibility, that the knowledge is now in the databanks and not just in large bulging heads. The crucial question he asks is: in the postmodern condition, who has access to this knowledge? I think we need to keep asking that question because what serves the interests of late capitalism is that the corporations and the governments should be the only people with access to it and the rest of us should just get on with changing our clothes a lot and stumbling around Los Angeles hotels worrying about not being able to find our way out of them. It seems to me that we need to do something much more important than that, which is to demand access to knowledge, and to demand that access, we have to get together. In other words, we have to acknowledge our differences but also to suspend them temporarily; we have to make alliances and devise strategic fronts in order to say we want that access. We want to tell our stories and we want to listen to other people's, and we want power-knowledge to be redistributed. The Enlightenment legitimated the rule of white, Western men. Now the postmodern condition recognizes no reason why power should belong to one group of people rather than another.

Could we turn to another aspect of Critical Practice *which has been very influential, and that it is its assault on the classic realist text. You say, for instance: 'The experience of reading a realist text is ultimately reassuring, however harrowing the events of the story, because the world evoked in the fiction, its patterns of cause and effect, of social relationships and moral values, largely confirm the patterns of the world we seem to know' (p. 51). That process of confirmation is seen in* Critical Practice *as a bad thing, and it is bad because the picture of the world that classic realism presents is false. But it seems to me that then actually reproduces quite a traditional literary-critical criterion – indeed one might say a Leavisite criterion – for judging the quality of realistic fiction, which is, precisely, the criterion of the veracity of a fiction's insight into the real relations of life. It's true, of course, that traditional literary criticism, or Leavisite criticism, uses that criterion to differentiate good classic realism from bad classic realism, whereas you use it to demote all classic realism. But given the poststructuralist premise of the textuality of reality, it's surely inappropriate to condemn classic realism as false. Would you agree with that?*

Yes. Totally. I'm not absolutely persuaded that I did condemn it quite as clearly as that, but those were the days of Althusser and Macherey. Macherey, brilliant as his book *A Theory of Literary Production* is, still had a residue of the notion of ideology as false consciousness, and Althusser spent his whole life struggling with the question of whether ideology is false and whether there's something which can be opposed to it which is science. I think he knew at a theoretical level, as a good philosopher, that you couldn't sustain that distinction, but as a Marxist he longed to keep it, and the uncertainty about whether you could sustain it runs all through his work. Now that was as far as I'd got in *Critical Practice*, and so I tried not to say, there is a truth by which we can measure the classic realist text and find it wanting. If there are lapses from time to time, I think it is because of the precise historical moment of *Critical Practice*. I finished it in '79, which was quite a long time ago, and I certainly wouldn't take that line now. But I think and hope that you could also detect running through *Critical Practice* the view that what classic realism encourages is not so much illusion as complacency. The reader of classic realism is offered a picture of a world which turns out in the end to be coherent, non-contradictory, easily intelligible. At the end of the story we know what happened and why. All our questions are answered and our uncertainties resolved. So I suppose in that sense you could say I'm claiming classic realism tells lies but what I'm really wanting to say is that it discourages thinking. Now what I also, I hope, went on to say about classic realism is that if you read it differently, if you don't just go alone with its closures, if you look for the moments when the fiction doesn't quite hang together, for the precariousness, the instabilities, then it tells a whole different story. So I never meant to condemn it and I think it probably really is a misreading, not on your part but on the part of endless reviewers who laid into me for this, to suppose that I hate classic realism. I love it. Its exact seductiveness is what I wanted to draw attention to. I read it in bed. I can't do without it. I don't really enjoy a lot of post-modern fiction. I want to read George Eliot and *Gone with the Wind*. So what I was trying to do was identify the powers of, precisely, per-suasion, but persuasion if it's read in a conventional way or in the way that was conventional in the sixties and seventies. Then it simply reaffirms what we already know. Now to have what you already know reaffirmed is not challenging, it's not exciting, it's not stimulat-ing, it doesn't make you critical of the world you inhabit, and that's so even when the content is overtly radical. In *Critical Practice*, I wanted to ask the question: how do I get people who do read George Eliot – and I want them to go on doing that – to sit up and think instead of being left with their questions answered and their com-monplaces confirmed.

Let me address then precisely that point about complacency. In Crit-ical Practice, *one characteristic of classic realism that you identify is, as you say, that it confirms a world we seem to know. But isn't that true of any text that presents, through fictional or non-fictional techniques, a picture of the world with which we happen to concur? For example, you yourself talk in your 1989 essay 'Towards cultural history – in theory and practice' (*Textual Practice, *vol. 3, no. 2, pp. 159-171) of 'the classic texts of poststructuralism' (p. 170) and it does seem to me that when we now read Althusser or Lacan or even Barthes, we do encounter a picture of the world that has become rec-ognizable and familiar to us, even if we don't agree with it, so that their texts are, in that way, confirmatory. Isn't the confirmation of what we seem to know by a text not a feature of a particular kind of text but a relationship that we can have to any text, even the most theoretical and radical?*

No. I see what you're saying – that if we move into a poststructuralist world, then the texts of poststructuralism become classic realist texts in a sense. I don't think it's necessarily the case and I think the differ-ence I want to gesture towards is a question of mode of address. Clas-sic realism works not only by confirming, by making propositions that you recognize, but also be effacing its own textuality. It sets out to construct for the reader the illusion – and this really is an illusion, this is false – that these events are really happening in a real identifi-able three-dimensional world which might be located at a different moment in history – people might be wearing different costumes – but which resembles yours. Classic realism requires a particular kind of reading which contributes to this process of confirming an extra-textual characteristic, an extratextual quantity, which is the truth of the fiction. Now what's striking about Althusser, Lacan and Derrida is that they're extremely difficult to read; they aren't transparent in any sense of that term. Derrida and Lacan write in a way that won't let you efface the textuality of the text. You have to keep on at it, asking does it say that, can it say that, and if it says that, can it be true, can it be right? Of course the question, can it be true, can it be right, cannot be answered. I think ultimately perhaps it's Lacan who is the least transparent, the most plural; he has a set of terms that he uses – Other with a capital 'O', other with a small 'o', the imaginary, the *objet a* – all of this vocabulary which seems to construct a system, but try to systematize it and you're lost because the words are not used in quite the same way the next time, there's a slippage.

One could argue then that these texts, for you, are doing something similar to what classic realism is supposed to do, as Leavis saw it. In Critical Practice, *for example, you call Lacan's 'Seminar on "The Purloined Letter"' an 'extremely dense, complex and perpetually surprising critical text [which] is not readily summarized' (p. 140). Now those laudatory terms are Leavisian – they are the kind of terms Leavis would apply to Conrad or James or particularly to Lawrence at what he saw as their best.*

Yes. But wouldn't he have, on the other side of this density, a truth, a metaphysical truth, which if you were perceptive enough, if you struggled long enough, you could get to? I would say with Lacan and with Derrida there is nothing that you get to. Now I don't mean you don't get to meanings, you get some meanings, but 'meanings' plural. There is no coherent system, there is no univocal truth, there is no single paraphrasable meaning.

But that was Leavis's point about Lawrence, surely – that you couldn't paraphrase and systematize what Lawrence had to say and that any attempt to do so would inevitably be disastrous?

Wouldn't that be an analogous to negative theology – to saying that wherever we try to locate God, with whatever figures we try to define God, he's not there, he's somewhere beyond everything we can say about him? Isn't that, for Leavis, where this truth ultimately resides, beyond language? Now I don't think that is the case with Lacan and Derrida. It's not that they possess a great truth which is so complex that it's ineffable. On the contrary, it seems to me what they propose is a set of meanings which slip and slide in such a way that you can never rest. It isn't that you can't rest in pursuit of something which is always beyond the text, but simply that you can't rest in pursuit of what it is this text could be put to work on behalf of, because if the Other keeps moving, there's an elusiveness which keeps you sitting up to find out where it is now and what it signifies now, and to see if you could in some way put it to work. It's not because in Lacan's head, if only we could get there, there's some ineffable wonderfulness that we want to possess.

Could we come on to this question of the subject, of subjectivity, which has been so prominent in poststructuralism and in your work – particularly in your book The Subject of Tragedy, *published in 1985, which aims to construct a history of the construction, so to speak, of the liberal humanist subject in the sixteenth and seventeenth centuries. The notion that the human subject is a construction, rather than an essence, has now become very widely disseminated, but an adequate account of how this process of construction occurs still seems to me to be lacking. There are a number of problems of which you'll be aware – for example, how does such an account avoid assuming the existence of what it sets out to explain? This is Paul Hirst's critique, in* On Law and Ideology *(1979), of Lacan's theory of the mirror stage, that in order for the infant to misrecognize himself as a unified subject, the constituents of subjectivity must already be there in the first place. Arguably the idea of interpellation runs into similar difficulties. And if one actually follows through that metaphor of construction, one might ask, for example, what are the materials out of which this construction is made and how and by what is it accomplished? To put the question in its most general form: don't we have a mere set of persuasive speculations rather than an adequate or coherent or scientifically informed account of how we come to be what we are?*

First of all I think it's important for me to say – this is something you didn't mention – that the reason why the subject is so crucial to my project is not simply that the subject is constructed, but that the subject is the lynchpin of the free west. The whole legitimation of the supremacy of the free west depends upon the idea of the unique autonomous individual consciousness choosing, and the reason why we had all those nuclear weapons pointing at the Soviet Union was that the Soviet Union didn't let people be unique subjects who chose. So the subject was very important, and still is. I think Hirst's demolition job, although attractive, is not right. I don't think it sticks. It seems to me that what all this is about is meaning and difference. The subject is what speaks, and in order to be able to speak, it has to take up a position in the language which is in circulation in the world it's born into. That language is already in circulation when the infant makes its first appearance in the world so that from the very instant that it's born it's surrounded by difference, and difference is crucial. Language is a system of differences with no positive terms and difference is the condition of meaning – meaning is only the trace of what isn't meant, what's excluded. Difference is the key, and I think Hirst's clever idea that there has to be a subject in place to say 'That's me' is wrong. All there has to be is the beginning of difference such that the infant can see a difference in the mirror image – can see that it is and isn't, as it were, the same as its mirror image, can grasp the possibility of the mirror image being two things at once, being other than the infant and being the same.

In relation to the question of the subject, you make a lot of play in your work with the idea of the subject as 'subjected'. But if one accepts the view that the subject is a construct, one might ask what is being subjected. Doesn't the idea of subjection entail the notion of some prior or co-existing something – not necessarily an essential self, but at least, say, a set of potentials – that is being constrained?

It's a pun, of course, it is exploiting the plurality of the meaning of the word, but I think the answer to your question is that what is being subjected is what we've left out of this discussion so far – the body, as Foucault would call it, or maybe what we need to call the human animal. On my theory, there isn't a *cogito*, there isn't a fully formed person, but there is a human animal which learns to speak and which could speak differently. It seems to me that Foucault's identification of the body, as having sensations however we interpret them, textualize them, is useful to feminism, though Foucault doesn't put it to work in that way. Think of how one set of meanings dominant in our culture until very recently – that men were the ones who went out to work and had cars, and women were the ones who stayed at home and did the shopping and the washing up – actually had implications for women's bodies. I would see women coming out of Tescos weighed down with shopping bags because their husbands had the car, and stooped over sinks which were Victorian and too low, and getting arthritis from sewing because it was a woman's work to do those things. So if we want a sort of ultimate, there is a body, there is a human animal on which this subjection is imposed. Maybe in a sense it subjects itself, insofar as it internalizes the meanings in circulation or fails to resist them; on the other hand it's not so easy just to say no to those meanings, so the degree of subjection is multiplied insofar as the meanings are identified as single, univocal and closed. In a period when what it means to be a proper woman is one thing and one thing only, what choice do you have? You can refuse to conform – and they'll lock you up.

One might seek to remove that subjection of the body, of the human animal; but a further point which seems very crucial to your project is that subjects can be reconstructed in a radical direction. One could acknowledge – indeed some conservative thinkers would acknowledge – that the subject is a construction, but would say that it doesn't follow that you can reconstruct the subject in any radical way and would point to the fact that attempts to do so have not, so far, proved successful. Can we assume that subjects have the degree of plasticity that your project of radical reconstruction seems to require?

I think there's a danger of my having given the impression of a great binary opposition; either we're fixed or we could be just anything. I don't think that's quite what I mean to imply. It isn't that we could simply choose to be something different tomorrow. But we have for a long time thought of the individual, the personality, as given, and, if given, unalterable. Now when you say that I say the subject can be reconstructed, it sounds like 1984, it sounds very disturbing. That isn't what I mean. I would put it more simply: I would say that the subject can change. There's been a lot of thinking on the left and on the right in terms of some sort of fixed truth of human nature: people are competitive, therefore we need a social system that takes account of that, or a sort of soft left position that people are naturally good. Now I don't think they're naturally anything; what they are therefore is produced by the culture they learn to inhabit. I think cultural differences are perceptible and that when you go to a really different culture you do see people thinking in different ways and with different assumptions. This suggests that people are products of a particular set of cultural circumstances, and that seems to suggest in turn that a different set of cultural circumstances from ours would produce different kinds of values, different sets of objectives, different modes of behaviour. Now I think that the free west has found it hard to believe that in practice. I think it has felt that everybody aspires to the condition of late capitalism. You saw this with the triumphalism over the fall of the Berlin Wall, and it's still going on even though we now know that this means massive unemployment and deprivation: still people are saying, see, all along these people have really wanted capitalism. Well, maybe, but there are good propaganda reasons why they wanted capitalism, because they've seen Hollywood movies and thought it was all like that, for instance. But it's not because there's a fundamental human nature which aspires to capitalism. So when I talk about the subject being able to change, it is precisely in order to challenge, again, what seems to me to be a kind of a dominant commonsense understanding that people just naturally are somehow, and if they naturally are somehow you should build a society which conforms to that. I think, on the contrary, we should think what kind of a society should we like to have and assume that it would be possible to fit in with it.

It's certainly true that one can identify cultural differences over human history and across the world today, but that does not necessarily mean you could have a culture which would inculcate, let's say, more socialist cooperative kinds of values. One of the startling things about Eastern Europe and about the USSR, even to some conservatives, is that the collective ethic, however distorted it may have been in practice, did not bite much deeper into human subjectivities than it seems to have done; how easily it caved in to capitalism. Doesn't that suggest that one may have to face up to the fact of certain limits to the range of differences we can hope to achieve?

I think anybody who made a plea for classical Marxism at this moment in history would be out of their minds, basically. But having said that, and having seen exactly what kind of a disaster, in many ways, those East European economies were, nonetheless I think we'd want to say, wouldn't we, that you can see exactly the moments at which they all went wrong. They were the moments at which they subscribed to a view that there was an élite vanguard which can decide on behalf of the people what's right for them, and the State took control. Now the State taking control is not cooperative, and sharing doesn't come into it. The bureaucracy simply takes over and tells you what to do, and this produces some good things and some bad things – mainly bad things, but also good childcare facilities and cheap rents and full employment and a lot of things that people in Eastern Europe are now beginning to miss a great deal because they didn't realize they'd lose them. We do need of course to recognize the importance of that repudiation by Eastern Europe of state Communism and we need to think very sceptically about the claims of classical Marxism, which was a nineteenth-century theory, but I think we can't take it that Eastern Europe demonstrates that there's no alternative to capitalism, that only capitalism can work. I think we can see very good reasons why what went wrong in Eastern Europe went wrong and we could learn from it and start again, not with a blueprint, not with a clear utopian model that we aspired to, but with ideas of what we won't do next time. And one thing we won't do next time, I hope, is have a vanguard that makes decisions for the rest of us.

You've stressed the importance of cultural work in making a contribution, even if only a modest one, to change. Could I ask you, in conclusion, what you are working on at the moment?

I'm working on a book about desire. I want to engage with the politics of sexuality. Groups of people – homosexual men, lesbians, and others – have started to insist on being heard and I'm glad of it, but what I've noticed throughout feminism, and in these movements which I fully support, is an unwillingness to problematize what I want to call desire itself. To say 'itself' suggests some kind of Platonic absolute again – it's just so hard to use the language at all without appearing to make another bid for metaphysics and I don't want to do that – but I think there is desire which is gender neutral and which can be talked about independently of object choice. It seems to me that we haven't paid sufficient attention to that. Literary criticism, whether radical or conservative, very rarely attends to the sexual desire which is the theme of so many of the texts. If you read nothing but the critics, you'd think Shakespeare's comedies were about morality or politics: you'd never guess they were about love. Our culture attributes a very high value to love. It privileges private life and personal experience over politics, with the effect that it keeps people off the streets. More even than Evangelical Christianity in the nineteenth century, desire is the solvent of class struggle in the twentieth. And yet this love we value so highly is very rarely discussed, except in anecdotes and gossip. People talk about sex – sexual preferences, and sexual practices. But apart from psychoanalysis, we don't have a vocabulary for talking about desire. As a result, what I'm doing is very speculative. I want to historicise desire. Obviously, I can only do it textually. I'm reading love stories from Chrétien de Troyes to Jeanette Winterson, and ranging from Henry James to Barbara Cartland. I want to suggest that this very private, intensely personal emotion has a history, that even in this most intimate area people have changed. There are no universal truths, even about sexual desire.

Marina Warner

London
19 March 1992

NICOLAS TREDELL: *What do you feel the decisive influences on your early development were?*

MARINA WARNER: I suppose there are two very decisive ones. One is that I'm a foreigner by formation, because I was brought up abroad until I was 12. My mother is truly foreign and speaks English with a foreign accent. She is Italian, from the South, and interestingly she is also a marginal foreigner in that Southern Italy belongs in a despised category, or did until recently. So there was this sense of not only coming from a background which made me different from my father's – as it were, the mainstream background – but also of coming from a part of Europe which rightly or wrongly – probably quite wrongly – I felt from an early age needed to be explained, because English people would assume that my mother was a Tuscan, and then when you'd say no, Apulia, when you'd say Bari, they would say, ah, Bari, with a sort of slight look which indicated that this wasn't the Italy of romance, or the Italy of sophistication, of the Renaissance, which they had expected. This was the Italy of Carlo Levi, this was where Christ stopped. My father was a bookseller, first in Cairo after the war, and then in Brussels, and as a child I spoke English only with adults. I spoke Arabic with my playmates when I was a little girl and French because I went to French speaking nuns in Cairo and in Belgium, and my English was therefore peculiar when I first came to boarding school in England. It was really learnt from books more than from people. I was terribly teased when I got to my school for my peculiar language; I didn't understand any of the slang. So I have had an experience of being different. Then the other, tremendously important influence is Catholicism, which comes from my mother. My father was a kind of social Protestant, in the sense that he felt you should know the vicar and you should go to church because it was part of the life of the English community and of the historical community. He had a tremendously strong sense of history. Very often what I write about is being divided in some ways, and I think that I do carry that sense of division within myself, that I am both Catholic and Protestant by formation, that I am both English and not English.

What was your experience of university education?

I went to university when it was hard for women to go, in the sense that we were outnumbered. This led to a sense of embattled female position within the universities – that's all changed now, which is wonderful, and it's one of the major changes of course. I wanted to go to Oxbridge. The new universities were only just starting then – this was in 1963 – so you had to be bold to go there, and anyway I had a rather strong sense of tradition – my father and grandfather had been to Oxford. I wanted that privilege and historical continuity. I chose a soft option, which was Modern Languages; I did have some other interests – I quite wanted to read Chinese funnily enough, but I simply didn't dare and I don't know that they would have accepted me. So I read French and Italian and there was a very strong medieval and philological accent then, you couldn't get out of it. My main love was poetry, and really contemporary or near-contemporary poetry. I loved the Italians – Quasimodo and Montale and Pavese and so forth – and I was completely obsessed with Baudelaire and Rimbaud and all the symbolists. So I was very reluctant to do the medieval work, which I found hard, but now of course I'm terribly grateful. It made a huge difference and it really led straight into all my preoccupations because it gave me the ability to read, really quite quickly, medieval materials, which I've used consistently ever since. So that was very lucky, and it makes me, in some ways, rather a conservative in terms of university syllabuses, because I do think that students should in a way not be asked too closely what they want. There should be some way in which they're made to discover areas which they might be reluctant to enter, because they could then be led on to other interests. I'm even grateful for the philology because it gives you a way through certain difficulties.

How did the relationship with Catholicism develop as you grew older?

As a child, I was really saturated in Catholic devotion, more than thought, though we were rather well taught. We did have special lessons in Church history, for instance, and of course we had lots and lots of New Testament stuff, but it was really the devotion rather than the thinking that affected me, and that also shows in my later interests. We had all these Catholic Truth Society pamphlets, which I still collect, and many edifying tales of heroic women and victims, because all the nuns had the names of saints so they would tell you the stories of their patrons. I've just been doing a lot of work on a saint called Dympna who is the patron saint of the insane and has intriguing connections with folklore: she's an example of an early medieval story which returns as fairy tale. Now the first place I ever came across Dympna was through one of our 'lay' nuns, the nuns who did the work and who used to bathe us when I first got to school, and she used to tell me about her saint. So there was this sense of storytelling behind the nun's imaginary lives. I used to be very against nuns, but I'm now more interested in them in a more tolerant way. They create their own identities. They break with their past life and when they make that break they invent a character for themselves, which is marked by the new name. That whole idea of making yourself anew in a symbolic way was, I think, very alive amongst the nuns. We were directed towards Mary, certainly rather than God the Father; we were directed a little bit towards Christ but Christ in relationship to Mary — he didn't really exist as an intercessor or in any kind of vivid way at all except as Mary's son, as a baby, as the victim in her arms in the Pietà and so forth. The whole accent fell on female imagery and female functions in terms of mercy, motherhood and then, obsessively for the nuns of course, sexual purity, which has faded very much for me as I've got older but was for a long time a desperate source of unhappiness. And so much of my work comes out of that.

We had a very strong topography in the convent: a grotto, for instance, which was made of cork oak from the Holy Land, and was entirely hung around with blessed rosaries, with Our Lady of Lourdes in the middle of it. We were only allowed into it on special feast days so it became a very desirable place. Then all the hockey fields and the tennis courts had different shrines of Mary, so as you walked through on a summer evening, with the long shadows, you would go through a series of as it were stations in the gardens punctuated by the presence of Mary. As far as I remember there was almost no other presence and of course within as well there were all the holy water stoups and the staircases and hundreds of pictures of her. She was the most dominating presence. The calendar of the year was entirely marked by her feasts. That liturgical calendar laid down a certain map in my mind which remains. We had a very good choir, and the Reverend Mother, who was very old, was a composer, and we used to sing masses for St Cecilia's Day that she had written. It was a very rich cultural life, and I now see it as more valuable than I see as negative the moral burden which was, I felt, imposed on me, so I've become more mellow talking about it. Certainly when I first started looking at Catholic imagery and beliefs about women I was more interested in the victimization aspects. Now I'm more interested in how, within systems, within structures of relationship and hierarchy, the low category – occupied by a figure such as the lay nun whose job it is to bathe the little children of privilege – is actually constructing something for herself. It's not just a story of oppression, it's a story of something else as well.

One review of your extensive study of the Virgin Mary, Alone of all Her Sex, *published in 1976, called it 'perhaps the best illustration since Joyce's* Portrait of the Artist as a Young Man *of the helpless love-hate relationship between a lapsed Catholic and the faith'* (Economist, *vol.260, no.6943, September 1976, p.135). How do you respond to that?*

It's far too much praise, of course, and if only it were a novel I would be much happier. I think that it isn't a novel due to the undermining of confidence that happened because of the kind of moral education I had. I had a sense of having to prove myself which has taken me a while to overcome in my practice and which I still feel intensely. By taking on a polemic against the nuns, I felt I was transgressing profoundly, and I couldn't transgress with any justification if I did anything as frivolous as write from the imagination. It was only by dint of expiating my transgression by doing an immense amount of research, for 12 hours a day, and really quarrying the Fathers of the Church, really breaking my head on them, that I would then justify this sinful act of defiance. Anything like the pleasure, to me, of writing from the imagination would be too lazy, too easy. This is not to say that writing fiction is an easy practice, but it would be seen like that. To write a novel about my relationship to Catholic views of sexual purity would not have expiated the act of disagreement fully enough. The love-hate relationship is extraordinarily powerful: I really thought that I had managed to set it aside or at least that by doing all that work I would exorcise it, but it continues. I'm still surrounded by images of Mary and there are many ways that I still find her very powerful and I am very drawn to her. In a sense, I'm still following some obscure pilgrimage. Mary is also a very important repository of stories about female language and female functions which she has absorbed into herself. This is partly an effect of the Reformation, because even Catholics obviously responded to cleansing processes, and simply gave over to Mary the attributes of a whole pantheon of female figures. So there's a revival of interest, a secular interest, in Mary as a source and resource.

In relation to that question of secular interest, could I ask you what relationship you think it is now possible for a secularized society, or secular people, to have to images like that of the Virgin Mary, to that whole repertoire of religious imagery which was once so powerful? What kind of relationship to such images is possible for those who no longer have the faith which was once associated with them?

It's such a deep question that it's very difficult to talk about. In what senses are myths alive in a society if they're not believed in? It's a philosophical question about belief. I think we're living in a time when in a way secular mythology is a kind of stand that we make against fundamentalism. I feel that if we build up our spiritual resources from history and culture in a secular mode, we may then develop riches with which to withstand the righteousness and lack of doubt of the Christian and other sectarian kinds of believers. I think they are very dangerous and I do take quite a firm stand on that. Indeed we see in Christians like Le Pen the danger of this form of righteousness. Julia Kristeva remarked at a conference that we must be able to say Chartres Cathedral is ours. We mustn't let Le Pen say it is his. We must be able to claim it. In a sense that was Péguy's stand too on Joan of Arc at the end of the nineteenth century. He was saying, as a socialist and a different kind of Christian from Le Pen, that Joan of Arc is a figure of the people, she's not a figure of royalist reaction and xenophobia. One mustn't surrender these hostages, these cultural points of collective memory and shared mythology, but continue to expand and absorb them. It's a very difficult position, though, to believe in Mary, but only as some kind of symbolic figure.

Doesn't it in fact drain such images of the power they once had when they were associated with faith? Can there be a secular body of myth – even if it's one that draws on traditional religious imagery – that can really stand adequately against those bodies of imagery which offer more fundamental kinds of identifications, the traditional identifications of faith?

If you look at how the Greek pantheon worked for the Renaissance, you have a sense of how this might be possible. I think I'm looking for a sort of Renaissance situation with regard to Catholic Christian images. I suppose it's a matter of allegory rather than belief. But the trouble philosophically is what happens when there is no-one who believes them – if you arrive at a point where no-one believes in Christ or Mary and these are simply signs floating free of that basis. Do we need someone to believe in them for them to work? I think psychologically we do. I personally do. For instance, I find *ex-votos* giving thanks for miracles performed very moving. I don't believe in the miracle, but I believe in the power of faith experienced by some-one who believes in the miracle. It's a sort of displaced activity. And yet I'm also very distressed by it. I've been to many holy places and seen many pilgrims, and have been very distressed by their faith because I think that they're fooling themselves. And yet faith in itself communicates a human affirmation of hope.

What do you think of attempts, by feminist theologians for example, to rehabilitate Christianity for feminism? Can it be done or is Christianity irredeemably patriarchal?

I take a practical line on that. I think their work is very valuable but not because of its relationship to some sort of intrinsic truth. This is a pragmatic line on Christianity itself, because I don't believe it's revealed truth, but I believe that it is a continuing process of thought, and as it's so important to social arrangements in many countries where its writ runs, this kind of feminist work is extremely valuable. The Church's record in terms of women is deplorable, but we've seen a lot of shifting of ground. For instance, when I was a child, we were not allowed on the altar because we were considered to pollute its holiness. Now you go into a Catholic Church and women are read-ing the lessons. The idea that the Word of God can be spoken by a woman at all is a tremendous advance, and it is an effect of radical pressure from within. So if women could achieve greater influence within the Church or gain the ear of some of the more influential people without being cashiered by the Pope – because of course that's what's happening at the moment, the radicals tend to get excluded and stopped from teaching, silenced – you would get move-ment on the basic humanitarian questions, and contraception above all, which have such an effect on women's lives. But quite a lot of feminist revision of previous religious interpretations seems to believe that it is going to arrive at some *Ur*-truth, and there it crosses

Jungianism – the idea that there is one goddess to be found, that there is some true picture, some *vera icon*, of the feminine. Now I absolutely part company with that. I think we are always in a continuum of contesting 'true images'. There is no *Ur*-truth. You can't scrape back to the archaeological first foundation. The very process of trying to do that lays another layer on the edifice. The question is who builds that layer, who gains the audience for the new *couche*. That's the struggle.

What would you say of the Catholic contribution to English culture in the twentieth century? There does seem to be a strong presence in the fields of literature and the humanities of people who either were brought up as Catholics, like yourself, or of Catholic converts such as Waugh and Greene.

I suppose there's an immediately broad difference between three groups. One consists of the old Catholic families and that legacy, which is connected to ideas of a fracture, the result of abandoning the medieval world, the world of the monasteries. I would see it as an abandonment of, for want of a better phrase, a concept of mixed genre. Medieval culture expresses itself very strongly in comedy, romance, folklore, fable, types of festivity, carnival, certain notions of the popular. This is set aside by Reformed England, and it affects language, it affects the play of high and low in language. Then you have a tremendously strong and important aspect of Catholicism: foreignness. Possibly, this also relates to ideas about mixed genre, or high and low that I'm interested in. Catholicism comes in with the Irish or, as in the case of my mother, with the Italians. There are early waves of immigration which bring Catholicism back to some extent. It's interesting now in Britain, because a lot of Catholics are Africans: the British Empire returns partly in a Catholic form.

Now the elected and self-appointed Catholics, the Graham Greenes and Evelyn Waughs, I find quite puzzling in terms of culture. Evelyn Waugh himself of course is such a peculiar and difficult voice. It seems to me that he was not in the least bit interested in the old medieval world of the popular, but he was interested in the snobbish idea of continuity, so that there is a sense in which recusancy gave him a desirable lineage. The desire for a kind of pure English lineage brought him to Catholicism, although it was a marginal lineage and an odd choice for someone who desired to belong to the centre – a perverse way of establishing himself as central. Graham Greene connects very strongly with the ideas of foreignness and universality in

Catholicism – the sense that there are no national borders in the Church. This relates to Greene's whole interest in colonies and former colonies and their attempts to define themselves in relation to the colonizing power – whether it's Americans in Vietnam or French in Vietnam. That whole colonial interest is bound up with the question of national versus international. Graham Greene is also a very good example of how English Catholicism differs from Mediterranean Catholicism in that his is really a Protestant conscience at work. The guilt in Graham Greene, though we use it very much as a quick way of talking about Catholic guilt, is actually not very Catholic, as you can see if you compare it to the way Catholicism is represented, say, in *The Leopard* or indeed to the Reformers' view of Catholicism – the way that the Leopard can go to confession after leaving his mistress and then go straight back to his mistress is what was reproached against the whole Catholic idea of responsibility, whereas Graham Greene has a deeply Protestant sense that you can't be absolved so easily.

Could we explore a statement you make towards the end of Monuments and Maidens: the Allegory of the Female Form *which came out in 1985. You say there: 'Biological sex cannot be the ring-fence in which the imagination lies wingless. Writers cleared it before painters; but visual representation, sculpted and painted, has continued to reify women in a manner some writers of fiction overcame some time ago' and you cite Shakespeare, George Eliot, Henry James, Edith Wharton and Willa Cather. (1987 edn, p. 333). But have writers, especially male writers, cleared that ringfence as much as you suggest? Doesn't Henry James, for example, for all the sensitivity and subtlety of some of his portrayals of women essentially show them as passive victims? James doesn't, to take a phrase you use in your study of Joan of Arc, extend 'the taxonomy of female types' (1983 edn, p. 28) and in some cases – in* The Bostonians *for example – he is clearly hostile to women's attempts to redefine their identities in certain ways.*

I think what I said was a bit sweeping. I was writing it at the time against a lot of polemical feminism of a separatist kind, so I made an argument against gender determinism perhaps more strongly or less subtly than it should have been made, because I was trying to challenge some received ideas. It was at the time extremely controversial to use the Tiresias image as I did and to claim that the imagination was androgynous. It was old-fashioned, a kind of Virginia Woolf position. I thought that I would be greatly attacked for it but interestingly enough it was never taken up. The feminists who liked the book just seemed to ignore that conclusion. I don't think that portraying women as passive victims is necessarily a male thing to do. I've just read *What Maisie Knew*, which I hadn't read before. There are a number of extremely unsympathetic portraits of women in that novel and you feel, through Maisie, Henry James himself all the time, but nevertheless it is an astonishing picture of a child's sensibility, and her gender is rather important. She couldn't be a boy. Her relationship of charm and compliance and the sexual *frissons* that occur with the men, including her own father, make her a very realized female figure of that age. And Willa Cather's very good on men, I think. It's interesting that they're both homosexual – this is really quite important and I haven't read anything very good on how homosexual sensibility contributes to crossing gender boundaries in writing.

Given then that some writers, have been able to clear the ringfence of biological sex in a way that visual artists haven't, or hadn't perhaps until recently, how have they been able to clear it? Why has it been possible in writing and not, in the past, in visual art?

We have to think about forms and the relation of the user of the form to the form. I would say at a guess that when you have a subjective voice posited in a written work you are likely to have more of a relationship between the work and the sex of the creator, so that I don't think you'd get many lyric poems in the first person which are able to transcend biological sex – possibly why quite a lot of medieval poems should be ascribed to women. With painters and sculptors, one would say that when their sense of themselves as creators is formed, there is a way – and it still continues, it's endemic to contemporary artists – in which they come to see themselves as heroic geniuses, and it's their ego, rather than any kind of migration of their imagination, which gives them their relationship to their material. They're almost all novelists that I listed in the passage you quoted, and I should have been more specific and said that the novel is the form in which the migrating imagination can work more freely. This is not true of some *Bildungsromane* and so forth, but the form of the novel often demands that the writer enter another personality, and I don't think that painting does this on the whole – though possibly some medieval painting of religious subjects dissolves the presence of the author. It's to do with 'I's' and 'eyes', it's to do with 'I beheld' and with the whole idea of vision, of summoning up – you see with your own eyes. There is an implicit authorial eye in painting. The act of looking is not imagined from another's view. And when you are the spectator, you spectate from your position and that is made up of a lot of things that you are. I like very much Kundera's remark that a novel is 'the territory where no one possesses the truth...but where everyone has the right to be understood'. It is the great arena in that sense. It's a little bit like the Greek theatre used to be – a dramatist like Euripides is a very good example of someone who migrates through many gender positions, who is very capable of seeing the female point of view. In *Medea*, you have the great chorus, then Medea's own justification of herself, then Jason's horror – you go through the whole moral debate. I think that, from the eighteenth century onwards, fiction in a way became the place in which this was possible.

Do you think the development of feminism in recent years has opened up new possibilities for women in literature and the visual arts?

I think that the amount of theoretical development in the field of gender studies has helped women's inspiration. Women have a lot of material to work with. Men, through having been generic for so long and then losing their generic status, have actually missed a gender category which would give them material to work with. There is a sense of a void in men's visual fantasy and I think, to some extent, in some male writers as well. Authors looking for subjects today tend to be male. The women are not suffering from that. They may not be such powerful stylists but they're not worried about what to write about. Some of our most successful male writers, with the most fantastically vigorous style, brilliant wit, astonishingly inventive syntax and wonderful ear, are short of material. This is rather sweeping – of course there are men who have a subject but sometimes I do feel that there's wasted talent. I think this is why Robert Bly has such a success with his book *Iron John*. It's really a lot of tosh but it has achieved huge popularity because it's a pebble thrown into this gigantic chasm that men feel. A good example of a book that escaped this problem because, in a sense, it faced it fully frontal is *A Child in Time*, Ian McEwan's book about being a modern man, which explores the issue in terms of his own relationship to his mother, and being born and being a father, and politics and boyishness and heroism, and that whole notion of authority and maleness which runs through the book and is reflected in the politician who becomes a child again.

*Could we turn to a general question about your cultural histories,
and then move on to your novels. Those histories are characterized
by superb ecphrases, verbal evocations of the paintings and other
artefacts that you discuss – as, for example, in your account in*
Monuments and Maidens *of walking through Paris and encounter-
ing the various statues. In that respect, it seems to me, your work
joins the tradition of Ruskin and Pater, in which aesthetic and cultural analysis becomes itself a kind of aesthetic construct. Your cultural histories also combine impressive erudition with a clarity which
makes them accessible to an audience outside the academy. Do you
consciously aim to write in such a clear and evocative way, or are you
just doing what comes naturally?*

I think I've always had a slight tendency to preciousness and of
course I loved Pater, and Ruskin, so you've put your finger on it.
There is a danger that the ecphrasis becomes a kind of screen which
conceals rather than reveals. But without wanting to be too mes-
sianiac I do feel that we have been given this unbelievable language;
I love dictionaries and I love words and so I want to use them as much
as possible. It's an almost musical thing. And I have always thought
that there should be no difference between the enterprise of imaginative writing and the enterprise of biography or essays, and indeed the
model practitioners, in my view, don't make a difference. James
Baldwin was a wonderful essayist who creates living stories when he
writes an essay. His essays are documents of imagination as well as
of history or polemics. And there are many others. I was excluded
from the academy, or to some extent I voluntarily excluded myself,
because they wanted me to stay – but to do medieval French which I
didn't want to do – and anyway I didn't like academe, I felt it was
parochial. I didn't want to be watched and observed, I wanted the
freedom of London. And then I didn't really have a subject because
I began too soon for women's studies and cross-cultural studies and
comparative literature and that sort of thing – they didn't really
exist, not in Oxbridge anyway. I also have a journalistic interest. I
like to go out and see things and be in the world. I liked doing Paris
in the way that I did in *Monuments and Maidens* – it was an idea that
I had that I would just try and see the allegories of Paris rather than
sitting at home and studying them.

*You've said you don't see a gap between the enterprise of imaginative
writing and that of writing non-fiction. What relationship do you see
between your cultural histories and your novels?*

I think it's quite a close relationship which I've only really noticed myself rather recently: almost every novel I've written is a postscript to a non-fiction book. When I was writing *Alone of All Her Sex*, I became very interested in visionaries, but of course as that book was a criticism of the cult I placed the sympathy that I felt into the character of the visionary in the novel *In a Dark Wood*. *The Skating Party* has a Joan of Arc theme because the hostage, the witch figure, in that novel is used by the anthropologist to endorse his own principles, which is exactly the relationship of politicians and historians to the salvific figure of Joan of Arc, in that her person doesn't matter, her survival doesn't matter, she herself is of no account: what matters is the gloriousness of her death. With *The Lost Father*, the relationship between fiction and non-fiction doesn't seem quite as close, but the mainspring of that novel for me was the fact that my mother had been brought up a fascist. The 'lost Father' is meant to be both the truly lost dead man in the story and the imagined leader, the Mussolini figure, the dream of a figure of authority who will save you. The whole novel is meant to be a sort of parable about how you invent such heroic figures and how they are fraudulent. I don't know that it works or comes across, but that was what I had in mind. It is to do with the allegorical structures which represent a nation to itself, and how a nation erects in a sort of dream language its own ideals which it then can default on in reality because the dream sustains them. So here and there in the novel there are townscapes with statues and architecture built in this kind of rhetoric. I was trying to communicate the idea that while we do represent our ideals to ourselves, the whole process is fallacious, in the same way as the narrator tells us that the family has been telling itself a story about the father which is fallacious. I think there are two differences between fiction and non-fiction which have pushed me towards writing more fiction than I used to. One is that with fiction you are responsible to yourself and to your material, but you do not have to master the vast range of data that now pours out as you do when you research a non-fiction book. The other reason, which is more important and in a sense more interesting, is that I think fiction is a form of middle age or maturity. The kind of non-fiction that I was writing was quite prescriptive. I hope I accepted that I didn't have the answers, but there was a sense that there were answers to be had and that I might be producing a sketch of some of them, and it is, in a sense, rather youthful to feel that. Fiction is a much more open-ended and ambiguous terrain where you don't have to know, you only really have to observe and try and bring the issues to life in some way. You don't have to have a view. For instance, with *The Lost Father*, I was able to portray certain female strengths which if I had been writing a history of women under fascism, I would not have been able to praise. I was able to praise them because it was fiction.

One of the elements of your fiction which appears both as a theme and as an aspect of structure is a concern with time, with an interaction between the past and the present. How would you see the importance of that?

One of the themes of Derek Walcott's *Omeros*, which I've been reading recently, is the presence of memory, and the idea that the mark of the human is to remember and the mark of barbarity is to forget – we live as consciously unexamined people if we accept that things lie beyond memory, beyond reach. So a lot of the practice of writing is one of recording or calling back from oblivion the forgotten – Walcott talks about that a lot – but the very act of recalling can perpetuate the forms that are being brought back to life. So it is of itself to some extent a conservative practice. At times he cries out for the blank page and he talks about the sea as an ideal place where there is no memory and about language where there is no metaphor, the blankness in that sense also being redemptive. But of course that's not in any sense a human condition of culture – it can only exist as a chimerical ideal, to have no memory, to have a language that is pure because it has no metaphors, no lies, no fictions in it. We are the product of these buried forms and they must be called back in order to be questioned, but in the act of calling them back you risk reviving them.

All our present century has this problem. Modern Germany has to some extent decided not to remember, because the memory is too disturbing, but that creates a fracture in their consciousness. Even to be in Germany is very strange because there's this whole gap, there are no memorials. They don't have memorials to the dead of the last World War because it's so shaming, and yet if you build a memorial what kind of memorial do you build? That's a particularly acute problem for the German artist or writer but it is, in a sense, a model of all our problems. I think the clue to my approach to the relationship between past and present is that it is a Catholic approach. It arises in my work entirely out of my study of Mary. The New Testament is the book, the Old Testament is the prefiguration of the book, there is an Old Covenant and a New Covenant, and the New Covenant exists as not just a continuum but as a recapitulation in an actual form of the promises of the past. That sense is in my latest novel, *Indigo*, as well – the sense that we re-enact what was prefigured, that, without it being deterministic, there's some sort of divine plan, that the structures repeat.

Isn't there a tension, both in your fiction and non-fiction, between that conservative sense that structures repeat and a radical urge to break free of the past? Indigo, for example, is much concerned with the relationship between the colonial past and the present. But how far can we move out of the structures of that past, or of any past, and how far do we continue to recapitulate them in different forms?

I think that then what you try and do is tell the story in such a way as to shift its angle of vision, set it off balance, so that when the recapitulation occurs, you see it in another light. One of the things that happens in *Indigo* is that each of the fairy tales it contains is slightly off balance to what occurs, so that you think, for example, that Serafine, the childrens' nurse, is, as it were, telling the story that will be then fulfilled but in fact every position is slightly out of line so that the golden girl before whom everything lies is not Xanthe but Miranda – the story has shifted one position. I didn't think this out when I was writing *Indigo* – it was only thinking about it afterwards that I saw that was what I'd done, because I was actually slightly worried that the stories didn't match, and I thought, why do they not match? It was because I'd made them so neat in books like *In a Dark Wood* and *The Skating Party*. Frank Kermode said that in *The Skating Party* the relationship between the ecphrasis of the painting and the plot was inert, which is right – there is something inert because they match exactly. I think that *Indigo* is unsettling because you don't quite know where you are really, which may not be a satisfactory solution to the problem, but at least it's not inert – there is a sense of chemical reaction, of fizz, at the point where the stories and the supposed reality rub against each other.

Indigo is to some extent a postcolonial rewriting and revision of The Tempest. How did you yourself see the relationship between that play and your novel?

I did feel, as a person who's not Caribbean, who's white, privileged, middleclass etc, that I didn't have a right to enter this terrain of postcolonial exploration, but it seemed to me, in relation to *The Tempest*, that I did have a right simply because it's a body of story that is

held in common. *The Tempest* has passed into myth; Caliban and
Miranda are mythic figures now like Robin Hood. I had a sense of
Prospero's mesmeric centrality to the whole thing, and his very
domination of it as the pattern maker, the Magus, made me wish to
see if there was another way of patterning this set of figures. It was
to do I suppose again with a love-hate relationship with the play – of
being both completely enchanted by it whenever I've seen it and at
the same time wanting to contest it because of the complete silencing
of Sycorax, the brutality of Caliban's nature and treatment, and of
course Miranda's acquiescence – the father-identified daughter who
is so compliant with his designs. She is in a plot that's written by her
father and so I suppose I wanted to be her father, to write a different
plot for her or at least to show her that she is in a plot. My Miranda
in *Indigo* is in a sort of plot devised by her family, but something
again shifts one position, and instead of marrying a Ferdinand she
marries a Caliban.

An intriguing element of Indigo *is the game, played both by the col-
onists and colonized and by their descendants, called Flinders. Why
did you invent that game?*

Originally it was going to be cricket – it clearly is cricket in its function, and the name Flinders comes from a Ted Hughes poem about
cricket. But I realized that if it was going to be cricket, I would not be
able to give it its metaphorical value. It was important to transform
it so that it could be seen in a fantastic way which would actually
make it more real, and to strip cricket of the associations it has either
for *aficionados* or for people who yawn at the very word. I felt that
I wanted to escape that and turn it into a telling image. C.L.R. James
was my mentor and also Michael Manley. They were the two people
I read on cricket and Empire and I wanted to peel the associations
away from the game so that we could see it as a place where power
relations have been played out in one way, then another way, and
then a third way again. I wanted the game – the Imperial game which
did not cease to be an Imperial game but which became also the game
of those who had been conquered and colonized and their successors
– to be calqued exactly on the battle I describe between the indigene-
ous inhabitants of the island and the first colonizers, because I
wanted to show the irony that the most civilized sport is actually
born out of conflict. And I wanted it to be the case not only that the
nomenclature of the game should recall this forgotten battle – that all
sorts of historical associations should have decayed into the very

names of the positions in the game and so forth – but also that the game should be more violent than cricket in the way it was played. So I put into it a little bit of the Sienese *palio*, the horse race which turns the town of Siena into a kind of ferocious civil war twice a year.

As well as the strong sense in Indigo *of an originary conflict which continues in only partly sublimated form, the novel also expresses a desire for reconciliation that reminded me of E.M. Forster – for example, the ambiguous resolution provided by the baby which Miranda and the black actor produce recalls the ambiguous resolution, through the baby of Helen Schlegel and Leonard Bast, of class and cultural divisions in* Howards End. *That Forsterian quality leads me to ask whether* Indigo, *for all its evocation of the violence and hypocrisy of colonialism and its racist residues, isn't finally too benign – or whether in fact you wanted that benignity, that intimation of reconciliation, at the end?*

The ending is really inevitable because of the character of the book as fairy tale. It does express an eirenic desire that we should make a multicultural, multiracial society which moves to a different system of values, including colour values. This is why black is, as it were, the end colour of the book, and is the sum of all the previous colours. It's meant to be a symbol of hope. It is the rainbow. Of course, the traditional symbol of hope is the rainbow complete, but my rainbow is not white, which is what in fact the spectrum amounts to in physics. In *Indigo*, it amounts to blackness. That aspect of the novel is an attempt on my part gently to move the symbolism that attaches negativity to ideas of blackness, not just in the figure of Caliban himself, but more generally with the colour black. *Indigo* begins and ends in what the French call *le métissage*, interbreeding. I think *le métissage* is something we have a great cultural resistance to in spite of the fact that it is the existential condition. None of us is pure: it's an impossible position. In an essay [in *PN Review* 82, 18:2, pp. 15-17], I quoted Primo Levi's wonderful remark that without impurity the wheel cannot turn. In chemistry there is no possibility of life without impurity. He's talking about that in the context of Nazism's desire for purity, but there is still – I feel it myself – an ideological resistance to the idea of pollution, a fear of pollution, and we think of impurity and mixing as forms of pollution. And colour is one of the areas where this resistance to pollution is evident – we see it all too grievously in France at the moment for example, and in resistance to immigration and so forth. To write about *le métissage* as

I do in *Indigo* is a way of trying to shift the boundaries of what we think of as identity.

In relation to that question of shifting boundaries and identities, could I take up a remark you make in that PN Review *essay, when you say,* apropos *of the legend of St Cunera and St Ursula, '[t]here was a time when I would have attacked such a legend as a compendium of Judaeo-Christian bigotry, savage and sadistically misogynist …now I am more interested in reinterpreting it to yield up new meanings helpfully' (pp. 16-17). What sorts of forms do you think such reinterpretations, both by yourself and by others, might take?*

I think it is important to develop the relationship between mandarin and popular culture, and the sense of responsibility of the mandarinate to the popular. That relationship has already developed a great deal – if you think of how the universities thought about the canon before, there has been a fundamental change of feeling. Of course it does lead to some sort of sillinesses, like people leaving universities with degrees in Disney, but I think basically that spirit is right. I would say – and in a sense this is an old-fashioned form of socialistic humanism – that there could be an interventionist relationship between mandarin and popular culture, though not of a paternalistic kind. An important area to me seems to be television and I think we have a profound responsibility to television which at the moment we are hopelessly abandoning. Having built up a wonderful communications system in this country, we are letting it go. That's going to be terribly serious. I think that all the people who are involved in the arts in this country need really to pitch in to prevent the thoroughgoing commercialization of the networks.

One of the most serious cultural developments of recent times has been the introduction of cable television without any form of control at all. There is now a mysterious popular culture which has no monitoring of any sort; no relationship is being built between the people who watch it and the people with whom they live who don't watch it. Another aspect was highlighted by what Juliet Stevenson said in relation to the film industry – that we are not making our national dreams, we are importing our dreams. One dreadful symptom is the fact that now you have to have cable to watch the cricket and that this might happen with the football. These are national sports and they are religious in the old sense, of binding – *religio*, to bind. These common pursuits should be held in common. They should not be bought and sold along class lines, which of course is another aspect of cable which is very damaging indeed – that it's class bound, to some extent. I would like to see a tremendous investment in attempting to tell stories to ourselves on our broadcasting systems, and those stories could draw on the kind of folklore material that I'm interested in and also on revisionist history. But one of the interesting aspects of folklore is that when you go back and look at it, the national order is all dissolved. This is one of the hopeful things about it. It appeals to me because it shows the common structures of the human imagination across all kinds of geographical and racial borders. This is not to say that the stories are archetypal. They are records of experience, people making sense of their experiences to themselves. We have sympathy with Odysseus, we understand what he felt like wanting to go home, or living with Calypso and having to leave her. These things are held in common, we have a common material reality. So I feel that it wouldn't be a narrow-minded nationalistic kind of enterprise to try and create as it were a kind of British cinema on television. It requires money. But I think it's an important political thing to do to bind our community because certainly television programmes are very binding, people love to talk about the characters and so forth. So that's one area of responsibility for the so-called intellectual élite.

Could I take up another point you make in that PN Review *essay, when you say that taking what you call 'the tinsel casket of folklore, fancy, and myth – even of superstition – doesn't mean consenting to its contents or affirming them – the salt, the mustard which make the material live are irony and humour…scepticism and pleasure are not incompatible' (p. 17), But as you also very much recognize in that essay, the last decade or so has seen a great upsurge of the desire for fundamental identifications of a religious and nationalistic kind – it's bound up with the desire for purity, the fear of pollution, which you talked about earlier. In view of that upsurge, can we suppose that irony and humour and scepticism and pleasure – all those civilized qualities, all those Forsterian qualities if you like – can offer sufficiently powerful gratifications to enough people, especially to the relatively dispossessed, to cause them to abandon their fundamentalisms? And isn't there a kind of liberal fundamentalism in what you say which might be seen as a form of cultural imperialism – it's once again Europe trying to impose its notion of civilized values upon the rest of the world. Isn't this how some of the more articulate fundamentalist objectors to* The Satanic Verses *see things?*

I wouldn't be so Eurocentric as to claim that humour, irony and scepticism are European. Moslem folklore, and even some of the actual commentaries on the Koran, are full of extraordinary flights of fancy and humour which the fundamentalists, or the purists among the fundamentalists, have very much set aside. Rushdie himself is in this sort of Islamic tradition. What the purist fundamentalists present as *Ur*-truth is in fact a modern and a relatively recent interpretation which claims atavistic authenticity. This kind of theocracy is a new political development. I do think that it appeals in our culture because of a failure of community and representation and access and that the dispossession you mentioned is not just material, it's to do with who is heard. The Rushdie affair in Britain created a platform for people who were not normally heard and they should have been normally heard if they wanted to be. All those hundreds of thousands of people who demonstrated against *The Satanic Verses* were demonstrating out of a frustration that arises not at all from *The Satanic Verses* but from something else that lies very deep.

To go back to broadcasting, that's why, although it may seem paternalistic, and may be very clumsy, to have specified proportions of time allotted to representing minorities in something like the Channel 4 way, it is at least an attempt to gather up the voices that make up our community and give them a hearing. I think that the drift of what you're saying is that a lot of my reforming and rather strenuous and strained optimism is doomed. I think that's probably right. I do actually think that we probably are heading for some quite unpleasant, some very unpleasant, times. But quiescence would default on the responsibility I see, because history's placed me in a particular place at a particular time with a particular set of privileges. I've come to think that the apocalyptic evocation of our times by some writers – Martin Amis is a good example – does not shift as much as the more Rabelaisian festivity of a writer like Angela Carter. Martin Amis's popularity is due to a sort of quiescence that is involved in accepting his Calvinistic, depressed view of man's inhumanity to man. He writes extraordinarily powerful dystopic visions and his account of misogynistic people is completely searing and brilliant, but it doesn't move misogyny.

Do you think your aversion to that kind of vision relates to your early Catholicism?

Yes, it probably does. The sense that you can fall but find grace and be redeemed is a Catholic idea and I do often have Catholic reflexes

about certain things in the sense that I dislike their Calvinistic tendencies. I disliked *Twin Peaks*, for instance, because it seemed to me
to be steeped in a Calvinistic view of irredeemable evil. So, once a
Catholic, as they say.

You've drawn on your interest in folklore in our conversation, you
make much use of folklore material in your latest novel, and you're
working at present on a study of fairy tales. In conclusion, could you
tell us something about that?

I'm looking for the points of tension that will illuminate something
that looks inevitable and symbolic. I've got very upset about the
figure of the wicked stepmother, who is an absolutely endemic,
apparently essential figure of female evil that occurs regularly in
folklore. But looking at it and trying to see why such a figure might
exist in terms of social and material circumstances, I came up with
two possibilities. One is very obvious, which is that there were a lot
of wicked stepmothers because there were a lot of young mothers'
deaths; but that's not as interesting, because it would not be a reason
for the type to continue after those historical circumstances has passed. The second sort of model which I've tried to suggest is that the
people who tell fairy stories tend, as far as we can see, to be servants
or elderly relatives who are in charge of the children. They were, and
indeed to the present day continue to be, a very vulnerable group in
society – the old woman who has ceased to be strong, though she
may have household tasks and mind the kids, is vulnerable, economically extremely so, and dependent on the goodwill of the members
of the household which supports her. She is likely to have been displaced at some point by the new female head of the household, who
is likely to be the mother of the children, so the displacement activity
of the wicked mother in the stories is not, in my model, seen from the
point of view of the child who invents a bad mother in order to cope
with the stresses of their lives, which is a psychoanalytical model. It's
a social model in which the old woman seeks to win the allegiance of
the young in the household by portraying the person who has the
power in the household, the queen figure, as bad, and portraying herself in the figure of the old crone, who appears in many, many fairy
stories bringing boons. Fairy godmothers are usually old crones;
very often, interestingly enough, they are in disguise in the stories;
they're really fairies but they're disguised as old women, and it's only
the good child who recognizes and is kind to them. So this is, in a
sense, a utilitarian argument, a *cui bono* argument, that the wicked

stepmother is a figure of fantasy produced by a vulnerable woman against a more powerful woman. That means that the wicked step-mother is not a symbolic figure, she's a figure born of economic realities, and her present survival in popular culture becomes some-thing else, becomes a reflex of misogyny, as in Disney characters – Disney has very misogynistic iconography – and then continues in a terrifying way because it then feeds back on itself. Most children now are completely familiar with the figure of the wicked stepmother, at a time when stepmothers are increasingly common, no longer for reasons of death but for reasons of divorce, and this creates a very difficult symbolic wall against women. So I'm hoping that my theory is going to loosen the hold of this symbol by showing that it's not an inevitable projection of the immature mind's needs but is embedded in a certain sort of power structure.

Donald Davie

Omega Cottage, Silverton, Devon
6 May 1992

NICOLAS TREDELL: *Could you begin by telling us about the influences which you feel shaped you prior to going to Cambridge?*

DONALD DAVIE: I was born and brought up in Barnsley in South Yorkshire, and I am still aware, and was very much aware when I grew up, of being a Northerner, though in actual geographical terms Barnsley is really North Midlands. But we were invited to think of ourselves as Northerners and I still, sentimentally or not, do this from time to time. We all went to the Baptist Chapel, and although in my teens I drifted away from it so that, for instance, I was never baptised in that church, provincial nonconformity was the cultural milieu, and I'm aware of this and still have considerable affection for and loyalty towards that tradition. Those are two influences that I'm well aware of. It's also true that we lived on the west side of Barnsley which is already climbing up to the Pennines, and walking up to the moors and on the moors was a great matter to me in those days. It's not, of course, the most picturesque part of the Pennine Chain nor of the Peak District which begins only a few miles south of there. On the other hand, though, just for that reason, it was in those days, and I believe still is, very largely untracked grouse moor so that as a teen-age boy I and my friends, strange as it may seem from a blighted industrial town like Barnsley, could and did, in an hour or so on the bus, escape into what one would have to call wilderness. It isn't everywhere in England that you can have that experience. Politically, of course, Barnsley was in those days, and has remained, an entirely proletarian town. The only classes that there were in Barnsley in those days were a small bourgeoisie and a vast proletariat. By the same token, of course, Barnsley has always been, and is still, a Labour Party stronghold, with a majority of thousands which I'm sure the Labour Party managers would prefer to spread more thinly in other parts of the country. My father was a very small business-man and we always voted the other ticket but never with any hope of success. This did give me the experience, from quite early, of being in a permanent minority, and this I think has had its effect upon me in terms of some things that look like pugnacity in my later life. I made friends among the socialist majority, of course, and so in a sense I feel that I know and have always known the sort of character and habit of mind which produces – we're talking now about small town intel-lectuals, you understand – the socialist left-wing intelligentsia. This is worth remembering when I from time to time declare my antipathy to left-wing habits of thought in society and politics. I do it from the inside and I have sympathies therefore with certain intellectuals of that persuasion, although I'm quite clear why I oppose them.

I went to the local grammar school and, looking back it seems to me that I had a better than average schooling. My parents had a very funny attitude. They were proud of being West Riding people and very ready to resent slights upon it that they discerned in other people's conversation, and yet they were perfectly sure that I had a duty to get out of it if I could. It was a provincial backwater and we were made aware that a much richer, softer, more historical stretch of England lay to the south particularly and that to that extent Barnsley was impoverished – not economically, though it was economically impoverished too in those days, the Depression of the thirties – but culturally deprived. This was what fired my parents and me to the really quite fierce competitiveness in school which in fact did drive me out of Barnsley into Cambridge. It was an escape, it was thought of as such, and yet at the same time we were loyal to the place you had to escape from. It was a curious ambivalence.

I think the final thing is that I have to say that both my mother and father were very literary people – rather remarkably so, since both of them sprang from a level of British society in which that habit of mind was by no means common, but I see now that it must have been one of the things that drew them together. So I grew up hearing English poetry quoted unselfconsciously by my mother and/or by my father. That was an incalculable boon.

What kind of poetry was your mother particularly interested in? You've written that she was very interested in Browning, for exam-ple.

Yes, she was. But she knew by heart I think the whole of Palgrave's

Golden Treasury, which is what you would expect of her generation in her circumstances. Heaven knows, we all know what's wrong with Palgrave's *Golden Treasury*, it is a monument to Victorian taste, but it's not a bad introduction to the whole range of English lyric poetry from at any rate the Renaissance to the present day. My mother knew it all and quoted it repeatedly. Then it is true that she had a particular affection for Browning. When I was about 15, she introduced me to that and I started reading about Browning. I didn't realize at the time, though I do now, that this too was predictable because Browning is a nonconformist poet. One forgets that because he was a very liberal nonconformist, but he was brought up in a dissenting household, a very affluent one, and some of his poems, though not his best poems, do deal with that. I think that's what may, in the first instance, have attracted my mother. My mother also introduced me to some twentieth-century poets, to the Georgians, and Walter de la Mare was perhaps the first modern poet whom I fell in love with – it was as strong a feeling as that.

So you got out of Barnsley and you arrived in Cambridge in 1940. What was your first experience of Cambridge?

I was very considerably disoriented. I think that Cambridge had for so many years been the pinpointed target of my parents' and my aspirations that no place could have lived up to the golden expectations that I'd invested in it. On the other hand, I was certainly aware of the architectural beauty of the university part of the town. This was really very new to me. I met boys – not girls in those days – from different parts of the country who spoke differently from me and who came sometimes from more affluent homes and from what might be thought more elevated social ranks. I think of it very much in anthropological terms. It sounds crazy to say so about such a small island as ours, but even within England, let alone the island as a whole, there are, in an anthropological sense, more cultures than one, and my going from Barnsley to Cambridge was crossing the divide. I moved from one tribe to another, which was of course educational, but was also, in the first instance, rather deeply disorientating.

You talk about culture rather than class. Would you say it was a consciousness of cultural difference rather than a consciousness of class difference that you felt?

I think I would. It's certainly what I want to believe. There were fellow-students, among the more stupid ones, who would attempt to condescend to me because of my provincial accent and some provincial habits, and also because I had largely won my way and so I wasn't being supported by my father, but these were very few and far between. I'm struck by the comparison with Raymond Williams: Raymond Williams was almost exactly my contemporary and he came from the provinces, from the Welsh borders, as I came from the West Riding. Some of Raymond's experiences, as he recounts them, coincide with mine, but the class divide plainly was far more prominent for him than for me. I think the difference may be that my father was *petit-bourgeois* – very *petit*, but he was bourgeois – and we were made to think that we weren't part of the proletariat, whereas Raymond, as we know, saw his own roots as firmly in the working-class Welsh borders.

So you didn't feel that alienation at Cambridge that Raymond Williams and others of a later generation like Terry Eagleton (see pp. 126-7 above) have described?

Oh, nothing like it. I've read those accounts and I've always found this response strange. I now remember I did have friends who were a little exacerbated. But Raymond and people like Eagleton would have little patience with the other reaction that I was aware of from my contemporaries – boys from backgrounds not totally unlike mine in the provinces who were so taken with the glamour of Cambridge that they couldn't wait to scramble into it by one route or another. That seems to me just as common a reaction as the one Raymond describes – people carefully attempting to disguise their provincial accent and so on.

Your education at Cambridge was interrupted when you joined the Navy and went off to Russia. What was that like and what effects do you feel it had on you?

I regard my being drafted to North Russia as a bluejacket sailor as one of the great windfalls of my life. It happened, you see, at just the right time. I was 19, 20, which is when one is most susceptible. It was my first experience of a foreign country. I was already a bookish youth and I had read the odd Russian novel. The strangeness, the immense melancholy of the Russian spaces, of the vast hinterland behind the Northern ports where I was stationed, which one didn't of course experience but of which one was aware; the strange climate, the perpetual night for much of the year and the eternal daylight for a couple of weeks in the summer: all this was – what is the word I want? – like an enchantment. Then of course this was 1942, 1943, when the Russian nation was at its most harried, when the Germans had driven deepest into the Soviet Union and the Russians were short of munitions and food. One was aware of that too. You were there with a heroic nation fighting with its back to the wall. All of this affected me greatly. I learned enough Russian to make Russian friends, in particular a Russian girlfriend to whom I was really devoted – I suppose it was the first serious love affair in my life. Unlike the tourists who had been before and have been since, we were there, the few of us, for 18 months in the end, and not aboard ship but ashore, so we could and did sink ourselves, lose ourselves, in the mass of ordinary Russian life which again, looking back, was a wonderful privilege. I have never lost my Russian enthusiasm. During the first few years after I went back to Cambridge, I was so much in love with things Russian that it almost irked me that I was reading the English Tripos and not Slavic languages. Of course, that has tailed off over the years, but it's never entirely disappeared. I am lazy about learning foreign languages and I should long ago have perfected the Russian I picked up to the point where it is a secure possession, but I haven't done so. But I still like to tinker with Russian poems, and later on, the interest did extend itself and I took in some Polish as well.

Could you say more about what it was like coming back to Cambridge after the war?

Well, it was different in that, before the end of the war, I had married and we'd had a baby boy, so that I came back already a family man with responsibilities. It seems to me now that returning to Cambridge should have been more of a shock than in fact it was. Those years in Cambridge from 1946 to 1950 were crowded with the experiences of marriage and fatherhood – and of considerable penury, I may say – and my studies were reasonably enthralling. But despite all that, the life was infinitely less vivid than what I remembered from the Navy, chiefly in Russia though the Navy also took me to India. Obviously one was glad to be out of uniform and indeed glad to be back in Cambridge, and yet there was a curious sense in which it was unreal. Reality was what one had left behind in the Arctic Circle or in the Indian Ocean. It was a long time, I think, before that wore off.

You say in These the Companions *that between 1946 and 1950* 'Scrutiny *was my Bible, and F.R. Leavis my prophet' (p. 77). Could you say expand upon what Leavis's work meant to you at that time?*

First, I'll give the bad side of it. What *Scrutiny* did, for an ambitious undergraduate and subsequent graduate like me, was tell me about ever so many books that I need not read. Leavis, through *Scrutiny*, was creating a canon, and it was a very restrictive canon. To have someone cut a swathe through the otherwise unmanageable abundance of *English* Literature, to go no further, was an enormous benefit to a harried young man such as I was at that time. So that's one thing it did for me. The book by Leavis which mattered most to me then, and really since then the book that I most admire, had in fact been published before the war – *Revaluation*, supplemented by a frailer book but still an interesting one, *New Bearings in English Poetry*. By the time I got to Cambridge after the war, Leavis was lecturing on what became *The Great Tradition* which was concerned with the sequence of, as he would have it, the great masters of the English novel, and in *Scrutiny* at that time, he and some of his collaborators were similarly very much concerned with the novel. This was something that I dutifully followed him in, but it never spoke to my personal needs then, nor has it rested with me as has what he did in *Revaluation*, which is a sort of great tradition of English poetry. I suppose it's many years now since I reread any substantial part of it, but I should be surprised if I didn't find that many of the chapters, and less the chapters than the sort of appendices, wouldn't come to me as they did then, as a model of what I understand responsible and perceptive criticism of poetry to be. I never knew him personally – well, that's not quite true, I did go to one of his famous teas, but only once. I was not at his college and he was not my tutor or supervisor, so I knew him mostly from a distance in the lecture room. I'm inclined to think that this was fortunate, that if you were actually sitting at the master's feet during those years, and I think later too, it was too much of a burden for a still young sensibility to stand up under. Too many of the men that I knew who had been Leavis's pupils became almost parodies of him because of the intensity with which he lived the student-teacher role. The emotional weight of the man was more than was good for people and I was glad to escape it. I've known a couple of other people who had the same effect upon their pupils, and it gave me an ironic sense, which I have never lost, that some teachers can be too devoted for their own good and the good of their pupils. Much better, I think, to have a distance established between the teacher and the taught. It's better for the taught.

One doesn't get the sense from what you say that you were drawn to the Lawrencian life-affirming aspect of Leavisism which became very important as he grew older.

It was becoming important during those years, though it later became more marked. Again, I dutifully attempted to go along with this. I read *The Rainbow* and *Women in Love* and some other Lawrence books, trying to experience them in the way that Leavis had and sometimes persuading myself that I'd done so. Of course, there are certain stories by Lawrence which I could read again and again, the short stories, I think, more than the novels. But I couldn't, in the long run, buy the case for Lawrence which Leavis argued for, particularly because it took the form of Lawrence in, Eliot out. It's also fair to say that I knew many places like Eastwood around Barnsley, I knew the people who lived in those cottages and some of them were my uncles and aunts, so that the Lawrence boyhood in Eastwood did not come to me with the glamour of exoticism, as I think it did for Leavis himself and certainly for many of his pupils.

Could we move then into the 1950s and talk about the Movement? In previous PN Review *interviews, critics who were around at the time – Frank Kermode, (see pp. 18-19 above), Karl Miller (see pp. 44-5 above), Bernard Bergonzi, (see p. 95 above) – have all testified to the importance and excitement of the Movement. The two critical books you produced around that period,* Purity of Diction in English Verse, *first published in 1952, and* Articulate Energy: An Enquiry into the Syntax of English Poetry, *which came out in 1955, were important in, among other things, giving an intellectual backbone to the Movement which it otherwise might not have had. You yourself say, in your 1966 postscript to the 1967 reissue of* Purity of Diction: *'I like to think that if the group of us had ever cohered enough to subscribe to a manifesto, it might have been* Purity of Diction in English Verse' *(p. 197). But you have also written about the Movement critically, for instance in your 1959 essay 'Remembering the Movement', where you are very harsh about it, charging it with 'pusillanimity' and 'craven defensiveness' (*The Poet in the Imaginary Museum, *p. 72). How would you judge the Movement now, looking back on it from the 1990s?*

I'd be more indulgent to it now than I was in 'Remembering the

Movement'. It had its limitations, God knows, but compared with the movements of literary opinion – we won't call it taste – since, it looks like a land of lost content. You mentioned Bernard Bergonzi, and I was particularly struck in Bernard's book *Exploding English* by what he said about it – he was younger than I was. I was very won over by, for instance, his insisting that it was one period when the universities were the natural nurseries of ambitious would-be writers, and of readers too. It was a period therefore when the universities were central to English letters as they were not often before and have never been since. A great difference to me was the death of Philip Larkin. Philip Larkin was my friend, and I admire his poetry, though I am aware of its limitations. I'm aware too of how those limitations were self-imposed. In the last ten years of Larkin's life, he and his poetry were held up too uncritically for admiration, in my view. He was admirable and irreplaceable, and there was no-one like him, but you can still find some people of my generation judging the whole of poetry since 1945, of English poetry at any rate, by measuring it up against Larkin and finding it wanting. Now while that was going on, I was at my most alienated from the Movement because the defiant insularity and philistinism of Larkin and of his friend Amis seemed to me really deplorable, not just for literature but for the national life too. Larkin was neither philistine nor insular, but he chose to seem to be. Alas, when poor Philip died, that cause of irritation was removed, because although Kingsley Amis is still famously irascible, no-one elevates him seriously in the way that Larkin was elevated, and is still by some people.

The Movement did have these maddening aspects of philistinism and insularity, but now that those seem to have disappeared, except in some very unrepresentative, uninfluential people, I'm far more aware of what a good time it was. Apart from anything else, it was my experience of the *Zeitgeist* in action. People don't understand that the Movement was not a club that met and decided they'd start a Movement. There was somebody in Aberdeen and somebody in Tokyo and somebody in Swansea and somebody in Dublin and so on, and it wasn't until anthologists began to put us together that one discovered that 'this fellow's moving the same way that I am'. In other words, the spirit of the age really showed. It turned out that a dozen people at least, quite independently of each other, had been moving on the same point. That was very exciting while it lasted.

One aspect of the Movement of which you're very critical in 'Remembering the Movement' is its humility, its deprecating, ingratiating tone, even some of its characteristic phraseology in what you call 'the interstices of our poems…the metrical places wasted on inert gestures of social adaptiveness – "no doubt", "I suppose", "of course", "almost", "perhaps"' (The Poet in the Imaginary Museum, p. 72). But it would seem to me that all those qualities which you criticize in that essay are necessary to the distinctive nature of the Movement, that those reticences and retreats and uncertainties helped to make it what it was and that they were even, if you like, an echo of some lost civility, the best that was possible in the shadowed, constricted world of postwar Britain. Would you feel that to be so now?

Yes I would. Those inert gestures of social adaptiveness, of course, were in me, in my Movement poems. I'm criticizing myself in that essay, or the person that I was then. It is an aspect too of what was most touching about the Movement. The Movement poets really thought that there was a public of goodwill in the nation at large which could be brought back into the world of poetry at the cost of just a few social adaptations on their part. It looks to me now as if that was a dream, but it was one which, without quite formulating it, I think we all shared, and that explains those social gestures and even the pusillanimity which I talk about. The notion was that we cannot move these people too fast or we shall lose them. If we're to take them along with us, we must do it gradually. By the time I changed around and wrote 'Remembering the Movement', I was far more aware, firstly that the response had not been anything like so general as we'd hoped, and secondly that all sorts of more adventurous and enterprising sorts of writing were being crowded out and excluded by the Movement. The case that is best documented, by Blake Morrison in his book on *The Movement* and by others is, of course, Charles Tomlinson. I tried to get him into the Movement, but the Movement wouldn't have him because he did not have enough of the sort of protective coloration that was required. And then I think of some American writers and a few years later – I didn't know his work in 1959 – I became aware of Basil Bunting. Behind all these was the figure of Ezra Pound. Tomlinson and Bunting, to stay with those two names, are writers who in different ways show that they have read Ezra Pound and are attempting to learn from him. I was the only person in the Movement who would agree to read Pound. There was therefore that tension between me and the rest of them from the first, and I think it was what I was expressing when I spoke of timidity on the part of the Movement.

*Earlier in our conversation, you compared and contrasted yourself
with Raymond Williams, and there's a criticism of the Movement
and of Movement poetry in a verse called 'On First Looking into
New Lines' which he wrote in 1956 but which did not get published
till 1984 (Writing in Society, pp. 257-8). This verse actually takes
lines from two of your poems – 'Remembering the 'Thirties' (Collected Poems, pp. 34-5) and 'Rejoinder to a Critic' (Collected Poems,
pp. 73-4) – and I wondered whether you felt the criticisms it made
had some validity, in the light of your own criticisms of the Movement:*

> *'A neutral tone is nowadays preferred.'*
> *'How dare we now be anything but numb?'*
> *If neutral, how be anything but dumb?*
> *If passionate, yet anxious, what's the word?*
> *– Careful. At least you cannot be exposed.*
> *Is it not really this that you've proposed?*

That's all news to me. I've never read that before. But insofar as I
understand it, it does not seem to me the sort of criticism of the
Movement which I have made. It is the kind of hostile response that
we became quite familiar with. It's like '[You] use the snaffle and the
curb all right, / But where's the bloody horse?', which of course
belongs to a previous phase of literary conflict but was the sort of
thing that they were saying about the Movement: where is passion in
your poetry, in your attitude to life? And this came particularly readily to a person like Raymond Williams who was committed, with
however many qualifications, to revolutionary changes in society. I
at any rate, but I think the Movement in general, was not fazed by
that. We were contemptuous of easy 'passionate' surges of feeling in
poetry and in society, and I still think that was necessary and right for
that time. You remember that we were reacting against the passionate excesses of the London bohemia of the 1940s.

*Those two poems of yours from which Williams takes lines make an
interesting contrast, in fact, because 'Rejoinder to a Critic' is in a
sense very much a defence against that charge of lack of feeling, and
it could also be read as a rationale for an avoidance of explicit political commitment. 'Remembering the 'Thirties', by comparison,
seems rather more ambivalent towards the question of passion and
commitment in relation to the poets of the thirties.*

Yes. Quite right. I can't now remember which of them was written

first. Stephen Spender got very cross with 'Remembering the 'Thirties' and I had to point out to him that in fact it is, in the end, a tribute, a compliment, to him and his friends. 'You were silly, but you
were brave'. Really people don't read what you write, you know,
they read what they think you've written. So those two poems do
point in different ways. After all, this line that Williams uses first, 'A
neutral tone is nowadays preferred', is followed, in my poem, by
'And yet...'. 'A neutral tone is nowadays preferred', mm, that has its
virtues, but 'it may be better, if we must, / To praise a stance impressive and absurd / Than not to see the hero for the dust'. The other
poem, 'Rejoinder to a Critic', is, as you say, defensive, but the
accusation has been thrown at me time and time again that 'you
don't feel enough, that's your trouble, you're very intelligent but you
don't feel'. So I've always tried to defend myself against that – well,
not always, I did try to defend myself at that time and at other times,
but now I've learned to live with it. The odd thing is that the same
people who accuse me of lack of feeling also tut-tut that I lose my
temper. I must have a lot of *negative* feeling!

The two critical books you wrote around the time of the Movement,
Purity of Diction in English Verse *and* Articulate Energy, *have stood
the test of time in a way that a lot of the criticism of that period
hasn't. Their endurance, I think, is partly due to the very close attention you give to language, which makes your readings still vibrant in
a time when criticism has taken a strong linguistic turn. But there's
one issue which you don't explicitly address – perhaps inevitably,
given your stress on purity and intelligibility - but which is sometimes
implicitly raised by the very close reading you do. This is an issue
which takes us back to Empson and forward to Derrida – the issue
of ambiguity, and of diction and especially of syntax as those areas
where ambiguity becomes most pressing. What was your attitude to
ambiguity, both when you first read Empson and subsequently?*

At first I was dazzled, of course, and I felt liberated. Subsequently, I
came to think that there was not sufficient check upon the ingenuity.
If you isolate a line and a half of verse, you can winkle ambiguities
out of anything, certainly in our language. So in effect what we do,
whether we're aware of it or not, is place them in a larger context –
for example, this is by this poet and this isn't, so that isn't the sort of
thing this poet does. I've taken the view that there's no harm at all in
looking always for clarity and intelligibility since our language,
because of its peculiar structure, is in fact so rich that it is continually

throwing up ambiguities whether we seek them or not. So you might as well press as hard as possible for clarity and intelligibility, because the language of Shakespeare will always, in the end, defeat you. I'm tempted to say that your bad writer is always ambiguous. It is much more difficult to be unambiguous than to be ambiguous. The responsible eighteenth-century critic, who would for me be personified by Sam Johnson, would have thought ambiguities were flaws if he detected them, as of course Johnson famously did in Gray – he could mean this or he could mean that, why can't the fellow say what he means? That's just careless, it's slipshod writing. And of course this is difficult to maintain in the twentieth century, particularly after Empson. But certainly some critics, and very well-regarded ones too among my contemporaries, seem to me – the indulgent word is over-ingenious. They will winkle an extra meaning out of the most unlikely concatenation of sounds, for instance, and I feel with them, as with Empson when he indulges himself, that they do not have the check of commonsense on the one hand and of context on the other. And indeed I think it is one of the rather baneful legacies of Empson that the critics that I have in mind not only pride themselves on getting enormous mileage out of the merest preposition but also write intolerably fidgety critical prose themselves, in which you have to be alert to the puns and ambiguities that are being deliberately inserted. They have very interesting minds and they certainly read closely, but I feel there is something frivolous, ultimately, about much of that.

For all the linguistic concern of Purity of Diction *and* Articulate Energy, *you're also very concerned in* Articulate Energy *to stress poetry's relation to human reality, to the way in which poems mime – a verb you often use – human experience. In* Articulate Energy, *you attack Northrop Frye's essay 'Levels of Meaning in Literature' (Kenyon* Review *(Spring, 1950), vol. 12, no. 2, pp. 246-62) – an essay later incorporated into the second chapter of* Anatomy of Criticism *(1957) – for, among other things, its view of language as a closed, self-referring system, and you conclude your book with an affirmation of the mimetic truth of poetry. Your example is Wordsworth's 'Complaint of a Forsaken Indian Woman' and you say '[this poem] takes on meaning only as it is open to another world. Unless it refers to that other "real" world, it is meaningless. Its syntax articulates not just itself, not only its own world, but the world of common experience ... [the syntax of Wordsworth's poems] is not "pure" syntax because it refers to, it mimes, something outside itself and outside the world of the poem, something that smells of the human, of generation and hence of corruption... For poetry to be great, it must reek of the human' (pp. 164-5). I'd like to take that olfactory image and set it beside one of your own poems – the poem called 'July, 1964' from* Essex Poems, *first collected in 1969, which is both a meditation on death and on the loss that is entailed in the act of writing. The last stanza of 'July, 1964' begins:*

> *The practice of an art*
> *is to convert all terms*
> *into the terms of art.*
> *By the end of the third stanza*
> *death is a smell no longer;*
> *it is a problem of style.*   (Collected Poems, *p. 137)*

That poem turns on a paradox – almost, one might say today, a deconstructive paradox – which is that while art does mime reality, it also, inevitably, loses it, that presence drains away. The relationship between language and extralinguistic reality has been a much debated question in recent years, both within and beyond literary study. You affirm in Articulate Energy *the necessity of that relationship for poems or other kinds of literary works to be meaningful, and yet at the same time one can see in your criticism and perhaps even more in your poetry a strong awareness of a gap or a tension between art and the world that art seeks to represent.*

That's very true. I don't have the sort of mind that can handle highly abstract philosophical or epistemological or even semiotic problems – this is not deprecation, it is the fâct of the case – so that I can only say, yes, there is this thrust and counterthrust in my attitude to life and art, particularly life and the art of poetry, and they're both part of my experience. I do not know any way to reconcile them. The reconciliations which we are offered on the one hand purify the art to the point at which it doesn't need to rely upon non-linguistic reality at all – that's a sort of solution, but the price is just too high to pay – and at the other extreme pay no attention to the formal problems, just put down the brute, dismaying truth, and walk away. That too is a solution, but again at too high a price. I am, as surely everybody must be, continually aware of how presences leak away when they're made into art. I think it is extremely sad that this should be so, but it is so. The simplest example of this, and I have written poems about it, is the way that you in fact use people that are dear and near to you and put them into poems. It's a sort of nightmare which haunts me. Perhaps I am a person so specialized in his concern for languages and rhythms and cadences that the rest of my life, my most intimate relations, are just so much raw material to be fed into the machine so that it can produce a poem. When I think that, I am of course disgusted with myself and with what I have been doing all this time. At the other side of the equation, my poetry must always refer to a reality outside language. I do hear about, and to some extent understand, the arguments that say that this necessity, or even the possibility of it, cannot be proved. It is necessary to me to believe it in order to write any poems at all. It is not for nothing that my example in those last pages of *Articulate Energy* is Wordsworth, because Wordsworth, it seems to me, is the real bone that sticks in the gullet of those who would cut language free of reality. Wordsworth really is and always has been a marker for me – the Wordsworth of the Encounter Poems rather than the Wordsworth of *The Prelude*. I've never dared to strip my language of so much of its fineries and euphonies and felicities as Wordsworth does in those poems. But if I'd been as absorbed in non-verbal reality as Wordsworth was, I would, I suppose, have found the courage to do so.

Could we move on to the 1960s. In your controversial review of Daniel Weissbort's anthology in the London Review of Books *earlier this year (27 February 1992, p. 3), you seem to feel strongly that the English poetic legacy of the 1950s was not in fact taken up and developed in the 1960s – that a certain continuity was lost. Why do you think that loss happened?*

Some of the most talented and energetic men – I can't think of any women – then emerging on the English literary scene were a new breed of person in that they were above all impatient – 'I want it now'. They wanted instant gratification, and the notion that a period of apprenticeship, of making mistakes and putting them right, was necessary if one was to do anything worthwhile, was anathema to them. They looked around therefore for a short cut, and I argued in that review that some of them found this in poems in translation which came their way out of the languages of Eastern Central Europe. Michael Schmidt, referring to that in his latest *PN Review* editorial [*PN Review* 85, 18: 5, May/June 1992, pp. 2-3], pointed out that another way that some of them took, or that the same people at another time took, was into a certain kind of American poetry which we might associate with Allen Ginsberg and the Beat Generation. I would accept that point, although it is true that there were other American poets who were influential at that time who didn't offer the same opportunities for a short cut. And I think that notion of 'there must be some way of cutting through all this nonsense' has persisted ever since and become more influential, and spread from the restricted circles of poets in the 1960s into the populace at large or into that part of the populace at large which is interested in writing verse. This does seem to me a loss.

I think the sort of persons I have in mind actively dislike, in fact, the past of English poetry. Some of them can be found actually speaking of the past centuries of English lyric poetry as a terrible ball and chain that they have to drag around behind them, or as an obfuscating fog which they must somehow clear their way through. This seems to me deplorable. I think, as surely most people did up to a few years ago, that the poet rides upon the shoulders of his predecessors. To a degree, I would say this was part and parcel of other aspects of the 1960s urge for instant gratification – I want it now politically, sexually, pharmaceutically – I mean drugs. It was characteristic. The instant revolution we ought to have at the University of Essex, for instance. And I've said, of course, that I think that the 1960s was a terrible decade in British culture. Now I find that on the television and in the popular press it is recalled with nostalgia as a glorious and glamorous period when some of us were young.

You've mentioned the University of Essex, and I wondered if you could say, to begin with, what your hopes for that university were when you first went there? The fact that you did actually go there from Cambridge suggests a certain commitment and optimism at that time.

Very much so. In the first place it must be said that I was not alone. There were other persons ensconced in comfortable fellowships in Cambridge, and, I think, in Oxford who got up and went at the same time. And I imagine that some of them, at any rate, must have been impelled by the same thing that impelled me. I really did feel that the Oxbridge stranglehold over higher education in this country had to be broken, that those two ancient universities exerted altogether too much influence, on the curricula actually far more than on the social advancements of their students, though that too was part of it. So I welcomed the opportunity that I was given to take responsibility for the whole of literary studies in the university – and, as it turned out, historical studies too – and the free hand that I had to rethink, within reason, the entire curriculum. I could do this because the Vice Chancellor, Albert Sloman, was an old associate of mine from my Dublin days. He could give me this assurance, and he didn't go back upon his word. So there then ensued a period of extraordinary frenetic activity which was, however, very rewarding. I and my first colleagues, like George Dekker – I name him because he was my principal lieutenant to begin with – really did work out an approach to literary study on an entirely new plan, one which, for instance, broke through the artificial and sterilizing division between, on the one hand, School of English, and, on the other hand, School of Modern Languages.

Another division we were really required to break down, whether we wanted to or not, was between literary studies and certain social sciences. So that was another aspect. The courses in politics ('government' as they called it in Essex) and in sociology, were to be meshed with literary studies: and with linguistic studies, insofar as foreign languages were required and were offered. The working out of how this could be done was extraordinarily intricate and demanding. At the same time, I was recruiting my first six, eight, ten persons who, when this scheme was explained to them, were prepared to come and move. My bitterness about the Essex experience was that, after I and these others had invested so much, when the thing was just getting off the ground and when we were just proving to ourselves and the rest of the university that what we had proposed was feasible, the political temperature rose and these months and months of work and devotion on the part of many people was sacrificed, as I saw it then and as I see it now, to political gesturing for the sake of the cameras from Anglia Television and obscure wishes to dress up in fancy costumes. I am told that not everything that we had installed in Essex has disappeared, and I'm touched by this. It seems there are certain features of literary study in that university which are still different from what you can get anywhere else, and valuable for just that reason. It wasn't that we were going to show Oxford and Cambridge where they were wrong. It was to point out that there are other ways of slicing up the cake and that you might like to look at this other way. It was a bitter and tragic waste, I think, the 1968 so-called student unrest, which of course was pretty well worldwide really, but which Essex got just about the worst of in this country.

When you talk about the 1960s in Thomas Hardy and British Poetry *which appeared in 1972, you make one very specific diagnosis of the problems – that they were due to a breakdown of authority, a failure of nerve on the part of those who should exercise authority – and you draw an analogy from Sophoclean tragedy: 'Creon's is such a thankless role in modern Britain that there is no one left to play it with conviction' (p. 98). Would you stand by that diagnosis?*

Yes. That's why I refuse to buy the label 'student unrest'. Students are always restive if you let them be. What I saw in Essex was a capitulation on the part of their elders towards the students, a wish to curry favour with them, so much so that I really think the troubles didn't originate with students at all, but with – well, they paraded around under various disguises as graduate students, and as junior and sometimes not so junior lecturers. If the Essex University Senate could have backed the executive officer, the Vice Chancellor, firmly enough and had been prepared to go the distance, the trouble could have been controlled, but there was no such wish, no such will, on the part of the Senate. And I know that the same is true in other places; Cornell, for instance. The particular phrase that you quote about Creon derives, I'm sure, from an essay by Conor Cruise O'Brien who was an old acquaintance of mine from my Dublin days. It's very interesting, the way that the basic triangle of that Sophoclean play – Creon, Antigone, and Ismene – in fact turns out to be extraordinarily relevant and apposite to all sorts of things in the 1960s. I suppose that's one reason why we know Sophocles was a very great writer.

How do you relate your feelings about what you see as the breakdown of authority there to the earlier feelings expressed in that poem of 1953, 'Creon's Mouse' (Collected Poems, pp. 23-4), which you cite again in Thomas Hardy and British Poetry. *There is a sense in 'Creon's Mouse' that what you call there '[a] self-induced and stubborn loss of nerve' may not be altogether a bad thing, for example in a world threatened by nuclear war – that there might be times when the best course is* not *to exercise authority. Is there perhaps in* Thomas Hardy and British Poetry *a certain strain of self-accusation – as if you're not just saying it's all those people who couldn't exercise authority but also implicating yourself in a much more general cultural attitude in which the exercise of authority came to seem something that was almost impossible?*

It never occurred to me that that was so, but it probably is so. I do have difficulty with the notion of exerting authority, except in very, very special circumstances, in that, like any other English person of my generation and – here we might get to it – of my social rank, I didn't come from the governing classes which traditionally do exert authority. Non-commissioned officers was what we were, and they, of course, exert authority, but only under higher authority. So it is with reluctance that I reach the conclusion that a decay and abdication of authority is so general in British society today, never mind in the 1960s, that the nation has become largely ungovernable.

The idea of a breakdown of authority and of the need for its reaffirmation became very much a theme of Conservative and of Republican politics in Britain and the USA in the 1980s – much of Mrs Thatcher's project and style could be seen as precisely an attempt to reassert authority and to make the nation more governable in the terms that you're talking about. It's interesting therefore that you don't seem to regard that attempt to reassert authority as having been successful. What would be your judgement on the politics of England and America since the 1960s, particularly in relation to that question of authority?

First, let me say that I hold no brief for myself as an armchair politician. It isn't one of the things that I aim to know about or to study, so this is pretty well off the top of my head. To answer your implicit query, no, of course I didn't like the exertion of authority by Mrs Thatcher nor by President Ronald Reagan, not at all, and it wasn't what I had in mind. If you look back through the early numbers of *PN Review* to some of the editorials that I used to write in those days, you will find me welcoming Mrs Thatcher, apprehensively, but prepared to extend a warmish welcome to her at the beginning of her years of rule. But I totally lost sympathy with her long before the end. After all you could say she exerted authority on some people, but she didn't exert authority on property speculators, did she? It was a highly selective authority; she did exert authority over the universities, but not over takeover bids in the City of London. And the same is largely true of Reagan.

Although you say you're not a political animal, one finds, even if one goes back to Purity of Diction in English Verse *and* Articulate Energy, *that you're rather more willing to make connections between politics and literature than some critics of that decade might have been – you stress, for example, the link between the health of syntax and the health of a civilization. And by the time one gets to* Thomas Hardy and British Poetry, *one has a book that very closely interweaves poetic and political concerns. You don't seem to have shown in your work the reticence in regard to politics of which critics of your generation have lately been accused. Would you feel that to be the case?*

Yes. I have never been seduced by the notion that poetry could exist hermetically sealed from the society which gave it birth. In that sense, it goes back to Leavis. From that point of view, Leavis is a thoroughly political animal, though it is to be doubted that he ever voted for any British political party. I am concerned with politics in the sense of a concern with what articulates and holds together the *polis* – when we can say that we've got a *polis*; how, if we get it, we maintain it, and how, if we haven't got it, can we ever get it back? Those questions certainly interest me greatly. What doesn't interest me is who's in, who's out, and still less what I call marching up and down in fancy dress, demonstrations and suchlike. And I suppose it is true that ever since the Essex experience, which left me very considerably embittered, I have looked for trouble from my friends on the Left, and they pay me back in kind.

After the Essex experience, you went to America, to teach at Stanford, and it seems that your relationship, not only to Essex University, but also to England, became embittered too. Would you feel that to be so?

I certainly was embittered for many years, particularly consciously so in the first years after I left Essex. There's a long poem called 'England', which nobody likes except one Canadian, which I wrote soon after in Los Angeles and which is the bitterest of them all. Then I wrote a series of rather cumbrous jokey poems called *Six Epistles to Eva Hesse* in which I tried to control the bitterness by making it comic. I have, I suppose, come to terms with it in the years since, though again in the early numbers of *PN Review* you can still find me rather red in the face and apoplectic. When I say I've come to terms with it, I don't mean to say that I've exactly recovered hope. I've settled with myself that it's no good crying for the moon. The state of my nation is thus and so, and there is no tangible or likely possibility of its changing before I die, so it's no good worrying about it.

You don't feel you became too embittered?

I know people have said that and I can see how they might say it. I suppose the most indulgent way of looking at it is as the resentment of the rejected lover. If I hadn't loved my country and didn't still love it in some sense, obviously I would have been much more cool about the way it changed.

Couldn't it be said that it's one particular version of England that you're in love with and that there might be alternative versions of what England is – the radical, dissident England of E.P. Thompson, for example?

I think E.P. Thompson is a wonderful writer who is abundantly worth quarrelling with. And he's civil too, he plays by the rules. But I'm sorry, Edward Thompson, I think I know these people that you write about. You don't know them. You know about them and you know their history, but you've never actually grown up with them. They weren't your blood kin as they were mine. In the same way, you strike a plangent note when you say in *The Poverty of Theory*: here I am like one of the Old Believers 'who will not bare his head before authority' (p. 182). But in fact, you're an atheist. I *am* one of those Old Believers, and that was my family. In other words, with Edward Thompson, as with many much less creditable people on the Left, their proletarian heroes are romances. Life in the proletariat isn't like that and never was. That's how I felt about Raymond Williams too, though in fact Raymond did know that life at first hand.

Could we turn now to your relationship to America and particularly to American poetry? There's a sense in your work of great openness to certain aspects of America – to its expansive landscapes, to some of its traditions, to the work of some of its poets. Could you talk about how that relationship developed?

It's gone through several different phases. Sometimes I've felt more at home with America, at other times less. You're right about the American landscapes and the spaciousness of them. This corresponds to, and is a sort of image of, a similar expansiveness in the American character and in American social habits. The trouble is, of course, that this can get to the point where, as was said of somebody very broadminded, his mind is so broad that it has no edges to it. This is what you sometimes feel about American sensibility, and American society too.

The story would have to start with my going to Stanford, in fact even before that. You know this name that I'm going to mention – Yvor Winters. It's the name that comes up in my conversation along with Leavis. Yvor Winters was like an American Leavis in many respects. The two men were aware of each other, though never allied, because apart from anything else, both of them were rather jingoistic patriots. Certainly Leavis read *Pudd'nhead Wilson* and recommended some Henry James, and he had American students and

American friends, but he was really only interested in the history and the future of England. Winters was just the same the other way round, and he would never come to this country. He was hated and feared by his colleagues in the same way that Leavis was. The great difference was that Winters was a poet and his principal interest was poetry. He was the first modern American poet whom I was drawn to and admired, and I still admire him. He was very much *not* the expansive sort of American. He was extremely, perhaps most people would say excessively, tight in his verse forms and in what he demanded of others. Still, I admired him and emulated him, as did Thom Gunn, and as does to this day Clive Wilmer, for instance. I as it were graduated to Winters from my reading of Leavis. I wrote to him when I was a graduate student at Cambridge, and he replied with extraordinary generosity to this total stranger from overseas, not once but many times. I had 12 or 20 letters from him which I've now deposited where they should be, because they're memorials of a great man. I visited him when we first went to the States for a year in 1956-57, and he was extremely kind. He set up and ran the verse writing side of a creative writing school in Stanford which was quite unlike any other, independently funded from outside the university, unashamedly élitist, and very demanding. A surprising number of worthwhile poets came out of it. When he was dying, the question of his successor arose. Winters was, as you might expect, extremely authoritarian and he tried to be authoritarian about the choice of his successor too. It wasn't for him to say, but he was allowed to have his say. Nobody that the department could put before him did he approve of, and his own candidate was one of which the department couldn't approve. Finally Davie emerged as the compromise candidate. Winters, I am told, replied, 'I have less objection to Davie than to any of the others'; which is the nearest you would ever get from him to a laying on of hands. Stanford had already been after me when I was at Essex to go and take his position and I'd said no at first, but with the troubles the thing had become so impossible at Essex that I took the offer. I then had ten happy years in California in a very lovely part of that lovely state – wonderful climate, wonderful landscape – teaching poetry writing and also straight literature courses to graduates and undergraduates. My wife and children enjoyed it greatly.

After ten years, in 1978, I accepted an offer to move to Vanderbilt. I was drawn to it because of the history of American poetry. When Winters was a young man in the 1920s, the persons of whom he was most aware and with whom he corresponded were the then Fugitive poets of Nashville, Tennessee, Allen Tate and John Crowe Ransom. Winters quarrelled with them in the sense that he didn't agree with them, but at least he thought they were worth quarrelling with. So there was a connection there. Of course, that group had dispersed long before, but in its time the Fugitive and later the Agrarian movement was an extraordinary phenomenon, which I had been partly aware of before I even left Cambridge. So that intrigued me. The second ten years of my American stay was therefore in this very different part of America, Tennessee, the Upper South. When you get to the South, of course, the history is tragic. It is overshadowed by the fact that they lost the crucial war and that defines everything that there is about Southern civilization, or did until lately. There now is a great deal more mobility, but the shadow is still there to a great extent. It has been said that this is why the southern states have provided more than their share of the great American writers of this century. Their history gave them a tragic sense such as the north and west of the country had never known. I think that is true up to a point. So the pleasure that you take in going to southern places is very largely elegiac and wistful, but it is quite a piercing pleasure all the same. Cities like Natchez in Mississipi, Savannah in Georgia and Charleston in South Carolina are more beautiful really than any of the cities of the North. What's more the Southerners, by and large, don't monkey with the past. They don't try and tart it up and make it better than it was. The ten years I spent at Vanderbilt was also a rewarding period, but less intellectually strenuous than Stanford had been. Meanwhile, the changes in the national politics of Washington were not to my liking, so that I was glad to retire in 1988.

As well as your admiration for Yvor Winters, you've also shown an interest – a surprising one, it has sometimes been thought – in the work of Ed Dorn and Charles Olson. Could you talk about how that interest developed?

I had made contact with Ed Dorn when we were still in Essex. One of the literatures we had to concern ourselves with at Essex was American literature, and in those early, heady days, when opportunity was opening up all round, and there was even some money to spare, I prevailed upon Essex to let me bring over a resident American poet, having in mind Ed, whose work I had been introduced to by – this may or may not surprise you – Jeremy Prynne in Cambridge. Ed did come to Essex and a very momentous time it was for him and for me and for the students. Michael Schmidt sees it as a strange aberration on my part that I should have affection and admiration for Ed's poetry, because Michael holds that poetry to be remarkable for lack of refinement and semantic nuance [see *PN Review* 85 editorial], whereas the fact of the matter is that nuance is what Ed's poetry is full of, particularly his long poem *Gunslinger*. It's a continual running ripple of joke, pun, outlandish comedies, verbal comedy, very difficult because it's very American – I mean it's American speech, not British – but certainly not lacking in nuance.

I did spend a lot of time on Charles Olson, and I suppose I don't regret it now, but I was never at all so sure of him as I was of Winters or of Dorn, though Dorn regarded himself as a sort of pupil of Olson. Olson was a very large, generous, admirable man. He had splendid large conceptions, but he was like those impatient people that I was speaking of earlier. He couldn't wait to learn his trade before he got started on an epic poem, so the execution is pretty consistently sloppy. But of course, he was the one who insisted that space was the distinguishing American concern and this spoke very much to my condition. Space is the first thing about America that strikes anybody from Europe, unless of course you insist on staying in the middle of New York or Washington or Boston. But the minute you move outside, whether by car, by train, or by aeroplane, you are astonished. There is an explosion outwards of one's whole sense of the non-human creation. The entire ratio between the human being and the non-human creation is totally different from Europe, and this is both frightening and extraordinarily exhilarating. I think this is what Olson had got hold of. It's particularly apparent in *Call me Ishmael*, where the last prairie is the Pacific Ocean. And Dorn, at a time when he was still very much under Olson's influence, programmatically called one of his collections *Geography* and it does include poems about driving great distances, in the West for the most part. This spoke immediately to what I was interested in, and it produced two things. First, in the *Epistles to Eva Hesse* and indeed in some other poems, I was concerned with the great travellers and explorers, particularly those that Francis Parkman wrote about: La Salle, Montcalm, Henri de Tonty – their names are not known now. And then of course there were English explorers too whom I read about, not to speak of explorers by sea of the Pacific Ocean and of the Coasts such as George Vancouver and Cook. Some of my interest was of the most banal sort – *Boys Own Paper* stuff, dauntless heroes and all that. I don't pretend that there wasn't that element of, if you like, immaturity involved. After all, the question of whether the heroic still exists as a mode of poetry is one of fairly general interest, I would have

thought, and one which has concerned me somewhat. I was exploring all these things and exploring space and the meaning of space and
the meaning of the crossing of space. In another curious way, I was
also very interested in the space that you cover when you fly from the
West Coast to London over the Pole and over Greenland, and that is
the framework of the long poem called 'England'. Related to this,
though not in any very obvious way is the collection that I did called
The Shires. The difference of scale is comical, but it is trying to
explore English spaces in the way the Americans have explored
America. All of that was vastly liberating for me.

*Your experience of America and American poetry gave you new poe-
tic themes. Did it also exert a formal pressure on the way you felt you
wanted to write poetry?*

In a curious way. After all, Olson and Dorn were using large loopy
shapes on the page as well being concerned with those kinds of
spaces in their subject matter, and I was naturally interested by their
experiments and by hearing them talk about what it was that they
conceived themselves to be doing. Obviously I would have a go at it
myself. But, as it were, it never took with me. I didn't like the experiments that I made. And in a sense this shouldn't have surprised me,
and didn't, because I'd had that experience long before with another
American poet: Ezra Pound. I've been an admirer of Pound for forty,
perhaps fifty years, yet my poems don't look like the *Cantos*. But it's
not for want of trying. I admire it, but I can't do it, and if someone
were to say that's the difference between a European sensibility and
an American sensibility, a New World sensibility, I would say that's
probably true. On the other hand, Yvor Winters advocated a tighter
poetry than I was used to writing, and I tried to do that too. I wrote
a couple of poems which pleased me, but that didn't take either. All
these poets gave me a sense of new possibilities, some of which I
explored, but that didn't produce any poems that are particularly
adequate. But that's all right. And in fact my *Six Epistles to Eva
Hesse* are quite explicitly an attempt to do Charles Olson's subject
matter in a verse measure – rhyming octosyllabics – as far as possible
from his.

What is your view of William Carlos Williams?

This is something on which I differ from virtually all my friends –
friends as different as Thom Gunn and Ed Dorn and Winters. They

all admired Williams, and I tried to go along with them. I tried particularly to hear his rhythms, but I cannot do so. When I want to be diplomatic, particularly with American writers, I say, well, it's my British ear that can't hear his American cadence. But I don't believe it. I bought that for a long time, but now I've discovered the courage, when I'm not being diplomatic, to say, phooey, if I can't hear them, they don't exist as far as I'm concerned. There are some very early poems which Winters admired and which I do admire, but that's all. Williams was apparently a very nice, attractive man. I think he was an absolute simpleton. His own theories of metre and of diction are self-contradictory in the extreme, and the veneration of him on these counts has done enormous damage to American poetry in the last 30 years. You see, in a sense I ought to respond to him very fervently, because what he says about himself, and what his admirers say about him, is the sort of thing that I've been saying about Wordsworth. No doubt at all about the toughness of the non-verbal reality that the language is measuring up to. No doubt at all of the way in which he will fearlessly make a poem out of a casual encounter with an uninteresting woman in a back street. I ought to approve, and in fact I do approve of the theory, but in practice the poems hardly ever come off.

In the Foreword to Studies in Ezra Pound, *a collection of your writings on Pound that came out in 1991, you talk about your 'preoccupation' – you're careful to distinguish it from an 'obsession' – with Pound (p. 7). But back in the fifties, in* Articulate Energy, *you seem to want to dismiss him when you say: 'in Pound's verse the rhythm steps out alone and we must follow it in blind faith, with no metrical landmarks to assist us. Every reader must decide for himself whether he can make this act of faith. I confess for my part I cannot, and it seems to me that after scrapping the contracts traditionally observed between poet and reader, a poet like Pound substitutes a contract unjustly weighted against the reader' (pp. 128-9). How do you look back on that statement now?*

When I wrote *Articulate Energy* in the fifties, I thought I had settled my hash with Ezra Pound for good and all. What you've just read out is a sort of cryptic summation of how I had, not written him off, but, as I thought, laid his ghost to rest. But I never can. I never have. He always comes to life again. Some reviewers find *Studies in Ezra Pound* maddening because at the end, Davie is still oscillating between angry exasperation with this poet and adulation of and devotion to him. I'm sorry, but that's the way it's always been for me with Pound. The odd thing, I suppose, when I think about it, is why it should have happened to me in my generation and to no one else. Part of the difference, I truly believe, is this: as I've explained, I went abroad in the Second World War, but I never went to Europe, except insofar as Russia is Europe, until long after the war, in 1952, '53, by which time I was already 30. I think it was probably 1954 before my wife and I got to Italy and that too was a revelation – the things that architecture can do to you in an Italian light particularly, the whole centres of Italian towns, and not just the big famous ones either. My wife, who's a photographer, speaks delightedly of how the light bounces off that stone. And I do respond to that far more than I do to painting, let alone music. Now Pound, particularly in some of the *Cantos*, is the poet in the English language since Browning who has most honoured that and has given the most adequate verbal equivalent of it. Amis and Larkin paraded their refusal to go abroad. I was very happy to go abroad and so there was in that way a bridge to Pound such as some of my fellows in the Movement did not share.

Your last collection of poetry To Scorch or Freeze: Poems of the Sacred *was published in 1988, and is now incorporated in your* Collected Poems, *Could I ask in conclusion whether you're still writing poems?*

The answer is no, which distresses me a little, though not as much as people might think. I now realize that *To Scorch or Freeze* is indeed my last, and not my latest, collection, because what I'm really doing in that book is measuring myself up against David the Psalmist. I perhaps should have explained this in the book. I thought it would be clear to anyone who would read it, but the Scriptures, even when I print them in italics, are not part of the common furniture of even Christian believers' experience any more. So in general, people are baffled by this collection. I can't quite say it's what my whole career has been working up to, but I can't conceive of going any place else after having done that. I am talking about the holy and I am measuring myself up against the great ancient Hebrew poet and the great translators of him into English through the centuries. The collection doesn't seem ambitious. These look like rather scrappy, jokey poems, and some of them are, but the whole enterprise is in fact extremely ambitious, not to say presumptuous. It baffles some people and offends others. This is always the case with poetry that is thought to be religious, as if it is a work of piety or as if I am coming on as holier-than-thou, or as if I am trying to hustle people into the pew. I think if you give it a fair trial, you'll see that it isn't that. There are two or three poems in which the second person of the Trinity, Jesus, and the third, the Holy Ghost, do appear, but through all the rest the God that I talk about is the God of the Old Testament, Yahweh if you like. It is the God of Wrath. If it were to be really a work of Christian devotion, the God of Love and Mercy would have to bulk much larger. It is exploring what it means to be Godfearing, which is not a term very much used, though it's a usage in perfectly good odour – 'he's a Godfearing man'. But it is an emphasis that is very seldom heard from official spokesmen for any of the Christian faiths at the present day.

One of the old Tennessee poets I mentioned earlier, John Crowe Ransom, wrote a book called *God Without Thunder* in which he asked very pertinently: if God is not fearful, why should we worship him? That's really what I'm trying to explore. The God that I'm speaking of is the God who rules this universe and therefore He is fearful. We are in His hands. He made the poles and He made the equator, and it is characteristic of Him to run to extremes of logical rigour; hence, we may say, to scorch or freeze. So if we find Him placing us in a temperate zone we should be very grateful, because we don't deserve it. In fact we don't *deserve* anything of Him and therefore the notion that we can argue with Him or that we can expect Him to be just according to our ideas of justice, or kind according to our ideas of kindness, is a simple logical mistaking of categories. That's what all the poems are about really, if anybody cares to look. Of course, it is because God is fearsome that we need a Redeemer, an Intercessor, the second person of the Trinity. Of course that is so, but it isn't what I care to say, except by the faintest implication, in that book. That is what David – we call him David though he was probably a composite ancient poet, but still – that is what the poets then of the Psalms are going on about all the time, as far as I can see, just as is the author of the book of Job. To justify God's ways to man, said Milton. It's a nonsense, it can't be done. You might as well give it up. David never pretends to justify them. He just says, you're moving in a mysterious way, Lord, and I'm scared stiff, and let me escape, if I may, please.

Are you hoping that message will be heard in modern times?

Well, I'm hoping that people will read my poems and understand them, which is not quite the same thing. I think I renounced the hope that I could significantly stem or deflect the tide of modern culture some time ago.

But Donald Davie won't be silent, of course. You'll still perhaps be producing what you call, in These the Companions, *one of your favourite forms: Jeremiads.*

Probably, probably. When you've been running off at the mouth for as many years as I have, you don't soon give it up.

John Barrell

Kemp Town, Brighton
19 June 1992

NICOLAS TREDELL: *Could I begin by asking about the cultural and intellectual influences that you feel shaped you through home and school, prior to going to university?*

JOHN BARRELL: I think I was far more influenced by school than I was by home. Neither of my parents was university educated and though my mother was a voracious reader, so that good books were coming through the house, she didn't talk about them at home in any way which might have produced some kind of an interest in studying literature. I still think that probably the most decisive influence was studying Classics at school. I didn't do English 'A' Level, I did Latin and Greek, and most of the things I found myself interested in doing with literature when I got to university seemed to come out of the kind of interest in Greek and Latin versification, and the kind of concentration on syntax, which my teachers of Latin and Greek at school cultivated in me. I did the scholarship examination to Cambridge in English as a kind of spare-time hobby, because I'd decided I wanted to read English, and felt it would be a good way of preparing myself for that to try, while I did my classical 'A' Levels, to mug up on English and take the scholarship exam in that. But all the time I was reading, and to some extent I still do read, Latin and Greek for work or recreation.

What was your experience of university?

I went to Trinity College, Cambridge, where there were lots of people reading English, but English was very much of a poor relation of a subject. Much less supervision was done in English than was done in other colleges, so that in some terms I had no formal teaching at all except for what was happening in the lecture rooms. For the whole of my first two years, Terry Eagleton and I, who were taught in a pair, were supervised by a retired schoolmaster who was one of those people that are half on and half off the books of Oxford and Cambridge colleges – he didn't really have any official status. He was very charming but not very stimulating. So until Terry and I and some other friends persuaded Raymond Williams to put on an undergraduate seminar that we could attend in our third year, and until I got supervised by Donald Davie in my second to last term, it's almost true to say that the teaching I had at Cambridge was of no value whatsoever. But in my last year it was of very considerable value. I was already clear what teachers I was interested in following, and they were precisely Raymond Williams and Donald Davie, and I suppose that my work since bears the imprint of the attempt to hold my interest in those two different kinds of approach together.

Could you say more about how you felt your work developed the different approaches of Raymond Williams and Donald Davie?

I suppose it's as clear in the first book I wrote as in any. That's a book on the description of landscape which is mainly about John Clare, but is trying to look at how John Clare, as a rural poet and the son of a rural worker, found himself trying to describe landscape both in, and in opposition to, the eighteenth-century polite tradition of landscape description. What interested me was to try and see the whole problem of landscape description as a problem of finding an adequate syntax to describe the landscape. It seemed to me that the eighteenth century had produced some extraordinarily artful ways of describing landscape always from a certain kind of – the fashionable word would be hegemonic – position. It was a syntax that precisely described, or described with extreme vigour, the experience of looking at landscape across a wide terrain and from a high viewpoint in ways in which then, and still more subsequently, I've been able to identify as being quite consciously implicated in a certain ruling class way of looking at landscape. If that sounds crude, put as abruptly as that, it may be, but actually the metaphors of rule and domination involved in that notion of perspective and viewpoint are very clear and very explicit, and were much discussed, in the eighteenth century itself. So I was interested in the problem of what John Clare as a poet could do with a tradition of landscape description which seemed to employ a syntax which was apparently nothing to do with the kind of experience of landscape that he might have. In that, I was taking over, in particular from *Articulate Energy*, though to some extent from *Purity of Diction in English Verse*, Davie's concern with poetic syntax and with eighteenth-century poetic diction, and trying to understand it in terms of questions of class and power in the eighteenth and early nineteenth century in ways that I'd been taught to think about them by Raymond Williams. I was fascinated by what always fascinated Raymond Williams, which is how writers who feel excluded from the literary tradition, but also want to contribute to it and feel much stimulated and formed by it themselves, can somehow find ways of using it and making it correspond with their own concerns.

That desire to understand eighteenth-century poetic syntax and diction in terms of class and power and exclusion suggests that you're not one of those critics who approaches the eighteenth century with a nostalgia for an age of stability?

I'm not one of those critics of the eighteenth century who have a nostalgia for an age of stability, but I certainly think, though this would seem to me to be endlessly denied by my writing, that I approach the eighteenth century with a nostalgia which it's almost the purpose of the criticism to negate. If you're English and you work on questions of English landscape, and you imagine that your sole interest in doing this is to subvert and question the ways in which the English landscape has been a vital constituent of a notion of Englishness and that all you're doing is coming along quizzically, as if an alien, and saying what on earth is this extraordinary investment that English culture has in the landscape – if you do that, then I think you're really fooling yourself. We sit in this room which, as you can see, is full of images of English landscape which I much like living with. So there is a certain amount of nostalgia, but what I like to think of myself as doing is finding ways of talking about what's so desirable and affecting about a lot of the literature and the painting of that period which don't merely seem to reproduce what I regard as the more oppressive aspects of the ideology which appears to be involved in them.

You went from Cambridge to Essex to do a PhD at a time when Essex was a very new university. Why did you choose to go to Essex and what was it like there at that time?

I went there because Donald Davie was going there. Granted that I wanted to leave Cambridge, and granted that the two people whom

I thought could teach me most were Raymond Williams and Donald Davie and that only Davie was leaving, it seemed appropriate to go to Essex. It was very exciting at the beginning. It was exciting, for a start, to be in a university which had a Department of Literature rather than an English Faculty. Not only could one teach students and talk to colleagues very easily who were reading and teaching other literatures, but one could also actually teach those literatures oneself, so that I taught quite a lot of eighteenth- and nineteenth-century French literature while I was there and enjoyed that a great deal. Essex was also interesting in that, like Sussex where I am now, it was a university which had a commitment to interdisciplinarity even beyond the literary, though for the students that rather ran out after the first year. But it did mean that you found yourself, to some extent teaching but certainly arguing about and discussing, works of political theory and of sociology in a way that the extremely narrow English course at Cambridge hadn't permitted. So it really was very much of an opening out. I started reading philosophy, or, let's say, non-English philosophy at Essex which I'd never had never much occasion to read at Cambridge. So that was very important. After a while I felt things rather went off the boil. It did seem to me – this may not be true now of Essex – that after a few years there was a sense in which academics were finding the commitment to inter-discplinarity irritating and frustrating. They wanted to be more specialist than the ethos of the university wanted them to be and it seemed to me that, for example, in what was called the government department, and the sociology department, there was a kind of split-ting off and a loss of the commitment to interdisciplinarity. When that happened, and also I think probably when Donald Davie left, the feel of the place changed a great deal and I thought it was time to move on. It didn't make sense in terms of what I've just said to move back to Cambridge, though that was in fact what I did. I just felt it was time to leave.

What was your view of the political troubles at Essex?

I suppose there are two obvious ways of seeing what happened at Essex. One was that there was a quite simple injustice perpetrated by the administration who, faced with an attempt by some students to stop a talk on biological warfare, suspended people whom they rather arbitrarily picked out as the ringleaders and who later turned out, after a formal enquiry, not to have been so at all. So at one level it seemed to me that it was important to point out that the administration had acted rather panickily and punished students who were not particularly involved, or certainly not involved as ringleaders, in the demonstration. As far as what happened at Essex was part of a much more general movement in 1968, then I found myself both involved in and promoting it and finding it very interesting, while at the same time being rather alarmed at a lot of the versions of what was going on. I found it interesting because it did seem an extraordinary educational moment and I still think it remains that. It is a moment which did change universities quite considerably. I don't think much of that looks terribly important now, but it was certainly important through the seventies and the early eighties. It was educational in the sense that, without 1968, there wouldn't be much student representation, or at least that was the trigger which produced it. All kinds of ways in which students got to have a voice, and a very valuable voice, in talking about issues relating to their own education seem much related to that moment. They learnt how to think about what kinds of rights and responsibilities and duties they might have in the running of the institution and that was important. I think it was important in a much wider sense, in that it did suddenly mean that when you were teaching, whatever you were teaching, you were being invited, in ways that were sometimes immediately unproductive but in the long term certainly productive, to talk about the relevance of what you were teaching to what a student of the second half of the twentieth century might need to know. Clearly there's a way in which, on any particular occasion, that whole question of relevance could be extremely tiresome. Very often one would want to tell students that they shouldn't worry about it and that the more irrelevant they found what they were reading, the more that might help them to get some distance on their own culture, which is as educational as having an immediate sense of connection between what they read and their social and political lives. But that emphasis on relevance did seem to produce a kind of conversation between teachers and students which made it possible both to defend a concept of relevance and to defend and define the concept of strangeness – the strangeness between what you learn at university and your immediate life – in ways that were productive. I was, however, extremely uninterested by the notion that students were workers and were in the forefront of some kind of revolution, because the differences between students and workers, and the unlikeliness, in England, that the kind of things that were going on at Essex or the LSE would spill over into mass political action, were so obvious that it seemed pure silliness to believe that they could do so. But I found myself criticizing that from what you might think of as an ultra-left position rather than from a liberal position.

A pamphlet of your poems, Property, *was published by Northern House in 1966. Were you writing a lot of poetry at that time?*

I never wrote a lot of poetry, but for a few years at Cambridge and then at Essex afterwards, I thought of myself as a poet in some sense, and I used to publish poetry in little magazines. I never made a particular decision to give it up, but although I've written odd poems since, none for ten years or so, I probably gave it up in effect when I started writing my thesis. I think the worst thing you can say about my poetry, and there are lots of bad things you can say about it, is that the same energy which went into writing academic prose or literary history and criticism seems to have been the energy that went into writing the poetry, and once I'd started doing the one I didn't have any particular inclination to do the other, or sense of lack in not doing it. I think my poetry's eminently forgettable. Some of my poems were possibly quite well written, but they achieved that condition by being so scrupulously empty of content that they polished very easily. Perhaps not in *Property*, but certainly afterwards, they increasingly became proudly empty of myself or of anything else and consequently probably rather more polished. My interest in writing them was very much formal, more of an interest in achieving a certain kind of tone and diction than in the ways of which one talks of form in terms of metre or stanza shape or anything like that. It was a certain kind of syntax and diction which somehow it seemed satisfying to produce but which wasn't really enough to sustain my interest, so why it should be enough to sustain the reader's I'm not sure.

You were also taking an increasing interest in the study of the visual arts, especially painting – that's already evident in The Idea of Landscape and the Sense of Place, *which came out in 1972 and by the time you get to* The Dark Side of the Landscape, *which appeared in 1980, it's moved into the foreground. How did that interest develop?*

It was originally an extremely narrow interest which developed simply out of my concern with how landscape was described in poetry. I became interested in looking at how pictures were composed because I was trying to talk about syntax as an equivalent to pictorial composition. That's what got me looking at seventeenth-, eighteenth-

and early nineteenth-century painting. The process of looking at that must have meant that I was developing ideas on much different topics in relation to English painting without particularly knowing it, because the actual decision to write a book about painting happened in the course of five minutes and very much to my surprise. I'd spent two terms writing an enormous book about the representation of the poor in English poetry in the eighteenth and early nineteenth centuries. It had grown to a draft of about 100,000 words and I still hadn't come anywhere near Wordsworth, and it was incredibly boring. I was just churning out page after page and it suddenly occurred to me that I could write a kind of equivalent of that story as a political pamphlet if I wrote about painting. This was partly because I didn't know so much about painting, which meant that I wasn't going to be tripped up by the trivia, but it was also partly because it did seem to me that I could isolate moments of historical transition much more precisely in relation to painting than in relation to poetry, not because those moments themselves are more sharply evident in painting, but because I'd made such an exhaustive study for the previous eight years of the representation of the poor in poetry that I'd lost all sense of the wood. I could only see lots of trees. So in a way it was the degree of my ignorance about painting which made me able to write about it at that time. Insofar as the interest's developed, it's developed very differently. I soon felt that the kinds of social and political readings of landscape paintings I was producing were becoming rather predictable and easy for me and other people to produce. It was almost as though I had produced a political grammar of reading paintings which you could fit over almost anything. So when I wrote about painting again, it was in relation to quite different interests which had come from my study of other areas of literature, in particular the study of republican thought in eighteenth-century Britain. I suddenly realized how crucial that tradition of political theory had been in the formation of theories of painting in the eighteenth century.

There's a question which begins to arise in The Dark Side of the Landscape *and which has become more explicit in your more recent work and more generally in cultural history and analysis with a radical bent. An older kind of radical cultural history and analysis, such as E.P. Thompson's* The Making of the English Working Class, *the influence of which you acknowledge in* The Dark Side of the Landscape, *or Raymond Williams's* The Country and the City, *which you also mention there, seemed to counterpose what Williams called 'real history' with mystification. To quite to a large extent, The Dark Side of the Landscape continues in that tradition. Much of its force comes from the sense that you're demystifying, unveiling, exposing – all these rather macho terms come to mind. But there are also moments of doubt in that book as to whether 'real history' and mystification can so easily be distinguished and opposed. You take issue, for example with Raymond Williams's praise of Crabbe as offering 'real history', suggesting that Crabbe might rather be seen as working with an alternative set of conventions, and at the end of the book, you say, apropos of Anita Brookner's approach to Constable, that 'it comes close to Raymond Williams's notion of "real history" – what really happened…when we have stripped away the nostalgia and mythologising about Merry England or the organic community. But the myths really happened as well…' (p. 164). A scepticism about the possibility of discovering 'real history', as distinct from sets of representative conventions and from myths, is raised there. And by the time we come to your essay 'Visualizing the Division of Labour', in The Birth of Pandora, published in 1992, you say '[t]he past is available to us only in the form of representations, and it was, equally to the point, available to the past only in the same form' (p. 117). The problem which seems then to arise is: given that one only has representations, by what criteria do we decide that one representation is superior to another? The older argument – E.P. Thompson's argument perhaps – would be that representation was superior because it was more faithful to the empirical facts and possibly because its explanatory power was greater. The suggestion that all you have are sets of competing representations seems to undermine a certain kind of radical cultural criticism and analysis, including the kind you yourself were conducting in The Dark Side of the Landscape. How do you feel about this question?*

I was very aware of being undecided and of continually finessing that question in *The Dark Side of the Landscape* because on the one hand the book, in a way, has no meaning unless it thinks of itself as unveiling and stripping away and as saying, here are all these misrepresentations, but we know the truth really, don't we? On the other hand, every time I put it quite as clearly as that, I felt extraordinarily embarrassed because somewhere already then I thought that all we really do have is representations. It's not that I believe that there are no empirical facts, but as soon as one puts a series of empirical facts together one is producing a representation. I don't think I'm any more clear in my mind now about how to relate the kind of commonsense belief that we all do hold, however much we pretend that we don't, that the past and certain things in it really did happen, with the quite straightforward truth – it seems to me as near as a truth we do have about history – that all we have of the past are representations. I find I stress the second point more now according to the context which I'm in, which is only another sign of the sense that not only do I not have much of an idea about where I stand on the issue but that I don't quite know what it would mean to be able to take a stand. The 'Division of Labour' paper was first written for a conference of the Social History society, and the passage you've quoted was written a few hours before giving the paper as a response to what seemed to me, within the conference, an extraordinary sureness that a certain version of history was what really happened and everything else was ruling-class mystification. Now I'm full of that myself, as *The Dark Side of the Landscape* shows, and in other contexts it irritates me enormously to hear somebody behaving not only as though it's all a matter of representations but also as though what's at stake, or what was at stake, in producing one representation or another was of no particular importance – that what's interesting is studying the grammar of discourses or the relations of discourses, as though once one had decided that the past was simply a set of representations, one had emptied it of meaning or of conflict.

So what I tend to try and do is show that different people or different groups in the past were concerned with producing different representations of their lives and that there was a great deal at stake in those conflicts between representations. I don't think I'm likely nowadays to have much time for an account of the past which would say that history from below is what really happened. What I am more and more concerned to do, however, is not only to show history as a site of conflict between contemporary historians, but also to try and understand how conflicting positions were constructed and represented in the past from a fairly finite set of discursive resources. So the nearest I'm likely to come to talking about what real history would be is talking about conflicting narratives that really were in competition, which really meant something to those who were involved in those conflicts and competitions. I don't think it loses touch with a sense of people's aspirations, desires, struggles and anxieties to do away with some notion that any particular account of what went on in the past is absolutely true, as long as you don't lose a sense of what was at stake in offering one representation as opposed to another. As far as what one's doing as a historian producing a particular representation of the past is concerned, when you don't believe that there's some straightforward objective empirical truth about the past, then I think there are a lot of complicated determinants. Clearly one does tend to try and produce a representation of the past which appears to take account most adequately of the kind of texts and instances that you've been studying. Clearly the kind of work you choose to do and the kind of answers that you find plausible are influenced by your own political position. There's another determinant which is more and more evident to me. I find myself more and more thinking of myself as a writer of narrative and there seems to me a sense, when you're writing about the past, of having done the job well when you've told a story that seems to have all kinds of things that at times I've thought were bad things, like finish, and that seems to come to an end, even if only with a set of questions. In other words, there are certain kinds of writerly considerations which may not be the same kinds of considerations as those involved in saying that the most plausible story is the one which takes most account of the evidence. It's not that I think that the good story is one which leaves out certain accounts of the evidence, but there is no doubt that all writers, even those who are most suspicious of narrative history, are concerned to find ways of representing accounts of the past as stories which are far more influential on how you write history than most historians, anyway, would acknowledge. So I think there are political influences on what story you find the most plausible, there's a notion of being as responsible a historian as you can which means that you're trying to tell a story which seems to take most account of evidence and instances, but there are also and above that, and much more importantly than I previously recognized, aesthetic or literary constraints which probably make it easier to persuade yourself that you've told the most plausible story you can about the past if the story itself seems to be coming out right or seems to be satisfying you as a piece of writing.

In relation to that concern with representation, could we go back for a while to the 1970s when you were working in Cambridge and when ideas concerned precisely with questions of representation – poststructuralist and deconstructionist ideas – were beginning to enter Cambridge from France via people like Stephen Heath and Colin MacCabe. I wondered how you responded to those ideas then, and subsequently, because they don't, at that time, appear explicitly in your work.

No, and I'm not sure how much they do now. I do think that my work has changed in certain ways very profoundly through an increasing interest in, and acquaintance with, theory, but I was always a slow learner and it was certainly a slow process. On the other hand, I didn't feel associated with the kinds of targets against which structuralism and post-structuralism were introduced into the university, so I never felt that theory was the kind of threat which critics more committed to what came to be called a liberal humanist account of literature were likely to feel. I found that I lived very equably with literary theory without finding, certainly not for a long time, that it really changed my way of thinking about literature, but it was certainly influencing me, more, I think, through picking it up in the air and through conversation than through actually sitting down and reading theoretical texts. So when I look back to where I was, let's say, by the time of the Colin MacCabe wars, then I think I was in profound agreement with those who were interested in literary theory in insisting that, in a way, the main educational problem about literary criticism as it was taught in English universities was that students weren't encouraged to examine the presuppositions on which they approached it. They inherited a critical vocabulary which they were expected to deploy with skill but not to inspect much. That always very much concerned me and so it was very easy to make common cause with Stephen Heath, for example, on a question like that.

I also had much sympathy – indeed more sympathy than I have now – with the idea that the concentration on the author as the unit in terms of which you studied literature was extremely distorting. I wasn't terribly interested myself in authors as authors; I was interested in periods and topics and problems and modes of representation, and so though I couldn't make the metaphysical leap of believing in the death of the author – I believe that the author is really quite alive – I was always more likely to find myself, in any polarized argument, defending that kind of concern than arguing for authors as the organizing principle in terms of which literature should be studied. I was also – this goes right back to my PhD work and my interest in the way in which certain kinds of organizations of syntax and sentence structure could produce certain kinds of representations – I was also already very interested in notions of what I later learned to call discourse. I was interested in how certain kinds of linguistic conventions were likely to produce certain kinds of representations rather than those representations being willed consciously by the author. So I found myself a great deal in sympathy, as an educator, with what the theoretical boys were arguing, without it actually making a very obvious difference to my work. But it didn't seem to me that the concerns of my work, though they were very differently expressed, were actually as far away from those of people like Stephen Heath as they were from a more conventional and liberal humanist way of doing the subject. Since then, although it's very hard to be very precise about influences, Foucault was clearly a big influence at one stage, though I think I ended up using the word discourse in a very different way from the way he uses it and probably in a fairly conventional way. I think that although I've taken on little bits of Derrida – bits of the vocabulary and a few of the concepts, in particular the concept of the supplement – I haven't been terribly influenced by that kind of approach.

What was your own sense of the issues that were at stake in the Cambridge dispute of 1980?

It was fairly clear to me at the time that the more traditional literary scholars in the Faculty saw the question of Colin MacCabe's reappointment as an opportunity to make a stand against theory. There was a very revealing comment from one of the influential members of the committee which was responsible for recommending his reappointment which went: 'There's a war on. Colin MacCabe wouldn't give me a job and I wouldn't give him one.' It was seen in terms of a war and indeed a lot of those involved were *anciens combattants* from the Leavisite campaigns. The more traditional scholars saw poststructuralist theory as a very considerable threat, and quite rightly, to the kind of work that they did. They saw that it was producing a following among students which made them feel uncomfortable and challenged, and they decided that here was an opportunity to take a stand against it. It's very similar to the recent Derrida controversy in some sense. It was a taking of a symbolic stand, except that much more was at stake than whether or not somebody got an honorary degree. I think it's extraordinary because it was a debate which, insofar as it ever developed into a debate, was typically Cambridge in that it couldn't be had as an intellectual debate about the nature of the subject and about what we should be teaching. Universities generally, but especially diverse collegiate universities where you have very few institutional occasions on which you can converse together and in which there's very little sense of an intellectual community, only have occasions to debate their educational policies, their critical beliefs, around administrative issues. So this was a way of displacing a conversation that ought to be taking place as an intellectual dialogue within the faculty onto an administrative and career issue in a way that was grossly inappropriate and might have been extremely unfortunate, except that probably nothing better could have happened to Colin than losing his job at Cambridge. But one of the most extraordinary things about the whole invasion of the academy by theory is how, almost everywhere, dialogue has been displaced into questions about whether we allow this or that question on the exam paper, or whether we allow this person or that person to have a job. It's never about the merits of the case or even, usually, about the merits of pluralism.

Could we come back to your books and take up the question that for me arose particularly when reading your English Literature in History 1730-80: An Equal, Wide Survey, *which was published in 1983. That offers a very interesting discussion of various attempts in the eighteenth century – by Thomson and Dyer and Johnson and Smollett – to achieve a unifying vision and a unifying language – or at least to try and imagine what a position might be from which one could achieve a unifying vision and a unifying language. In some sense that's a theme which you take up again in* The Political Theory of Painting from Reynolds to Hazlitt: 'The Body of the Public', *which came out in 1986. In that book, you trace a range of attempts – by Sir Joshua Reynolds, James Barry, William Blake, Henry Fuseli, and Benjamin Robert Haydon – to revise and sustain a civic humanist theory of painting against the assaults of social change and the discourse of political economy. There seems, however, to be a certain shift in your work, because in* An Equal Wide Survey, *and even going back to* The Dark Side of the Landscape *and* The Idea of Landscape and the Sense of Place, *there's a strong sense that the attempt to achieve a comprehensive vision is mystifying and even destructive, if you relate it, for example, to enclosure as you do in* The Idea of Landscape and the Sense of Place. *But by the time we get to* The Body of the Public, *while you're still very aware of what the civic humanist discourse excludes – it cuts out most men and all women – there also seems to be a more positive sense of the value of such a discourse as opposed to what one might call the privatized approach to painting that you identify in Hazlitt. Do you feel that to be the case?*

Yes, absolutely. What I found so useful when I started looking at republican theory or the discourse of civic humanism generally, which first became important in *An Equal, Wide Survey* and which I talk about at length in *The Political Theory of Painting*, was the

notion of citizenship that it contained. Now it goes without saying
that the kind of notion of the active citizen which civic humanism
produced was always an exclusive one. In a straightforward sense, as
classical republicanism, it was an account which provided an
extremely convenient way of distinguishing the free man from the
citizen and indeed of justifying the existence of slaves, as those who
were not capable of behaving as citizens. But I was conscious at the
time that my interest in that discourse was in some senses as immediately related to my political awareness as *The Dark Side of the Landscape* had been when I wrote that. It did seem to me that the early
years of Mrs Thatcher's government had already made it very clear
that there was going to be an enormous attenuation of the degree to
which members of a democracy could feel themselves to be actively
involved and could feel themselves to be citizens. That was partly
because of the extraordinary professionalization of election campaigns – it does seem that to a large extent we have been disenfranch-
ised by the way in which democracy has been commercialized. But
there was also, for example, the attack on local government and the
way in which government was increasingly conducted by ministerial
fiat rather than by Act of Parliament. It seemed to me that one way
of thinking about what Thatcherism was doing, even in the early
eighties, was as an attack on democracy and on the notion of citizenship, the most obvious part of which was that strange, contradictory
claim to be returning power to the people while centralizing government by leaps and bounds. By the very early eighties I was not
becoming less of a redistributive socialist, but I was increasingly feeling that the first part of the agenda was to try and hold the line on
citizenship and on the right of everybody to participate in decisions,
and to try and find ways in which participatory democracy could be
strengthened – in many respects, the kind of programmes that Charter 88 has. So I think that the fascination with the discourse of civic
humanism very much grew out of my sense that citizenship was
being so quickly attenuated or indeed being privatized. There was
that whole period in which citizenship was precisely seen as being a
good, active, but not political member of a local community in ways
in which were beautifully summarized by the Neighbourhood Watch
campaign in the mid-eighties. This concern carries right through to
my present work. What I'm looking at now is radical political movements in the 1790s whose political programme was to say: we want
to find ways of constructing a politics which represents equal active
citizenship as one of the rights of man. It's not Painite natural rights
language, it's a kind of Jacobin language but one which says clearly

that this language of citizenship is in some sense the most valuable
political inheritance we have and we've got to find ways of making
it a democratic language and not an aristocratic or oligarchic language. So really that's what I've been thinking about for the last ten
years, though always of course in these rather oblique ways.

There's another question that arises from The Political Theory of
Painting. *In a sense, that book counterposes two possible attitudes to
painting: the civic humanist theory, in its various versions, which
sees the most dignified function of painting as the promotion of public virtue, and the attitude represented by William Hazlitt which sees
painting as a wholly private transaction between a genius, nature,
and the individual viewer of the canvas. But there would seem to be,
in the practice, if not in the theory, of late eighteenth-century French
painting, a possibility of a kind of painting which combines public
and private functions – which both addresses its viewers rhetorically
as citizens but also reaches into their most intimate psychic and bod-
ily recesses – I'm thinking of course of David, and of a painting like*
The Oath of the Horatii. *There's a sense in which your study might
seem actually to reproduce and sustain a kind of public/private
dichotomy – coming down on the public rather than the private side
but not adumbrating any possibility of fusing the two. Do you think
one could imagine, or even point historically to, the emergence of a
kind of painting that combines public and private modes of address?*

As far as the historical question is concerned, I'm not terribly happy
with the notion that paintings which show the enormous private cost
of acting virtuously in the public service really do represent some
bridging of that dichotomy. It would be impossible for David to
paint 'Horatius persuaded by his mother not to defend the bridge
and to escape with her into the safety of the countryside'. Integral
throughout this civic humanist tradition is the idea that the greater
the renunciation of private comfort and private solace, the greater
the representation of virtue, so that the more we agonize over con-
demning our sons to death or over leaving our womenfolk knowing
that we're doomed to extinction, the more virtuous we are. I think
we read it rather unhistorically, though that's not to say we read it in
some straightforward way wrongly, if we imagine that there's any
real openness in the outcome of those narratives. There's only one
decision that is paintable. It's only by looking at them with the kind
of concern for privacy which is made available to us by the loss of
that public rhetoric that we can conceive of this bridging of the

dichotomy. It's because we're not so steeped in those notions of civic virtue that we can read those pictures as acknowledging the value and the importance and the real pull of private life in quite the way that we do. It's not that they don't acknowledge that, but they acknowledge it only in order and always in order to show that nevertheless the renunciation of the private must be made by the civic hero. In a general sense, I think that in *The Political Theory of Painting*, I come down in favour of a way of thinking about painting which is asking questions about its relation to our life as citizens or as members of a society but that I'm not conscious myself of wanting a *painting* that does that. I'm saying that there is a danger of thinking, as it seems to me Hazlitt thought most of the time, that painting is something that addresses us in some room where we're not acting as citizens, and that it doesn't seem to me a very good idea to argue that it has that entirely private consolatory function. I certainly don't see any straightforward way of advocating a public painting. Public painting is something that happens within certain kinds of social and political situations. To imagine that one could invent a public painting, though the attempt must always be interesting and might always be worth doing, seems odd. I don't quite know what it would mean to say that painting itself ought to have a public function unless one could talk concretely about what a painting like that would look like, and the problem about the society we live in is that it's very hard to know what a painting like that would look like, as indeed it was quite hard in the late eighteenth century, because there was very little interest in actual works of history painting at the time, though there was a great deal of interest in the theory which talked about how they could be produced. So I'm not sure that I would be concerned to try and find a kind of painting that either was self-consciously and responsibly public or was self-consciously capable of holding together the public and the private spheres. I'm interested in saying that painting, of whatever kind, inevitably addresses us in our civic and public capacity as well as in our private capacity and that we ought to think about the kinds of languages in which we could talk about that. It's a demand for a certain way of talking about pictures, a certain set of questions that we ought to have in mind when we look at pictures, rather than for a particular kind of art.

Can we turn to poetry again and to your book Poetry, Language and Politics, *which appeared in 1988. You argue in your Introduction to that book that practical criticism rests on an ideology which values control, balance and unity, primarily as evinced in a fusion of form*

and content in those texts that it defines as literary, and which iden-
tifies those valued qualities as essential, transcendent and universal,
It's an ideology that presents itself as above politics and history but
that is covertly political, middle class, masculinist and historically
specific. It seems to me that the achievement of that book is, in a
sense, paradoxical, because you support your attack on the ideology
of practical criticism with the kind of close attention to syntactic and
semantic detail which was supposedly advocated by practical criti-
cism itself. You turn some of the techniques of practical criticism –
allied with discourse analysis and textual and historical scholarship
– against what you define as the ideology of practical criticism. But
that might also be seen as a recuperation of practical criticism under-
stood as a mode of reading which is defined, not necessarily by the
particular ideological components you identify, but precisely by its
very close bestowal of attention upon the minutiae of a text. Isn't
that technique of reading the real core of practical criticism and
doesn't your approach in some sense preserve that and occlude a
politics which may inhere in that very technique, in the very idea that
it matters in some vital way to pay that kind of very close attention
to texts?

There are two questions there. One is whether I do actually use the
techniques of practical criticism in my attack on practical criticism.
That's only true if we accept that practical criticism simply is anything that pays close attention to texts. What you're trying to argue
is that it is. What I would say in reply is that there are two obvious
ways in which I do close reading of poetry in that book: one is
through syntactical analysis and the other is through analysis of discourse. Practical criticism, it seems to me, was never very interested
in syntax. The kind of objective access to a text that the analysis of
syntax might offer was always rather alien to it – 'objective' in the
qualified sense that we could actually agree whether a reading of a
poem which was conducted in terms of its syntax was right or was
wrong or was half-right or partly right, at least at the level of description. It seems to me that practical criticism didn't have anything that
resembled the kind of debatable descriptive content that critics like
Auerbach or like Davie brought to their close readings of poems, and
because it didn't have anything like that it was able to praise and
blame without in any way taking responsibility for the descriptions
on which its value judgements were based. In some sense, they
weren't debatable and they were therefore capable of proceeding
quite uncomplicatedly from certain presuppositions which were also

not examined and which couldn't really be challenged because the description itself couldn't be challenged. The analysis of a poem in terms of its discourses is rather similar to the analysis of it in terms of its syntax in that we can, not with precision, but with at least some possibility of debate about a recognizable object, say that a poem is partly written within a certain discourse and partly written within another. That's something we can argue and convince each other about in a way which I don't think the kinds of descriptions which, let's say, Leavis produces, allow us to do. I don't think there's an object we can converse about and discuss and disagree and persuade each other about in the same kind of way.

So in answer to the first question, I don't think I'm doing practical criticism, I'm doing close reading, and I've got no kick against close reading whatsoever. I think close reading is the absolute basis of everything we do. In response to the second question, of whether there's a politics about close reading, I think the answer is no, or that there are many politics about close reading. There's no particular politics which you're always inevitably bearing out if you're doing close reading. I'm still, however, entirely persuaded by the kind of argument that someone like Leavis would use that the close attention to the detail of texts within the classroom or within the work of literary criticism has an extremely important educational function and that the recognition of the power that language has over us and of how we can become aware of and to some extent free ourselves from that power is absolutely crucial to a literary education and to the kinds of things that I think a book like *Poetry, Language and Politics* is doing. Insofar as that book has a politics other than that of its attack on practical criticism, it's a politics which says that you need to attend to the syntactical structures and to the historically specific discourses of texts in order to see the ways in which they are constructing reality and in order to question those ways. So I'm extremely traditionalist in that kind of defence of the value of close reading. But I don't think you can identify close reading with practical criticism.

Could I take up another claim you make in your Introduction to Poetry, Language and Politics. *This relates to the questions, much debated in recent years, of literary value and of the identity of literature as a distinctive category. You say '[i]t seems finally that the literary text, as constituted by practical criticism, has been constituted as such not by the kind of attention that it demands, and so by its intrinsic nature, but by the kind of attention that certain critics have chosen to bring to bear on it' (p. 11). That appears to suggest that, as it were, anything at all can be made into literature by practical criticism. The question which then seems to arise – a pressing educational question – is: what criteria should guide the selection of texts for study? The idea once was, to put it simply, that you should study the best literary texts. There was room for disagreement about what the best texts were and about the criteria for selecting them, but the idea nonetheless was that the selection was being made on a qualitative basis, even if that basis was bound up with particular social and political notions – the idea of 'Englishness', for example. If you open the field up and say any text, any discourse, is open to close reading, if you do away with the notion of some kind of qualitative criteria, by what other criteria are the texts that one ought to read going to be selected?*

To begin with, I'd better say that I have lots of anxieties about the introduction to *Poetry, Language and Politics*. In the first case you hit on an area that I wasn't anxious about, but this one I am, of course. I'm not at all happy with the suggestion in the particular bit you read out, though I think there's a lot of truth in it, that there aren't things that signal the literary and which announce that texts are functioning in a literary kind of way. I'm overstating my case there in my polemic. So we can reduce the field at least to some more manageable area by saying that. But not too much because as far as I'm concerned the more useful distinction is one between telephone directories and, let's say, discursive texts. I'm very happy to teach government reports or newspaper articles or whatever. It seems to me, however, that the main criterion that one needs to use in selecting texts is to make sure that students read those texts, or a representative selection of them, out of which our literary history has been constituted – whatever else they read, and they must read other things. This is why I believe in teaching the canon. I don't think that it makes any sense really to read non-canonical texts except in relation to a notion of what the canonical is and why it's canonical and how it's come to be regarded as canonical, though those questions about why and how may get different answers from somebody like me than they would from another critic. It would be quite ridiculous, as a teacher, to announce that the canon was ideologically bankrupt and that therefore one's students ought to spend their time reading non-canonical works, because that would mean the founding assumption on the basis of which you were offering them non-canonical works was one which they were never in a position to test because they'd never read the canonical works. As far as I'm concerned, it's absolutely crucial to any student's sense of the history of the culture that they're studying that they should read those texts that are regarded as canonical, or as many of them as leaves room for them to read other texts that question the notion of canonicity or enable them to raise questions about what's not in the canon as well as what is and about what is constituted as the literary and what isn't. Unless they read 'non-literary' texts with the same attention as they read literary texts, they won't be in a position to talk about the nature of literariness or to decide whether it exists or not. Unless they read non-canonical texts, they won't be in a position to talk about the canon or the non-canonical texts either. So the argument there seems to me quite straightforward and I'm certainly not at all struck by the notion that it's somehow oppressive to submit students to the authority of the canon.

But hasn't the authority of the canon broken down not only because it has been characterized as oppressive but also because it has become much more difficult to decide what is actually in the canon and what isn't?

Yes, partly because it's become much harder to talk confidently about literary value than it was before, but also for the much more profound reason that the industry of literary criticism and literary history has so expanded that our awareness of what's been written in the past and what's being written in the present has gone out of the control of any canon. Too much literature has been presented as literature worthy of study for it to be possible to make much sense of a canon that has anything other than an institutional and historical importance. So I don't think that there's a serious possibility of continuing with the notion of a canon other than as a selection of texts which have been canonized in the past and as a result have become so important to the history of literature that one is going to be seriously ignorant of their influence unless one reads them.

Can we come on to The Infection of Thomas De Quincey *which was published in 1991. That book shows your characteristically close attention to textual detail but it does also mark a departure in its use of psychoanalytic perspectives and in its concern with Imperialism. Why did you move into those areas?*

Well, there are different ways I can talk about it. I can talk about it as the effect of being at Sussex where the influence of Homi Bhahba and Jacqueline Rose was certainly important in directing me both to questions of imperialism and questions of psychoanalysis. I can talk about it in more general terms of the new opportunities for thinking about such topics which have been created in the last ten years or so. I can talk about it in terms of an increasing amazement, which built up over a number of years but only finds expression in that book, at how much of the literary history of England in the last 200 years has been written without any consciousness of Britain as an enormous world imperial power. It's extremely hard now to think how it could ever have occurred. But it is an extraordinary legacy, of both the kind of little-Englishness that has been very much at the centre of English studies, and the tradition of close reading as an exclusive rather than as a founding aspect of the subject, that until recently, and even on the Left, questions about imperialism in relation to English Literature had very rarely been raised – granted, there are obviously important exceptions. The way the book actually grew up was very different and very sudden in a way. When I was researching the essay on James Barry which appears in *The Birth of Pandora*, and becoming interested in Barry's use and awareness of oriental mythology, I was looking at De Quincey's *Confessions*, at the oriental opium dreams and suddenly I found myself seeing that there, the talk about the Orient was continually slipping into talking about very personal and familial issues and vice versa. You seemed to have a kind of knot in which imperialist imagery was related to anxious and disturbing accounts of personal experience. So that was the initial perception from which the book began. Now I hadn't read any Freud at all really since I was a graduate student, but it was perfectly clear that in order to think about this perception I would need to start reminding myself of Freud, and taking advice about what to read of him so that I could think about ways of connecting this recurrent imperial interest and imagery with the personal experience. Yet all the time, both briefly in the Barry essay and repeatedly in the De Quincey book, I was trying to find ways of neither privileging the kind of historical and/or 'discourse analysis' approach over the psychoanalytic, nor privileging the psychoanalytic over the other. I think both the success and the failure of the De Quincey book is the way in which I behave as though I'm entirely persuaded by the psychoanalytic reading of De Quincey that I'm producing, while at the same time I'm continually trying to hold it in place and saying that this mustn't be regarded as the whole story.

With regard to that relationship between the personal and the histor-

ical, how far did you want De Quincey's case to be taken as a representative one, as the subtitle of your book – A Psychopathology of Imperialism – suggests it might be?

The subtitle is intended to be rather canny – too canny by half, I'm afraid – in that it precisely is not 'the' but 'a' psychopathology, which is hedging its bets on whether it's individual or representative. This is a difficulty about close reading, isn't it, because the only way of writing a book like *The Infection of Thomas De Quincey* is through the kind of close reading that it does, through the immensely detailed analysis of individual incidents and the relating of them one to another. To argue the case at that level in relation to a whole range of writers would require that the same attention be paid to them as I paid to De Quincey, and because simply of the exigences of publishing, but also the exigences of time, it would be very hard to produce the kind of text which would make the case convincingly for more than one writer. From the considerable amount of reading I did in early nineteenth-century writings about India and the Orient at the time that I was writing the book, my sense is that this is a rather representative case study in the sense that the fear of the Orient is something which, at that period at least, is constituted very early and in relation to the family, to make a generalization no larger than that. I'm gambling on that being true and my hunch is, from all the material I've read, that it would be the case in relation to a large number of writers at that time.

You talked of trying to hold together the psychoanalytic and the historical in The Infection of Thomas De Quincey, *and you state explicitly near the start of your study that 'this book will avoid (I hope) the attempt to establish a hierarchy of precedence' (p. 21). That avoidance relates to what you call later in the book 'the unanswerable question of determination' (p. 169). An older kind of radical criticism, as well as believing you could distinguish between true and false representations, also believed it was both possible and necessary to establish the causes of things, to identify a hierarchy of precedence, in order not only to analyse the world but also to change it. That belief may have had harmful consequences in political practice, but it was also enabling and motivating. Doesn't the suspension of a reply to the question of determination effectively paralyse radical criticism and offer a rewriting, in more fashionable terms, of the old liberal humanist contemplation of delightful undecidable ambiguities?*

It's one thing to regret, as in a way I do, the sense that a secure notion of determination has been lost. It does however seem to me that it has been and that we are in a position where we can no longer advocate the confident causal narratives that used to fuel radical criticism. Of course that means that such criticism has now become much more uncertain and provisional. I don't think it has therefore become the same as liberal humanist criticism, because it's asking very different questions. To begin with, it's asking questions which to some extent it does accept now are undecidable, and that's not a characteristic of liberal humanist criticism. Liberal humanist criticism asks questions to which it believes there are answers. The question of determination is one which is undecidable but which is nevertheless a useful heuristic tool for talking about the relations between different kinds of approaches and for trying to give a kind of an authority, in a way that the old radical criticism couldn't, to personal and private experience in the formation of people not only as personal and individual creatures but also as political creatures.

You said earlier in our conversation that you'd become increasingly interested in writing plausible narratives, and The Infection of Thomas De Quincey *is particularly absorbing to read. It combines the structure of a Freudian case study and of a kind of detective novel. There's a lot of enigma and suspense, and you often intimate the possibility of revelations, though I'm not sure how fully they are delivered. You say in your introduction 'I have thought of rewriting the book, and of allowing each chapter an equality of knowledge concerning the direction the story is taking. In the end I decided against this, not because I want to keep my readers in suspense, but because the story that eventually emerges is so disturbing (at least I find it so) that I would not ask anyone to believe it who had not watched it come together from the hints and fragments scattered across the most disparate range of texts' (p. 23). That seems implicitly to acknowledge that the persuasiveness of the book rests not only on the evidence that you adduce but also on the way that you adduce it — it rests, that is, on a set of rhetorical techniques which might be used as effectively in fiction as in a critical study or a case history. And although you don't come to definite conclusions, those techniques arouse the same suspicion that one might have, let's say, in regard to Freud's 'Wolf-Man' essay — I'm thinking particularly, of course, of Stanley Fish's account of it. There's a sense as one reads the book of a deeply pleasurable manipulation. But, in the end, are we meant to believe that it's true?*

Let's start from the deeply pleasurable manipulation. Among the people being manipulated was me. When I sat down to write that, I thought I was writing an essay which was intended to be about 8000 words long and would become part of *The Birth of Pandora*. I sat down and literally in three weeks I'd written the full draft of a book. It's written in that sense as discovered – that's to say, chapters almost end when I suddenly see, gosh, I hadn't realized that before. I was continually shocked and pleasurably horrified by what I was discovering. Whatever I wrote about not wanting to keep my readers in suspense, I think I'm quite pleased to be thought to be manipulating the reader, but it felt as though it was a matter of not rewriting or not reordering material rather than of being consciously manipulative. Are you meant to believe it? You're meant to believe that there's a continual and noteworthy slide in De Quincey's texts between images of eastern horror and images of the anxieties of childhood, and you're meant to accept the book as a plausible account of how that slide happens. But a great deal of it is only as believable as the Freudian theory itself. I didn't attempt to argue with Freud or rewrite Freud or develop a para-Freudian theory of my own. I'm fairly agnostic about how much I believe that Freudian psychoanalysis has a particularly persuasive grip on how we develop. But what intrigued me was how extraordinarily appropriate it seemed to be for explicating this particular body of material. The book says, here are some ideas which I have at secondhand from Freud which might make sense of this. If you find Freud plausible then you might find this account of what's going on in De Quincey plausible. But I can't say you're meant to believe it because, as we've already said, the book stresses indeterminacy, so you would then have to believe, not only in a particular account of determination which is Freud's, but also in a particular indeterminacy.

In your moving and fascinating memorial piece for Allon White in the London Review of Books *(29 August 1991, p.21), you discuss an essay he wrote called 'Why am I a literary critic?' in which he suggested, by your account, that writing criticism might be a way of dealing at a distance with deep and unresolved psychic conflicts which would however return, in some form, in the criticism. You then explore the possibility that your study of De Quincey might be looked at in such a light and you say at the end of that piece '[i]f I did not quite believe in the adequacy of Allon's account of why he was, or I might be, a literary critic, I did come to understand how much more convenient it is to get off on the psychic work done by someone else than to dig up your own patch. But I also learned to acknowledge as mine these things and thoughts of darkness – to be aware at last of the beast stamping on the distant shore, if only so as to be better at not confronting it' (p.21). Let me put Allon White's question to you and ask you to respond to it in both private and public terms: what do you think drives you to write literary and cultural criticism – is 'drives', indeed, the right word – and what do you see as your public critical role?*

'Drives' seems to be the right word because I certainly feel compelled to do the work I do. On the other hand I don't think it would follow that the compulsion would always be the same. Certainly it looks to me as though the compulsion behind a book like *The Infection of Thomas De Quincey* is rather different from the compulsion behind, say, *An Equal, Wide Survey* which is an altogether cooler performance. Insofar as I can identify the compulsion, it is a political one. When I look at the range of my work and at the kind of concerns that animate it, it seems as though what compels me is the desire to tell a different story about the politics of a text or a period or a question than has been told about it so far. Although this may not have always been foregrounded in the books, I think, looking back on them, that the particular things I find myself wanting to write against are moments where the polite culture of England represents itself as the whole of English culture. But it's never simply a political compulsion. It is also a passion for finding out that is bound up with a passion for writing in a way that seems to tell a very full story, and the actual process of finding a language and a way of conducting an argument in relation to my material has its own fascination which may have as much claim to be the driving compulsion as the political one. Whether I'm also driven by the kind of things that Allon wrote about, I'm not sure. Writing the De Quincey book certainly felt like an intriguing exploration of another person's psyche which had a good chance of being both an exploration of my own and a displacing of it on to somebody else's, both a confronting and a non-confronting. But the difference between that book and the others makes it reasonable for me to think that it would only be in a fairly indirect and much displaced way that one could talk about the body of my work as having the same kind of compulsions as Allon talks about. I was nearer the De Quincey book when I wrote that piece. I feel further away from psychoanalysis now, as I work on law and politics, and I'm not sure that the displacements wouldn't be so many that it would be difficult to locate much psychic anxiety driving my present work.

Insofar as one has a public role as a critic, that seems to me something that you both construct and have constructed for you. You construct it by the kinds of books you write and by the kind of address you adopt in them, but it's also constructed for you by the kinds of invitations you get on the basis of your writing to do this or to write that or to speak there. I think that the kind of 'neither one thing nor the other' feeling that people have had about the political in my writing – that it's somehow never absent but yet never present – probably describes rather well at least the perception of me or the kind of position I occupy as a critic. That's to say, everybody who thinks of me at all as a critic thinks of me as being on the left but I don't have much of a presence, nor have I particularly sought one, as a journalist or a speaker on political questions. I feel very uncomfortable talking about politics in conversation. It's not at all that my understanding of political issues is so complex that I find it difficult to articulate what I think within the kind of animated conversation in which politics tends to be discussed, but my sense, at least, of the complexity of political questions is such that talking about them always embarrasses me because I'm immediately aware of what it is that I haven't said. I think the context in which one finds oneself talking about politics is one that requires a much greater simplification and a much greater ability to speak in coherent and confident sentences than I'm capable of. I think probably that at every point in what I write where it might seem that I should turn from the rather intricate consideration of a particular issue to make a contemporary political point, there would be a loss of persuasiveness if I did so, because there would be a loss of the opportunity for care and for discrimination. This sounds terribly fastidious, but I think it probably is what I think. Granted that the books I write are really about the past, to be making political asides or to be sketching, or hinting at, or even developing in a paragraph here or there, points about the relation between this story about the past and the present, would always involve a loss of the kind of argumentative and evidential care with which I try to write about the past. If I wanted to make those kinds of political points, it would be appropriate to another kind of writing altogether. When I get the opportunity to do that other kind of writing, I'm often quite happy to do it, but it feels like a different kind of exercise. I'm quite happy to be thought of as a critic who makes his politics clear and who's identified as being in a roughly left-wing and radical position, because my anxiety always tends to be the other way – why aren't other people more upfront about their politics in their work? – but I'm not sure that I've got the right kinds of talents to represent my politics more in public than I do.

Colin MacCabe

British Film Institute, Stephen Street
London 6 July 1992

NICOLAS TREDELL: *Could I begin by asking about your formation through home and school, prior to going to university?*

COLIN MacCABE: My parents are Irish and came over to England just after the war and just before I was born. In that sense, and I think it is of some importance, I'm a first generation immigrant, though obviously Ireland's different to other immigrant communities. I went to a Catholic school in Ealing called St Benedict's, and it's a pardonable exaggeration to say there were no English people there. Because it was a Catholic school, there were a lot of Irish, Poles and Italians. It was a public school which was founded by Downside at the beginning of the twentieth century, I suppose to deal with the problems of suburban Catholics, and it got an incredible lease of life in the post-war period because of the shortage of schools. This meant that something like half the places, from eleven onwards, were paid for by various local councils, and the school was effectively a super grammar school for bright Catholic boys. It was an odd mixture of a very bad school – it had many of the features of a third-rate public school – and a very good one. I got fantastically good teaching there, particularly in the senior school before I left, and especially from a history master called Steve Walker who was phenomenally successful at educating children and then getting them into Oxbridge. Chris Patten is probably his most notable success. In that sense, my childhood was that of a lower-middle-class boy in London in the fifties and sixties, and of course by the end of my schooling, in 1966, one was fully in the sixties. That's to say one of the very important influences on me outside school was rock music – the Rolling Stones and the Who were local groups – and the other great influence outside school was television. It seemed to me then, and in retrospect nothing has changed my view, that it was a fantastic moment of television. I learnt an incredible amount from television as well as from my school.

Would you still maintain, as you suggested in your South Bank Show Lecture of 1987, that television at that time brought you education and entertainment on a scale you could not have otherwise obtained (See The Listener, *119: 3049, 11 February 1988, p. 10)?*

Yes, I think so. If I think back, for example, to the Potter or Mercer plays, or to *Z Cars*, one did sit down to watch them with a sense of great expectation. Television really was a fantastic influence on me at that time. I have thought that it was just fond memories of youth that made it seem so good. In retrospect, having produced two television programmes, one of which, last year, was about television in the fifties and sixties, I've come to think that there really was a moment of television, which I described in the South Bank Show Lecture, which not only hasn't been repeated but is unlikely to be repeated.

How did your interest in television and rock music relate to more traditional activities, to reading for example?

I think the point is that it didn't. I had this fantastic interest from a very early age in poetry and in fiction of all kinds, and then I had these more contemporary interests, but at that stage they were just held in different parts of one's mind. There was zero encouragement, there was zero, as we would say now, discourse in which one could talk about one's interest in pop music or television in the same way that one could talk about one's interest in T.S. Eliot or *Henry IV Part 2*. I think, though – this is slight retrospect, everything else I've said up to now was actually what I felt at the time – that I was very determined even then to make it all come together. I wasn't going to downplay one in favour of the other and certainly in the last 20 years, that's been a very conscious decision. In a sense, in academic terms, I'm as anti the traditionalists who want to know nothing about the contemporary world as I am equally against those who are only interested in contemporary cultural forms – it seems to me that without some kind of historical perspective you really can't tell the wood from the trees.

What was it like going to Cambridge in the sixties?

I went up to Cambridge in October '67, having spent a year between school and university mainly in Paris, and I was astonished by a whole number of things when I got to Cambridge. The first thing that was very striking to me was the intelligence of my contemporaries, and also the fact that this intelligence was much more wide-ranging than I expected. If you take rock music – not so much television, but particularly rock music – I was suddenly in a world where there was a discourse, where people were spending a great deal of time thinking and talking about rock music. And there's also the fact that I went up as a lower-middle-class kid from the London of the sixties, in the period of the Labour government, and I thought this was really a moment of historical change, that we were going to see real changes in Britain, real changes in class structure. I went up to one of the ruling class institutions and I was very struck by those aspects of it and found them – I wouldn't say simply repulsive, they have an attraction and repulsion which is difficult to describe, but I thought by and large they were aspects which would disappear. I quite seriously thought that all these institutions were going to be transformed very radically in the next two or three years. Now in retrospect there are two things one can say about that. One obvious thing to say is how idiotic could one have been, because of course, literally within ten years – that's to say, when I first took up my job as an assistant lecturer at Cambridge in 1976 – everything was completely back to normal. But the other thing to say is that probably there was a moment when there was more give within the social and institutional fabric. It wasn't all illusion. There was a real moment of change. One of the reasons for that was the success of the grammar schools, and there's a deep historical irony in that. For if there was one thing in 1966 which I thought was going to change Britain, it was comprehensive education, and I now think that if there was one thing that actually reinforced the class structure, reinforced all the institutions, it was comprehensivization. It actually took all the pressure off. But that's a thought I really didn't have for another twenty years.

Intellectually Cambridge was exciting, though in rather traditional ways. I wanted to do philosophy first and then switch to English, and philosophy was dominated by Wittgenstein. My own concerns were to try and hold together the force of that tradition with a lot of the more speculative philosophy around the student movement. I had very many good teachers, but there wasn't a figure like Wittgenstein around. Then, as I'd intended, I switched to English and there was then a quite striking moment, which came when I attended Stephen Heath's lectures. I remember his lectures on realism in the novel very clearly, because here was something that was both new and wasn't like, say, Marcuse. In my first two years I was caught up in a ferment of ideas, but with little idea how to put them together, and then suddenly I came across this new world of Derrida, Althusser, Barthes. The names are now completely familiar, but they were completely unfamiliar then, and they seemed to offer a way of articulating all the diverse ideas of the late sixties. Intellectually, I then spent the next four to five years entirely, in a sense, working through various theoretical problematics, still very influenced by Wittgenstein and the analytic tradition but in the perspectives of those French thinkers. After I graduated this work focused on a thesis on Joyce. Joyce seemed perfectly to match my own particular interests, in relation to Ireland, in relation to politics, and in relation to the analysis of new forms of literary language. In that period, which lasted four or five years, I worked very hard indeed in this particular way. I spent a year at the Ecole Normale in Paris and I attended Althusser's classes very carefully.

In your 'Realism: Balzac and Barthes', published in your Theoretical Essays, *which came out in 1985, you say 'At the intellectual level, whether Althusser, Lacan and Derrida will come to seem merely historical curiosities – scholarly footnotes in studies on the influence of Marx, Freud and Heidegger – or whether their thought will prove genuinely fruitful, is still difficult to determine' (p. 132). The ideas of those thinkers have certainly, as you said, permeated intellectual life in the humanities. How would you now assess their importance?*

I think it's still very difficult. Let's take the clear-cut case first, which is Althusser. Great man in a way as he was – a tragic figure, but great man as he was – I think the philosophy has very little importance now. The project of the elaboration of a truly scientific Marxism is dead and buried. It is a curiosity. Its importance was almost entirely in bringing ideas from the philosophy of science into Marxism, which I wouldn't necessarily link simply to Althusser, and in terms of a political project which was to allow people within Marxist perspectives to use a much wider range of intellectual traditions. Now that was tremendously influential, but it was the influence of a very specific political moment. If you go back and read Althusser's texts – *For Marx* or *Reading Capital* or 'Ideology and Ideological State Apparatuses' – I think one can definitively say that none of that holds up.

Lacan is the most interesting figure. My guess, and it is really a guess, is that his work will last, that it provides a series of insights into the psychic which probably are as important as Freud's. It's difficult at the moment, though, because it seems to me his ideas are stuck, though in a different way, where, in a sense, psychoanalysis was always stuck, which is at the problem of how you produce its concepts in such a way that they give you any grip on a social reality. It's been the most basic criticism of Freud for a very long time, but it still applies to Lacan. The psychoanalytic account is all very well, but it gives a priority to the family which is questionable, particularly in the twentieth century. If you look at a small child in a house today, surrounded by radios, television, computers, it's not clear at all that Mummy and Daddy play quite the role that they did in the nineteenth century. But given that hesitation, I think Lacan is important.

With Derrida, I really don't know. Reading Derrida was one of the great intellectual experiences of my life. I've been continuously appalled, however, at what happened to Derrida in America, where deconstruction turned into a clever way of reading the traditional texts which redeemed you from having to read anything else because you could endlessly read anything new out of those texts. There's also no doubt that Derrida seemed to go along with that. One can understand it at a personal level. Derrida was and indeed still is continuously rejected by the philosophical establishment in France, and in that sense to go to America and be fêted must be personally gratifying. Intellectually, though, I really do not understand what he thought he was doing with the deconstructionists. But it also has to be said that I have not followed the later work closely enough to even begin to try and assess it, and when I've looked at the later work I've always got the feeling that, on the whole, it's repeating material that's been done before. I saw recently, though, that he'd done work in the early eighties on the national character of philosophy which I had missed and which sounds very interesting indeed. So I may be misjudging him. Derrida's the most difficult case. It seems to me a lot of these ideas have to be judged by the work they produce. Both Derrida and Foucault have become very dominant within American literary studies. The Derrideans have produced lots of individually brilliant readings, but I'm not sure that brilliant readings can't be produced in lots of ways. It seems to me that, by and large, the Foucauldians have not produced interesting work. Foucault's own historical work was very interesting, but what gets produced by those who work within Foucauldian frameworks are pale imitations – it's not new, original historical work.

What about Barthes?

Of all of them, Barthes was probably the person I read the closest. With Barthes, it's both easier and more difficult to give an assessment. It's easier to say that he is one of the three or four greatest critics of the twentieth century and one of the century's great writers. Of that there is no doubt and his later work merely confirmed it. *Camera Lucida*, his last book, is for me a really great and moving book. But if you want to judge him as a theoretician producing a science of texts, which was the claim of the sixties, I'm not sure that any of Barthes's work really stands up at all. In this retrospect, Barthes is a brilliant literary and cultural critic, but of a kind that goes back to Michelet. The interest is in a critic of a very traditional kind, a position he embraced at the end. So I suppose my problem with Barthes is not the question of the greatness, it's the question of how one would categorize the work that he did, how far it marked something new and how far it's not new at all but the continuation of very traditional kinds of critical activity. And my worst thought is that a lot of those claims to scientificity in the late sixties and early seventies was actually the last cry of an intellectual class which felt itself losing its culturally privileged position.

How did the work of Barthes and the other figures of that period relate to your own research at the time?

The heart of the *Tel Quel* position, at the point at which *Tel Quel* informed me, was that there had been this radical change in writing, this radical change in the uses of language, and that this modernist revolution had to be understood politically. But the more I studied it the more empty that claim became. Kristeva offered a kind of historical account in *Revolution of Poetic Language*, but I was desperately – unconvinced is the wrong word, but I felt that I didn't have sufficient grasp of the history of the language or of linguistic theory really to talk about changes in language in a serious way. When I took up a research fellowship at Emmanuel in 1974, I said that I wanted to look at the odd linguistic fact that the Authorized Version in 1611 is written in a language that is 50 or 60 years out of date, that is to say it's written almost entirely in the language of earlier translations. I thought that there was some research to be done on why that choice was made, why by 1611 a fully contemporary translation would have actually revealed the kind of different religious positions that were there at the time. Although I thought and still think it to be a very good research project, I quickly became aware that I was not a linguist of that kind and I wasn't going to master the Greek and the

Hebrew, and indeed I probably wasn't a scholar of that kind either. But I became interested in the whole question of that crucial moment in the history of English, which is the moment of the formation of early modern English and the moment at which you get these great literary texts which quite clearly seem to be engaged in a kind of political and ideological project. So that was what I was working on and at that particular moment, the Cambridge English Faculty advertised a job in the modern history of the language which I applied for and got. Then after I was kicked out of Cambridge I went on to Strathclyde and continued that work, setting up a Master's degree in literary language, literary linguistics. So for about ten years from 1975 to 1985, that was where my attention was. And in some sense I'd say that my strong interest in what then came to be called theory probably ceased about 1975. It wasn't that I didn't occasionally read it, but it seemed to me that it had those problems which I've pointed out, and I was much more interested in trying to trace one specific history and one specific, more concrete set of problems. I think, to a certain extent, I did that. I published various papers on the subject, most of them rather difficult to find, and I'm trying to write that material up into a book called *Broken English* at the moment.

The most famous notion that emerged from the poststructuralist theoretical ferment was that of the death of the author. You've returned to this question and tried to find a way of conceiving of the author that is non-idealist and yet allows him or her some kind of role. In your 'Digression on Authorship' in Diary of a Young Soul Rebel, *you suggest that film-making can offer an account of the author as somebody who is a site of discourses but who is not thereby wholly eliminated. How would you want to approach the question of the author now?*

The problem of the author comes in various ways. It comes most practically, for me, from becoming a film producer. At a phenomenological, experiential level, despite the fact you have 60 or 70 people making a film, there is an author, and if you don't have an author you're in trouble. This isn't just with art films. The reason directors get paid enormous sums of money in Hollywood is that they've got exactly the same worry there. So there's that experiential problem. From another perspective, the problem relates back to my increasing feeling that television is, by and large, very uninteresting at the moment, and then thinking that if you really wanted to differentiate between the television of the early sixties and television now, one of the major differences would be the way in which in the television of the sixties you did have strong definite visions – either individually, for example from Mercer or Potter or collectively from Troy Kennedy Martin, John McGrath etc. – the people who made *Z Cars*. In the latter case, you had a collective authorship, which already complicates the notion of author a little bit. But you did have personal if not individual visions. So this is a very traditional position: that what makes great art is great artists. Art which is entirely designed for an audience, which is simply repetition, may have certain virtues. I don't want to say it's completely without interest. But one's really interested in those moments when somebody actually makes something count. But if you're dealing with models like film and television, the amounts of investment involved are such that, whatever that individual vision is, it's got to be very heavily tempered all the time by the demands of an audience. I'm interested now in trying to find ways of theorizing that dialectic in the media and also of going back into literature and writing, where of course it's much less obvious. It's much less obvious for two reasons.

First of all, writing does look like the activity of one person. There's the phenomenological fact that it seems quite clearly that a writer is one person. Of course, if you look closely at the activity of writing, it's not so simple. Here I think Sartre's biography of Flaubert would become one of the great texts, but you can see it in Benjamin and Barthes as well. Even with Beckett, you can quite clearly see Beckett as the site of a set of familial dialogues. The author is not a multiplicity of persons, but you can break up the notion of the author as being one. But as I say, it's not so easy with writing as with film. There's at least a kind of obvious sense in which the author who is writing is alone in a way in which the director in film is not.

Then there's a second problem which is technological. All you need is the price of pen and paper to write, and even if you take the publishing, of, say, a poet like Jeremy Prynne, you might get published on the basis of a very small audience. It's none the less the case that I want to pose across those questions the whole question of how one is to analyse the relation between audience, technology, and individual. And I think what I said in *Diary of a Young Soul Rebel* or in a slightly more theoretical paper I wrote called 'The Revenge of the Author' are probably roughly the terms that I want to talk around. On the other hand, I think the elaboration of those will not come theoretically. It will come with a much fuller working out of particular cases, and the particular case where I hope to do it is with Godard, whose biography I've begun research on. It would really be in relation to that, because Godard himself is a very interesting example of someone who, despite having passed through this whole discourse of the death of the author in the late sixties and early seventies, actually has, in the way that *Cahiers du Cinema* had in the fifties, a very unreconstructed romantic account of the author. I want in some ways to revise and alter that account, but there's now something within it which I want to retain. And of course if you take Barthes, who produced certainly the most elegant statement of all this, you find that *Camera Lucida* is the most personal work and you can then in retrospect read all his work in a very different way. So that's where my intellectual concerns are at the moment and they bring together, in a way perhaps that I never felt was brought together before, both my practical and my theoretical interests. It's not that, in your practical day-to-day activity, you need to have answers to these questions, but in your practical day-to-day work on making and producing something, you are dealing with these elements all the time, because as a producer you're constantly having to draw a fine line between badgering the director to give up that which is merely personally idiosyncratic, while at the same time trying above all not to make them give up that which is absolutely essential to making the work their work. So it's something one's negotiating at a very practical level but which at the same time I want to reflect on theoretically, though I think the theoretical reflection is probably much better done in a historical and closed mode where, apart from anything else, you can get much more information about what the various elements at play were.

Could we pursue this question of audience? In James Joyce and the Revolution of the Word, *which appeared in 1979, you make the point that Joyce's audience, certainly for the later part of* Ulysses *and for* Finnegans Wake *is simply the Joyce scholars and that this part of his work hasn't really got a wider audience, or not very much of one anyway. In your 1980 book on Godard, you discuss his period with Tziga-Vertov films when he had a sense of a small but coherent audience that he was addressing – an audience which, as you point out, very quickly dissolved. Let me put this as a general question: can one either point to historically, or imagine, a work which is both formally experimental and politically radical but reaches a wide audience?*

I don't think you have to imagine. I think Spike Lee's *Do the Right Thing* is a very good example of a work that does it. It was a phenomenally important movie in the States. When they write the history of America from 1982 to 1992 I would have thought that that movie would be seen as a crucial moment in certain kinds of articulation. It's formally relatively radical, in particular at the moments at which they hurl racial insults, and when at the end it rolls the Martin Luther King and Malcolm X quotations. If it's not extremely formally innovative, to call it Brechtian, which is not the term I would now use all that often, is really not inaccurate. And it was very popular. Lee is able, in a way which almost nobody else that I'm aware of at the moment is, to summon $20 or 30 million budgets from Hollywood, and they don't give you those budgets because you're politically correct, they give you those budgets because they think they're going to get their money back. So there's an example.

In more general terms, I would want to try a kind of postmodern answer. If you go back to Brecht or to the great modernists, the idea was exactly to find the kind of formal devices that would break open everything. I think that you have to face up to the fact that this is all within a kind of revolutionary or radical perspective which conceives of totally differing states of consciousness as it were on one side and the other of an artistic divide and gives an importance to art which I now find very difficult to grant. I think that today, instead of seeing art within a grand narrative within which there is going to be this crucial break, it's much more a question of always looking at the specifics – if we look at any particular piece of art, in what context does it occur? So the point is not simply to ask about poetry in general, because poetry in Britain occupies a very different place from poetry, say in Nicaragua. You then have to ask why that is, and ask exactly how the various artistic forms relate together, and then I think you'd probably have to say, now where does the formal experimentation come in, how does it relate to the whole social, cultural and political situation? You would ask much more, to use a postmodern world, local questions about art and its function. On the other hand, that doesn't get you away from what you might call the Frankfurt School problem of why is so much cultural production such rubbish? This does seem to me the great problem. There are two crude ways of answering it. One is the Frankfurt School answer, which is that it's all rubbish and everybody consuming it is full of rubbish. That is unacceptable democratically because it effectively discounts the vast majority of people. On the other hand, the populist response that this is all wonderful is manifestly untrue. I think then you probably need again a very careful account, a kind of ethnography of art. You need to ask why people want this kind of rubbish in certain parts of their lives, where actually in other parts of their lives they probably wouldn't be willing to accept it. So it's not a question of saying that if they accept this they're full of rubbish, it's a question of why they like this kind of rubbish, or why I like this kind of rubbish in this particular context. It then seems to me not impossible to allow of people in contexts so degraded, so awful, that they get nothing but rubbish, but they become a minority rather than a majority. What you've got to look at, time and time again, is how art is being used. The questions about the author, on the one side, and about popular forms, on the other, are not new questions but there was a moment, whether you call it the Derridean or the Barthesean moment, which looked as though it had proposed a new kind of radical solution through the medium itself. It didn't work. It's not that we didn't learn a lot more about various things but we're back to those problems. We haven't achieved that kind of leverage by which we were going to find some kind of pure form that would solve all the problems for us.

As well as the questions of the author and the audience, a third question which has been important in your work has been that of realism as a mode of representation. How do you feel today about the issue of realism?

I think realism continues to be a major mode. But here I must admit that I feel much less certain than I did about the other questions because I think we're moving into an area of subjective aesthetic judgement. I like realism, so I want to avoid the trap of simply turning my own aesthetic prejudices into generalizations. But I would say at the least that realism continues to count. And I think my answer to the question of realism is much more in terms of audience than it ever was before. If you take *Do the Right Thing* once more, one of the striking things about that film is that Lee takes a mainstream form and he shows to an audience which has never seen them the realities of a street corner in Bedford Stuyvesant on a hot summer day, but probably as importantly he takes that mainstream form and he shows it to the people who live on Bedford Stuyvestant. There's something about that double operation which is crucial to the film. It becomes more problematic with a film like *Boyz in the Hood* which I think is at every level – the soundtrack, the dialogue, the characterization – much less original and well thought through than Lee's film, but which in some ways is slightly more powerful. Whereas *Do the Right Thing* concentrates on *the* problem area of South Central Los Angeles, and in that sense becomes, particularly a

year later, very prophetic, *Boyz in the Hood* is slightly more powerful because it says, here is a set of lower-middle-class American
families which are completely like all other lower-middle-class
American families except that the young men kill each other. There
is a kind of power in that very corny melodramatic story which I
think you can only describe by an appeal to realism. Realism now for
me is much more question of audience and conjuncture and also, as
with Lee's film, about this idea of the double audience. It's about
showing things to people who've never seen them at the same time as
you show them to people who've seen them but have never seen them
in that artistic form. There's something there which I think is still
very important in art and still very important in fiction. Of course,
poetry is much more difficult, because realism in poetry is not a
realism of representation at all but of forms of language, and it's a
realism which is somehow much further back, at the moment at
which thought or emotion first takes shape. If you were to produce
an analysis of poetry in terms of realism, it would be a matter of
focusing on juxtaposition, on ways of speaking and so on which have
not yet been fully grasped and articulated. But as I say, I'm a little bit
less happy about all of that than about the author or the audience
because apart from anything else, many of the people I've worked
with, many of the directors I've worked with, are very anti-realist, so
I'm kept much more on my toes about my own prejudices. I think
that, by and large, I can probably learn to appreciate and see what is
at stake in various kinds of more aesthetic forms which do not use
realism as a justification, but realism is very much my take on art.

*From 1973 to 1981, you were a member of the editorial board of the
magazine* Screen, *and a significant contributor to its pages. How do
you look back on* Screen *at that period now?*

I look back on it in a variety of ways. It was phenomenally exciting.
It's very important to say that. The intellectual pleasure and excitement of that moment should not be forgotten. But we were involved
in a fundamental contradiction. On the one hand – and I think this
is true of almost everybody there – we genuinely thought that we
were engaged in the analysis of ideological forms within a political
perspective – this was a very Althusserean problematic. What we
were actually doing was academically establishing a discipline with
all that it entailed, including all that it entailed in terms of jobs, material prospects etc. Now I think those two things went hand in hand.
It isn't simply to say that people were saying one thing and doing the

other. They were doing both things at the same time, thinking that above all they were doing the first while vaguely aware that what they were actually doing was the second. Obviously the politics of that time now look extremely dated. In particular, there was within that a kind of traditional intellectual position that wanted each work of art to measure up to certain kinds of political or ethical standards. That now seem to me completely to ignore the very diverse ways in which art works. On the more positive side, it still seems to me that if you go back and look at that moment of *Screen*, there is a production of ways of reading film which has not been surpassed. Stephen Heath's reading of *Touch of Evil*, for example, remains for me the single most brilliant reading of a film ever. *Screen* was the moment at which a whole lot of things came together and enabled an engagement with how a film text worked which had never happened intellectually before, although of course film-makers had made the same engagement practically.

The ideas developed in your work with Screen *and the French poststructuralism associated with* Tel Quel *came into conflict with the ideology of English studies that had become entrenched at Cambridge, and in 1980 the refusal to upgrade your temporary lectureship into a permanent one served as the flashpoint for bitter controversy. You were the man at the centre of the storm: how do you look back on that controversy now?*

It's still something that's it's very difficult for me to give a full-scale account of. When something like that happens to you, I'm not sure you ever get over it, but it's certainly the case that I find it incredibly difficult, even at this distance, to separate out the local petty jealousies from any larger serious questions. It's been said that the virulence of academic disputes is in direct proportion to the unimportance of the issues. In some ways, my temptation is to say that the Cambridge controversy was insignificant. Obviously it was personally important for me, and it was important in the particular institutional history of the English Faculty, but it wasn't about anything of larger importance. Another part of me perhaps would say that it was about something quite important, which was the attempt to transform English into Cultural Studies. There was a very concerted attempt in Cambridge in the mid-seventies to have a fundamental rewriting of the Tripos which would have produced something like a Cultural Studies degree. It nearly happened, but it failed to happen. Now while it's very nice to say that it failed to happen because we lost, which we did, I also think, looking back, that we didn't have a clear enough idea of what we wanted to do. I could now articulate it much more clearly, but that's after running postgraduate programmes and audiovisual research centres in Strathclyde, it's after producing films, it's after experience of American universities. That's just me – I'm not talking about all the various experiences that other people would have had. But even with that reservation that we perhaps didn't have a clear enough idea of what we wanted to do, there was a chance of a very new kind of degree which might have well been a better model than anything else currently existing to which I can point. That chance went, but it left an incredibly bitter and divided faculty, not least because, putting it very crudely, it was all too clear that the brains, energy and enthusiasm were all on one side and not on the other. That generated a situation in which people were willing to go to extraordinary lengths effectively to prove that this wasn't the case at all, that those who looked as though they had intelligence, energy and enthusiasm did not. As is the way of these things, that backfired much more seriously on them, and it seems to me, insofar as I still follow it, that the English Faculty at Cambridge has not yet quite recovered from that controversy – not because of me, but the fact that within two or three years of the affair, many of the most interesting people had left.

After Cambridge, you were Professor of English at Strathclyde University from 1981 to 1985, and, as you've mentioned, you helped to set up new courses there. You then came to work for the British Film Institute, so you're now very much involved with modern media. In relation to that involvement, could we turn to a matter about which you've written and which has recently become very significant: the future of public service broadcasting. In what you've written about public service broadcasting, you've stressed the importance of giving people the opportunities, the right as it were, to create their own images, to be producers of images as well as consumers of images. Could you say something about how you feel that might be facilitated over the next decade or so in the world and the society we now have?

I have both an incredibly pessimistic and a relatively optimistic view on this. The incredibly pessimistic view is that public service television as we know it is being destroyed. It seems to me that, wherever you look, the commmercialization and the commodification of television proceeds apace. I wouldn't like to say that nothing is going to stop it because there would be many people trying and Jeremiahism is very easy and what normally happens is something a little bit more complicated. I'm not saying there'll be no public service element left. But by and large, whether I look at film or I look at television, the logic which favours the international production of big budget fiction with very wide audiences continues apace. Whatever the strengths of that kind of thing, and there are occasionally strengths, there are a lot of weaknesses, and above all it continuously works against local production. Against that, the actual technology now favours individual production. You can now buy a camcorder for between £1000 and £2000 and you can produce images and sound of a considerably better quality than you could on broadcast television in the sixties. That is now used almost entirely for home movies. The question is whether there any way in which one can make that very cheap production of material more widely available. One obvious way we got was Rodney King. There's a kind of straightforward reportage way in which, against the these extremely expensive news operations, there is now, it seems to me, what Enzenberger Utopianly hinted at about twenty years ago. You can quite seriously imagine people producing other accounts of events, certainly if you take public disturbances.

It becomes much more difficult with fiction. I recently saw in the 'Black and white in colour' season on TV, the 1965 production of *A Passage to India*. Practically no exteriors, all done in terrible tacky sets, but a brilliant production, very clearly bringing across, particularly compared with David Lean's film, the impossibility of friendship across the Indian-English divide, even with the best intentions on either side. In its own kind of soft-centred, liberal way, *A Passage to India* is a very tough book, and the production was very tough and got it right. Now you might say, given that we've now got the equipment with which we can make films for very little money, why can't we just go ahead and do it? You then run into the problem that if you produced a film like that today, the audience would not accept it. As the technology has got cheaper on the one hand, the desire for production values has gone up on the other, so what you now would have gained on the side of the camera you would lose on the side of production, design, costume, a whole set of things which people would demand in order to watch it. So I don't want to get too carried away with the possibilities of this cheap technology but it does seem to me that it is through that cheap technology, and above all through the schools, that we may change the nature of broadcasting.

I think this is where it links back to what I'm doing now, as Head of Research at the British Film Institute. I would say that the ability to record and edit audiovisual material is an ability which should be part and parcel of going to school, which you learn just as you learn to read and write. And it may be that the schools will be the place where this stuff will get out. If so, it will be like the school play, but instead it will be the school video. There are ways of distribution, in the sense that you can imagine both on a very local level – parents watching it – or if you look at America, where there's much more decentralization of transmission, you can imagine it perhaps being broadcast on cable stations at two o'clock in the morning. All I'm trying to do is to describe what I see as the whole scenario: whereas on the one hand you see the ever increasing dominance of capital, on the other it seems to me that there are developments within the technology which might enable one to think more optimistically and to imagine slightly Utopianly, in five or ten years time, the production of works, some of which would break through the various levels and reach much wider audiences. In a way, if I thought that was going to happen, that might be fine. That might be all one wanted. It's not that you want to stop the making of *Batman*, say; some big budget films are awful, some are very good. The problem is not at that level of production, it's what happens lower down and above all it's important to give people the ability to produce and comment on and edit material themselves.

Could you tell us more about the work that you've done at the British Film Institute?

I was Head of Production from 1985 to 1989, and that was entirely a production job. Other than being a member of the senior staff of the Institute, I had no contact with areas like publications and education which I'd had contact with before, through *Screen*, for example. I was simply a producer, and I had the thrill of working with people like Derek Jarman, Terence Davies and Isaac Julien, and the pleasure of getting involved in certain kinds of entrepreneurial fund raising, which was an activity, as I'd already discovered from Strathclyde, which I quite liked and was relatively good at. So I spent four years producing films, enjoyed it enormously and had considerable success at it. Then the new Director of the BFI, Wilf Stevenson, asked me whether I would consider turning the Institute into a proper research institute, complete with postgraduate degrees and the lot. Now unlike the request to become Head of Production, where it took me about three seconds to decide that I wouldn't mind doing it, this was much more difficult, because on the one hand it wasn't what I wanted to do next – what I wanted to do next was to produce my own films – while on the other hand, it was the opportunity of a lifetime in the sense that an awful lot of what I'd done over the last 20 years, such as my work on *Screen*, had been made possible in one way or another by the Institute, though I hadn't realized it, and the Institute provided the basis for setting up proper research on the moving image. So in the end it was an opportunity I thought I couldn't refuse. But it was effectively going into a kind of mixture between university administration and being a sort of Managing Director of a small company. So it wasn't entirely pleasurable.

But we've relaunched *Sight and Sound*, we've reorganized the publishing operation, we've launched a postgraduate degree which takes its first students in September, and we've started various programmes of both external and internal research. Although we've been very successful to date, I think the longterm aim is a very ambitious and possibly unrealizable one, which is to create a new kind of academic institution, that is to say an academic institution which is very closely linked to all aspects of the moving image. At the BFI, we archive, we curate, we produce, we distribute, we exhibit, and the aim is to produce an intellectual reflection on this which is tied into those operations. For example, the crucial distinctive part of the postgraduate MA degree is a four month research placement in which students work in one of the parts of the Institute, while engaging in an intellectual reflection upon that work. In talking about this, I use the metaphor of the telephone and the library. Universities are places which effectively enable you to be in a library for a very long period of time without interruption from the telephone. For a series of historical reasons, they've grown up as the place where research is done, and certainly they enable you to do research. But by taking you away from the telephone, they effectively disconnect you from a great deal of contemporary life, which is particularly damaging, it seems to me, if you're engaged in contemporary cultural studies or moving image studies. On the other hand, if you're on the telephone, you may be involved in the modern world, but you never have a moment to reflect on anything you're doing, to produce the kind of research you need. We're trying here to produce a kind of library with telephones in it or at least a library from which you can exit to use telephones. Now I don't know whether this is going to be possible, either administratively, or, much more importantly, in a personal way. Academics will all tell you that you can only do a proper piece of research by dropping all other concerns and going off for a period of six months or a year. We're trying to set up here something whereby in a sense you will do that on a daily basis. That's to say, half your day will be spent doing research and half your day will be on spent working in administrative matters. The question is whether that will work, and I think the jury will only return on that in about two or three years time. But that's the aim.

What are your own future plans?

Personally I hope that I will only remain fulltime doing this job through the first two years of the postgraduate course, which starts in September, and then, since I've had most of my energies engaged administratively in one form or another since 1981, I hope to see a significant reduction of my own administrative activity. I then want to complete *Broken English*, the book I mentioned earlier, to work on the biography of Godard, which is where I think theoretical issues such as the concept of the author can be explored, and to do that in conjunction with producing films on my own initiative. How far any of that will come to pass is quite another question, but that's the ideal future.

Richard Hoggart

Park Court Hotel, Lancaster Gate, London
18 March 1993

NICOLAS TREDELL: *In the first volume of your* Life and Times, A Local Habitation, *published in 1988, you say, when you're describing your time at Leeds University in the late 1930s that '[m]y own emerging intellectual life had three main focusses: politics, documentary and poetry' (p. 194). I wondered if we could look at each of those interests as they've interwoven with your life and work – starting with poetry first of all, which has been a constant concern of yours, though in your multifarious activities it's not always been the concern that's been most noticed.*

RICHARD HOGGART: I have always thought that poetry is the queen of the literary arts. Indeed, I used to write poetry at the university and had some of it published in a student magazine. I had a friend – we wrote a joint poem which was banned by the professor on the committee of the university magazine – who threw everything up and went down to London to become a poet. He became one – a minor poet, but a poet he was devoted to being. I never had that strength of conviction or feeling, or that kind of courage perhaps, but I remain fascinated by poetry, thinking it the most important literary form, more so than fiction. It's the most taxing linguistically and also intellectually and imaginatively. For whatever reasons, I stopped writing or trying to write poetry – it was never more than trying to write. Of course, I went to the war, but even in five and a half years as a soldier I could still have written poetry. But I retained my interest in poets, and the first book I produced was on Auden. I wrote 30,000 words of that as a soldier in Italy, with no access to books of any kind except Auden's poems. When I came home I wrote much more and sent it to Chatto; Day Lewis read it and said: 'Would you make it full book length; if so, we'll publish it.' That's how that happened. I didn't

start again writing poetry, and I really don't know why. I became
interested in writing about poetry, then I became interested in writing about society. The funny thing is, though, that the passages
which most people find impressive of any I've written – I don't say
there are many – are always passages which remind me that I would
once have liked to be a poet. I don't want to say this in any boastful
way, but I met Betjeman once and he said: 'You know, you're a better poet than I am.' That does seem very odd but I think I know what
he was meaning – he was meaning that sometimes the way I look at
things and the way I try to capture them in words is rather like what
a poet tries to do – I wouldn't say more than that. In the book I've just
finished, which is about the Surrey town where we now live, Farnham, I deliberately sign off saying – this is the last book I will write
about the nature of societies, using people as representative bodies as
it were. I don't know what I'll do now but would like to think I'd
start writing poetry again. But I don't know.

*Could we turn to the second of the intellectual focuses which you
mention, politics? In* A Local Habitation, *you say that '[t]he politics
were socialist, as they still are' (p. 194). Socialism has become very
beleaguered of late, not least in England. What do you feel to be the
roots of your continuing socialist convictions?*

I can tell you that because it's at the front of my mind. This latest
book has an opening chapter saying why I'm writing a book about
this town. I say it's Cobbett's town, it's George Sturt's town, and living there now, I can feel the impulses which made them look around
and try to capture it; there's something peculiarly English, for good
and ill, in towns like that. Then I talk about how I set about writing
the book. You start as if you're going to write one kind of book and
you end writing a book which you could never have predicted. But
the big thing is not to resist your impulses. If something takes hold of
you, let it run away with you. It's like the novel – you know that
lovely phrase of Lawrence's, that if you try to nail the novel down,
the novel gets up and walks away with the nail. One of the things that
has come out of this book, and I spend ten pages in an Introduction
explaining how it happened and why, is more about my political position. I realize that my socialism is a moral socialism. It's a humanist,
liberal, ethical socialism which requires a great deal more from its
adherents than is required from Tories, because it's based on the
sense that we belong to one another. I shall never break from that,
I'm sure. This phrase 'belong to one another', with references to

Orwell and all such, runs through this new book, as it should. The result is that in the course of the book I criticize Conservatism a great deal, because Farnham is a conservative town and a lot of it's not very pleasant, is very snob-ridden. I then find myself, in an Introduction, criticizing left-wing attitudes strongly, with more force than I expected.

A lot of left-wing writing today is violently abusive to a degree that's not needed. You've only to pick up some of the left-wing journals to find that they can be illiberal, unimaginative, intellectually shabby, and that they foreshorten argument by abuse. There's also a certain kind of sentimentality. One event I can't take to is the final session at the Labour Party conference where they all stand up and sing the Red Flag. That's bogus. It's self-deceit of a very high order. That's not English socialism, not at all. Equally the big trade union leaders talk about my lads – 'my lads won't stand for this' and all that kind of stuff. Once or twice, people much more to the Left than I am and have always been, criticize *The Uses of Literacy*, even though they may pay compliments to it, because they think it presents a picture of working-class life which they find rather sentimental. I don't accept that. Those people are usually middle-class by origin and they want to have a working class which is either fiercely political, brawny armed and ready to beat the bosses, or ground down by the mass media. They don't want to hear what I stressed, that there were certain quiet strains of comeliness, neighbourliness and all that, in working class life. I wasn't the first to point that out – Orwell did it and so did many another – but they find that very hard to take.

The more substantial criticisms I have of the Left concentrate on two interconnected issues. One is anti-racism. I'm anti-racist – who isn't, if in good faith? – but they carry their anti-racism to a point where it's illiterate, and this is where it links with the other issue, which is political correctness in language. You can hardly say anything, you mustn't say what is an absolute fact, if it can be construed by somebody else as racist, even though you don't mean it that way. That is a new kind of censorship. I can give you an instance of that – I could give many. In the second volume of the *Life and Times, A Sort of Clowning*, I talked about having an accident on a mountain road in Tunisia during the war. The driver skidded on a wet clay road – it was a rotten road anyway – and we went right off and overturned and we were bleeding quite badly. It was about five in the morning and we stood on this road waiting for something to come – there was no civilian traffic, it was 1943 – and an American jeep came along and we waved at it, just assuming they'd pick us up, and it went

whoosh around us. Inside it were two black soldiers. My driver –
they always knew these things – said: 'Of course, they've been out on
a drug run, that's why they can't stop.' He may have been wrong, he
may have been right. They were certainly out illicitly. But when I said
'two black soldiers' in the draft, that was edited out on the grounds,
not that I was being racist, but that I would be accused of being
racist. So that is not in the book and I regret it. I should have put it
in because it's part of the picture, and when you start editing out
because somebody else might misconstrue it, you're actually producing a kind of negative censorship.

I'm afraid that those are treacheries of the clerks on the left; but I
expect more from the Left. I'm not suggesting that I spend all my time
in this new book attacking the Left but I certainly do say, and end by
saying, that ethical, moral, humanist socialism is an English tradition
of long standing and I'm not willing to lose it. I am a socialist and I
always will be a socialist, but not very ideological. I'm a socialist who
recognizes first and always that the world is muddy and qualified,
and that we're all fallible.

The third of those early focuses you mention in A Local Habitation,
*and one which has clearly been very important in your writing, is
that of documentary. How did that interest develop?*

The immediate origin of it was the fact that the thirties were a great
period for documentary, from Mass Observation to the films of
people like Grierson. There was a lot of very good documentary writing about coalminers and all sorts of things, and I liked it very much.
I don't think it's on a par with what great novelists would do; I'll cite
George Eliot any day and say that there you have a different sort of
achievement and a much higher one. I think one of the origins of my
interest in documentary was growing up as an orphan with no
money. I was immensely well looked after by all kinds of people who
were very powerful in my life, and I hope I've paid them due tribute
in the books, but the part of background also was that if you were a
working class orphan in a city like Leeds, you suffered constant
snubbings from local officials. Not always – there's always one who
helps you, or did me anyway – but often. And even when a friend at
school took you home, and they knew you were an orphan, they
looked at you and knew your socks were made out of shoddy and the
trousers had cost about ten bob in Woolies and things like that. You
lived with an awareness of this and you built up a sense of: 'I'll show
you, I will not have this.' So I think that's one of the origins of my
fascination with intonation and accent and style.

My own documentary writing began without my thinking. I had come back from the war and we were at my wife's home in Stalybridge near Manchester. It was just before I started work in the extramural department of Hull University. One morning I went down to the Magistrate's Court and did a little documentary piece about the whole style of magistrates. In those days – I think they've improved a lot – they could be very stupid, very much the people who ran the town as of right. But I didn't write about them angrily, I just did a portrait of them at work, and sent it to *Tribune*. Orwell had been its literary editor, but at that time it was Orwell's friend, T.R. Fyvel. Tosco Fyvel wrote back and said: 'I'm publishing that and will publish anything else you write of that sort.' So I then went into a public library reading room and did a portrait of what it was like as a refuge for old men, and men out of work, and men living in single rooms. That went into *The Uses of Literacy*, much modified. That's how I started. But that didn't make me actually decide to write documentary. *The Uses of Literacy* started as an attempt to write a textbook of the sort that Leavis and Denys Thompson had done – that's to say, I was going to find examples of popular journalism and popular fiction – magazine stories, sex-and-violence novels – and discuss them, and use this as a textbook for extramural work. So the second half of *The Uses of Literacy* was written first.

I then felt increasingly that – this was a good insight to have, and was a revelation to me – you can't write about this material without relating it to the people who read it. These people aren't blank slates and they're not two-dimensional. They have a background, they have a culture, they have a whole world in which they live and into which this material comes. It was partly inspired by the admiration I had for Leavis and for Mrs Leavis and for studies such as *Fiction and the Reading Public*, but also by very grave doubts about the fact that she tended in that book to look at the material as though she was holding it at arm's length in studying it, and as though it impinged on its readers without as it were intermediary attitudes. So I decided that I would try to recreate the nature of working class life as I'd known it, as honestly as I could; and that became the first half of the book. In a sense, the determination to do as it were a cultural social-cultural background and then start dealing with the material arose from my feeling that there was something missing in Mrs Leavis's approach, much as I admired her. I discovered much later on – you know she became rather disgruntled – that before she died she said that Raymond Williams and Hoggart had climbed on the back of her work and made themselves fortunes from it. Two things are wrong with that. Obviously one is that we didn't climb on her back – Raymond Williams certainly didn't and nor did I, but we were each different in our approach. The other thing is we didn't make fortunes either. Just after I got back from America in 1957 – *The Uses of Literacy* had come out in February that year – I was asked to Downing College to lecture. The Leavises weren't there – they sent apologies – but the place was crowded and I discovered afterwards that people had appeared because the word had gone round that I was going to deliver a resounding attack on the Leavises. Nothing was further from my thoughts. I began by saying how much I'd learned from them. That audience must have been very disappointed.

In A Sort of Clowning, *you mention that 'F.R. Leavis is said to have remarked that [*The Uses of Literacy*] had some value but "he should have written a novel"' (p. 206). The* Uses of Literacy *does evoke 'felt life' in a way that sometimes calls a novel to mind. Given your views on the superiority of the novel over documentary, did you ever in fact consider producing it as a novel?*

I tried to write a novel. I remember a remark by Trilling to the effect that there are two kinds of writers: one is the centripetal writer, the other's the centrifugal writer. Tolstoy is one of the great centrifugal writers, who goes into different personalities and characters, and Joyce is one of the great examples of the centripetal writer who turns round on his own axis. In that sense, allowing for differences of scale of course, I'm nearer in type to Joyce than to Tolstoy. But I am interested in different characters and different types of people. That wasn't the problem. I know that I can create physical setting quite well and that I have got a reasonable ear for speech and gesture. One doesn't have to be boastful to say this, because you must then go on to say what you haven't got. Apart from what may be many other failings and limitations, one thing I found when I started to write a novel was that I forgot that I had people in rooms moving around in three dimensions and having relationships. I just set them talking and forgot all about it and left them there, which also told me that I'd never write a play because I have no sense of movement, and that is the essence of the dramatic spirit. It's also important in the novel. Good novels are always dramatic in many senses.

Let's take one of the great novels of our language, *Middlemarch*, and the point when Mrs Bulstrode realizes that her husband has been corrupt. At the moment when she goes into his room, the novel brings together not only the great sense of what it all stands for, what it signifies about rural bourgeois life in the mid-nineteenth century, but also an enormous sense of moral conviction and moral struggle. I can't read that without thinking, gosh, what a power is there. There's a passage in which George Eliot says something to the effect that Mrs Bulstrode was a very moral woman and she could not forgive her husband because he had done wrong, but that on the other hand she loved him and he was her husband and she would stand by him. I'd give my eye-teeth to be able to write like that, but I don't think I could sustain the, as it were, thematic thread.

I have been reading a lot of Nadine Gordimer recently and wondering why is she so impressive. The first thing is that there's such a depth of texture in her writing. Nothing is simple. When she's talking about blacks and whites in Africa, the whole thing is not programmatic, not polemical, not ideological. You feel these are real people who are suffering and living and facing problems, moral problems. Sometimes I think I'll have another go at a novel, to see if I can do it. Raymond Williams did it several times but I don't think his novels work. They're interesting in their own way but you can see the schematic bones sticking out. If I started a novel and I suddenly found I'd forgotten what I thought I was doing, that it had taken off, I'd be delighted. If I found every morning that I went to it and that I was cranking up the machinery, I'd think it was not working.

I'm slightly tired – though I'm not going to make a fuss about it – of the excessive attention paid to the novel in England today. There's a certain kind of pride assumed in writing fiction which I'm not prepared to honour myself. If you read the reviews of what are perfectly ordinary novels, they're all wonderful, the best of the year and all this kind of thing. But some are very feeble. I'm not being arrogant, but I feel I could write one like that. There are some very inflated reputations. Of course there are some interesting novelists, but manifestly very few who will last. By contrast, it's a good period for biography, though I think that phase is beginning to pass. Autobiography is disregarded, and that's partly the fault of the autobiographers who are usually trying to be cosy and twee. But many of the problems of autobiography are as difficult as, and similar to, those of fiction. A character in an autobiography can run away with you. In an autobiography, unless you simply want to say: 'I was born in London in 1856 on a wet day', and then carry on chronologically, you have enormous problems of structure, of selection, of tone and angle. So now I'm stressing again the importance of what we used to call documentary – I'm not on the whole addicted to the word – of social descriptive non-fictional writing. Just before he died Trilling said he thought we were going to move into an era where socially descriptive non-fictional writing would reveal its strengths again, which had been disregarded; I hope he was right.

Isn't one of the problems with that kind of writing that it leads sometimes to unwarranted inferences and generalizations? Doesn't this happen at times in The Uses of Literacy *– for example, in your memorable description of the juke-box boys in the milkbar, where you say: 'Compared even with the pub around the corner, this is all a peculiarly thin and pallid form of dissipation, a sort of spiritual dry-rot amid the odour of boiled milk. Many of the customers – their clothes, their hair-styles, their facial expressions all indicate – are living to a large extent in a myth-world compounded of a few simple elements which they take to be those of American life' (Penguin 1958 edn, p. 248).*

No, I stand by that description. It may be over-rhetorical, a bit over the top, but it's basically right. A man of 37 whom I know and like was talking about it and told me: 'You don't recognize the richness of their culture.' But he hadn't realized he was talking about a time 15 to 20 years after the one I was talking about. The description of those people in that milk bar in Goole was written in 1952, and I believe its documentary nature is accurate. I said to this man: 'What you've done is skipped a couple of decades. You want to assert that English working-class pop culture is vibrant and vivid and all that sort of thing. I'll argue about that as it was in the sixties and seventies with you if you like, but don't use it to criticize me when I describe the fifties, because it was not true then.' Now we come to a more important point, which is what I call the 'stay as sweet as you are' syndrome. There are several books which describe present-day aspects of working-class culture – whether it's music or motorcycle gangs or whatever – and suggest that they have a rich fecund imaginative life. We may all want to believe that. One father of that approach is William Labov in New York, who made studies of the language of street gangs. Labov I admire; he has done some very interesting work. But to translate that into motorcycle gangs in Birmingham is to take a very tiny part for the whole and to do a cultural translation or transposition which is very tricky. It does tell you that you can't just write these groups off – they have a language of their own and they have a set of styles and attitudes – but then to father on them a maturity of outlook which is adequate to what is needed to live in an open, sophisticated democracy is romanticism. Some of that writing came from the Centre for Contemporary Cultural Studies at Birmingham.

That prompts my next question, because you're the great founding father of cultural studies in England. The Uses of Literacy *is one of its great founding texts, and you began the Centre for Contemporary Cultural Studies at Birmingham at a time when there was nothing else like it. Much of the work you've just described, and criticized, is precisely the work which comes out of modern cultural studies. What do you think of the way that discipline has developed?*

Let me go back a little. I gave an inaugural lecture at Birmingham – it's been collected in Volume 2 of *Speaking to Each Other* – trying to lay out what I was up to. My impulse was to set up a postgraduate Centre for Cultural Studies which would essentially use the methods of literary criticism and analysis – listening to words, to the different textures of language – and apply them to the study of society. That was my central point. I learned a lot from Leavis though I was modifying his approach along the way. I thought and think that literature, the language of literature and the insights of literature, are a key way of understanding a society. People had said to me apropos *The Uses of Literacy* and the setting up of the Centre: 'the sociologists will slay you'. They didn't. On the whole, they were very generous. There was the odd number cruncher who said, 'Oh, mere impressionism', but most sociologists didn't. The French ones were marvellous because they were reacting against their own theorizing; they were much more receptive. If anybody grumbled it was the English literary people. I remember one very snobby professor saying: 'Well, of course, your graduates won't get jobs.'

I asked Stuart Hall to join me in running the Centre. I admired Stuart, though I knew he was more left-wing than I, and more theoretical – I'm not theoretical at all. Stuart and I worked together extremely well. We were great friends and never quarrelled. But when I'd gone off to be an Assistant Director-General of UNESCO for, at first, three years, and Stuart was holding the fort as Acting Director of the Centre, a PhD candidate – a middle-class, bright girl – said that they no longer had any time for the 'Matthew Arnoldian liberal humanism of Hoggart'. I thought that was a considerable compliment. She was right in a sense; I was proud to have those words as a description of me. But she felt the Centre was a 'Red Cell' and must only take in people who were already committed to the Left. I thought that was profoundly wrong. You take people because you think they're of quality and will have something to say eventually. Stuart and I did not question people's politics. Several of the people we took – we didn't know their politics then, but they weren't in fact left-wing – produced some of the best work in cultural studies. On that girl's criterion, they wouldn't have been admitted unless they'd run up the 'Red Cell' flag. I think that's illiberal. But what did happen was that with Stuart Hall as Acting Director, the Centre was being run by a considerable theoretician of the Left and so attracted more left-wing and theoretically inclined people. The Centre became the place to go to and therefore it stabilized itself much more as that kind of place. Once I agreed to stay on at UNESCO beyond my original three-year term, I resigned from my Chair at Birmingham and from the Directorship of the Centre. The Vice Chancellor was very miffy about the Centre and before he gave Stuart the job set up a committee chaired by Jo Grimond to look into the workings of the Centre. The Report of the committee was very positive, but they made two criticisms and I think they were both fair. One was that the Centre people's theses too often picked up the jargon of various kinds of cultural studies, whether it was French or American or whatever, and the other was that there was too much emphasis on group work being put in for first postgraduate degrees. One of the tests of postgraduate work, at the beginning anyway, is that you discover things on your own, go through the trials and tribulations of independent research. In the later seventies and the eighties, the Centre became committed to theory – for me, with my cast of mind, over-committed to theory. It picked up a mixture of Marxist theory and sociological theories of a cultural kind. That can be very interesting, but sometimes what they were doing was just throwing up new balls in the air and enjoying it, incestuously almost. But the Centre did a lot of good work professionally, and that Professor's comment that 'your people won't get jobs' was wide of the mark. The people from the Centre and their descendants are all over the world, and the best of them are very good.

There's now a strong movement in higher education and indeed in schools to assimilate the study of literature into cultural studies, so that literature will no longer have the autonomy and high prestige that it once enjoyed. What do you think about that?

I resist it. I think those who promote it are wrong, and it's certainly not what I sought. I'll tell you what we used to do at the Centre; Stuart and I did it together. This used to startle our students. They thought they were going to start by having a wonderful time talking about cartoons in relation to politics. We used to give them a very tough poem, such as a John Donne, and sit down for two hours and talk about it. We used to take comparisons too from difficult fiction. Nothing but the best, not trash. If they don't understand the best, if they don't know the intensity and depth of texture of the best writing, they're not going to do anything good when they're writing about popular fiction. They must have a benchmark. We wouldn't let them get away until they understood this. Then they could go and and talk about soap operas, but would have a sense of scale and dimension and relative quality. Some of the courses that are being put on now in what were the polytechnics, and in FE, are ragbags organized by people who would find it very hard indeed to talk with real weight and penetration about a good poem, and as I say if they can't do that they're not going to get very far talking about cartoons or popular fiction. I remember once writing a deliberately polemical article where I made the crack that all literature aspires to the condition of *King Lear*— which I would quite happily defend any day, as a remark – and saying, 'Look, you may enjoy the music of the Beatles or whoever it may be, and there are some interesting things to be said about these as there are about television comedy and television plays and so on. I may be an admirer of some of those, but won't mix them up. Don't say they're all as good as one another, and don't even use the other cop-out which is, "it's good of its kind".' I then received the usual bundle of abusive letters saying: 'Hoggart's always going on like that'; the funny thing was that the people who wrote were mostly middle-class Oxbridge graduates. It's sometimes a bit of *nostalgie de la boue*.

You've also attacked that kind of abrogation of value judgements in the public library service. Could you talk about that?

Yes, it's going on now in the public libraries, and I've gone into battle with that, waving my snickety-snick. They're saying libraries are falling down because they haven't much money. They *are* short of money, but that's not the real problem. The real problem is that they don't know why they're there. They don't know that the libraries have always stood and should still stand for something, which is that there are differences in quality between books and that if they merely follow majority taste and flow with the wishes of people who regard books simply as a soporific, they'll end buying twelve Jeffrey Archers and not one work by many better writers. I've gone on and on about this all over the place. You then receive marvellously abusive letters from schools of librarianship saying things like: 'Does Hoggart not realize that the libraries *were* a soporific invented by the bourgeoisie to keep the workers quiet?' I thought it was the other way round; I thought they could be seen as revolutionary. Or these librarians take refuge in Information Technology; for some people that's rather like opting for Anglo-Saxon in English decades ago – it saved them from dealing with the more intangible things. I don't know what their training is but many come out of library schools reciting ideological gibberish. It isn't so much that there's *no* truth in what they say. There may well have been some people who thought that libraries would keep the workers quiet. There were also many people who thought they would arm the workers to have better control of their own fates. Another thing the defenders of the libraries' populism say is: 'Does Hoggart not realize that the so-called great novels of George Eliot are in fact no more than a celebration of bourgeois hegemony?' Of course the novels of George Eliot are bourgeois. It was a bourgeois society. The workers didn't read her, not least because they couldn't afford a three-volume novel or often couldn't read. But you have to consider taking the step of saying: 'Yes, these are the cultural roots of production of those novels but at the same time they transcend those roots and become something which talks about human nature not just in this time and place but also in universal terms.'

But if you use this kind of language today, many modern theorists of literature will look at you and think you are out of your innocent mind, that is not what literature is about, it's a thing constantly remade by readers. I think they're deeply mistaken. I think there's a countermovement now setting in, from recent statements by Bergonzi and Kermode. But for the moment you have deconstructionists on the one hand and Marxists on the other, and when you get the two together it produces an extraordinary brew. You are being told that you can't ever utter words of value about literature. If you can't do that, you are lost. I know this as well as many because, although I've never written a novel or a play, I have written books in which I've tried to come face to face with my own imperceptions and perceptions and vulnerabilities and prejudices, and I know that the attempt to write any book except a railway timetable or something such as that is a deeply difficult moral problem for the writer.

You've been much concerned in your work with the quality of a society's conversation with itself. In your more recent writing, particularly in the third volume of your autobiography, An Imagined Life, *there's a strong sense that you feel that the quality of that conversation and indeed the quality of life in this society has deteriorated a great deal in the 1980s.*

Yes. One of the things I'm very sad about is that the British intellectual classes, or whatever you like to call them, don't pick up their role here. I hate that phrase which was invented by a journalist, 'the chattering classes', but there's a sense in which it's true. What is the real test for the intellectual classes? The French call them the clerks and Coleridge called them the clerisy and sociologists call them the gatekeepers, but that's a neutral – a lesser – tag. It means those who read the books and open the gates for the new ideas. That's not only what the clerisy is. The clerisy is saying, this is so, is it not – you know Leavis's phrase – and this is good and this is bad; believe me if you will, in a democracy I can't force you, but here are issues which have tentacular roots in your sense of value and virtue and so on.

Apart from the public library debate, where very few are engaging properly (they'll all sign a petition to government saying give more money to libraries but they won't engage with the libraries themselves) the worst case is broadcasting. The new Broadcasting Act is appalling. It will destroy public service broadcasting as we know it; it has already started. It wasn't difficult to predict this. People are even now throwing up their hands and asking: 'Why didn't we know?' But before the Act came into force, how many among the intellectual classes in England ever objected to or wrote about the threat? How many long articles were there, in the journals, about the nature and implications of the changes? There was a movement called the Campaign for Quality Television which did good work, but it was run by people who are in quality television, such as Melvyn Bragg. That didn't destroy what they were saying, but it meant that they were interested parties. Other than that, you have this vision of people, often with high Oxbridge voices, trotting weekly up to Broadcasting House to chat on Radio 3 about the new book, the new play, the new exhibition, picking up their 50 quid and trotting back again; and the ground's being cut from under their feet and they don't know it. There's a sense in which the English could learn from the French there – to get out into the streets and argue.

C.H. Sisson

Moorfield Cottage, The Hill, Langport, Somerset
9 July 1993

NICOLAS TREDELL: *Could we begin by looking at your early days in Bristol? What elements of your childhood and schooling do you think have been important in your subsequent life?*

C.H. SISSON: You start with a very difficult question, of course, because how do I know really? Whatever happens to one – certainly whatever happened to me at that stage – is unremarkable in a sense. One goes on into different places and times and one begins to realize where one *has* been, so to speak. When I went out into greater Bristol, I began to know a bit about what Eastville was; living abroad you begin to know what England is, and sure enough I began to feel what Europe is by being in Asia. I noticed somewhere someone says 'born in a working-class suburb' and it's supposed to be rather posh to claim affinity with the working classes these days. Eastville, the district of Bristol where I was brought up, was a working-class suburb all right, but although my family on both sides were certainly not particularly well off, we were quite respectable by Eastville standards. My father was an optician and we were rather somebody than nobody, though nobody much. Both my mother's and my father's family had quite long histories of their own which certainly weren't what you might call proletarian. My mother's family were all farmers for generations and my father's family had a comb mill in Kendal. Unfortunately my grandfather died when my father was only eleven, otherwise that might have gone on. But the comb mill went back to the late eighteenth century at least. So they're both what you might call petit-bourgeois families.

You went to what you call, in On the Look-Out, *'a county secondary school [in Bristol], ranking somewhat above the worst of these establishments in the city and well below the best' (p. 202). Alan Ross, who quotes that remark in his TLS review of On the Look-Out, goes on to remark 'but by the time, after six years as a pupil, Sisson was ready to go to Bristol University, he had studied French, Latin and English, in his spare time read Rupert Brooke and the Sitwells, acquired* The Waste Land *and developed an obsession with Dante Gabriel Rossetti. Not many boys from public schools leave with such a wide taste and addiction to literature' (*TLS *October 6-12 1989, p. 1091). Would you agree with that profile of yourself at that stage of your life?*

What you've got there is roughly correct, though I had to wait for my copy of Eliot until I got my leaving prize in my last year at school, so I got it just before I went to university. But I had certainly heard of him. In those days the BBC was worth something; they had some lectures by Harold Nicolson on the radio, and published a pamphlet to go with them which had an extract from *The Waste Land*. That was how I first came across those electric lines.

What about writing poetry of your own at the time? Were you doing much of that?

Not much, but I did write poems as a child and I continued them as an undergraduate. So the answer is yes, though we shouldn't give the impression of someone thinking about writing poetry. I was thinking about getting to university really.

When you did get to Bristol University, what was it like?

It was the only university known to me, but from my point of view it was very good. Of course there weren't anything like as many students as there are now. The university had a neo-Gothic tower which we used to sneer at somewhat, but the library was perfect really. It was divided into bays which each had a solid oak table and chairs. Each bay was roughly a subject bay. The books were very well chosen, extensive enough for anyone's needs at that time, and I could use it during the vacation as well. As for the teaching, I did a joint course in English and Philosophy. In the first year, you did the language as well as the literature, and philosophy too. My only regret about the first year is that I didn't pay as much attention to Anglo-Saxon as I might have done, because it was well worth doing. But I was determined I was going to do the philosophy and I got into that all right.

The philosophy school had an excellent professor called Guy Cromwell Field, who wrote a book on Plato. Because the school was so small, you had tutorials where he would sit on one side of the table with a book and he read a bit of Kant, say, and then stop and you had to explain it. The English professor, John Crofts, was a softer character, rather handsome, I suppose, with a lovely voice. He used to like to read Sir Thomas Browne. He was basically a good chap, though of course his discrimination stopped short of T.S. Eliot. But then so did most people's. It's not so long ago that people didn't read Eliot. So one had to make one's way and I think there's a lot to be said for that really.

Did you have any sense that you were missing out in not having gone to Oxford or Cambridge? Any Jude the Obscure-*like hankerings?*

It never occurred to me that I could go there. I thought I was doing jolly well in getting to Bristol University. It was three well-spent years on the whole – it can't have been all well spent, but you know what I mean. My sense of Oxford and Cambridge was rather of the silliness of Auden, Spender and Day-Lewis – the social silliness, I was interested in the poetry they were putting out. The rest would be only incidental to my general political orientation.

With regard to politics, you say in On the Look-Out *that when you were a student you 'shared some of the emotional attitudes of the left' (p. 195) and you were strongly aware of unemployment, seeing the queues outside the Labour Exchange and passing the unemployed in the street as you walked to and from the university. Was there a process of moving towards a certain political position?*

As far as I can recall, I didn't resist the general movement of the time. There was something to be said for it in a way. It was full of hunger marches and that kind of thing and the students' sympathy was naturally with these. But there were one or two theoretical people about and I was rather less taken by their view of the Communist thing. By the time I took my degree, I think I could say I had reached an agnostic point of view as far as politics were concerned. I wasn't at any point a real party man. It never occurred to me join the Party – there was only one Party – it never occurred to me to join that lot, but it wasn't for any particular reason – my reflections didn't come to a point in that way at all. So much of the general political talk was about unemployment at home, and abroad it was a thing called fascism which was alleged to be everywhere. But anti-fascism in itself was just silly really, like anti-anything. The whole thing was focused so much more sharply when I went to Germany that everything before that seems rather vague.

Could you talk about your experiences in Germany?

A trouble was that I hadn't really done any German so I had to try to learn some. I started with a month in Hamburg and went to courses and that was all right as far as it went. I was there with a friend from Bristol and we were there with Herr Radel and Frau Radel – he was a retired wholesale butcher, I believe, and she was, well, a piece of meat really. My friend then went on to Marburg or somewhere and I went to Berlin – I was a very isolated young man, twenty or so. I stayed with people in Berlin who had a flat which was quite small – not quite an Earls Court kind of building, but that sort of thing – but very well situated just off the Tiergarten and within walking distance of the university. In this flat there lived Herr Doctor Bargel. Bargel seemed to edit some Nazi Labour Front journal. He was a First World War veteran who had been down on the Silesian border afterwards and when he was in his cups he would describe how there was always peace in the countryside in the daytime and at night they took their guns and went out hunting for Poles. Then there was Doctor Mohrhoff. Mohrhoff worked in an office of some heavy industry and went to illegal 'courses' with the Reichswehr. Perhaps because he had a slightly Jewish nose, he was madly pro-Nazi. There was also a relatively harmless boy, Schmid, who was training to be an actor. But the devil was that none of these people could be induced to speak German. They were all going to learn English from me and that did me real damage in time, but that was quite common. I never really learnt as much German as I would like to have done or could have done, but still I was deeply instructed as to the nature of Nazism.

I'd already been to a labour camp when I was in Hamburg, but in Berlin I was really in the clutches. The Nazi presence was entirely pervasive. No-one got near a university unless he was acceptable, and in the streets it was everywhere. The thing I always remember is the Saar plebiscite. You would hear this song everywhere: *'Deutsch ist die Saar, / Deutsch immerdar, / Und deutsch ist unser Flusses Strand / Und ewig deutsch das Heimatland'*. When the result of the plebiscite was announced, posters appeared all over the place saying there would be a spontaneous demonstration the same evening in front of the old Reichstag building. I went there with Schmid and

Mohrhoff. Goebbels spoke, and afterwards the procession moved out with all the torches and flags and *Sieg Heils* and salutes. I stood to attention – I thought that was enough – but Mohrhoff kept pushing my elbow, trying to get it up in a salute. Afterwards he said: 'Sir would not greet the flag!' Well, I thought, enough is enough. I did have my own back on that sort of thing on one occasion in Munich. We went to a museum and as we were coming out there was a chap, a perfectly harmless doorkeeper, more or less snoring, and I couldn't resist it, as I went past him I said 'Heil Hitler!' and he leapt up in shock. But that was the only occasion when I officially gave way. Then I went to Prague and that was fascinating, but again I went with introductions to Nazis. When I left Prague for Nuremberg, my German friends came to see me off, and they brought quite a lot of pamphlets and pictures showing where the frontier would be redrawn in Bohemia. I just bunged them inside my case and thought, I'd deal with them later. There was a great deal of currency smuggling at that time, it paid you to get registered marks out of Germany, and the customs and police would usually turn out people's cases just like that. But when I got to the frontier, they opened my case, saw this wonderful propaganda inside, and smiled and let me through. I could have smuggled thousands of deutschmarks. So then I went on to Munich and ended up in Freiburg. But being in Germany left me in no doubt what everyone was after and I just hoped the French were up to it, because I knew that at home at that time, the talk was all of peace ballots and that sort of thing.

From Germany you went on to France. What was that like?

It was a wonderful change. I was lucky because I was at a student pension, run by Monsieur and Madame Duchemin, which was just behind the Pantheon, perfectly placed. There were quite a large number of people there, perhaps three students, and the mother of one of them, and a daughter who was married to an actor who was also there. I had a good reading knowledge of French at that time, but I could hardly understand or utter a word. There were two long meals a day and I sat there throughout these and they all talked at once and an understanding of the language just dawned on me in time. Monsieur Duchemin was a schoolmaster who taught English. He never spoke English to me – I don't know why – but he was very good to me and asked me questions in French that I could answer. But then we got on to more complicated things like politics. I took to reading the *Action Française* which he hated. Everyone there was against it, with one possible exception. Monsieur very much hated having the *Action Française* in the house, but none the less he would say to me: 'Et qu'est-ce qu'il dit ce matin, votre Monsieur Maurras?' And I would tell him what Monsieur Maurras had said that morning, and the conversation went on from there and the other people all joined in. It was an excellent place to be in and of course right in the middle of the Latin Quarter with bookshops and all that. All this time – this is the great joke of it all – I was supposed to be doing a thesis. I never did.

Were you writing any poetry at that time?

I wrote it up to the time I left Berlin. I remember that the last poem I wrote – they weren't all like that – was vaguely Audenesque, though it was anti-Auden really as well. On the Potsdamer Platz or some-where close by, I decided to give up writing poetry. I just wasn't good enough. The last thing I wanted to do was to 'be a poet' as they say. I didn't see that as my future. I thought I'd better forget it. I didn't in fact start writing poetry again until eight or nine years afterwards, when I was on a troopship. So it was a genuine voluntary gap, a wil-ful gap, I might say. There was plenty to preoccupy me in my travels in Germany and France. It was a most valuable time to me and jux-taposed like that it has marked me for life really.

Could you say more about how your interest in Maurras developed?

I must first have heard of Maurras and the *Action Française* through the pages of *The Criterion* and I read *L'avenir de l'intelligence* when I was still an undergraduate, but that was only by the way. Then when I was in Germany I did read the odd copy of the *Action Fran-çaise* – when I saw one I bought one. Maurras was a fantastic jour-nalist – not of the kind we mostly have now, which I think nothing of. He was deepening the analysis of the political situation, at a time when there was a lot of rubbish being talked – it was the time of all those goings-on at Geneva which came to nothing, and there was the Abyssinian war. As for the Russian influence, Maurras didn't bother his head unduly about the so-called ideals of the Left, he bothered himself about national politics, and how right he was in relation to Russia. It was at this stage that I became quite convinced that this Communism/Fascism business did not represent the guts or the real-ity of what was going on, and I suppose Maurras did make me think in English terms really. He indicated certain ways of thinking which had been absolutely obscured by the general sloppy left-wingism and liberalism in this country. It was new, whereas what the left-of-centre or vaguely left papers in France said was really of no great interest because it was what the papers in England said. Reading Maurras was an education, and in a way it joined up with the very different world of the English seventeenth century, which I knew a bit about anyway. So that really my general position is out of one by the other, so to speak.

In the opening paragraph of your first published essay, 'Charles Maurras and the Idea of a Patriot King', which appeared in the New English Weekly *in 1937, you say 'Inevitably, both poetry and political analyses are the worse for the lack of political doctrine' (English Perspectives, (1992), p. 15). How do you look back on that observation?*

That's rather a grand statement. I don't know that I can really justify it at my age. 'Political analyses' perhaps explains itself, but as to poetry I think that's rubbish really. It was no doubt written with, once again, the Spender Day-Lewis mob in mind and so it was in effect a crack at them. It doesn't stand up as a general truth. Make the usual discount for youthful enthusiasm there.

But that statement does suggest that you didn't think of poetry and politics as existing in completely separate spheres?

Oh no, I don't think I've ever thought that.

When you came back to England you went into the Civil Service. What was that like – both getting in and your early experience there?

Getting in was interesting because in those days, in the examination for the Administrative Class, you had some compulsory papers and then you had to choose from a vast menu. It really meant an ordinary honours degree wasn't enough. I saw when I went to do the exam that quite a lot of the candidates were from public school and most of them had gone to crammers after university to prepare. But in addition to my degree subjects I was able to do French Language and French Civilization, which I'd read up on in Paris, and I did German as a supplementary language – I was more than good enough for that. There was also an interview. I was a very unsuitable person for the interview and I was marked accordingly; having myself sat on many interview panels since, I see it differently now, but at that time I went along in my innocence and I'd no idea really what was expected of me. We had this curious mixed interview panel, a Civil Service Commissioner, a retired ambassador or somebody, an Oxford don, and people like that. They would ask me a question and I just answered them plainly; I thought that's what was wanted. Someone who had been on the interview panel said to Field, the philosophy professor at Bristol: 'I don't think we've been able to do very much for your chap, you know.' But I did well enough in the written exam to get in all the same. I was unsuitable in a sort of way, but only in the sense of student background. In those days, people in the Civil Service came mostly from Oxford, some from Cambridge, a few from London, and there were always one or two Scots, but nobody came from other British universities.

First of all I was dealing with unemployment benefit. It was all very mysterious because it was highly legal – it was all a question of appeals, mainly on points of law. I went along to a Tribunal with a senior official, and I found myself innocently chatting with the National Unemployed Workers' Union man. The official made it clear that he didn't think much of that, that if you were going to a Tribunal you didn't really fraternize and you'd better keep your mouth shut. It wasn't a very good place to begin, and I hadn't been there very long when the First Division association, which was a sort of Civil Service Trade Union for the administrative class, got me transferred. My Principal then was a chap called De Villiers, a very Oxfordy sort of man, who obviously summed me up immediately as someone needing to be told everything. He told me I should raise my hat – and I wore a hat, believe it or not – every time I passed the Cenotaph. I must have mentioned Maurras to him because he ignorantly said it should be pronounced 'Maurra', without sounding the final 's'. We had Humbert Wolfe as Deputy Secretary and De Villiers said how inferior he thought Yeats's later poems were to Wolfe's, how much better Humbert was. That wasn't my view of the matter.

So the war broke out, and you undertook the passage to India, which you evoke in the central section of On the Look-Out. *In 'Autobiographical Reflections on Politics', originally written in 1954 and first published in* The Avoidance of Literature, *which came out in 1978, you say: 'Amidst the evasions of a Hindu world it was possible to see something of what was meant by saying that Europe had been affected by Christianity. When on the way back [from India] we put in at Gibraltar it was not merely the Rock that stirred me, though no*

*Englishman, I hope, can see that for the first time without emotion.
The coast of Spain was the frontier of the Latin and Christian West
and England was, in its odd and insular way, part of that. After my
stay in India I knew better than from Massis what there was to
defend' (p. 142). Would you say that your passage to India strengthened your sense of yourself as both an Englishman and, in a certain
way, a European?*

Yes, it's what I was saying earlier about how one learned about England by going to Europe. And in this case it linked up with classic
Europeanism.

*In your account of India, one element that comes across very
strongly is your aversion to Hinduism.*

It never attracted me, let me put it that way. What I say about it
wouldn't be terribly well-founded, because I don't claim to know
what I'm talking about really. What I feel about it is not superficial,
it's deep, but it is ignorant, and it must be mixed up with the climate
and general depression. But of course I took quite a bit from the Abbé
Dubois whose book is a fascinating account of what went on. What
I really objected to in Hinduism is that it gives the impression that it
can take in anything, so to speak – take in Christianity as just another
bite. Instead of the idea that there is one thing somewhere, it's the
idea that everything fades into everything else, this endlessly evasive
spirit, this so-called profound philosophy. It is the old pagan world
really.

*When you got back to England after the war, you went back into the
Civil Service at a senior level, so you were well-placed to observe
what was going on in the period of the 1945-51 Labour Governments. What were your feelings about that era?*

I probably didn't have general feelings. I was so glad to be back anyway, and at work. I reacted to this and that, but I didn't say, in the
way I do now, what a ghastly age we live in. The government tried to
do some quite sensible things, I thought. But of course, rubbish is
never very far from politics. I did take against the bureaucratic over-
lay and the determination to suck everything into the management of
the State, turning all voluntary things into a sort of State function. I
suppose it was a general dislike of *Gleichshaltung* really. There are
traces of that in some odd articles I wrote at the time, around 1950,

and also in the pamphlet called 'The Curious Democrat' I published in 1950 under the name of Richard Ampers.

Your book on twentieth-century English poetry starts in 1900 and ends in 1950. In the fifties, you had this new generation of poets – part of what has come to be called the Movement – of whom Donald Davie was one, and others like Larkin and Enright. What did you think of those poets at the time?

They didn't really mean much to me. I've always said, truly enough, that it's the poets immediately before one who mean most to one. *English Poetry 1900-50* should really have ended in 1940 because it was at that point, partly through my age, partly because of what was happening at that time, that, in a sense, my significant discovery of contemporary poetry ended. I put in the extra ten years at the request of the publishers who wanted to make the period covered by the book up to 50 years. In the 1950s, there was generally this 'back to Hardy' notion, back to the English after all these Yankees like Eliot and Pound. As far as I was concerned, Eliot and Pound were the crucial bearings. It's not that I don't admire Hardy, but you can't just go back to Hardy after those two.

You contributed to the magazine New English Weekly, *which ran from 1932 to 1949 and was edited by Philip Mairet. Could you recall that magazine and Mairet for us?*

The *New English Weekly* couldn't exist at present, and couldn't have existed for some time past. It was really the victim of the first great post-war inflation. Otherwise I think it could have gone on for a time – it never had a vast circulation but it was solidly established. It followed A.R. Orage's *New Age* really. Eliot was on the board and it had a certain respectability. Philip Mairet was an extremely intelligent, gifted and extraordinary person. He had been engaged at one time in making stained glass windows. The *New English Weekly* had been interested in Social Credit but by the time I was connected with it, that wasn't really a living thing, though people like Mairet had seen enough of it to be critical of the financial system: as to the alleged solutions Social Credit offered, that's another matter. With the magazine, it wasn't a matter of a group of writers getting together: I suppose this might have been true of the older ones, but on the whole the *New English Weekly* collected up odd people from odd places. It was truly independent. Mairet would just ask you to do something or let you do something that no-one else would have dreamed of letting you do. There was a certain amount of vague socializing and the odd meeting. I did meet quite a few people through the paper but I didn't acquire any great social connection there. But it was the only connection I had. In a way, really, that was characteristic of my career. I never was a literary man in the sense of being in with literary people, except perhaps for that short spell with the magazine X. I worked long hours on the whole, and I was just able to write an article now and again.

In the opening sections of On the Look-Out, *you have this vivid description of yourself, in 1964, 'organized as a dichotomy' (p. 18), as you put it there, moving between your Civil Service office in St James's Square and the* demi-monde *of poets' pubs. Did you experience that movement between those two worlds as a tension or a pleasure?*

It was a pleasure and an interlude. It would be unfair to put it as two sides of a dichotomy because my real life was in the Civil Service, and I feel now that I'm a retired civil servant really. But it was interesting and pleasant to meet the people I met, David Wright first of all, who then introduced me to various others. I used to go and have the odd pint now and again on the way back from the office but it was nothing like George Barker and others who really made a thing out of mucking about in Soho.

Could we talk about your novel Christopher Homm, *which was first published in 1965? The most immediately striking technical point about that novel is its reverse chronology, telling the story of its eponymous protagonist from death to birth. Can you say why you chose to do that?*

I don't know why. I had no sort of definite plan. It just happened, but then the things one writes tend to happen really. Once you had begun it seemed clear which way you were going. At one point the Gaberocchus Press, who had brought out my first novel *An Asiatic Romance*, thought they might publish *Christopher Homm* and asked if I could alter it and put it round the right way. I looked at that and it didn't work very well, because in a sense the novel is the explanation of how the hero got where he is in Chapter I, and the explanation comes afterwards.

The narrative stance you adopt in Christopher Homm *pins down its protagonist and the other characters remorselessly. It's very effective, but might it not be said that it's too remorseless? Christopher is allowed no voice of his own – when he does speak, his words are always placed by the overall narratorial position.*

I suppose that's true, in a sense. If I had ideas about novels at the time, they would be based as much as anything on Wyndham Lewis's external approach. It was meant to be that sort of approach in *Christopher Homm*, though there's nothing very Lewisian about the novel. But it was definitely not confessional. It was meant to be people seen from the outside – which after all is as likely to be true as what you see from the inside. But *Christopher Homm* does represent precisely a juncture in my development. It's partly a book – although it might not pass for such – not exactly about the Church, but about human life as a whole, and it was written at the time when I was interested in the possibility of a Christian nation, so to speak.

In On the Look-Out, *in the section where you're talking about the impossiblity of saying how you became a Christian, you conclude by saying that you were writing* Christopher Homm *at that juncture of your life (p. 54). Was the vision of human disappointment that* Christopher Homm *expresses so powerfully an element of your movement into the Church?*

I'd long given up having any particular confidence in the way the human race carried on, and that dates rather back to T.E. Hulme than anything else. I don't think joining the Church was because of that. It was because – it might sound absurd and it is absurd and I say it again in the Preface to *Is There a Church of England?* – that it seemed to me that it was the Creed or nothing, and that I hold these two possibilities in my mind. *Christopher Homm* does represent a vision of the world and of mankind really, but it's only an illustration, so to speak, not an absolute everyman.

Could we turn from your fiction to your many translations – for example, of Heine, Virgil, Dante, Horace, Lucretius, Du Bellay. What has translation meant to you?

The first bout so to speak, the first notable bout anyway, was the Heine, and that can be best explained in social terms. It was during the war, I had this one volume of Heine with me and the Army round about me, and the two combined. It was something to do. The second major bout was the Catullus and that was quite different. I'd written quite a bit by then, but I was still hankering after some kind of directness and plainness, and I thought it would help to go to something so blindingly clear as Catullus. I was very busy in the office, working long hours, and I used to read a poem of Catullus at night and translate it with my tea in the morning. The influence of that does show up, I think, in various things in *Metamorphoses* and the next volume after that. All the translations I've done have left some mark, but then I've only translated things I've really known, or which I've known partly, for a long time, and wanted to know more about, like the Lucretius. You have to have a sympathy with the subject matter before you do a translation. I have much enjoyed doing those long translations in recent years. I'd never read Dante through continuously until I came to translate *The Divine Comedy*. It was a marvellous thing to sit down with it day after day, and it gave a continuity to life which you begin to lack when you grow old. I really have regarded Dante as the perfect performer ever since I saw Eliot's essay on him when it came out. Of course one doesn't begin to say one's influenced by Dante, that would be ridiculous in a way; but at least it tells you what not to do, and then you go and do it. It is the perfect model for direct speech if ever there was one. In the case of Virgil's *Aeneid* it's different. My translation was a matter of trying to say it in contemporary language, and it's not bad in its way, but one couldn't think of the *Aeneid* as a book to model oneself on at this time of day. Then some of the minor things, like the Du Bellay, I enjoyed doing. I felt I had a certain affinity with Du Bellay in his office in Rome, doing a job. So much in my life answered to that. He's so gracious and so easy a writer. It's a reasonably straightforward translation, but it's not entirely so, it's Du Bellay remade so to speak. I think I was in Cambridge when a girl who was obviously deep in these ways – she was probably a graduate student – said I was using Du Bellay much as Du Bellay had used Horace. I often translate bits of French Renaissance poets. I was working on Chassignet recently whom I've never really dealt with before and who is rather fascinating.

Could I put to you some observations of Robert Nye on your own poetry – he's specifically talking about 'The Usk', but it relates to a more general concern of your poetry and of your essays, which is that poetry is not an expression of self, not least because there isn't very much of a self to be expressed. Nye says 'a thing which Sisson has made expressly his own [is] a scepticism regarding the persistence of consciousness in any real individual sense at all other than through the Incarnation in which God as it were consented once more to be broken up into man, His own image. This theme of a divine flux being all there is for us in the way of hope is recurrent in Sisson' (Audiocassette: 'Robert Nye on C.H. Sisson and David Jones'). Do you feel those are valid observations?

I wouldn't put it quite like that myself, but I can see what he's saying, though I think 'broken up' is very difficult to understand in that context. But one of the connections between the Incarnation and my general point of view is that the notion of disembodied spirits means nothing to me, and when people talk about personality they very often mean something like that enduring, going on. An elderly lady once said to me: 'Surely you think that the personality will survive?' I don't know what that means at all. I can understand the conception of Resurrection, which seems to make sense as far as it goes – whether it's possible or not is another matter – and of Incarnation. After all, the Resurrection follows the Incarnation as the day the night. Again, it's that or nothing, and nothing is easily conceivable. It's not a question of hope or non-hope but of what turns out to be the case. I'm not very good on the afterlife really.

Could we explore the relationship between metre and rhythm in your poetry? In Under Briggflatts, *referring to a remark of yours about syntax, Donald Davie says '[t]he truth seemed to be in 1980 that Sisson could afford to be so permissive about syntax…because he was very exacting indeed about something else: about rhythm, and more precisely about* inventiveness *in rhythm. Though Sisson sometimes writes verse that can be scanned, in his theory he is very much a free-verse poet. Most of his poems, like most of the nursery-rhymes he so much admires, resist scansion according to any of the standard accentual-syllabic metres' (p. 185). What do you feel about the relationship in your poetry between rhythm and the use of standard accentual syllabic metres?*

This is true Donald, of course. I suppose that what really guides me when I'm writing about anything is rhythm. Words come up and whether they're right or not probably depends largely on whether I think they are when I write them down. People make so much of this matter of regular or irregular verse, but in fact the kind of free verse I've written is all against a background of ordinary scansion. It's a question of how far you depart from that, and the answer is, at some times more than others and for some purposes more than others. I have no use for the sort of free verse that is so free you can't tell that it's verse at all. An awful lot of this is written, but I don't think there's any of mine that's like that. I've never had to teach anyone about these things, unlike Donald, so I just go on.

Could we take up the question of structure in your poetry? In a generally admiring essay in Critical Quarterly *in 1979, John Pilling points to what he calls your 'comparative disregard for structure, especially in longer poems' (vol. 21, no. 3, p. 78). How do you respond to that charge?*

'The Corridor' is the only thing I can think of which blatantly responds to Pilling's comment, and that is a sort of departure. 'The Corridor' was written in a very curious way. I felt a bit tired of the forms and rhythms I'd been using and I was trying deliberately to get away from them. I started writing various things which were later included in 'The Corridor', but only bits, mostly small bits, and I think I went on for some time. I must have sent them to David Wright and it reached a point where he said you can make a long poem out of these, and that became 'The Corridor'. It is a special case.

What about the question of obscurity in your poetry? One can think of a certain kind of poetry which might initially seem obscure but of which one could generate a reasonable if necessarily inadequate prose paraphrase. With some of your best poems, such as In Insula Avalonia, *one feels that would be much more difficult. Are you happy to produce poems that might be seen as obscure in that kind of way?*

The trouble is I don't think about what I'm writing. I write what I write at the time and looking back, the clarity varies. *In Insula Avalonia* is partly about my terrible days in the office when I was thoroughly fed up with what was going on, although this is necessarily not a public meaning. But not all my poetry is obscure. I once had to read to rather young schoolkids – I don't really know why, my poetry's highly unsuitable to read to children – and I chose a few poems about places and started off with the early ones about India. Those few little poems of India aren't obscure; they are clearly me all right, but they are the poems of someone who's been educated by Pound. My latest work tends to get away from obscurity and to be rather more lucid. But lucidity isn't everything, and when I try to understand the poetry I've been writing this year, I'm still puzzled over some of it. Whether that's because it's not lucid enough or because it's like that, I can't say really. A lot of my poetry deals with precisely the questions of the relationship of body and mind and between people, and the old question of identity. But it's not quite the same as if I had a grand theory to expound on any of these things. It's a question of feeling one's way around this literally endless puzzle, in this way at one time and this different way at another time. In a sense – there are exceptions, of course – the material doesn't change so much as waver over the years. But then it's all written by the same chap, so what can you expect?

The end of Christopher Homm *sees the protagonist in the womb about to emerge and the narrator observes: 'if he had known how bitter the journey was to be he would not have come' (1984 edn, p. 239). Your life has been very different from Christopher Homm's; but if you had known what your journey was to be, would you have come?*

That's a hypothetical question.

Lisa Jardine

London
13 October 1993

NICOLAS TREDELL: *Could you begin by telling us about your formation through home and school the cultural and intellectual influences
which you feel shaped you prior to going to university?*

LISA JARDINE: I had a really intellectual childhood – I think that's
something that's probably dawned on me only since I've been teaching very underprivileged students. My father was an intellectual of
some visibility and our house was full of extremely glamorous
people. I was the eldest child, and my father made no secret of the
fact that he would have liked one of his four girls to have been a boy,
so I stood in from a very early age. I can remember I sat up for dinner
with people like Aldous Huxley from when I was nine. Furthermore,
my father told me that these were people I should remember having
met, and I kept an autograph book. In other words, I was in no doubt
as to the importance of this circle. It was a very Central European
version of intellectual importance and the only other place that I've
really seen it is in New York where now I find families who still continue that tradition. So it was very privileged really.

From a very early age it looked as if I was going to be a mathematician and unfortunately, it looked as if I was going to be a prodigy, so
I was nurtured towards mathematics through my little state primary
school. Then at the point at which I was to go to secondary school,
with no reference to me, my parents panicked about the local girls'
grammar school and put me in for the scholarship exam at Cheltenham Ladies College, which was the local school. That exam is one
of my first most vivid memories. It was a complete nightmare. I sat
in front of these maths papers in which the mathematics was of a
kind I'd never ever encountered, of a sophistication that presumably
young women being groomed in their prep schools could deal with.

So all I did was about one question on each paper, and I had to work out the answers from first principles, and as a result they gave me a scholarship.

What was Cheltenham Ladies College like?

I got a fabulous education as a mathematician. The Principal was a mathematician and I was taught by young women who had recently finished at Oxford and Cambridge. It was an extraordinary situation for a girl. The environment was a total confusion for me because I was a day girl, so I lived at home in a left-liberal household with a mother who was a very bohemian sculptor and a father who was by that time a radio and TV figure, and at school I absorbed all the snobberies and class formations of the British upper classes. I think I turned into a most obnoxious girl. I cannot imagine how obnoxious I was at 14. I learnt all kinds of important things, like assertiveness. We got public speaking and assertiveness training. We were all supposed to become doyennes of the local community. It's terrifying to think of how beautifully it prepared me for a life in the public eye. So that's a period of my life that was very formative. And it was wholly intellectual in the classroom. The ambition of the school was to turn out very intellectual young women, and some of my closest friends are still women who went through that sort of formation.

So you then went on to Cambridge?

I have to backtrack slightly to say that the first stumble in my career in this golden childhood – it's comic in a way – was that I didn't get into Cambridge on the first try, I only got into Oxford – that was my father's version of it. Clearly I was under this terrific patriarchal influence because, again with no reference to me, it was decided that I therefore wouldn't go to Oxford but would take a second year and try Cambridge again. So I went out to work for the Consumers Association for the year, and then I retook Oxbridge Entrance and I did get into Cambridge. But I got in by a whisker and by that stage *I* was becoming very uncertain about my competence as a mathematician. I suppose I didn't let it show, and I arrived at Cambridge to read a subject I no longer really wanted to read and as a very outwardly confident young woman who had suddenly become extremely insecure about her academic ability. So my first year at Cambridge was very contradictory. On the one hand, I immediately went into the Labour Club and became very active in left politics, or as active as girls were allowed to be then. In other words, we made the tea and we typed the pamphlets and we supported the men and we wrote to prominent political figures to ask them to come and speak and we took them to dinner – I remember taking people like Dennis Healey and Shirley Williams to dinner. On the other hand the maths went very badly. So I was schizophrenic.

Did you resent or accept the subordination of women within the Labour Club at that time?

I think it was invisible to us. It was very unsettling because we got double messages constantly and we tried to negotiate the double messages. That's the thing that one now reads quite a lot about with women who grew up in the sixties.

Did you find this subordination of women in other areas of university life?

Only in the mathematics department. The first time anyone ever said to me that girls don't do as well as boys was in the first introductory supervision I had at Newnham. I remember phoning my father virtually in tears and saying I've just been told that girls won't do as well as boys. He was absolutely furious. But that wasn't the case elsewhere. For instance, I sang in several small chamber choirs, so you could sing and you could be very successful at that, and you could be in politics and you could be very outspoken – it's just that you never made major office. I was in a women-only college, and that's very important. At that time women at Newnham had a very strong sense of their own ability to achieve. But it was within the discipline that I'd chosen, unfortunately, that the signals were extremely strong that women would never succeed. But I don't think it ever crossed my mind that I wouldn't succeed in life, not once.

With the breakdown of the mathematics for you, what happened then in terms of your intellectual course?

I behaved very badly, which is a kind of marker all down my career, I suppose. That's part of having been an obnoxious 14 year old – I suppose I did learn that being obnoxious could sometimes be quite effective. At the end of the second year of mathematics, I was so unhappy, and my results were poor, so I went to my Director of Studies in maths to ask to change subjects. When I was told that

I couldn't, I announced I was leaving. So Newnham was coerced into allowing me to shift subjects. They wanted me to shift to economics and again my father intervened – it's a very patriarchal story. My father came to Cambridge and we sat and talked for hours, and he said, why don't you read English for the last year? There's a long good tradition of doing English. He was a near-contemporary of Graves and Empson, and Empson in particular did mathematics very brilliantly and then did the English Tripos. So Newnham in a sense had no option – they could have let go of me, but they didn't. But Ruth Cohen, who was Principal, made it quite clear that it was under duress and they didn't approve, and indeed subsequently they didn't allow me back to Newnham to do research.

How did you adapt to the change of subject?

It was a delight. It was the life that I'd lived, it was like studying your life. Plus the enormous change of being taught in a context where your teachers wanted to relate to you. That was the most striking thing about the shift from sciences to arts. In two years doing mathematics, no teacher had ever known the first thing about me. You went in with the paper problems that you'd worked on, you went through the technical errors, you went through better solutions, you went away again, and you came back if you had problems with the lectures. In my first supervision with Jean Gooder at Newnham, she sat me down in her kitchen with a cup of tea and said: Now tell me all about yourself. I was actually fairly panicked by that, but as I eased into it, it became clear that this really was, as I say, a course in your life. So for instance, it's in dramatic contrast for me with Raymond Williams's idea that literature was where he first discovered inequality. Literature was where I discovered equality. I was absolutely centred in that culture, in spite of my father being an immigrant Jew.

How would you sum up the underlying assumptions and procedures of the Cambridge English course at that time?

I escaped the procedures. I literally can't tell you about the pressure of Part I English, which I think hasn't changed very much down to now. I took Part II, so I took the final year course. I never did any Anglo-Saxon, I never did any Middle English, I never did compulsory Shakespeare, I never did the compulsory period papers. I took the English Moralists, Plato to Marx, I took a paper in Jonathan

Swift with Dennis Donoghue who was a Visiting Professor, I took the Tragedy paper as it had just been redesigned by Raymond Williams, and I took a Practical Criticism paper and was taught by Jeremy Prynne. It was a wonderful bouquet of the best that Cambridge had to offer at that time.

What happened after Cambridge?

I was refused permission to go on to research by Newnham, which I now discover was completely improper. They had no right and had I applied to the university I would have been accepted. The refusal was directly related to my political activity. The year before I left, I and some others had spearheaded a campaign to allow Newnham women not to pay full commons and eat all their meals in. The College had insisted on a referendum and had issued documents to show that the cost of food would go up by (say) 20% if the reform went through. But we'd discovered by slightly illicit access to the College finances that the cost of food was to go up 20% anyway. So we issued a flyer and we won the referendum and effected the change. I received a letter from the Principal which said that she had on reflection decided that my ability to distort the truth made me unsuitable to do research. So I went off to Essex, which was a brand new, volatile, experimental university, and I did the MA in Literary Translation with Donald Davie for a year.

How was that year at Essex?

It was another political year. Essex was incredibly political and it confirmed my growing belief that there was an intrinsic relation between literary studies and politics, not really based on theory but on the practice, the fact that this was where you found polemic and the struggling with class and culture. So it was a good, interesting year. I don't know how formative it was. I think it was a time of transition.

What was your view of the political troubles at Essex?

It was the year before the troubles, but it was clear that the troubles were coming and we were more highly politicised than any other context I've ever been in. One was immersed in the political troubles and I did go back and sit in and all that stuff. Any view I have is with hindsight, but with hindsight – because it happened again later with Bernard Williams at Kings, Cambridge – if you put liberal-left authority figures in, they are the most hurt and distraught when they discover that students still oppose them. Really the opposition to Sloman at Essex was about the fact that he felt that the students ought to understand that he knew best because he was basically a liberal, whereas of course the students just thought he lived in a big house surrounded by a lake and paid no attention to the political ferment in the world.

How would you have defined your own politics at that time?

I was conscientiously Labour Party. I joined the Labour Party from the Labour Club at Cambridge and I've belonged to it ever since. A lot of my friends were anarchists and various forms of extreme left. I fell in briefly with *New Left Review* and I did the same making tea and typing things there as I'd done at the Labour Club in Cambridge. I was completely captivated by Juliet Mitchell and Perry Anderson as a couple. I wanted to be in a couple like that, they were just everything that I wanted. At the same time I remained absolutely stolidly within the Labour Party.

You mention Juliet Mitchell. Was feminism entering into your consciousness at this point?

I didn't have the faintest inkling of feminism and I remember when Juliet Mitchell published 'Women: The Longest Revolution' in *New Left Review*, I fear I was on the side of Quintin Hoare, who attacked it, in the sense that I couldn't understand what she was trying to do. I wrote about that later in the book I and Julia Swindells produced, *What's Left*, in which there's much more autobiography than is visible. It's probably fairly obvious that my own formation took me far too hard against the male edge. What I always tell my own students is: make no mistake, I got where I am by being a pretend man. So I guess until after I got my job at Cambridge I was still achieving fairly systematically as a man.

Could we turn to your PhD at Cambridge and the book which emerged from that, Francis Bacon: Discovery and the Art of Discourse, *published in 1974. How did you become interested in Bacon?*

I was accepted to do my PhD on literary translations of the Bible and I was allocated to Derek Brewer as supervisor. I was very interested in interdisciplinary work, and I already knew that I had a facility with languages, so I wanted a topic that used languages, and literary translations of the Bible was acceptable to the English Faculty. But six months into it there was a real Road to Damascus moment where Derek Brewer and I were sitting in the Varsity cafe opposite Emmanuel College. We were talking about my PhD very animatedly and suddenly somebody said 'Excuse me', and we looked up and there was a woman who looked exactly like Mary Poppins, with a navy hat fixed firmly on her head with hatpins. She said 'Did I 'ear you talking about the Bible?' and she proceeded to launch into passionate Evangelism. Derek Brewer looked at me and I looked at him, and that was the moment when I knew that I was on the wrong topic. When Derek Brewer went on leave for a term I was allocated to Robert Bolgar. Within three weeks, he had identified that I'd done a lot of work on Francis Bacon, because he was part of the 1611 translation team for the King James Bible, and within half a term he had steered me towards a topic in intellectual history.

How far do you feel the work that you did on that has continued to underpin your researches?

It underpins one arm of my researches and it gave me a most incredible grounding. I often think of it as a sort of investment account, which means that every time someone says 'Lisa Jardine's sounding off', they have to say, 'but she's an awfully good scholar'. I fear that that also goes back to my childhood – that I knew that the people who sounded off most vehemently and were listened to all had impeccable credentials in some field so difficult that the hack reviewers couldn't shoot them down. That sounds as if it were done deliberately, but it wasn't. The thing is, I love scholarship. It probably gives me my stability. There is nothing more wonderful than sitting in an archive with a really difficult text doing the detective work that's needed to bring it alive.

Is Francis Bacon: Discovery and the Art of Discourse *a book you would, not necessarily rewrite, but see differently today in the light of some of the changes that have come about in Renaissance studies?*

It's always a mistake to publish your PhD. That book smacks of PhDishness. You can tell it's a PhD because it keeps veering in the wrong direction. Just when it starts to be interesting, it gets buried in footnotes, and all its most interesting ideas are submerged. I think that you're right in suspecting that therefore some of those sub-merged ideas then form the basis for things that I did later. I have actually been asked several times to rewrite that book. It's not in my nature ever to backtrack so I couldn't do it, but I think that I do now at this precise moment in my career believe there is a field waiting which is called the new intellectual history and which I probably will do my next piece of work in, which would be the regrounding of intellectual history such that that book wouldn't be so broken-backed. It kept having to hover around literary text studies and the study of so-called non-literary texts. It doesn't quite know where the literary is, but then nor did the discipline at that point.

You were a post-doctoral Research Fellow at the Warburg Institute in London from 1971 to 1973. What exactly is the Warburg Institute?

The Warburg Institute is called an Institute in the Classical Tradition. Its brief is the study of any area of culture either in text studies or plastic arts which is grounded in some explicatable way in the classical heritage. Given its spread, this actually means ancient cultures which would include Islamic and Judaic cultures as well as those of Greece and Rome. It was founded by Aby Warburg, the youngest son of the banking family in Germany, who had a library which he had to remove from Germany under Nazism and which the University of London gave a home to. When I was there Ernst Gombrich was its head, Francis Yates had the next office to me and D.P. Walker helped me when I got into difficulties with my work. It was quite extraordinary.

After the Warburg, you taught at Essex, spent a year as a Research Fellow at Cornell, and then returned to Cambridge to research and teach. Could we explore your relationship with feminism during that time? You said earlier that you had no inkling of feminism in the 1960s. In the 1970s, feminism was a growing force, How did it impinge on you in those years?

I think if you were brought up as the son that your father never had and if you then succeeded in male fields – and I may not have been a prodigy but I know I have a most ludicrously classically logical mind – you were living feminism, in a sense. I was constantly aware of con-tradictions in the work I was doing in relation to myself, but I lived them rather than explicated them. Now that's not entirely true, because I first started being involved in women's groups at Essex, and by the time I was teaching at Cambridge I was helping to run groups of that kind. Like many women, I was involved with the activism side of feminism long before I actually confronted feminism in my work. I do have to say that I think that I wittingly waited till I had enough seniority for it to be difficult for people to resist those arguments when I made them. There was a little bit of care about that which some people might read as self-protective caution. I was also extremely deeply involved in Labour Party politics in Cambridge and in pressure groups, for instance on conservation issues. So I have to say rather sheepishly that, aside from my women's groups where I did keep attending, I didn't have time. I'm not a very good advertisement for a perfectly well-formed feminist.

The 1970s was also the time when other new ideas in literary and cultural criticism and theory, particularly from France, started to cross the Channel, if slowly and tardily. What was your own sense of those when you were teaching in Cambridge then?

I'll start from the fact that because I was hired to teach what was crudely called Renaisssance background, this excluded me in some way from the English curriculum. I taught Shakespeare and I taught the Renaissance, and because of the Warburg, because of my training which was European – the other thing to say about the Warburg Institute was *it* was Central European – it is my firm belief that Renaissance studies had already to some considerable extent absorbed European currents of thought. So whilst my colleagues were struggling to get theory into the curriculum, we pottered on with the Renaissance, and those few students in those days who went on to do Part II papers in the Renaissance were so committed and so broadly read that it was where I certainly learned most strongly that if you're going to transmit high theory, it has to be absorbed into practice. That seemed to me to be already somewhat the case with Renaissance studies. However, we did line up very very strongly behind the theory faction, if you like. I spent one year at King's which had appointed me to a non-university teaching job, and as soon as I got my university job I moved to Jesus College which at that time had Howard Erskine-Hill, Raymond Williams and Stephen Heath, so that we really were a site of struggle. It was as fierce a site of struggle as the Faculty and I stood up to be counted on Stephen's side.

The Cambridge struggle comes across as a very macho *contest. What role did feminism play in it?*

Let me go to the centre of it, to Christopher Ricks's attack on Colin MacCabe. We all knew where we lined up. That is to say, there was the progressive wing of the English Faculty. There were Raymond Williams and Frank Kermode – and by that time of course, I'd worked with Frank Kermode at King's – who were the great touchstones. They were never there – in fact we made badges which said 'Has anybody seen Raymond?' at one point – but they were – the *éminences grises* would be the polite way of putting it. In every Faculty meeting we turned out in force and voted for Colin. We also became the *bêtes noirs* of Christopher Ricks who was obsessive in his dislikes, and our students became targets of his vindictiveness. But the moment when it became clear where feminism stood was when I was sitting in the Buttery on the Sidgwick site at Cambridge with Suzanne Kappeler and with Stephen Heath. Over on the other side there was a gaggle of students who were being interviewed by a reporter from the *Sunday Telegraph*, and one of the students came over and said the *Sunday Telegraph* would like to speak to you. We said to him, go back and say to the *Sunday Telegraph* that if the *Sunday Telegraph* wants to speak to us, the *Sunday Telegraph* can come over here, which he didn't do. At that point Stephen said: You do realize that were you to introduce a feminism paper at this moment it would go through on the nod. So Su and I sat up all of that night, then we consulted Stephen and then we consulted Gillian Beer and Jill Mann, and we ran around Cambridge to find support, and we produced a document that was tabled on the following Thursday at the Faculty Board and went through on the nod. That was how the Literary Representation of Women paper entered Part II of the Tripos. It just beautifully reflects the state of feminism in Cambridge. Feminism was no part of the poststructuralism debate and therefore feminism entered Cambridge under cover of darkness.

So that, in a sense, was one consequence of the dispute. In other respects, what was the aftermath?

I think the aftermath for me at Cambridge was that it was part of the build-up of my understanding that you were not going to be able radically to alter the curriculum there. Ricks had very cannily identified the issue as being whether Oxbridge would be the permanent repository of a particular view of English studies, just as it is the permanent repository of a particular view of classics. I think we did see that this was what was happening and, for instance, that a paper like Literary Representation of Women would be allowed its six-year run and then it would go again and something else would replace it. So it was the beginning of that understanding for me. In larger terms, it's just been tiresome because the press developed a taste for high theory but never educated itself. It was not an accident that it got into the national press. It got into the national press because Colin was so well-connected, and so the press never did try and figure out *why* they were interested and what it was all about. It meant that a whole generation of figures in the media who are now in positions of prominence know the buzzwords without any understanding of what the issues are. That's persisted here, and it's about to rear its head again over the PC debate which is rather tardily appearing in Britain. The editors know they want to run it, because it's a sexy topic and it's done well in America, but they're not taking the time to understand it.

Could we move on to your book Still Harping on Daughters: Women and Drama in the Age of Shakespeare, *which first came out in 1983 and is now a standard text. How did that come about?*

The *London Review of Books* sent me, as a Cambridge Shakespearean, five feminist books to review. I took a lot of trouble over it and wrote a long review, and I sent it to the *London Review of Books* and it came back with a slip from the editor saying you must understand we could never publish this. I was completely taken aback. I could not for the life of me understand why. I was also very upset. One of the persistent features of my career is that I do obstreperous things and I'm incredibly upset by the consequences. I'm publicly very thick-skinned but I'm not privately. But I'd been doing some reviewing for *Quarto* and so I mentioned it to the editor of *Quarto* and he said we'll publish it. When it appeared in *Quarto*, Sue Roe of Harvester Press phoned me up and said I've just read your review, how long would it take you to write the book, and I said, I can do it in three months. And I did.

In the opening chapters of Still Harping on Daughters, *you attack what you see as an over-sanguine view of women's increased freedom during the early modern period, as evidenced by new ideas of marriage or new ideas of secular humanistic education for women. For example, you say: 'I have been arguing that in spite of the wider range of opportunities which became available to (some) women during the Renaissance and Reformation, attitudes towards women did not perceptibly change – may in fact have become somewhat*

hardened as individual women challenged traditional roles' (p. 58).
This gives a sense rather like that produced by a certain Foucauldian
approach – I'm not suggesting any direct influence here – in which
what is claimed as liberation is revealed to be not only illusory but
also to be a reinforcement of subjection. There's a kind of disparage-
ment of those feminist critics who made claims for women's greater
freedom in that period.

That disparagement was what I rued in my preface to the second edition. The new preface was partly an apology, and in a way that's
probably the most visible evidence you've got of my after-the-event
realization that I'd been a man for a very long time, because I had
offended a lot of women critics. I'd grown up in that male tradition
of strenuous polemic. I hadn't grown up in an intellectual environment such as American feminists had of covering one another's
backs, and they heard what I had to say as extremely highanded. But
intriguingly that disparagement did come from a position of high
theory and after all might well have been written by Terry Eagleton.
It says that feminist writing at this time about women in the early
modern period had inadvertently reverted to intentionalism, to
biological determinism, to all the things which we'd been taught by
theory were no part of the critic's perspective. I found myself incredibly impatient reading these feminist books on Shakespeare, because,
of course, I had missed the whole debate, internally to American
feminists in particular, about where they would find women's voices.
And of course it's persistently the case that, just as here we know
absolutely nothing of American cultural history, so inevitably those
who are writing about Shakespeare from North America know a
great deal less about the cultural formation of the early modern
period than we do. So it's tempting to be a little bit high-handed from
time to time. As far as the early modern period goes, I am working on
a book that will be finished at Christmas called *Reading Shakespeare*
Historically, one of whose themes is how dangerous it is to imagine
that our Whiggish versions of freedom emancipated groups or individuals in these repressive, authoritarian periods in which they lived.
So I continue to want to point up the danger of romanticising freedom.

Your attack on over-sanguine estimates of women's increased eman-
cipation in the early modern period in Still Harping on Daughters,
sometimes invokes a distinction between the actual, and the apparent
or theoretical. For example, you say: 'Justifications for subjugation

*altered towards sophisticated mutual consent theories, but the actu-
ality of the woman's role in the household remained, as far as one can
discover, unchanged' (p. 43). But perhaps a certain uneasiness is
indicated by that concessive, and one might ask how far a distinction
between the actual and the apparent can be maintained in our current cultural situation, where there is a strong sense that all we have
of the past are textual traces.*

That's why the concessive is there. If I were more Williamsite in the
language I use I would speak of the everyday. It would be, as it were,
either the visible cultural form or the textual residue which carries
that down to us. That is the opposition. I told you this was a book
that was written fast and also a book that was written on the way to
arriving at the position that I'm now at. But I by no means mean
'what really happened'.

In chapter 5 of Still Harping on Daughters, *which is about dress
codes, sumptuary law and natural order, you discuss the boom in the
publication of pamphlets and treatises on the woman question between the 1550s and the 1640s and you say: ' "Controversy", however, is too strong a word for the stylised and rhetorical exchanges
these publications contain. There is a solidity and a smugness about
them (whichever camp the author attaches himself or herself to)
which betrays a lack of real urgency in the debate. It has, as readers
fresh from the "woman question" debates of the nineteenth century
are likely to overlook, a strong traditional precedent in "controversial" themes admitting of rhetorical elaboration on either side of the
question. And its rhetorical bias is betrayed by the ruthless borrow-
ing by successive generations of pamphleteers from the major origi-
nals in the field' (p. 162). Aren't you yourself making an underlying
assumption there – which itself might be seen as a rather nineteenth
century Romantic one – that stylized and rhetorical exchanges are
incompatible with real urgency?*

No, I think it's the absence of anything else in those pamphlets. That
is, their reference is exclusively other pamphlets, and in a period
which is dense with controversies in absolutely every realm, that's
generally a danger signal. If what's referred to is always the same
ruff, and if it was first used by a bestselling pamphleteer, and if we
never get another example, then one is suspicious that this is a textual
exchange which has an eye more closely to the market than to the
bone of contention. I do say elsewhere, however, that I think the

women question is a displacement of social and economic debate and therefore I would want to say, and I hope that in a fuller working out of that argument I would say, that bestselling controversies have their finger on the pulse of an issue that is worrying the community. However, I don't believe that what's worrying them is women's dress.

Your point about displacement leads on to my next question. Immediately after the paragraph I've just quoted you say: 'In trying to find an answer for why this particular issue [that is, of women usurping or affecting male attire] should find so eager an audience in this particular period, we must return, I think, to the highly sympto-matic relations between women, their dress and behaviour, and their place in the social hierarchy. Women bore the brunt of a general social uneasiness, I believe, because the fear of the inversion of authority between men and women has a primitive force which is not to be found in the threat of the upstart courtier to usurp his "right-ful" lord. To point a finger at woman's affecting of the badges of male office – dress, arms, behaviour – was to pin down a potent sym-bol of the threat to order which was perceived dimly as present in the entire shift from feudal to mercantile society' (p. 162). Now there you offer two linked explanations for the prominence of this particu-lar kind of woman question: one is this 'primitive force' and the other is the shift from feudal to mercantile society. It's the notion of that primitive force I'd like to address first of all because one can imagine it being criticized today as rather loose and untheorized.

I think you may not quite have understood it. It's not two explana-tions. The unease is a symptom of the shift – I wouldn't unfortu-nately any longer describe it as from feudalism to mercantilism, but the shift into mercantilism. Actually I don't think it's shifting, I think it's more strongly in transition in this period than we had thought while we were still vulgar Marxists. And the ease with which you can use instability to trigger fear is something which perennially can be done by invoking woman or race. Look at the British National Party.

But why does that happen? Why does an anxiety about social and economic change become focused on race or on women?

It happens because what is not sufficiently structurally clear in the shift into a trading and merchant society is how you establish hierar-chical order, and three of the clearest metaphors for the establishing of hierarchical order are those of man over woman, father over children, and king over state. They are three perennial ones that come up in controversies of this period. Remember this is a book about women, and therefore I'm drawing attention to the fact that this is *one* of the displacements. I fear that it's bound to appear in this book that it's *the* displacement, but this was a polemic in reply to people who had overly privileged this as being about the real. I would have equivalent things to say about my anxiety now about my first chapter about cross-dressing, the one that as it were disparages, in some sense, single-sex love, because after all the critics I was coming back at were absorbed with male/female relationships. I would write about it differently elsewhere. Your worry is that I don't sufficiently explain or account for why it should be *this* debate. The answer is that it isn't just this debate, it's this debate in this context. Even though my work, I hope, has got a bit more sophisticated, I continue to think that culture displaces its anxieties over order on to key relationships which have perennially figured in cultural production, and women versus men is one of them.

Do you think psychoanalysis offers a useful way of talking about that kind of displacement?

I have yet to be persuaded that a theoretical frame that comes out of late nineteenth-century Viennese culture can without a great deal of tucking and pinching be made to apply to a culture which suckled and reared its children differently. Of course I don't have to be persuaded that you can do very valuable things by using psychoanalytic theory as a frame, because with my mathematical training I know that all models which are systematically used can be turned to advantage on disparate material. But it isn't a model which yields for me the kinds of insight that I'm after, which still seem to me to be too materialist to be grasped by psychoanalysis.

In your 1989 Preface to the second edition of Still Harping on Daughters, *you make a point about agency which I'd like to take up. You say that 'in my case, the move* forwards *towards a new fusion of methodologies and materials from cultural history and text studies was made in order to retrieve* agency *for the female subject in history … Just as the social historian combs his or her archival material for the textual trace of those on the margins, so I have dredged the documents for textual evidence of the presence of women in the early modern community. Furthermore, insofar as I have been successful in giving back to her a place in contemporary events, this retrieval of agency has been achieved by my treating the individual female subject in the drama as a "cultural artifact"...Like the anthropologist, I look for the subject in history at the intersection of systems of behaviour, customs, beliefs, out of which, I consider, personal identity is constructed' (pp. viii-ix). But does the retrieval of the textual traces of the past necessarily demonstrate anything about agency, particularly if you have a view of the subject as a construction produced in the intersection of systems of behaviour, customs and beliefs? With that model, agency is superadded, not explanatorily necessary: it may be morally uplifting and politically motivating but it doesn't emerge from the traces themselves.*

But I mean agency very literally, in an almost vector form, as an account, as it were, which puts back the fact that even an obstructive object acts. Of course I was led in that direction by the new social historians and by Lawrence Stone and Keith Wrightson and Eric Hobsbawm. I would openly acknowledge their influence on that thought, particularly that of Keith Wrightson, who was my colleague at Cambridge in my last years there while I was writing that Preface. What seemed to me tricky about the historical reconstructions of women in past time was that because history, apart from social history, always privileged the successful actor, it couldn't even articulate those who stood in the way and altered the course of history. In line with my general feeling that we ought not to attribute too much romantic effect to women in this period, it is the construction of a system of influences and presences such that when a woman is in the room you can't behave as if the outcome would have been the same if she'd not been there.

In a footnote to your new Preface to Still Harping on Daughters, *you recall first hearing yourself described from a public platform in 1984 as a 'new historicist' (p. x). Is that a description you're happy to bear?*

We've adopted a form of words this year of referring to certain sorts of writing as 'what used to be called the new historicism' – one of my graduate students taught me that. It's interesting that North America needs labels for movements affirmatively, whereas in this country labels are always used derogatorily. Nobody would call themselves a poststructuralist, it's used as a term of disapproval, and I think that goes for all the critical movements here. But in North America, because intellectuals in universities are actual money earners and because job descriptions stipulate intellectual movements as well as fields of study, the label was about academic prominence. I remain a great admirer – I am teased for remaining a great admirer – of Stephen Greenblatt. I think his *Renaissance Self-Fashioning* changed the tide of academic history for Renaisance studies. One day we had three students and the next day we had 300 students, and I'm not prepared to knock that. Brilliant students now want to do Renaissance studies rather than twentieth century studies and that was due to Stephen Greenblatt. His book has all kinds of flaws, but it was written in 1980, and 1980 is a watershed. He coined the phrase new historicism. I'll accept it. I don't like cultural poetics, I'm not a cultural poeticist. I don't want to reject the new historicist label because I admire several of the practitioners, but I'm not sure that it is a coherent school and I don't think I really belong in it. I was flattered for a short time to be put there. Ultimately new historicism remains too literary for me. I think I'm just a hybrid text studies historian. I'm a Professor of English in England and a Professor of History in America. I like that.

Could we come on to your latest book, Erasmus, Man of Letters, *which argues that Erasmus's charisma was a careful and complex construction by himself and a network of his contemporaries. In your Introduction, you say the book 'has proved an unexpected one, both in its conception and in the direction of its development' (p. 3). You talked earlier in our conversation about your love of sitting in the archive doing this kind of detective work. Could you explore how this book came about?*

It's another phase in my own history. North America has provided me at regular intervals with an inspiringly supportive context for being able to be polemical, populist and scholarly. My life changed in 1974 when I went to the Society for the Humanities at Cornell University and discovered that working on the nitty-gritty of Renaissance logic could get you audiences of 50 students and the local radio station might want to talk to you about it. That somehow brought together all the facets of my personality. The struggle about whether I wanted to be Jerome in his study or Erasmus masterminding book circulation was resolved there. It was resolved more completely by Princeton, where I've been on several occasions, and in fact the Erasmus book was wholly written at Princeton. Some of the additional research was done in London and in Cambridge, but I couldn't have

formed that book in my mind and I couldn't have kept my confidence
that you could be iconoclastic and scholarly, outside that milieu. The
fact that the Princeton History Department contained Natalie Davis,
Robert Darnton, Lawrence Stone and Tony Grafton sums it up
really. As to why I came to work on Erasmus, I said it was by accident, but it wasn't by accident really. It is of enormous importance to
me at this moment to show how gendered the intellectual figure in
Western Europe is. All the work on Erasmus is about how he isn't
me, how I do everything as it were in that tradition, but how the
whole elaborate way in which he constructed a presence of the secular intellectual constructs him as male. So I think that's why I became
absorbed in the way in which this was a construction and therefore
one couldn't say it had happened by accident. When I did my inaugural lecture at the University of London on Erasmus, I projected
above myself the Metsys diptych – magnified images of Erasmus and
his friend Pieter Gilles – and as the lecture finished, one of the
graduate students in the department was stopped by a senior
member of another department who said to her: "I'm surprised Professor Jardine didn't do a feminist lecture.' She said to him: 'It *was* a
feminist lecture'.

Do you feel that gender concern comes across in the book?

I don't mind if it doesn't, because the great thing about having
become, if you like, a visible figure in intellectual life is that you then
have the luxury to have just that juxtaposition the graduate student
noticed. I think it would have been self-indulgent and would have
diminished this book to have made explicit why a woman who was
known to be *now* a prominent feminist wrote a book exclusively
about men. It had to some extent been true about the Bacon book but
it is much more so and much more self-awarely so about the Erasmus
book. In other words, I certainly knew what I was doing. I considered saying something in the Preface and discarded that, but I put
my daughter prominently into the Acknowledgements to make clear
that daughters had played their part.

*Your detective work on the way in which Erasmus's charisma was
constructed is fascinating – at moments it feels as if one is reading a
novel by a combination of Umberto Eco and Thomas Pynchon,
experiencing a sense of paranoia and disorientation at the revelation
of what might, or might not be a complex and intricate plot. This
leads me to ask what degree of consciousness we are supposed to be
attributing to those who engaged in this construction?*

If the book has anything of Eco and Pynchon in it, I'm more than happy. I think that the narrative strategy was supposed to alert the reader to the difficulty in locating the source of construction. Except in very few rather banal circumstances, I don't think I would want to venture a judgement on how consideredly or systematically Erasmus or anyone else was doing this.

At one point in the book you say: 'there is an Erasmian agenda, as it were, which sees to it that the life of the paradigm Christian textual editor and exegete conforms to the expectations of a sixteenth-century humanistic audience. In other words, it is the agenda, rather than any desire on Erasmus's own part to be seen as "like" Jerome, which draws Jerome's life away from hagiography and towards that cluster of exemplary sacred/secular activities best represented for Erasmus by the combination of Lorenzo Valla's annotations on the New Testament and his Elegantiae' *(p. 74). Could you say more about the nature of this agenda?*

The agenda is to emulate the successful dissemination of a particular set of ideas of the kind that the early Church Fathers apparently effected *vis-à-vis* Christianity. That is a model that was available to Erasmus of the extraordinary international dissemination of secondary works on the Christian corpus where as it were almost tangible figures like Jerome and Augustine are present in the study of the student studying them. But I do think the agenda is in the process of being transformed into a secular one, and of course Erasmus would have been the last person to recognize that because he hadn't even appreciated that the Reformation had taken place, let alone his own place in it. And I would love to take on the issue of Christianity and humanism because I think that my work is beginning to show that you can't talk about the Reformation separately from all of this. This kind of work has been done in the past by wonderful scholars, many of whom I've drawn on doing this book. What they don't do is see where that work is inevitably leading. I think if I have any kind of gift, it's for seeing the implications of shifts in scholarly interest. That's what's novel about the book. I always cause annoyance when I suggest those implications but there's a curious way in which then the discipline seems to accommodate them. What I'm intrigued by so far, vigorously touching wood, is that people seem prepared to consider these implications seriously in this book of mine for the first time, as it comes off the press so to speak. I love the reviews I'm getting because they are by people who struggle with the book and are reluctant to accept its implications. It's very precious to me when someone like Anthony Levi, who is not of my party as it were theoretically or anywhere, is struggling because he feels, I have to take this on board, I just don't like what it's saying. He's worried about what this will do for the images of these hallowed figures (*Literary Review*, no.180, June 1993, pp. 10-12). That's a new thing for me. It's both flattering and very heartwarming. Not surprisingly, the one real hack review I had in the *Evening Standard* just says, she has to be wrong, course she's wrong, which you would expect.

In your Introduction to the Erasmus book, you say: 'We twentieth-century advancers of learning have altogether lost any such confidence [of the kind projected by the Eramus charisma] in grand designs. We are painfully aware of an apparently flagging eminence, a diminished stature, a waning of a world in which men of letters made the agenda, and worldly men then strove to pursue it.' (p. 4). You continue in this rather eloquent vein, and then you partly retract it by saying that there never really was a golden age, that this is nostalgia. Perhaps there's some ambivalence there. You have, as you've said, a scholarly formation and a love of scholarship. In some ways, you're a scholar of quite a traditional kind, and one might thus see you as somehow sharing that sense that the humanities are not what they used to be. But in many of your public statements that I've read – for example about the future of literary studies – you come across as a very optimistic progressive. What then are your feelings about the position and the nature of the humanities today?

I think what I want to say about Erasmus and myself is that engagement in the contemporary is a vital part of scholarship. I want to retrieve that energy and that desire for change. When I talk about a a flagging confidence on the part of scholars, I mean the retreat of scholars into minutiae, their plangency about how nobody understands them any more, how nobody wants to do the work. I recall Tom Greene at a dinner party saying that at Yale in the fifties you had very clever students and that now nobody wants to put in the hard work. I said to him, don't you think maybe that comparative literature's got rather boring and that's why they don't want to do it? It isn't engaged with anything. I feel that my own persona is like that of Erasmus in a total engagement in the here and now, in its politics, in its controversy, and in its desire for change, coupled with the privilege of having the in-depth training which allows you to pursue that through in minute detail.

Could we take up one particular issue here? You're a Latinist posses-
sed of a classic literacy which is increasingly marginal in modern edu-
cation. There is an argument – posed eloquently by George Steiner –
that if you lose that classic literacy, you also lose a whole range of
resonance and allusion in English writing from Chaucer through to
Derek Walcott. Do you regret the now virtual disappearance from
curricula in schools and universities of that kind of classical training?

No, and I would give you a cogent account of why that is not a position to which I would ascribe. The sort of central European that
George Steiner is – enormously admirable – is the displaced and
transient member of an intellectual diaspora who is therefore quite
explicitly not any longer politically engaged. He's engaged in the
intellectual sphere in about that domain which is like the controversies about dress code and sumptuary law in the early modern period.
It's conducted in an extraordinarily rarefied atmosphere. It doesn't
ground itself in any particular place where you want change to happen in the here and now and in the politically actual. I know that any
graduate student of mine who needs Latin can get it up in six months,
that the pedagogic tools like Francis Cairnes's computer programme
which will allow them to have access to it mean that it's irrelevant
whether they've got it. To try and give it to a nine-year old child when
they don't need it and don't know what it's for, is just boring and
tedious and probably will turn them off it for life. So tradition as formative seems to me to be somewhat spurious. I believe in being
grounded – this is a bit Habermasian – in the overlapping circles, the
life-worlds which you inhabit. I'm always told I've invented Habermas and that I'm a Jardine Habermasist, but my Habermas I ascribe
to, namely that you inhabit life worlds and if you're Indo-Caribbean,
Afro-Caribbean, South-East Asian, you carry with you bits of your
life world and then you engage with the life world in which you find
yourself. Derek Walcott and Toni Morrison come out of those sorts
of intersections. To have taught them something culturally specific at
school seems to me not quite to the point.

Could we move on to the teaching of literature today? On Sunday
you were interviewing Gore Vidal for Radio 3's Making Waves
programme, and there's an interesting moment when he says: 'I have
observed in my lifetime…that as we lost the Common Reader we
lost the Common Critic, and English departments have now pretty
much got rid of literature itself and replaced it with literary theory.
Well, I'm not going to be thrilled by that'. At this point, you interject

strongly 'But we haven't', and the conversation then takes another turn. Nonetheless there is a widespread perception that literary texts have been displaced either by theory or by being dispersed into a whole range of other texts or discourses. When I interviewed Frank Kermode, he said that 'the abolition of literature is definitely on the agenda' (see p. 36 above). Would you like to take up that point now?

Gore Vidal and Frank Kermode are not contemporaries but they're close in terms of attitude. The signal there is the death of the Common Reader. There isn't a Common Reader any more. There are readers from overlapping circles. The Common Reader was a wonderful security blanket presence, namely that of the nicely self-educated, maybe grammar school boy. The Common Reader is a grammar school boy, I think, and he's no longer the unique reader. You can't address your classroom studies to that unique reader any more, so the strategies used in academic departments of literature have much more to do with the diverse cultural backgrounds of their student population and with a lack of conviction on the part of many of us that we have any self-evident right to claim the priority of one tradition. All of that seems to me to be very liberating. Gore Vidal is terribly good on every other topic except classrooms. Unlike George Steiner, he is deeply engaged with the political at the everyday level, and that's why my response to that exchange was disappointment that he nevertheless has a weak spot for old literary studies. My riposte to Gore Vidal was that I doubt we read any fewer literary texts and I suspect we read rather more in depth. John Barrell once said to me what a terrible task students now have to master the range of kinds of writing, types of approach, and disciplinary frames that you need today to become competent in literature – what a contrast that was with the sixties. The students are better trained than they ever have been. It's now a discipline which ranks – I've said it before – with philosophy in the complexity of thought, the self-awareness and the intellectual rigour that it expects of its students. I see nothing to complain about. I would have to say that we now expect a student to read the whole of *Clarissa* whereas Cambridge expected us to read a bit. In other words I think the idea that English departments have got rid of literature is one of those convenient falsehoods and I'm not quite sure what it's supposed to serve. My optimism is enormous about the field that I'm in.

But haven't you yourself suggested one of the problems by pointing to this enormous extension of the field – that the range of possible texts and of theoretical and critical approaches means that the subject has lost its coherence? It may acquire a coherence at specific institutions like your own, Queen Mary and Westfield College, but it's lost it more generally and it has also in some sense become cut off – except perhaps as an entertaining spectacle, say in David Lodge's novels – from people who might otherwise be interested in reading and thinking about literature.

I don't feel that. It seems to me simply not to reflect my experience and I do after all move around departments of literature a lot. I think what is maybe misleading is that because of the range of possibilities for any student entering the discipline we now, like philosophy, tend to teach the fundamental skills and methods needed for going to any chosen area and accessing it. In other words we try to prepare students for whatever their chosen area of study is. Now that is what philosophy does and it's what sociology or anthropology do to some extent. Literary study is much more like an 'ology' now in that it's a professional training from which you will embark into whatever field you subsequently move into. Hence the misunderstanding, I think, about how much grounding is given, as opposed to reading your way systematically from Chaucer via Shakespeare, Spenser, Milton, Pope and whoever down to now.

If you have courses centred on a body of skills and concepts rather than a body of texts, doesn't that mean that you don't necessarily have to read any of the old conventional literary texts at all?

No. To go right back to the beginning of our discussion, I said that the Renaissance studies I did had absorbed theory, and therefore students learnt the complexity of the theory through practice. Now that is the brilliant technique that's used in all good English departments. Of course you don't teach Foucault. You take eighteenth century literature and you look at it through the prism of Foucault. You always set your students to read literary texts and then you engage with literary texts with a particular set of skills. Most progressive departments don't have an isolated theory course. Only conservative institutions have add-on theory. So Cambridge has add-on theory, but Queen Mary and Westfield College doesn't have a theory course anywhere. It only has the practice of reading informed by a particular theoretical frame which will be made explicit. I do think that's a profound misunderstanding and that you'll find that any literary critic over 45 will have difficulty with that, while a literary critic under 40 will find it easy to grasp.

You talked earlier about your belief in an intrinsic relation between literary studies and politics, about your political activities and commitments, and about What's Left, *the book you wrote with Julia Swindells about some of the problems of socialism. In a recent* Times Higher Education Supplement *special on English teaching, you're quoted – I don't know how accurate this quote is – as describing yourself as 'a plain old-fashioned radical socialist' (11 June 1993, p. 17). But all those terms now beg questions: what do they mean today?*

That was a joke in that when your back's against the wall, you revert, and I revert probably to a vulgar materialist. I still comfortably believe in socialism. I don't have any of the problems some socialists have about the demise of Russia. Because I'm an intellectual historian, it doesn't seem to me that, because the practice failed in one location, that means I have to discard it as an aspiration. I probably didn't say 'radical', that's been put in, but I think I did say 'plain old-fashioned socialist'. 'Old-fashioned' means that however many times I go into an election booth with an intellectual conviction that I ought to do something strategic, I always vote for the Labour candidate. I still believe in a party. I am not a freethinker politically. That shows that I'm a died-in-the-wool politician. I once was on the 'B' list for a parliamentary seat and decided after serious reflection, mostly with Julia Swindells, that I didn't think I could toe the party line enough day-to-day. But I still believe in the party as the only way that you can help the poor and the disadvantaged. I really do believe in group consciousness. I really do believe that individualism is a terrible stumbling block in effecting change on behalf of the disadvantaged. It's a luxury of the élite that we cling to as intellectuals, but I have no faith in it as guiding our future action, and I think that Conservatism has wickedly fragmented us into a collection of self-interested and self-absorbed individuals. So I'm old-fashioned in the sense that I can't be persuaded that anything other than group action will effect change. I'm modernizing within the Labour Party in that of course, in any of the discussion groups I'm involved in, the position of women is crucial, the position of British nationals who are not Anglo-Saxon, and so on. My relationship to the unions is difficult, although of course I belong to my own and wouldn't dream of not doing so. I'm nearly 50, so I belong to the sixties generation that did believe that we wanted political change and that this could only be effected by groups, and the group that I subscribe to is still the Labour Party.

In the remarkable range of your activities – scholar, socialist, feminist, teacher, broadcaster – you might be seen as a modern Renaissance figure. Could I ask, in conclusion, how you yourself would define the links between all these Lisa Jardines?

First of all, I think it does matter to be a woman. I don't think a woman believes in disinterestedness. Her whole life has been lived under the pressure of gender. Even at the stage I'm at, I still can't walk into a room without having to establish that my gender does not exempt me from being taken seriously, and it'll happen for the whole of my life. Now that doesn't happen to men. So you live with this. I think it's crucial that one's network is probably more diverse than the corresponding networks that men belong to, for that same reason. There are somewhat fewer of us in my generation, though that won't last long, and we stick together and we protect each other's rear on public platforms. I'm now part of a network that I absolutely love of other successful women. Probably the women I admire most at the moment are Natalie Davis the historian, Helena Kennedy the QC, Michèle Roberts the novelist and Julia Swindells the political activist. All of them are part of my everyday life. I've left out there the lesbian separatists, Suzanne Kappeler who's one of my old friends. It's all always there, so your profession is inevitably tied in with that. I think again a woman doesn't separate her profession from her persona, and the separation of private and public has proved such a catastrophe historically for women that most prominent women will not observe it. I will not leave my children out of public debate. I drive the BBC crazy by referring to my entire life rather than pretending to be depersonalized. The bottom line is that I can never be universal man, so I don't actually want to be called a Renaissance figure because that's always universal man. What I am is an absolutely typical representative of intellectual curiosity in the late twentieth century and of a passionate commitment to change.

Bibliography

Christine Brooke-Rose

FICTION
The Languages of Love. London: Secker and Warburg, 1957.
The Sycamore Tree. London: Secker and Warburg, 1958.
The Dear Deceit. London: Secker and Warburg, 1960.
The Middlemen: A Satire. London: Secker and Warburg, 1961.
Out. London: Michael Joseph, 1964.
Such. London: Michael Joseph, 1966.
Between. London: Michael Joseph, 1968.
Go When You See the Green Man Walking (short stories). London: Michael Joseph, 1970.
Thru. London: Hamish Hamilton, 1975.
Amalgamemnon. Manchester: Carcanet, 1984.
The Christine Brooke-Rose Omnibus: Four Novels: Out. Such. Between. Thru. Manchester: Carcanet, 1986.
Xorandor. Manchester: Carcanet, 1986.
Verbivore. Manchester: Carcanet, 1990.
Textermination. Manchester: Carcanet, 1991.

NON-FICTION
A Grammar of Metaphor. London: Secker and Warburg, 1958.
A ZBC of Ezra Pound. London: Faber, 1971.
A Rhetoric of the Unreal: Studies in Narrative and Structure, Especially of the Fantastic. Cambridge: Cambridge University Press, 1981.
Stories, theories and things. Cambridge: Cambridge University Press, 1991. Chapter 12 is called 'Palimpsest History' and was originally a paper delivered at Cambridge following Umberto Eco's Tanner Lectures of March 1990. Another version of 'Palimpsest History' was published as Chapter 6 of Umberto Eco, with Richard Rorty, Jonathan Culler and Christine Brooke-Rose *Interpretation and Overinterpretation*. Cambridge: Cambridge University Press, 1992.

Frank Kermode

NON-FICTION
Romantic Image. London: Routledge and Kegan Paul, 1957; 1961.
Wallace Stevens. London: Oliver and Boyd, 1960.
Puzzles and Epiphanies: Essays and Reviews 1958-1961. London: Routledge and Kegan Paul, 1962.
The Sense of an Ending: Studies in the Theory of Fiction. The Mary Flexner Lectures, 1965. Oxford: Oxford University Press, 1967; 1968.
Continuities. London: Routledge and Kegan Paul, 1968.
Shakespeare, Spenser, Donne: Renaissance Essays. London: Routledge and Kegan Paul, 1971. Republished as: *Renaissance Essays: Shakespeare, Spenser, Donne*. London: Fontana, 1973.
Modern Essays. London: Fontana, 1971.
Lawrence. London: Fontana, 1973.
The Classic: Literary Images of Permanence and Change. The T.S. Eliot Memorial Lectures, 1973. London: Faber, 1975. With corrections and new Preface by the author: Cambridge, Massachusetts: Harvard University Press, 1983.
The Genesis of Secrecy: On the Interpretation of Narrative. The Charles Eliot Norton Lectures, 1977-78. Cambridge, Massachussetts: Harvard University Press, 1979.
Essays on Fiction 1971-82. London: Routledge and Kegan Paul, 1983. Published in the USA as: *The Art of Telling: Essays on Fiction*. Cambridge, Massachussetts: Harvard University Press, 1983.
Forms of Attention. The Wellek Library Lectures, 1984. Chicago: University of Chicago Press, 1985.
History and Value: The Clarendon Lectures and the Northcliffe Lectures 1987. Oxford: Clarendon Press, 1988; 1989.
Poetry, Narrative, History. The Bucknell Lectures in Literary Theory. Oxford: Blackwell, 1990.
An Appetite for Poetry: Essays in Literary Interpretation. London: Collins, 1989.
The Uses of Error. London: Collins, 1991.

ESSAYS AND ARTICLES
'Burke to Orwell'. Review of Raymond Williams, *Culture and Society* (1958). *Encounter*, vol. 12, no. 1, January 1959, pp. 86-8.
'Peter Ure 1919-1969'. C.J. Rawson ed, *Yeats and Anglo-Irish Literature*. Liverpool: Liverpool University Press, 1974, pp. 1-39.
'On Being an Enemy of Humanity'. *Raritan*, vol. 2, no. 2, 1982, pp. 87-102. Response to Helen Gardner's attack in *In Defence of the Imagination* (1982).
'Introduction' to Stephen Haggard, *Nya* (first published London: Faber, 1938). Oxford: Oxford University Press, 1988, pp. 1-8.

Karl Miller

NON-FICTION
Cockburn's Millenium. London: Duckworth, 1975.
Doubles: Studies in Literary History. Oxford: Oxford University Press, 1985. Oxford University Press paperback edn, with corrections: 1987.
Authors. Oxford: Clarendon Press, 1989.
Rebecca's Vest: A Memoir. London: Hamish Hamilton, 1993.

EDITED
Writing in England Today: The Last Fifteen Years. London: Penguin, 1968.

ESSAYS AND ARTICLES
'The *London Review of Books*'. C.J. Rawson ed, *The Yearbook of English Studies: Literary Periodicals Special Number*, vol. 16. London: Modern Humanities Research Association, 1986. Pp. 203-12.

A.S. Byatt

FICTION
Shadow of a Sun. London: Chatto and Windus, 1964.
The Game. London: Chatto and Windus, 1967.
The Virgin in the Garden. London: Chatto and Windus, 1978.
Still Life. London: Chatto and Windus, 1985.
Possession: A Romance. London: Chatto and Windus, 1990.
Sugar and Other Stories. London: Chatto and Windus, 1987.
Angels and Insects. London: Chatto and Windus, 1992.
The Matisse Stories. London: Chatto and Windus, 1993.

NON-FICTION
Degrees of Freedom: The Novels of Iris Murdoch. 1965.
Wordsworth and Coleridge in their Time. London: Thomas Nelson, 1970. Republished as: *Unruly Times: Wordsworth and Coleridge in their Time*. London: Hogarth Press, 1989.
Passions of the Mind: Selected Writings. London: Chatto and Windus, 1991. Includes the 'Nature Morte' essay, first published in David Kelley and Isabelle Llasera eds, *Cross-References: Modern French Theory and the practice of criticism*. London: Society for French Studies, 1986, pp. 95-102.

George Steiner

FICTION
Anno Domini. London: Faber, 1964.
The Portage to San Cristobal of A.H.. London: Faber, 1981.
Proofs and Three Parables. London: Faber, 1992.

NON-FICTION
Tolstoy or Dostoevsky: An Essay in Contrast. London: Faber, 1960; 1980.
The Death of Tragedy. London: Faber, 1961; 1963.
Language and Silence: Essays 1958-1966. London: Faber, 1967. 2nd edn, with new Preface by author, 1985. Abridged edn, Penguin, 1969.
Extraterritorial: Papers on Literature and the Language Revolution. London: Faber, 1972.
In Bluebeard's Castle: Some Notes towards the Redefinition of Culture. London: Faber, 1971.
The Sporting Scene: White Knights of Reykjavik. London: Faber, 1973.
After Babel: Aspects of Language and Translation. Oxford: Oxford University Press, 1975. 2nd edn, with amendments and new Preface by the author, 1992.
On Difficulty and Other Essays. Oxford: Oxford University Press, 1978, 1980.
Heidegger. Modern Masters series. London: Fontana, 1978.
Antigones. Oxford: Clarendon Press, 1984.
George Steiner: A Reader. London: Penguin, 1984.
A Reading against Shakespeare: The W.P. Ker Lecture for 1986. Glasgow: University of Glasgow, 1986.
Real Presences: Is There Anything in What We Say? London: Faber, 1989.

ESSAYS AND ARTICLES
'What is an Educated Man Now?' *Conference*, vol. 12, no. 1, February 1975, pp. 5-10.
Untitled contribution to symposium on 'Modern literary theory: its place in teaching'. *Times Literary Supplement*, no. 4062, 6 February 1981, p. 135.
'Ecstasies, not arguments'. Review of translations of Mircea Eliade's *Journals*, vols. 1-4 and *Youth without Youth and Other Novellas*. *Times Literary Supplement*, no. 4565, 28 September-4 October 1990, pp. 1015-16.

Bernard Bergonzi

POETRY
Descartes and the Animals: Poems 1948-54. London. Platform, 1954.
An English Sequence. Manchester: Manchester Institute of Contemporary Arts, 1966.
Years: Sixteen Poems. Hitchin: The Mandeville Press, 1979.

FICTION
The Roman Persuasion: A Novel. London: Weidenfeld and Nicolson, 1981.

NON-FICTION
The Early H.G. Wells: A Study of the Scientific Romances. Manchester: Manchester University Press, 1961.
Heroes' Twilight: A Study of the Literature of the Great War. London: Constable, 1965. 2nd edn, London: Macmillan, 1980.
The Situation of the Novel. London: Macmillan, 1970. Penguin, 1972. 2nd edn, London: Macmillan, 1979.
T.S. Eliot. Masters of World Literature series. London: Macmillan, 1972. 2nd edn, 1980.
The Turn of a Century: Essays on Victorian and Modern English Literature. London: Macmillan, 1973.
Gerard Manley Hopkins. London: Macmillan, 1977.
Reading the Thirties: Texts and Contexts. London: Macmillan, 1978.
The Myth of Modernism and Twentieth Century Literature. Brighton: Harvester, 1986.
Exploding English: Criticism, Theory, Culture. Oxford: Clarendon Press, 1990.
Wartime and Aftermath: English Literature and its Background 1939-60. Oxford: Oxford University Press, 1993.

EDITED
Innovations: Essays on Art and Ideas. London: Macmillan, 1968.
T.S. Eliot: Four Quartets: A Casebook. London: Macmillan, 1969.

David Caute

FICTION
At Fever Pitch. London: Deutsch, 1959.
Comrade Jacob. London: Deutsch, 1966.
The Decline of the West. London: Deutsch, 1966.
The Occupation. London: Deutsch, 1971. Vol. 3 of *The Confrontation* trilogy.
The K-Factor. London: Michael Joseph, 1983.
News from Nowhere. London: Hamish Hamilton, 1986.
Veronica or The Two Nations. London: Hamish Hamilton, 1989.
The Women's Hour. London: Paladin, 1991.

DRAMA
The Demonstration. London: Deutsch, 1970. Vol. 1 of *The Confrontation* trilogy.

NON-FICTION
Communism and the French Intellectuals 1914-1960. London: Deutsch, 1964.
The Left in Europe since 1789. 1966.

Fanon. Modern Masters series. London: Fontana, 1970.

The Illusion: An Essay on Politics, Theatre and the Novel. London: Deutsch, 1971. Vol. 2 of *The Confrontation* trilogy.

The Fellow-Travellers: A Postcript to the Enlightenment. London: Weidenfeld and Nicolson, 1973. Revised edn, with new subtitle: *Intellectual Friends of Communism*. New Haven: Yale, 1988.

Collisions: Essays and Reviews. London: Quartet 1974. Pp. 12-40 contains 'Crisis in All Souls: A Case History in Reform' originally published in *Encounter*, vol. 26, no. 3, March 1966, pp. 3-15. In *Collisions*, 'Crisis in All Souls' is followed, on pp. 40-5, by a 'Postscript, January 1973'.

Cuba, Yes? London: Secker and Warburg, 1974.

The Great Fear: The Anti-Communist Purge under Truman and Eisenhower. London: Secker and Warburg, 1978.

Under the Skin: The Death of White Rhodesia. London: Allen Lane, 1983.

The Espionage of the Saints: Two Essays on Silence and the State. London: Hamish Hamilton, 1986.

Sixty-Eight: The Year of the Barricades. London: Hamish Hamilton, 1988.

Joseph Losey: A Revenge on Life. London: Faber, January 1994.

FORTHCOMING (FICTION)
Dr Orwell and Mr Blair. London: Weidenfeld and Nicolson, June 1994.

Terry Eagleton

FICTION
Saints and Scholars. London: Verso, 1987.

DRAMA
Saint Oscar. Derry: Field Day, 1989.

FILMSCRIPT
With Derek Jarman. *Wittgenstein: The Terry Eagleton Script, The Derek Jarman Film*. London: BFI, 1993.

NON-FICTION
Shakespeare and Society: Critical Studies in Shakespearean Drama. London: Chatto and Windus, 1967.

Exiles and Emigrés: Studies in Modern Literature. London: Chatto and Windus, 1970.

Myths of Power: A Marxist Study of the Brontës. London: Macmillan, 1975. 2nd edn, 1988.

Criticism and Ideology: A Study in Marxist Literary Theory. London: New Left Books, 1976. Verso, 1978.

Walter Benjamin or Towards a Revolutionary Criticism. London: Verso, 1981.

The Rape of Clarissa: Writing, Sexuality and Class Struggle in Samuel Richardson. Oxford: Blackwell, 1982.

Literary Theory: An Introduction. Oxford: Blackwell, 1983.

The Function of Criticism: From The Spectator *to Post-Structuralism.* London: Verso, 1984.

William Shakespeare. Rereading Literature series. Oxford: Blackwell, 1986.

Against the Grain: Essays 1975-1985. London: Verso, 1986.

Nationalism: Irony and Commitment. Derry: Field Day Theatre Company, 1988.

The Ideology of the Aesthetic. Oxford: Blackwell, 1990.

The Significance of Theory. The Bucknell Lectures in Literary Theory. Oxford: Blackwell, 1990.

Ideology: An Introduction. London: Verso, 1991.

The Crisis of Contemporary Culture. An Inaugural Lecture Delivered before the University of Oxford on 27 November 1992. Oxford: Clarendon Press, 1993.

INTERVIEW

'The Practice of Possibility'. Terry Eagleton interviews Raymond Williams. *New Statesman*, vol. 114, no. 2941, 7 August 1987, pp. 19-21. This interview is collected, under the title of 'The Politics of Hope: An Interview', in *Raymond Williams: Critical Perspectives*, ed. Terry Eagleton, pp. 176-183. Cambridge: Polity Press, 1989.

Roger Scruton

FICTION

Fortnight's Anger. Manchester: Carcanet, 1981.

Francesca. London: Sinclair-Stevenson, 1991.

A Dove Descending. London: Sinclair-Stevenson, 1991.

Xanthippic Dialogues: Comprising: Xanthippe's Republic; Perictione's Parmenides; *and* Xanthippe's Laws; *together with a version, probably spurious, of* Phryne's Symposium. Subtitle on dustjacket: *A Philosophical Fiction.* London: Sinclair-Stevenson, 1993.

NON-FICTION

Art and Imagination: A Study in the Philosophy of Mind. London: Methuen, 1964. 2nd edn, 1982.

The Aesthetics of Architecture. London: Methuen, 1979.

The Meaning of Conservatism. London: Macmillan, 1980. 2nd edn, 1984.

From Descartes to Wittgenstein: A Short History of Modern Philosophy. London: Routledge, 1981.

The Politics of Culture and Other Essays. Manchester: Carcanet, 1981.

Kant. Past Masters series. Oxford: Oxford University Press, 1982.

A Dictionary of Political Thought. London: Macmillan, 1982.

The Aesthetic Understanding: Essays in the Philosophy of Art and Culture. Manchester: Carcanet, 1983.

Thinkers of the New Left. Harlow: Longman, 1985.

Sexual Desire: A Philosophical Investigation. London: Weidenfeld and Nicolson, 1986.

Spinoza. Past Masters series. Oxford: Oxford University Press, 1986.

A Land Held Hostage. London: Claridge, 1987.

Untimely Tracts: Articles Originally Published in The Times. London: Macmillan, 1987.

The Philosopher on Dover Beach: Essays. Manchester: Carcanet, 1990.

EDITED

Conservative Thinkers: Essays from the Salisbury Review. London: Claridge, 1988.

Conservative Thoughts: Essays from the Salisbury Review. London: Claridge, 1988.

FORTHCOMING

The Classical Vernacular: Essays on Architecture. Manchester: Carcanet, 1994.

Modern Philosophy. London: Sinclair-Stevenson, 1994.

Robert Hewison

NON-FICTION

John Ruskin: The Argument of the Eye. London: Thames and Hudson, 1976.

Under Siege: Literary Life in London 1939-1945. London: Wiedenfeld and Nicolson, 1977.

Ruskin and Venice. London: Thames and Hudson, 1978.

Irreverence, Scurrility, Profanity, Vilification and Licentious Abuse: Monty Python – The Case Against. London: Eyre Methuen, 1981.

In Anger: Culture in the Cold War 1945-60. London: Weidenfeld and Nicolson, 1981. Revised edn, Methuen, 1988.

Footlights: A Hundred Years of Cambridge Comedy. London: Methuen, 1983.

Too Much: Art and Society in the Sixties 1960-75. London: Methuen, 1986; 1988.

The Heritage Industry: Britain in a Climate of Decline. London: Methuen, 1987.

Future Tense: A New Art for the Nineties. London: Methuen, 1990.

Stephen Heath

NON-FICTION

The Nouveau Roman: A Study in the Practice of Writing. London: Elek Books, 1972.

Vertige du déplacement: lecture de Barthes. Paris: Fayard, 1972.

Questions of Cinema. London: Macmillan, 1981.

The Sexual Fix. London: Macmillan, 1982.

Gustave Flaubert: Madame Bovary. Landmarks of World Literature series. Cambridge: Cambridge University Press, 1992.

ESSAYS AND ARTICLES

'Ambiviolences: notes pour la lecture de Joyce (I)'. *Tel Quel*, no. 50, Summer 1972, pp. 22-43 and *Tel Quel*, no. 51, Autumn 1972, pp. 64-76. English trans. by Stephen Heath in Derek Attridge and Daniel Ferrer, eds, *Post-Structuralist Joyce.* Cambridge: Cambridge University Press, 1974, pp. 31-68.

With Philippe Sollers. *Finnegans Wake* (extract). *Tel Quel*, no 54, Summer 1973, pp. 19-24.

'Théâtre du langage'. *Critique*, no 331, December 1974, pp. 1053-1081.

'Changer de langue'. *Magazine littéraire*, February 1975, pp. 18-19.

'Film and System: Terms of Analysis. Part I'. *Screen*, vol. 16, no. 1, Spring 1975, pp. 7-77. 'Part II'. *Screen*. vol 16, no. 2, Summer 1975, pp. 91-113. Contains analysis of Orson Welles's film *Touch of Evil* (1953). Sections reprinted in Terry Comito ed, *Touch of Evil.* New Brunswick: Rutgers University Press, 1984 pp. 259-74.

'Difference'. *Screen.* vol. 19. no. 3, Autumn 1978, pp. 51-112.

EDITED

With Colin MacCabe and Christopher Prendergast. *Signs of the Times: Introductory Readings in Textual Semiotics.* Cambridge: Instantprint, 1971.

Barthes, Roland. *Image-Music-Text.* Selected and trans. Stephen Heath. London: Fontana, 1977.

With Teresa de Lauretis. *The Cinematic Apparatus.* London: Macmillan, 1980. 2nd edn, 1985.

Brian (C.B.) Cox

POETRY

Every Common Sight. London: London Magazine Editions, 1981.

Two-Headed Monster. Manchester: Carcanet, 1985.

Collected Poems. Manchester: Carcanet, 1993.

NON-FICTION

The Free Spirit: A Study of Liberal Humanism in the Novels of George Eliot, Henry James, E.M. Forster, Virginia Woolf, Angus Wilson. Oxford: Oxford University Press, 1963.

Joseph Conrad: The Modern Imagination. London: Dent, 1974.
With Raymond Williams. *The Arts Council: Politics and Policies.* 1981
W.E. Williams Memorial Lecture. London: Arts Council, 1981.
Cox on Cox: An English Curriculum for the 1990s. London: Hodder and
Stoughton, 1991.
The Great Betrayal. London: Chapmans, 1992.

ESSAYS AND ARTICLES
'Editorial'. *Critical Quarterly*, vol. 3, no. 4, Winter 1961, pp. 291-2.
'Editorial'. *Critical Quarterly*, vol. 4, no. 4, Winter 1962, pp. 291-2.
With A.R. Jones. 'After the Tranquilized Fifties: Notes on Sylvia Plath and
James Baldwin'. *Critical Quarterly*, vol. 6, no. 2, Summer 1964, pp.
107-22.
'Editorial'. *Critical Quarterly*, vol. 6, no. 3, Autumn 1964, p. 195.
With A.E. Dyson. 'Word in the Desert'. *Critical Quarterly*, vol. 10, nos. 1-2,
Spring and Summer 1968, pp. 1-7.
'Pop Goes the Poetry'. *Critical Quarterly*, vol. 10, no. 4, Winter 1968, p. 307.
'Editorial'. *Critical Quarterly*, vol. 13, no. 3, Autumn 1971, pp. 195-8.
'Editorial'. On the Cox Report. *Critical Quarterly*, vol. 32, no. 4, Winter
1990, pp. 1-6.

EDITED
With A.E. Dyson. *Black Paper One: Fight for Education: A Special Issue of*
Critical Survey. London: Critical Quarterly Society, 1969.
With A.E. Dyson. *Black Paper Two: The Crisis in Education: A Special Issue*
of Critical Survey. London: Critical Quarterly Society, 1969.
With A.E. Dyson. *Black Paper Three: Goodbye Mr Short: A Special Issue of*
Critical Survey. London: Critical Quarterly Society, 1969.
With A.E. Dyson. *The Black Papers on Education.* Revised edn. Contains
selected papers from Black Papers One, Two and Three. London: Davis-
Poynter, 1971.
With Rhodes Boyson. *Black Paper 1975: The Fight for Education.* London:
Dent, 1975.
With Rhodes Boyson. *Black Paper 1977.* London: Temple Smith, 1977.
The Cox Report: Department of Education and Science and the Welsh
Office. *English for Ages 5 to 16: Proposals of the Secretary of State for*
Education and the Secretary of State for Wales. Otherwise known as the
Cox Report. London: HMSO, 1989.

Catherine Belsey

NON-FICTION
Critical Practice. London: Methuen, 1980.
The Subject of Tragedy: Identity and Difference in Renaissance Drama.
London: Methuen, 1985.

John Milton: Language, Gender, Power. Rereading Literature series. Oxford: Blackwell, 1988.

ESSAYS AND ARTICLES
'A Space in the Syllabus?' *LTP: Journal of Literature Teaching Politics*. No. 1, 1982. Cardiff: University College Cardiff, pp. 58-65.
'Literature, History, Politics'. *Literature and History*, vol. 9, no. 1, Spring 1983, pp. 17-27.
'Anti-Imperative: Questioning the Old Order'. *PN Review* 48, vol. 12, no. 4, 1985, pp. 26-8.
'Towards Cultural History – in Theory and Practice'. *Textual Practice*, vol. 3, no. 2, Summer 1989, pp. 159-71.

FORTHCOMING
The Metaphysics of Desire. Oxford: Blackwell, 1994.

Marina Warner

FICTION
In a Dark Wood. London: Weidenfeld and Nicolson, 1977.
The Skating Party. London: Weidenfeld and Nicolson, 1982.
The Lost Father. London: Chatto and Windus, 1988.
Indigo or, Mapping the Waters. London: Chatto and Windus, 1992.
The Mermaids in the Basement. Stories. London: Chatto and Windus, 1993.

NON-FICTION
The Dragon Empress: The Life and Times of Tz'u-hsi 1851-1908, Empress Dowager of China. London: Weidenfeld and Nicolson, 1972.
Alone of All Her Sex: the Myth and Cult of the Virgin Mary. London: Weidenfeld and Nicolson, 1976.
Joan of Arc: the Image of Female Heroism. London: Weidenfeld and Nicolson, 1981; Penguin, 1983.
Monuments and Maidens: the Allegory of the Female Form. London: Weidenfeld and Nicolson, 1985; Picador, 1987.
Into the Dangerous World. Subtitle on front cover: *Some Reflections on Childhood and its Costs*. Counterblast pamphlet no. 5. London: Chatto and Windus, 1989.
'Imagining a Democratic Culture'. A Manchester Paper. London: Charter 88 Enterprises, 1991.

ESSAYS AND ARTICLES
'A Few Thoughts about Europe and its Legacy'. *PN Review* 82, vol. 18, no. 2, November/December 1991, pp. 15-17.

FORTHCOMING
From the Beast to the Blonde: On Fairy Tales and their Tellers. London:
 Chatto and Windus, 1994/5.
Managine Monsters: Six Myths of our Time. The BBC Reith Lectures, 1994.

Donald Davie

POETRY
Collected Poems. Manchester: Carcanet, 1990. Contains: *Brides of Reason*
 (1955); *A Winter Talent and Other Poems* (1957); poems from *New and
 Selected Poems* (1961); *A Sequence for Francis Parkman* (1961); *Events
 and Wisdoms* (1964); *Poems of 1962-1963*; *Essex Poems* (1969); *More
 Essex Poems* (1964-1968); *Los Angeles Poems* (1968-1969); *Six Epistles
 to Eva Hesse* (1970); *The Shires* (1974); *In the Stopping Train and Other
 Poems* (1977); *Three for Water-Music* (1981); *The Battered Wife and
 Other Poems (1982); To Scorch or Freeze* (1988); *Uncollected Poems*
 (1990); *Goodbye to the USA*.

CRITICISM
Purity of Diction in English Verse. London: Chatto and Windus, 1952.
Articulate Energy: An Inquiry into the Syntax of English Poetry. 1955. 2nd
 edn, 1976.
Purity of Diction in English Verse and Articulate Energy. With new
 Foreword by the author. London: Penguin, 1992.
The Heyday of Sir Walter Scott. London: Routledge and Kegan Paul, 1961.
Ezra Pound: Poet as Sculptor. London: Routledge and Kegan Paul, 1965.
 Now included in *Studies in Ezra Pound* (see below).
Thomas Hardy and British Poetry. London: Routledge, 1973.
Pound. Modern Masters series. London: Fontana, 1976.
The Poet in the Imaginary Museum: Essays of Two Decades. Manchester:
 Carcanet, 1977.
*A Gathered Church: The Literature of the English Dissenting Interest 1700-
 1930*. The Clark Lectures, 1976. London: Routledge, 1978.
Trying to Explain. Poets on Poetry series. Ann Arbor: University of Michi-
 gan Press, 1979.
*Dissentient Voice. The Ward-Phillips Lectures for 1980 with Some Related
 Pieces*. Ward-Phillips Lectures in Language and Literature, Volume 11.
 Notre Dame, Indiana: University of Notre Dame Press, 1982.
Czeslaw Milosz and the Insufficiency of Lyric. Cambridge: Cambridge Uni-
 versity Press, 1986.
Under Briggflatts: A History of Poetry in Great Britain 1960-1988. Man-
 chester: Carcanet, 1989.
Slavic Excursions: Essays on Russian and Polish Literature. Manchester:
 Carcanet, 1990.
Studies in Ezra Pound. Manchester: Carcanet, 1991.

Older Masters: Essays and Reflections on English and American Literature. Manchester: Carcanet, 1992.

The Eighteenth-Century Hymn in England. Cambridge: Cambridge University Press, 1993.

AUTOBIOGRAPHY

These the Companions: Recollections. Cambridge: Cambridge University Press, 1982.

EDITED

The New Oxford Book of Christian Verse. Oxford: Oxford University Press, 1981.

ESSAYS AND ARTICLES

'Their Witness'. Review of Daniel Weissbort, ed. *The Poetry of Survival: Post-War Poets of Central and Eastern Europe* (1992). *London Review of Books*, vol. 14, no. 4, 27 February 1992, p. 3.

John Barrell

POETRY

Property. Newcastle-upon-Tyne: Northern House, 1966.

NON-FICTION

The Idea of Landscape and the Sense of Place 1730-1840: An Approach to the Poetry of John Clare. Cambridge: Cambridge University Press, 1972.

The Dark Side of the Landscape: The Rural Poor in English Painting 1730-1840. Cambridge: Cambridge University Press, 1980.

English Literature in History 1730-1780: An Equal, Wide Survey. London: Hutchinson, 1983.

The Political Theory of Painting from Reynolds to Hazlitt: 'The Body of the Public'. New Haven: Yale University Press, 1986.

Poetry, Language and Politics. Manchester: Manchester University Press, 1988.

The Flight of Syntax: Percy Bysshe Shelley and Tom Raworth. The William Matthews Lectures delivered at Birkbeck College, London, 14 and 15 May 1990. London: Birkbeck College, 1990.

The Infection of Thomas de Quincey: A Psychopathology of Imperialism. New Haven: Yale, 1991.

The Birth of Pandora and the Division of Knowledge. London: Macmillan, 1992.

EDITED

Painting and the Politics of Culture: New Essays on British Art 1700-1850. Oxford: Oxford University Press, 1992.

Carnival, Hysteria and Writing: Collected Essays and Autobiography of Allon White. Oxford: Clarendon Press, 1993.

ESSAYS AND ARTICLES

'Death on the Nile: Fantasy and the Literature of Tourism 1840-1860'. The F.W. Bateson Memorial Lecture. *Essays in Criticism*, vol. 41, no. 2, April 1991, pp. 97-127.

'Diary'. On the late Allon White. *London Review of Books*, vol. 13, no. 16, 29 August 1991, p. 21.

Colin MacCabe

NON-FICTION

James Joyce and the Revolution of the Word. London: Macmillan, 1978.

Godard: Images, Sounds, Politics. London: Macmillan, 1980.

Theoretical Essays: Film, Linguistics, Literature. Manchester: Manchester University Press, 1985.

With Isaac Julien. *Diary of a Young Soul Rebel*. With Screenplay by Paul Hallam and Derrick Saldaan McLintock. London: BFI, 1991.

On the Eloquence of the Vulgar: A Justification of the Study of Film and Television. A Lecture given at the National Film Theatre on 13 October 1992 to inaugurate the MA Degree Course Being Offered by Birkbeck College and the British Film Institute. London: BFI, 1993.

ESSAYS AND ARTICLES

'Is Television about to Enter the Dark Ages?' Edited version of South Bank Show lecture. *Listener*, vol. 119, no. 3049, 11 February 1988, pp. 10-12.

'Language, Literature, Identity: Reflections on the Cox Report'. *Critical Quarterly*, vol. 32, no. 4, Winter 1990, pp. 7-13.

'The Revenge of the Author'. *Critical Quarterly*, vol. 31, no. 2, 1989, pp. 3-13.

EDITED

The Talking Cure: Essays in Psychoanalysis and Language. London: Macmillan, 1981.

James Joyce: New Perspectives. Hemel Hempstead: Harvester Wheatsheaf, 1983.

High Theory/Low Culture: Analysing Popular Television and Film. Images of Culture series. Manchester: Manchester University Press, 1986.

With Olivia Stewart. *The BBC and Public Service Broadcasting*. Images of Culture series. Manchester: Manchester University Press, 1986.

Futures for English. Manchester: Manchester University Press, 1987.

Richard Hoggart

NON-FICTION

Auden: An Introductory Essay. Chatto and Windus, 1951.

The Uses of Literacy: Aspects of Working-Class Life with Special Reference to Publications and Entertainments. London: Chatto and Windus, 1957. Penguin, 1958.

Speaking to Each Other: Essays. Volume I: About Society. London: Chatto and Windus, 1970.

Speaking to Each Other: Essays: Volume II: About Literature. London: Chatto and Windus, 1970.

Only Connect: On Culture and Communication. The BBC Reith Lectures, 1971. London: Chatto and Windus, 1972.

An Idea and its Servants: UNESCO from within. London: Chatto and Windus, 1978.

An English Temper: Essays on Education, Culture and Communications. London: Chatto and Windus, 1982.

AUTOBIOGRAPHY

A Local Habitation (Life and Times, Volume I: 1918-40). London: Chatto and Windus, 1988.

A Sort of Clowning (Life and Times, Volume II: 1940-59). London: Chatto and Windus, 1990.

An Imagined Life (Life and Times, Volume III: 1959-91). London: Chatto and Windus, 1992.

ESSAYS AND ARTICLES

'The Abuses of Literacy'. *Guardian*, 27 June 1991, p. 21.

'A Public Library Is Not a Burger Bar'. *Independent on Sunday*, 30 June 1991, p. 22. Originally published under title of 'The Pursuit of Quality' in *The Bookseller*, no. 4460, 14 June 1991, pp. 1700-03.

'Populism Rules – OK?' *Library Association Record*, vol. 94, no. 1, January 1992, p. 24.

'The Mission and the Vision: Education'. *Guardian*, 4 March 1992, p. 21.

'Where Have the Common Readers Gone?'. *Times*, 6 May 1992, 'Life and Times' section, p. 1.

FORTHCOMING

Townscape with Figures: Farnham, Portrait of an English Town. London: Chatto and Windus, 1994.

C.H. Sisson

POETRY

Collected Poems. Manchester: Carcanet, 1984. Contains: Early Poems and *The London Zoo* (1961); *Numbers* (1965); *Metamorphoses* (1968); The new poems from *In the Trojan Ditch* (1974); *Anchises* (1976); *Exactions*

(1980); miscellaneous poems since *Exactions* (1980-83); *Night Thoughts and Other Chronicles* (1982-83).
God Bless Karl Marx! Manchester: Carcanet, 1987.
Antidotes. Manchester: Carcanet, 1991.
The Pattern. London: Enitharmon, 1993.
Who and What. Manchester: Carcanet, 1994.

FICTION
An Asiatic Romance. London: Gaberbocchus, 1953.
Christopher Homm. London: Methuen, 1965. Manchester: Carcanet, 1975.

NON-FICTION
Under pseudonym of 'Richard Ampers'. *The Curious Democrat.* Emergency Pamphlets no. 2. London: Peter Russell, 1950.
The Spirit of British Administration and Some European Comparisons. London: Faber, 1959. 2nd edn, 1966.
Art and Action. 1965.
Essays. 'Sevenoaks Essays'. Sevenoaks, Kent: C.H. Sisson, 1967.
English Poetry 1900-1950: An Assessment. London: Hart-Davis, 1971. Revised edn, 1981.
The Case of Walter Bagehot. London: Faber, 1972. Now included in *The Avoidance of Literature* (see below).
David Hume. Edinburgh: Ramsay Head, 1976.
The Avoidance of Literature: Collected Essays. Manchester: Carcanet, 1978.
Anglican Essays. Manchester: Carcanet, 1983.
In Two Minds: Guesses at Other Writers. Manchester: Carcanet, 1990.
English Perspectives: Essays on Liberty and Government. Manchester: Carcanet, 1992.
Is There a Church of England? Reflections on Permanence and Progression. Manchester: Carcanet, 1993.

AUTOBIOGRAPHY
On the Look-Out: A Partial Autobiography. Manchester: Carcanet, 1989.

TRANSLATIONS
Versions and Perversions of Heine. London: Gaberbocchus, Black Series, no. 4, 1955.
The Poetry of Catullus. London: MacGibbon and Kee, 1966.
The Poetic Art: A Translation of Horace's Ars Poetica. Manchester: Carcanet, 1975.
The Poem on Nature: A Translation of Lucretius's De Rerum Natura. Manchester: Carcanet, 1976.
Some Tales of La Fontaine. Manchester: Carcanet, 1979.
The Divine Comedy: A New Translation of Dante. Manchester: Carcanet, 1980.

The Song of Roland. Manchester: Carcanet, 1983.
Les Regrets of Joachim du Bellay. Manchester: Carcanet, 1983.
The Aeneid of Virgil. Manchester: Carcanet, 1986.
Britannicus, Phaedra, Athaliah of Racine. Oxford: Oxford University Press, 1987.

Lisa Jardine

NON-FICTION
Francis Bacon: Discovery and the Art of Discourse. Cambridge: Cambridge University Press, 1974.
Still Harping on Daughters: Women and Drama in the Age of Shakespeare. Brighton: Harvester Press, 1983. 2nd edn with new preface by the author. Hemel Hempstead: Harvester Wheatsheaf, 1989.
With Anthony Grafton. *From Humanism to the Humanities: Education and the Liberal Arts in Fifteenth- and Sixteenth-Century Europe.* London: Duckworth, 1986.
With Julia Swindells. *What's Left? Women in Culture and the Labour Movement.* London: Routledge, 1989.
Erasmus, Man of Letters: The Construction of Charisma in Print. Princeton: Princeton University Press, 1993.

FORTHCOMING
Reading Shakespeare Historically. California: University of California Press.

Index

Compiled by Angela Tredell